Ken Akamatsu

TRANSLATED BY

Douglas Varenas

ADAPTED BY

Peter David and Kathleen O'Shea David

LETTERED BY

Steve Palmer

LONDON

Published in the United Kingdom by Tanoshimi in 2006

1 3 5 7 9 10 8 6 4 2

First published in serial form by Shonen Magazine comics and subsequently published in book form by
Kodansha Ltd., Tokyo in 2003. Copyright © 2003 by Ken Akamatsu.

Published by arrangement with Kodansha Ltd., Tokyo and with Del Rey,
an imprint of Random House Inc., New York

Tanoshimi
The Random House Group Limited
20 Vauxhall Bridge Road, London, SW1V 2SA

Random House Australia (Pty) Limited
20 Alfred Street, Milsons Point, Sydney
New South Wales 2061, Australia

Random House New Zealand Limited
18 Poland Road, Glenfield
Auckland 10, New Zealand

Random House (Pty) Limited
Isle of Houghton, Corner of Boundary Road & Carse O'Gowrie
Houghton 2198, South Africa

Random House Publishers India Private Limited
301 World Trade Tower, Hotel Intercontinental Grand Complex,
Barakhamba Lane, New Delhi 110 001, India

Random House Group Limited Reg. No. 954009

www.tanoshimi.tv
www.randomhouse.co.uk

A CIP catalogue record for this book is available from the British Library

Papers used by Random House
are natural, recyclable products made from wood grown in sustainable forests.
The manufacturing processes conform to the environmental regulations of the country of origin.

ISBN 9780099504160 (from Jan 2007)
ISBN 0 09 950416 2

Printed and bound in Germany by GGP Media GmbH, Pößneck

Translator – Douglas Varenas
Adaptor – Peter David and Kathleen O'Shea David
Lettering and Text Design – Steve Palmer
Cover Design – David Stevenson

A Word from the Author

Please excuse my one month silence. I now bring to you Volume 2 of *Negima!*

You may think that what sets this manga apart is this: "Later, when you read it again from the first frame of the first story, the conduct of the various characters is consistent." But just as you're thinking that, contradictions are already arising in their dialect and expressions. Yikes! There are 31 people so

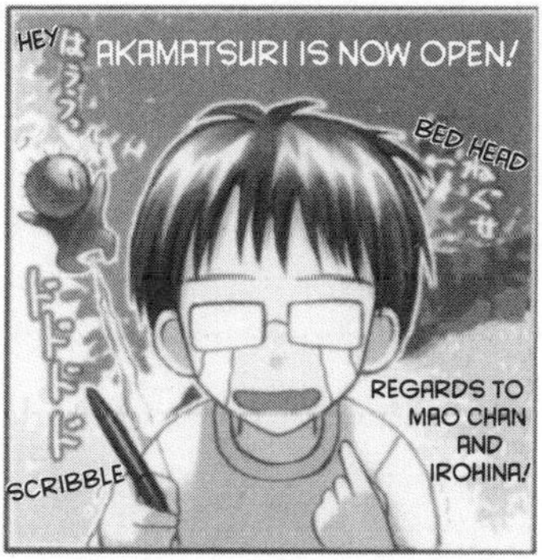
HEY
AKAMATSURI IS NOW OPEN!
BED HEAD
REGARDS TO MAO CHAN AND IROHINA!
SCRIBBLE

please overlook that a little. In any case, there are a lot of characters so it's tough remembering them, let alone managing them (ha ha!). However, the class rep, Chisame, and the like are favorites. There is a mountain of various characters and subplots that haven't been introduced yet, so everyone please imagine some various subplots of your own and enjoy! (If you think up any good ones please notify me by mail [ha ha]).

Ken Akamatsu

http://www.ailove.net

Honorifics

Throughout the Tanoshimi Manga books, you will find Japanese honorifics left intact in the translations. For those not familiar with how the Japanese use honorifics, and more important, how they differ from English honorifics, we present this brief overview.

Politeness has always been a critical facet of Japanese culture. Ever since the feudal era, when Japan was a highly stratified society, use of honorifics — which can be defined as polite speech that indicates relationship or status — has played an essential role in the Japanese language. When addressing someone in Japanese, an honorific usually takes the form of a suffix attached to one's name (example: "Asuna-san"), or as a title at the end of one's name or in place of the name itself (example: "Negi-sensei," or simply "Sensei!").

Honorifics can be expressions of respect or endearment. In the context of manga and anime, honorifics give insight into the nature of the relationship between characters. Many translations into English leave out these important honorifics, and therefore distort the "feel" of the original Japanese. Because Japanese honorifics have nuances that English honorifics lack, it is our policy at Tanoshimi not to translate them. Here, instead, is a guide to some of the honorifics you may encounter in Tanoshimi Manga.

-san: This is the most common honorific, and is equivalent to Mr., Miss, Ms., Mrs., etc. It is the all-purpose honorific and can be used in any situation where politeness is required.

-sama: This is one level higher than "-san." It is used to confer great respect.

-dono: This comes from the word *tono* which means *lord*. It is an even higher level than *sama*, and confers utmost respect.

-kun: This suffix is used at the end of boy's names to express familiarity or endearment. It is also sometimes used by men among friends, or when addressing someone younger or of a lower station.

-*chan:* This is used to express endearment, mostly toward girls. It is also used for little boys, pets, and even among lovers. It gives a sense of childish cuteness.

Bozu: This is an informal way to refer to a boy, similar to the English term "kid".

Sempai: This title suggests that the addressee is one's "senior" in a group or organization. It is most often used in a school setting, where underclassmen refer to their upperclassmen as *sempai.* It can also be used in the workplace, such as when a newer employee addresses an employee who has seniority in the company.

Kohai: This is the opposite of *sempai,* and is used toward underclassmen in school or newcomers in the workplace. It connotes that the addressee is of lower station.

Sensei: Literally meaning "one who has come before," this title is used for teachers, doctors, or masters of any profession or art.

-[blank]: Usually forgotten in these lists, but perhaps the most significant difference between Japanese and English. The lack of honorific means that the speaker has permission to address the person in a very intimate way. Usually, only family, spouses, or very close friends have this kind of permission. Known as *yobisute,* it can be gratifying when someone who has earned the intimacy starts to call one by one's name without an honorific. But when that intimacy hasn't been earned, it can also be very insulting.

魔法先生ネギま!

MAGISTER NEGI MAGI

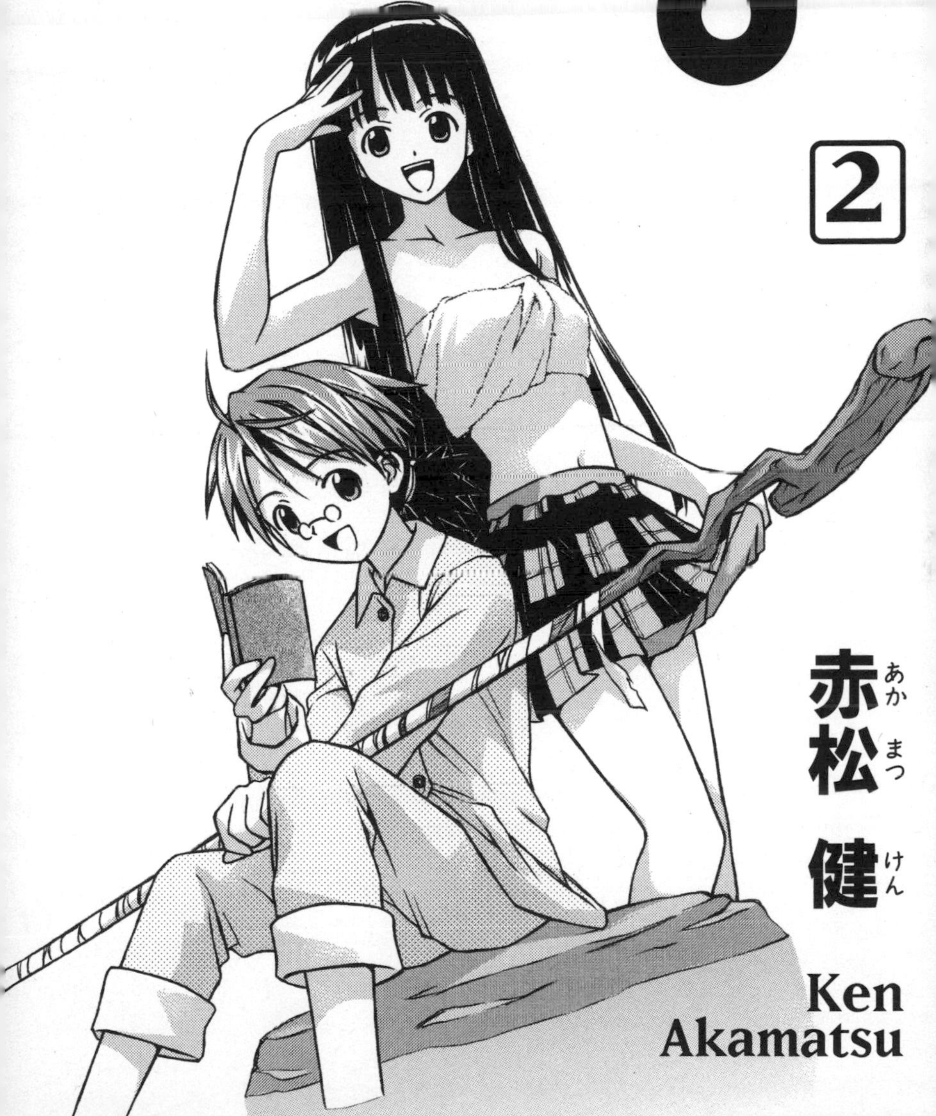

2

赤松健

Ken Akamatsu

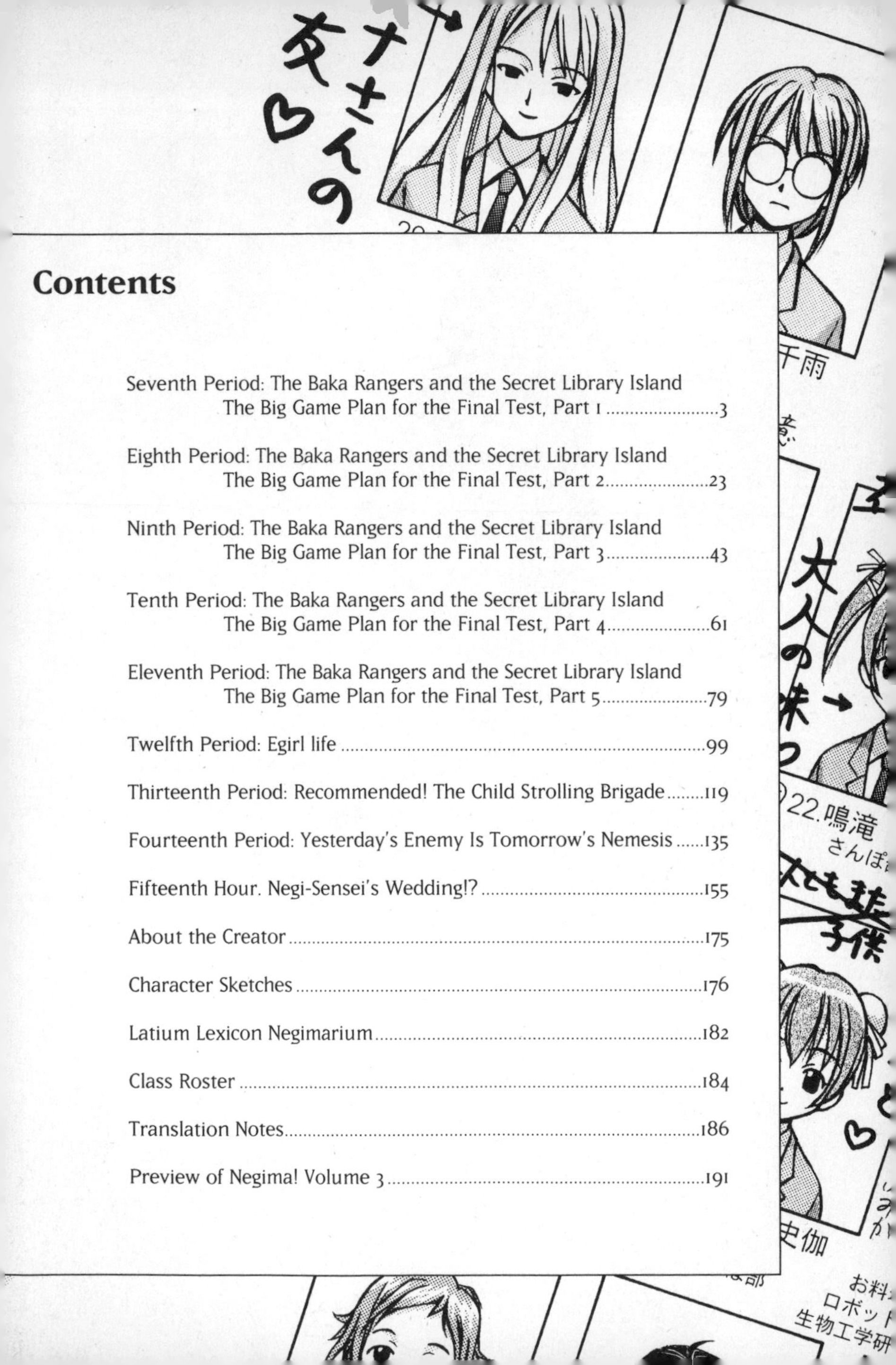
千雨
22.鳴滝
史伽
生物工学研

Contents

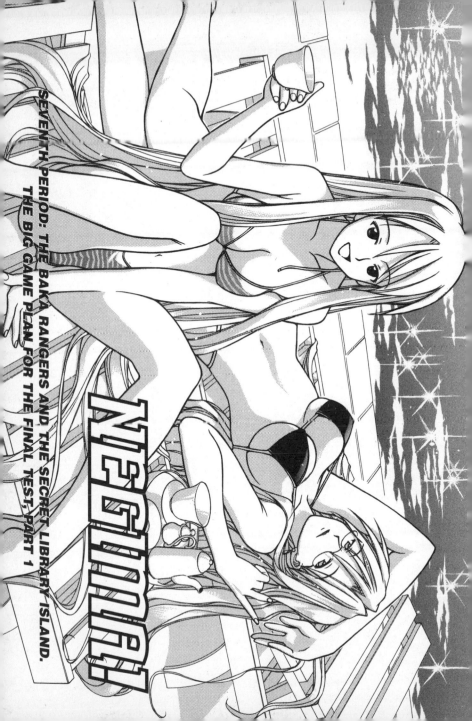

SEVENTH PERIOD: THE BAKA RANGERS AND THE SECRET LIBRARY ISLAND.
THE BIG GAME PLAN FOR THE FINAL TEST, PART 1

NEGIMA!

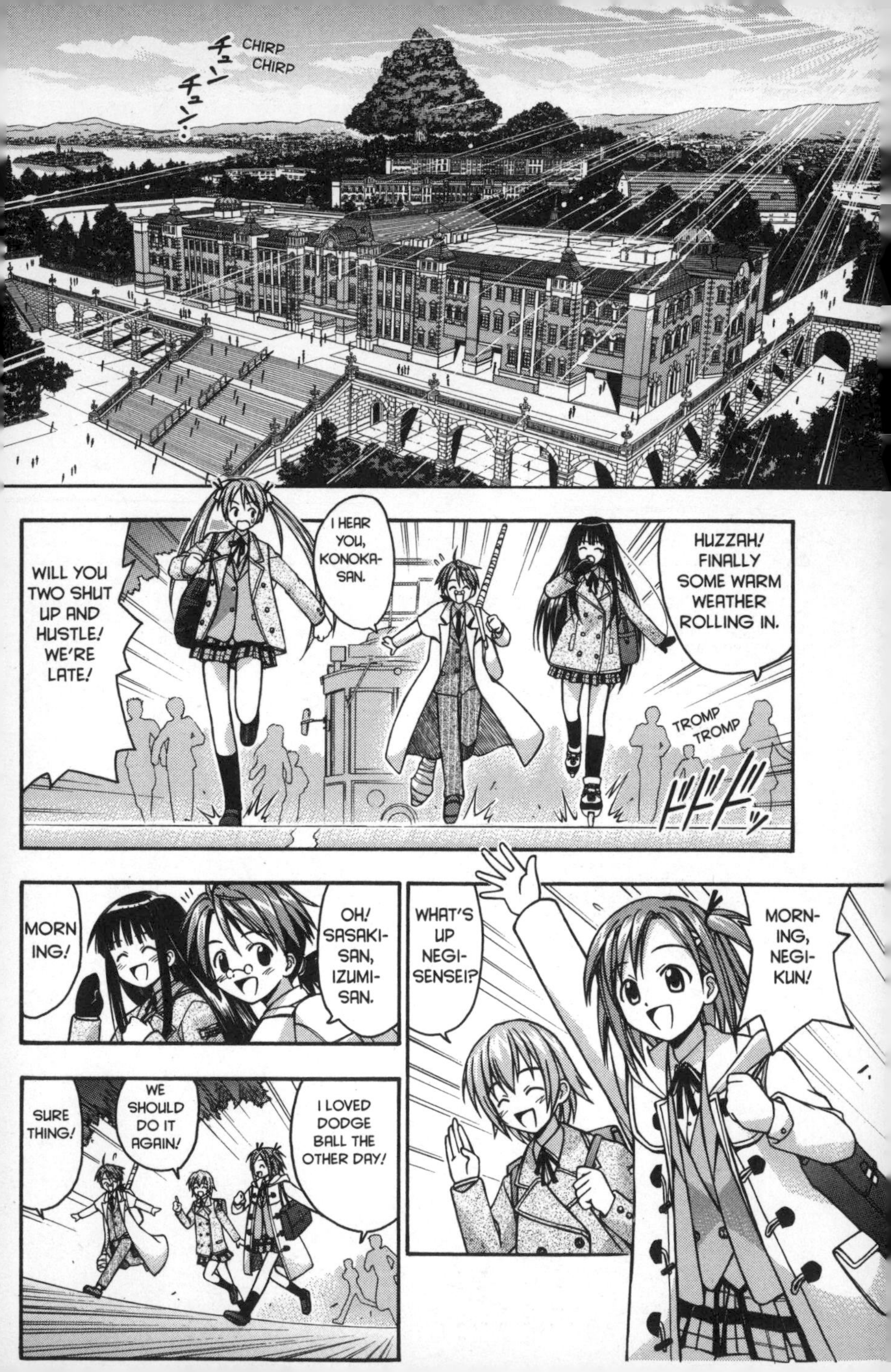
チュン チュン…
CHIRP CHIRP
HUZZAH! FINALLY SOME WARM WEATHER ROLLING IN.
I HEAR YOU, KONOKA-SAN.
WILL YOU TWO SHUT UP AND HUSTLE! WE'RE LATE!
TROMP TROMP
ドドドッ
MORN-ING, NEGI-KUN!
WHAT'S UP NEGI-SENSEI?
OH! SASAKI-SAN, IZUMI-SAN.
MORN ING!
I LOVED DODGE BALL THE OTHER DAY!
WE SHOULD DO IT AGAIN!
SURE THING!

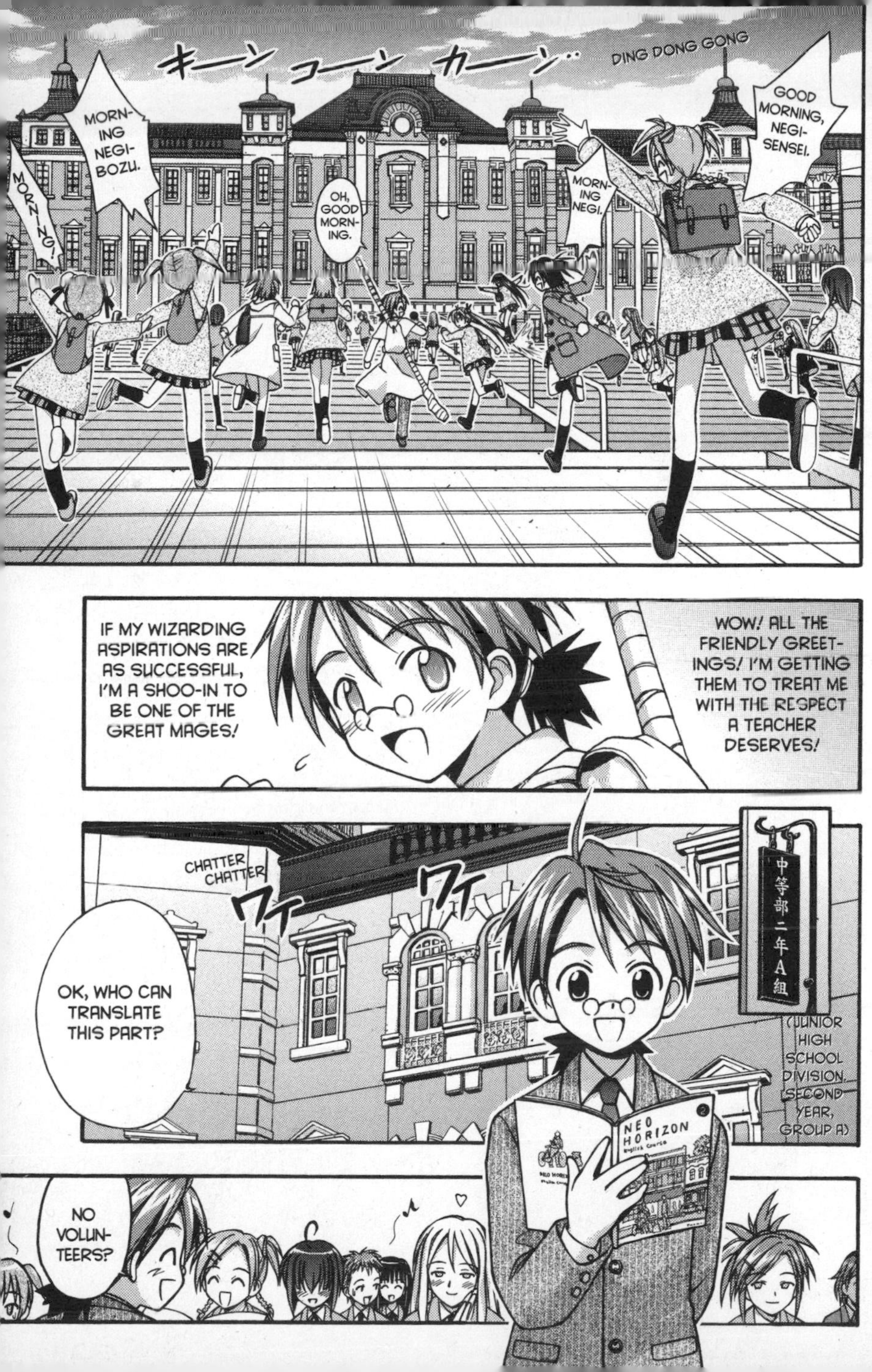

キーン コーン カーン
DING DONG GONG
GOOD MORNING, NEGI-SENSEI.
MORNING NEGI.
OH, GOOD MORNING.
MORNING NEGI-BOZU.
MORNING!
WOW! ALL THE FRIENDLY GREETINGS! I'M GETTING THEM TO TREAT ME WITH THE RESPECT A TEACHER DESERVES!
IF MY WIZARDING ASPIRATIONS ARE AS SUCCESSFUL, I'M A SHOO-IN TO BE ONE OF THE GREAT MAGES!
中等部二年A組
(JUNIOR HIGH SCHOOL DIVISION, SECOND YEAR, GROUP A)
ワイ ワイ
CHATTER CHATTER
OK, WHO CAN TRANSLATE THIS PART?
NEO HORIZON English Course
NO VOLUNTEERS?

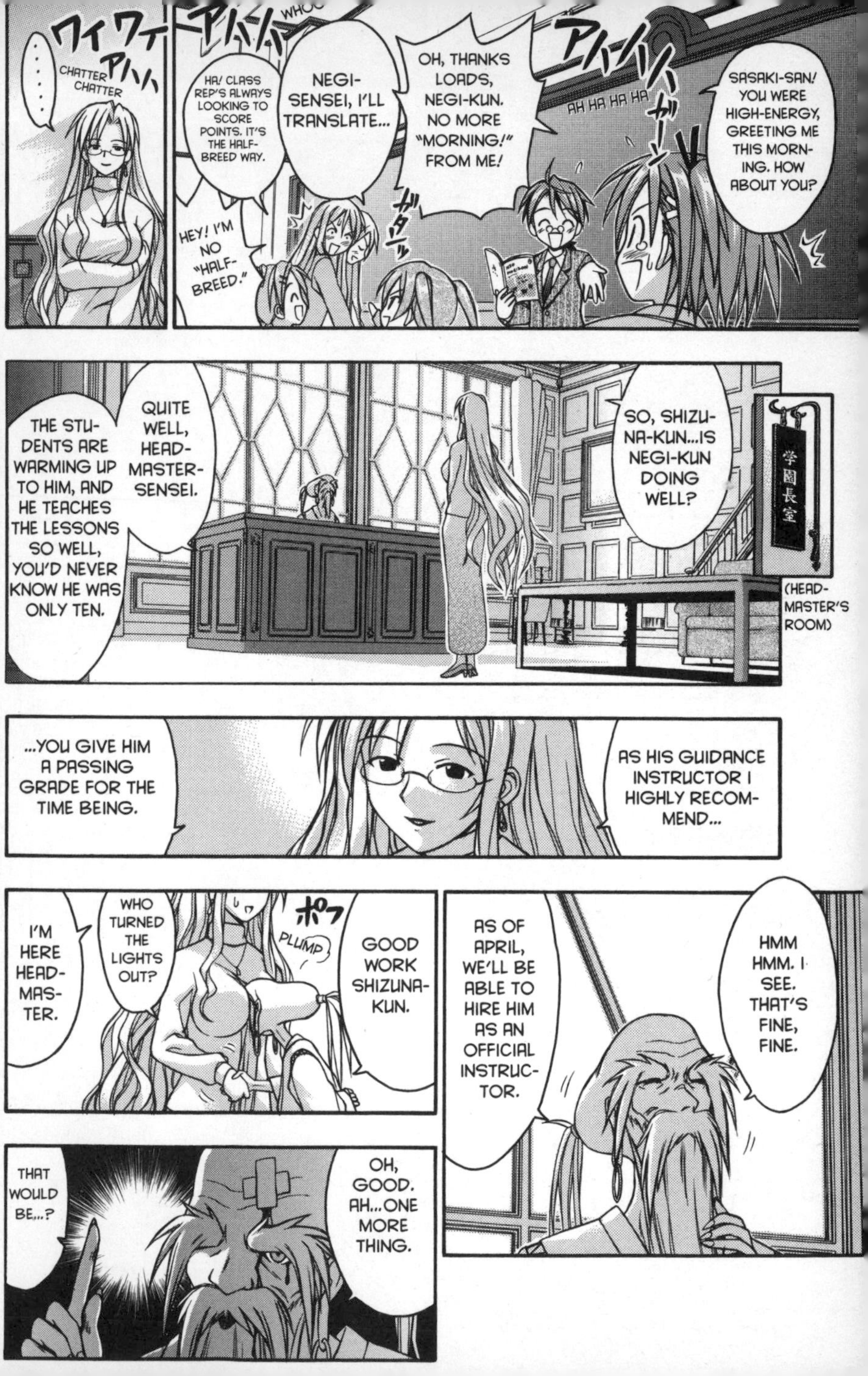
SASAKI-SAN! YOU WERE HIGH-ENERGY, GREETING ME THIS MORNING. HOW ABOUT YOU?
AH HA HA HA
OH, THANKS LOADS, NEGI-KUN. NO MORE "MORNING!" FROM ME!
NEGI-SENSEI, I'LL TRANSLATE...
HA! CLASS REP'S ALWAYS LOOKING TO SCORE POINTS. IT'S THE HALF-BREED WAY.
HEY! I'M NO "HALF-BREED."
CHATTER CHATTER
......
SO, SHIZUNA-KUN...IS NEGI-KUN DOING WELL?
(HEAD-MASTER'S ROOM)
学園長室
QUITE WELL, HEAD-MASTER-SENSEI.
THE STUDENTS ARE WARMING UP TO HIM, AND HE TEACHES THE LESSONS SO WELL, YOU'D NEVER KNOW HE WAS ONLY TEN.
AS HIS GUIDANCE INSTRUCTOR I HIGHLY RECOMMEND...
...YOU GIVE HIM A PASSING GRADE FOR THE TIME BEING.
HMM HMM. I SEE. THAT'S FINE, FINE.
AS OF APRIL, WE'LL BE ABLE TO HIRE HIM AS AN OFFICIAL INSTRUCTOR.
GOOD WORK SHIZUNA-KUN.
PLUMP
WHO TURNED THE LIGHTS OUT?
I'M HERE HEAD-MASTER.
OH, GOOD. AH...ONE MORE THING.
THAT WOULD BE...?

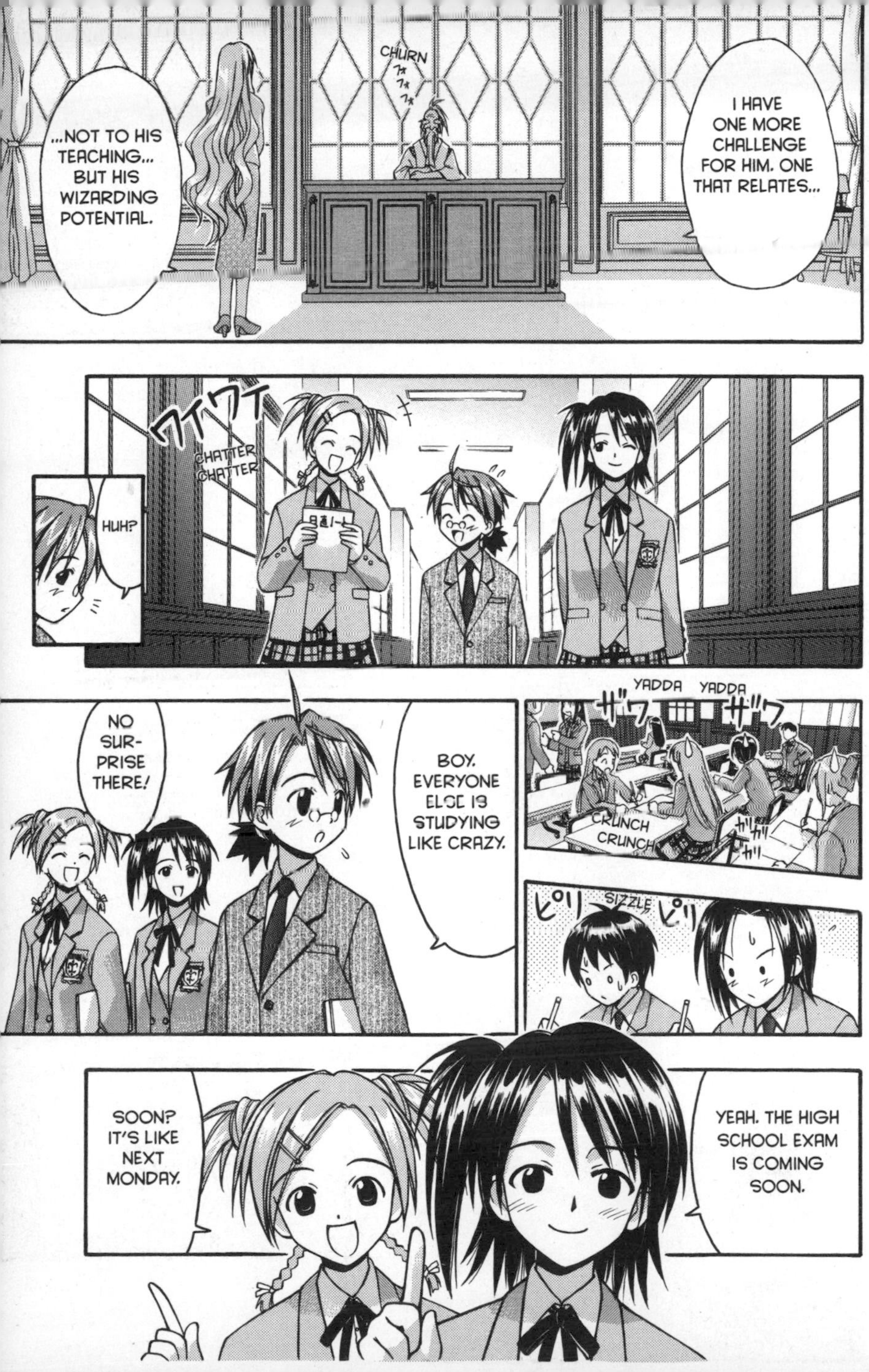
I HAVE ONE MORE CHALLENGE FOR HIM. ONE THAT RELATES...
CHURN
...NOT TO HIS TEACHING... BUT HIS WIZARDING POTENTIAL.
CHATTER CHATTER
HUH?
YADDA YADDA
CRUNCH CRUNCH
SIZZLE
BOY. EVERYONE ELSE IS STUDYING LIKE CRAZY.
NO SUR-PRISE THERE!
YEAH. THE HIGH SCHOOL EXAM IS COMING SOON.
SOON? IT'S LIKE NEXT MONDAY.

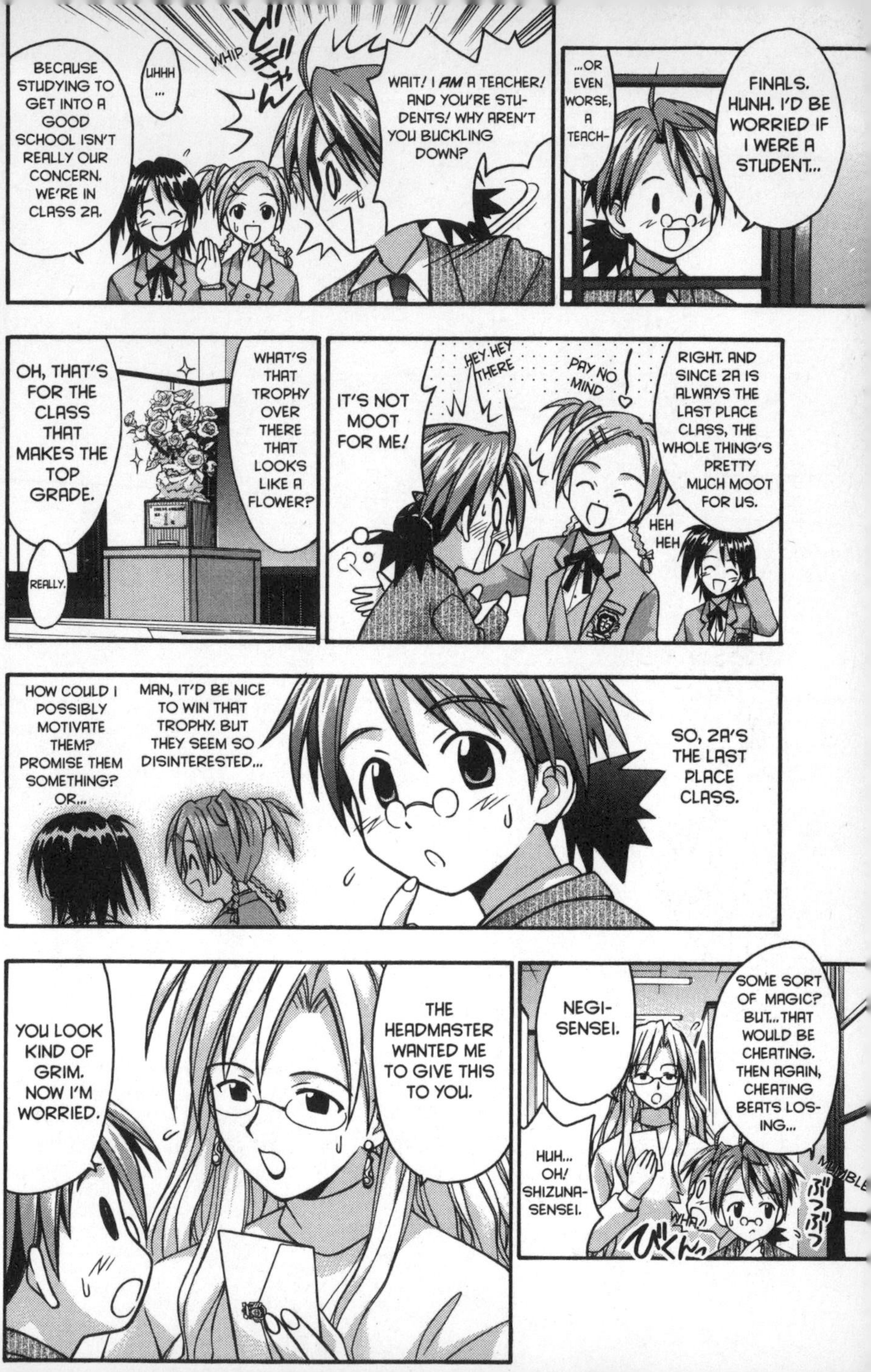
FINALS. HUNH. I'D BE WORRIED IF I WERE A STUDENT...
...OR EVEN WORSE, A TEACH-
WAIT! I AM A TEACHER! AND YOU'RE STU-DENTS! WHY AREN'T YOU BUCKLING DOWN?
WHIP
UHHH ...
BECAUSE STUDYING TO GET INTO A GOOD SCHOOL ISN'T REALLY OUR CONCERN. WE'RE IN CLASS 2A.
RIGHT. AND SINCE 2A IS ALWAYS THE LAST PLACE CLASS, THE WHOLE THING'S PRETTY MUCH MOOT FOR US.
HEH HEH
PAY NO MIND
HEY HEY THERE
IT'S NOT MOOT FOR ME!
WHAT'S THAT TROPHY OVER THERE THAT LOOKS LIKE A FLOWER?
OH, THAT'S FOR THE CLASS THAT MAKES THE TOP GRADE.
REALLY.
SO, 2A'S THE LAST PLACE CLASS.
MAN, IT'D BE NICE TO WIN THAT TROPHY. BUT THEY SEEM SO DISINTERESTED...
HOW COULD I POSSIBLY MOTIVATE THEM? PROMISE THEM SOMETHING? OR...
SOME SORT OF MAGIC? BUT...THAT WOULD BE CHEATING. THEN AGAIN, CHEATING BEATS LOS-ING...
MUMBLE
ぶつぶつ
NEGI-SENSEI.
HUH... OH! SHIZUNA-SENSEI.
WHA!
THE HEADMASTER WANTED ME TO GIVE THIS TO YOU.
YOU LOOK KIND OF GRIM. NOW I'M WORRIED.

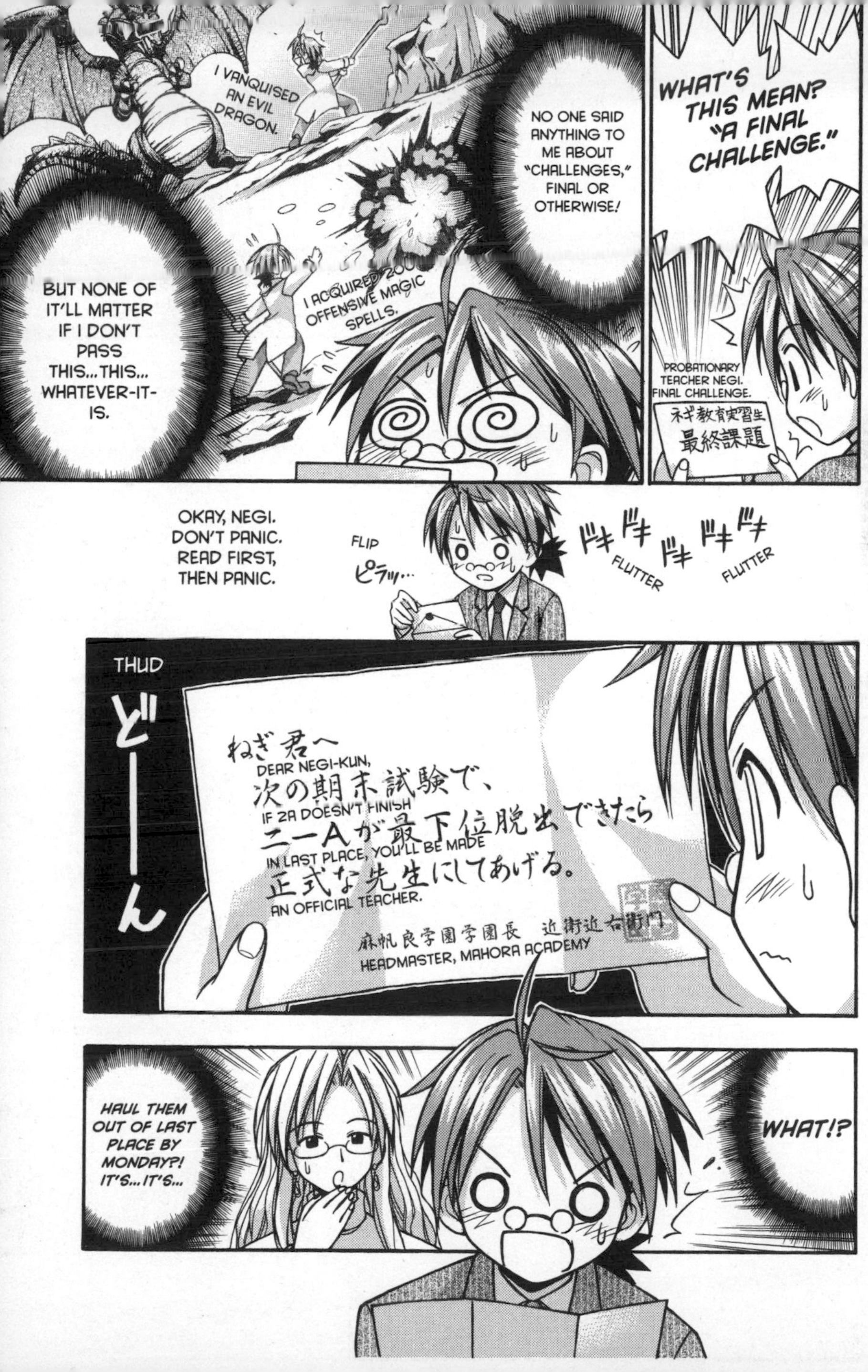
WHAT'S THIS MEAN? "A FINAL CHALLENGE."
PROBATIONARY TEACHER NEGI. FINAL CHALLENGE.
ネギ教育実習生
最終課題
NO ONE SAID ANYTHING TO ME ABOUT "CHALLENGES," FINAL OR OTHERWISE!
I VANQUISHED AN EVIL DRAGON.
I ACQUIRED 200 OFFENSIVE MAGIC SPELLS.
BUT NONE OF IT'LL MATTER IF I DON'T PASS THIS... THIS... WHATEVER-IT-IS.
ドキ ドキ ドキ ドキ ドキ
FLUTTER
FLUTTER
FLIP
ピラッ…
OKAY, NEGI. DON'T PANIC. READ FIRST, THEN PANIC.
THUD
どーーん
ねぎ君へ
DEAR NEGI-KUN,
次の期末試験で、
IF 2A DOESN'T FINISH
二ーAが最下位脱出できたら
IN LAST PLACE, YOU'LL BE MADE
正式な先生にしてあげる。
AN OFFICIAL TEACHER.
麻帆良学園学園長 近衛近右衛門
HEADMASTER, MAHORA ACADEMY
WHAT!?
HAUL THEM OUT OF LAST PLACE BY MONDAY?! IT'S... IT'S...

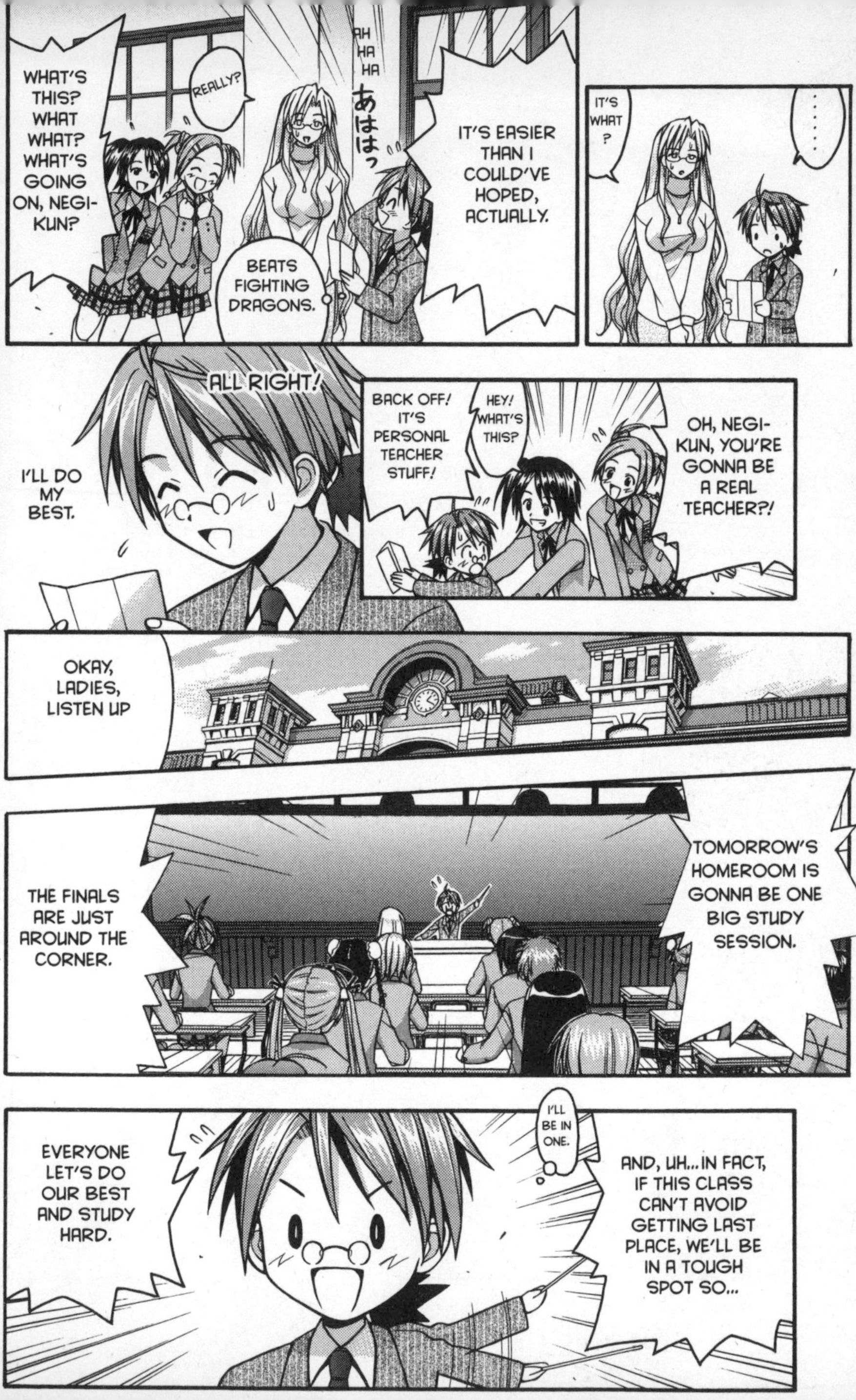
...
IT'S WHAT?
IT'S EASIER THAN I COULD'VE HOPED, ACTUALLY.
AH HA HA あははっ
REALLY?
WHAT'S THIS? WHAT WHAT? WHAT'S GOING ON, NEGI-KUN?
BEATS FIGHTING DRAGONS.
OH, NEGI-KUN, YOU'RE GONNA BE A REAL TEACHER?!
HEY! WHAT'S THIS?
BACK OFF! IT'S PERSONAL TEACHER STUFF!
ALL RIGHT!
I'LL DO MY BEST.
OKAY, LADIES, LISTEN UP
TOMORROW'S HOMEROOM IS GONNA BE ONE BIG STUDY SESSION.
THE FINALS ARE JUST AROUND THE CORNER.
I'LL BE IN ONE.
AND, UH...IN FACT, IF THIS CLASS CAN'T AVOID GETTING LAST PLACE, WE'LL BE IN A TOUGH SPOT SO...
EVERYONE LET'S DO OUR BEST AND STUDY HARD.

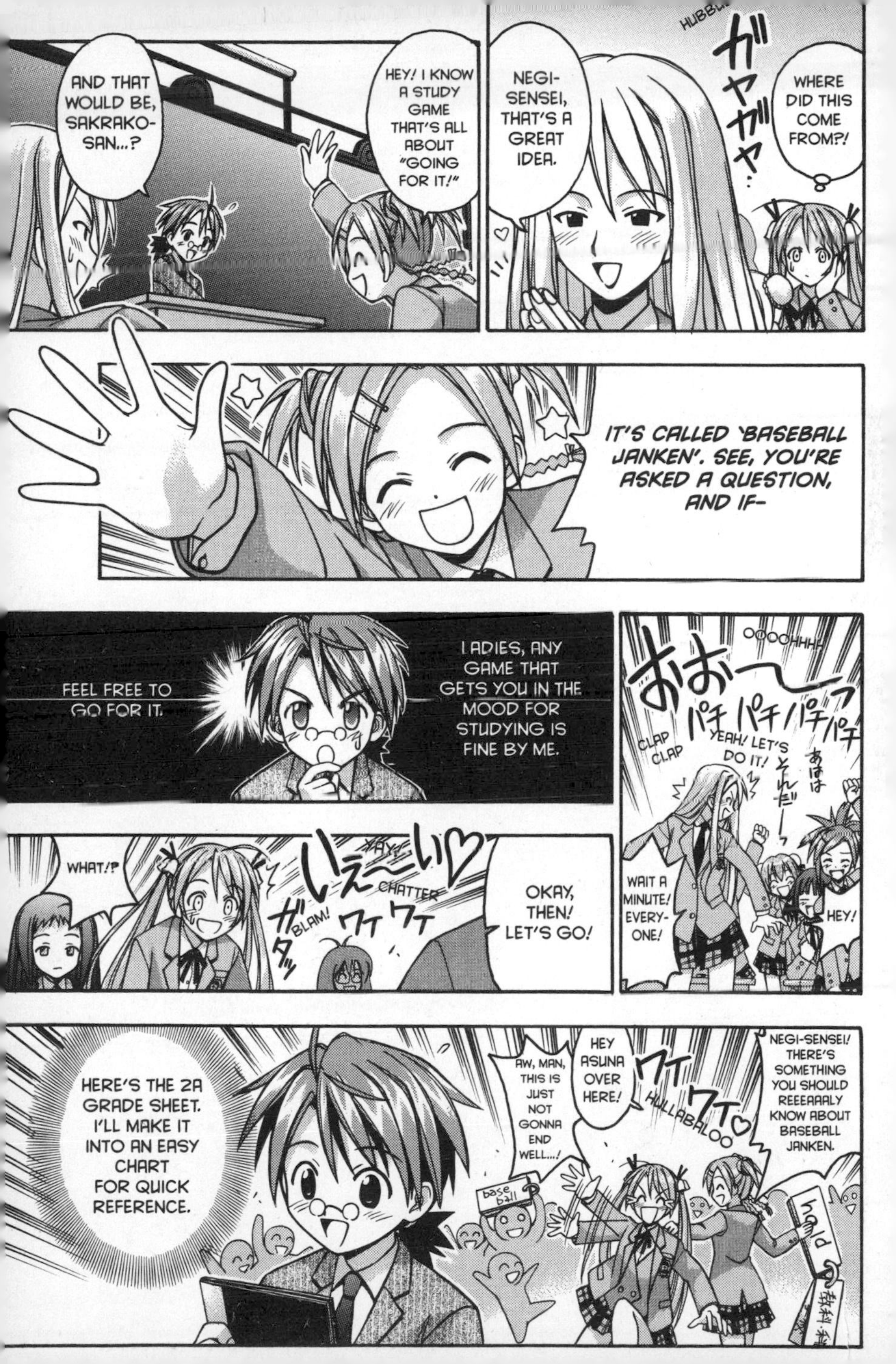

ガヤガヤ
WHERE DID THIS COME FROM?!
NEGI-SENSEI, THAT'S A GREAT IDEA.
HEY! I KNOW A STUDY GAME THAT'S ALL ABOUT "GOING FOR IT!"
AND THAT WOULD BE, SAKRAKO-SAN...?
IT'S CALLED 'BASEBALL JANKEN'. SEE, YOU'RE ASKED A QUESTION, AND IF-
OOOOHHHH
おおーっ
CLAP CLAP
パチパチパチパチ
YEAH! LET'S DO IT!
そんだーっ
あはは
WAIT A MINUTE! EVERY-ONE!
HEY!
LADIES, ANY GAME THAT GETS YOU IN THE MOOD FOR STUDYING IS FINE BY ME.
FEEL FREE TO GO FOR IT.
OKAY, THEN! LET'S GO!
YAY!
CHATTER
ワイワイ
BLAM!
WHAT!?
NEGI-SENSEI! THERE'S SOMETHING YOU SHOULD REEEAAALY KNOW ABOUT BASEBALL JANKEN.
HULLABALOO
HEY ASUNA OVER HERE!
AW, MAN, THIS IS JUST NOT GONNA END WELL...!
base ball
HERE'S THE 2A GRADE SHEET. I'LL MAKE IT INTO AN EASY CHART FOR QUICK REFERENCE.

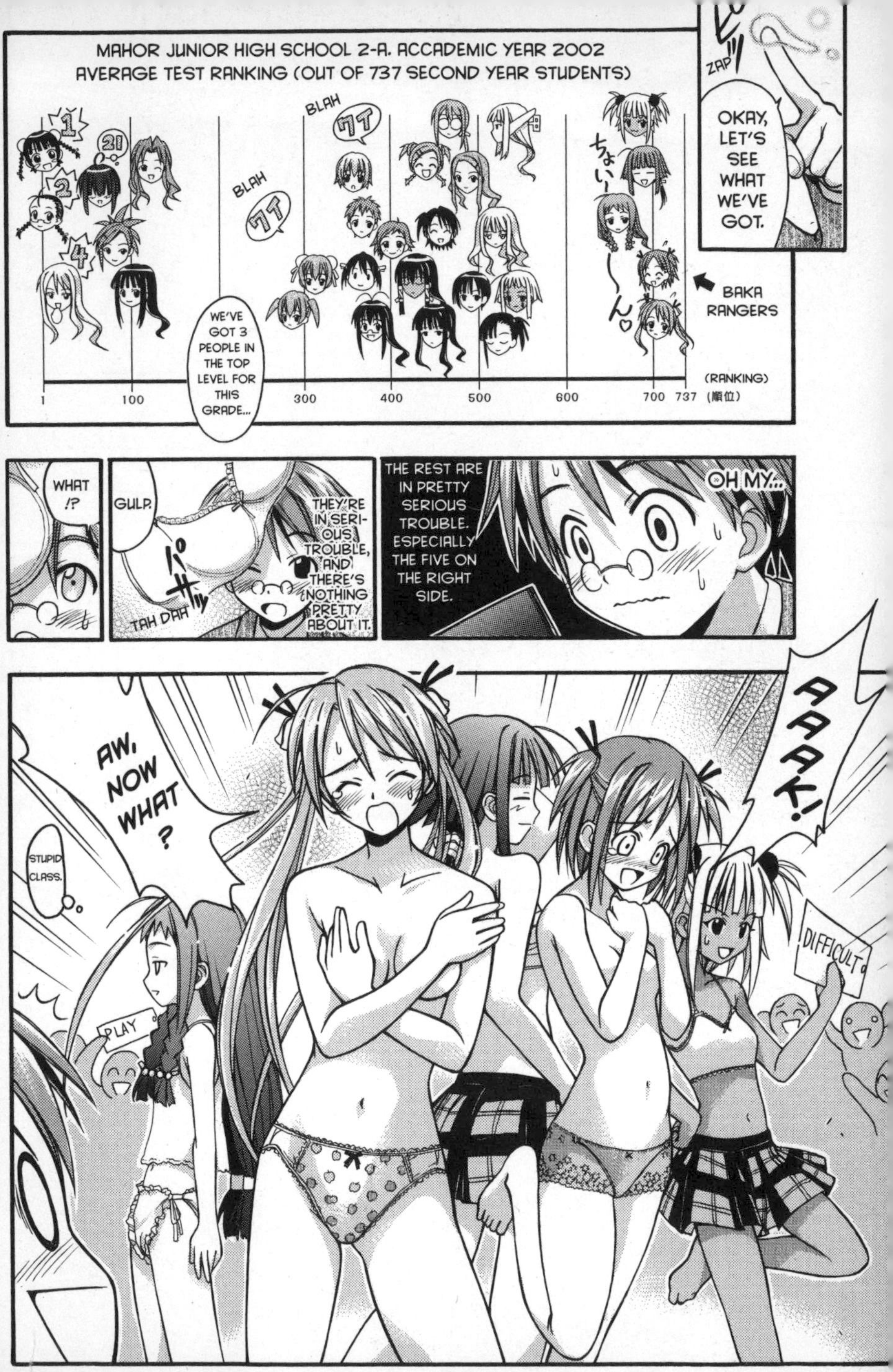
ZAP
OKAY, LET'S SEE WHAT WE'VE GOT.
MAHOR JUNIOR HIGH SCHOOL 2-A. ACCADEMIC YEAR 2002
AVERAGE TEST RANKING (OUT OF 737 SECOND YEAR STUDENTS)
1
21
2
4
BLAH
ワイ
BLAH
ワイ
ちょい~
BAKA RANGERS
WE'VE GOT 3 PEOPLE IN THE TOP LEVEL FOR THIS GRADE...
1
100
300
400
500
600
700
737
(RANKING)
(順位)
OH MY...
THE REST ARE IN PRETTY SERIOUS TROUBLE. ESPECIALLY THE FIVE ON THE RIGHT SIDE.
THEY'RE IN SERIOUS TROUBLE, AND THERE'S NOTHING PRETTY ABOUT IT.
GULP.
TAH DAH
WHAT!?
AAAAK!
AW, NOW WHAT?
STUPID CLASS.
DIFFICULT
PLAY

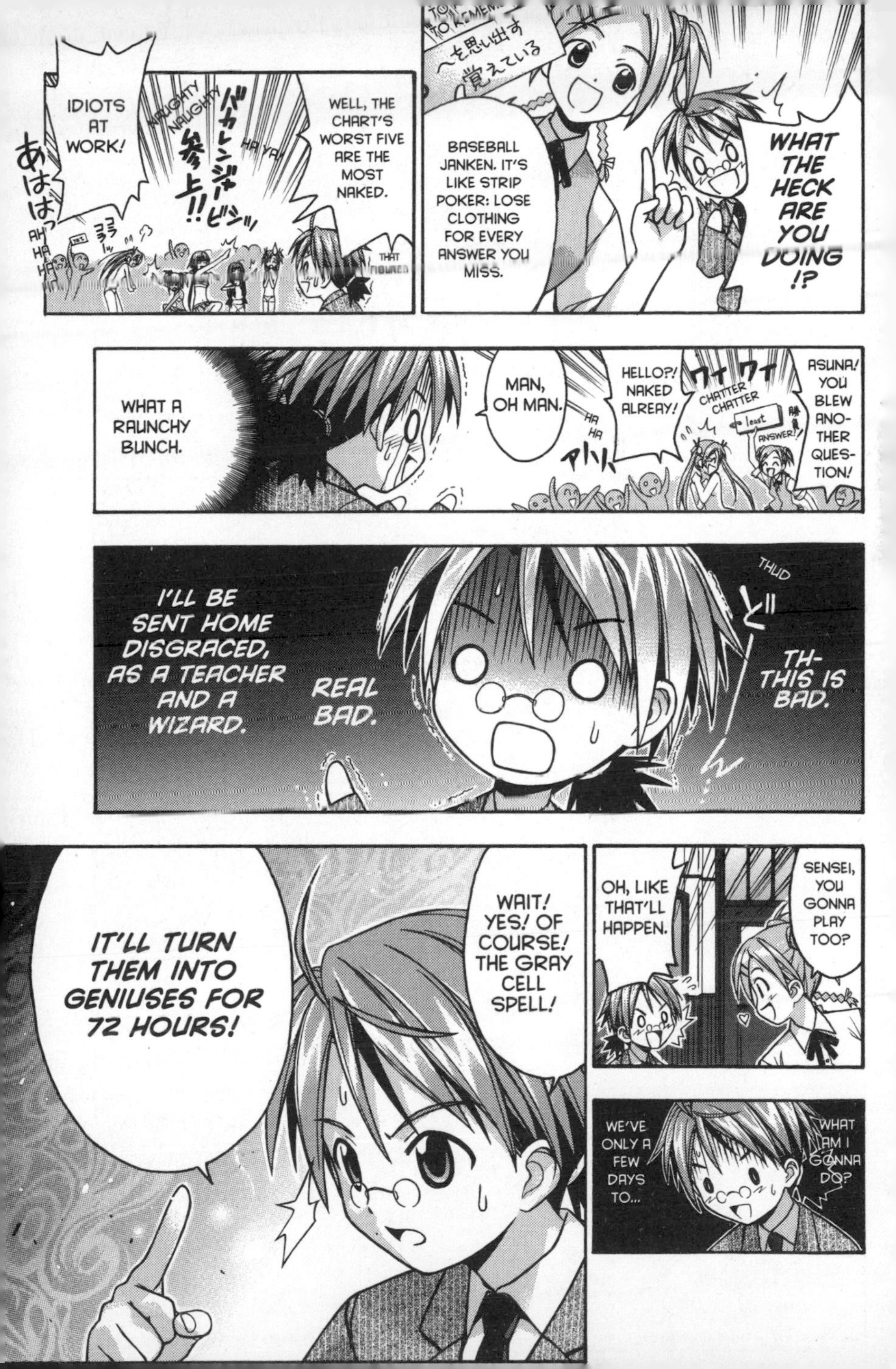
～を思い出す
覚えている
WHAT THE HECK ARE YOU DOING!?
BASEBALL JANKEN. IT'S LIKE STRIP POKER: LOSE CLOTHING FOR EVERY ANSWER YOU MISS.
WELL, THE CHART'S WORST FIVE ARE THE MOST NAKED.
バカレンジャー参上!! ビシッ
NAUGHTY NAUGHTY
HA YA!
IDIOTS AT WORK!
あははっ
AH HA HA
THAT FIGURES
ASUNA! YOU BLEW ANOTHER QUESTION!
ワイワイ
CHATTER CHATTER
HELLO?! NAKED ALREAY!
アハハ
HA HA
MAN, OH MAN.
WHAT A RAUNCHY BUNCH.
TH-THIS IS BAD.
THUD
REAL BAD.
I'LL BE SENT HOME DISGRACED, AS A TEACHER AND A WIZARD.
SENSEI, YOU GONNA PLAY TOO?
OH, LIKE THAT'LL HAPPEN.
WHAT AM I GONNA DO?
WE'VE ONLY A FEW DAYS TO...
WAIT! YES! OF COURSE! THE GRAY CELL SPELL!
IT'LL TURN THEM INTO GENIUSES FOR 72 HOURS!

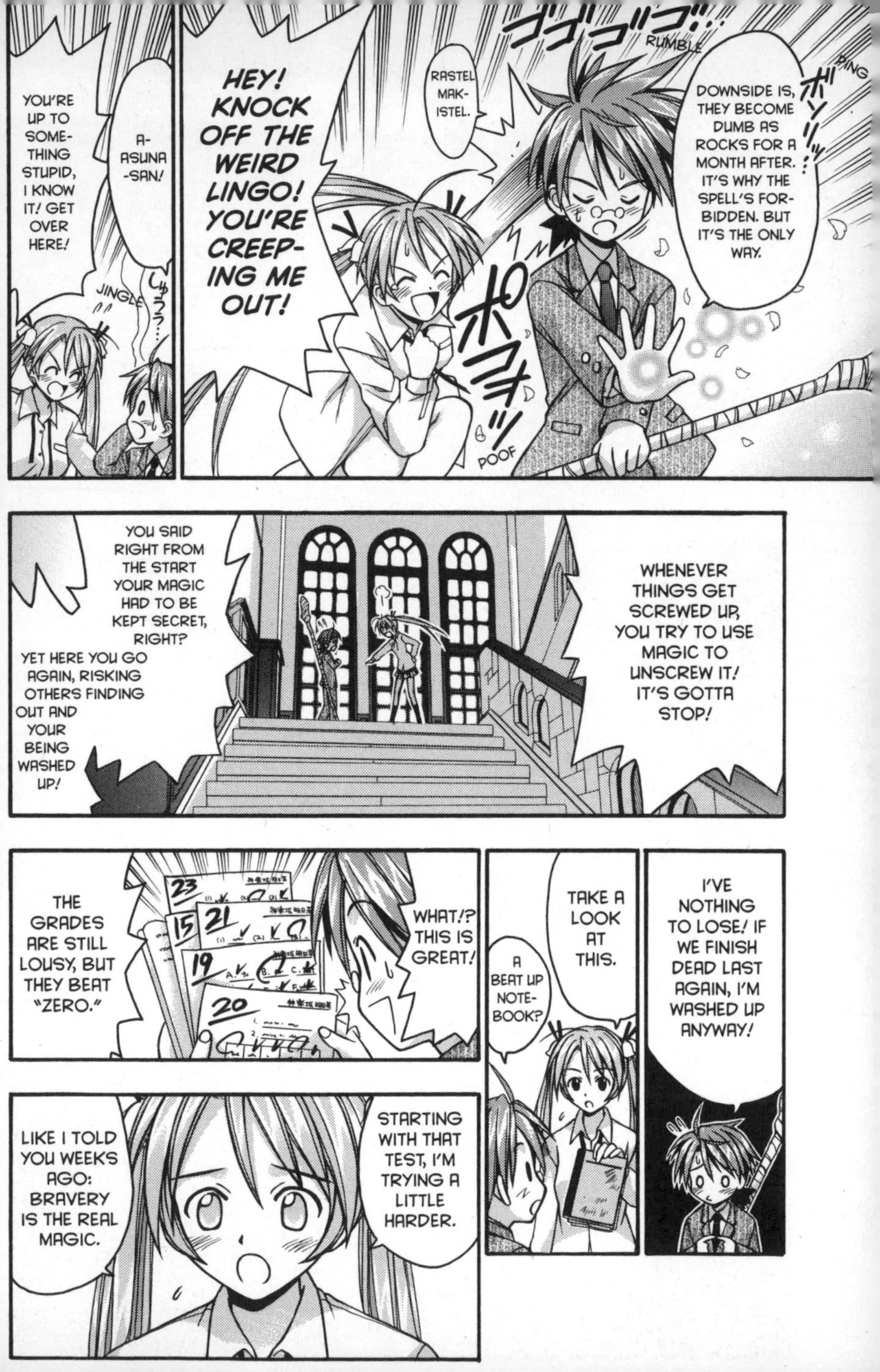
RUMBLE
PING
DOWNSIDE IS, THEY BECOME DUMB AS ROCKS FOR A MONTH AFTER. IT'S WHY THE SPELL'S FOR-BIDDEN. BUT IT'S THE ONLY WAY.
RASTEL MAK-ISTEL.
HEY! KNOCK OFF THE WEIRD LINGO! YOU'RE CREEP-ING ME OUT!
POOF
A-ASUNA-SAN!
YOU'RE UP TO SOME-THING STUPID, I KNOW IT! GET OVER HERE!
JINGLE
WHENEVER THINGS GET SCREWED UP, YOU TRY TO USE MAGIC TO UNSCREW IT! IT'S GOTTA STOP!
YOU SAID RIGHT FROM THE START YOUR MAGIC HAD TO BE KEPT SECRET, RIGHT?
YET HERE YOU GO AGAIN, RISKING OTHERS FINDING OUT AND YOUR BEING WASHED UP!
I'VE NOTHING TO LOSE! IF WE FINISH DEAD LAST AGAIN, I'M WASHED UP ANYWAY!
TAKE A LOOK AT THIS.
A BEAT UP NOTE-BOOK?
WHAT!? THIS IS GREAT!
THE GRADES ARE STILL LOUSY, BUT THEY BEAT "ZERO."
STARTING WITH THAT TEST, I'M TRYING A LITTLE HARDER.
LIKE I TOLD YOU WEEKS AGO: BRAVERY IS THE REAL MAGIC.

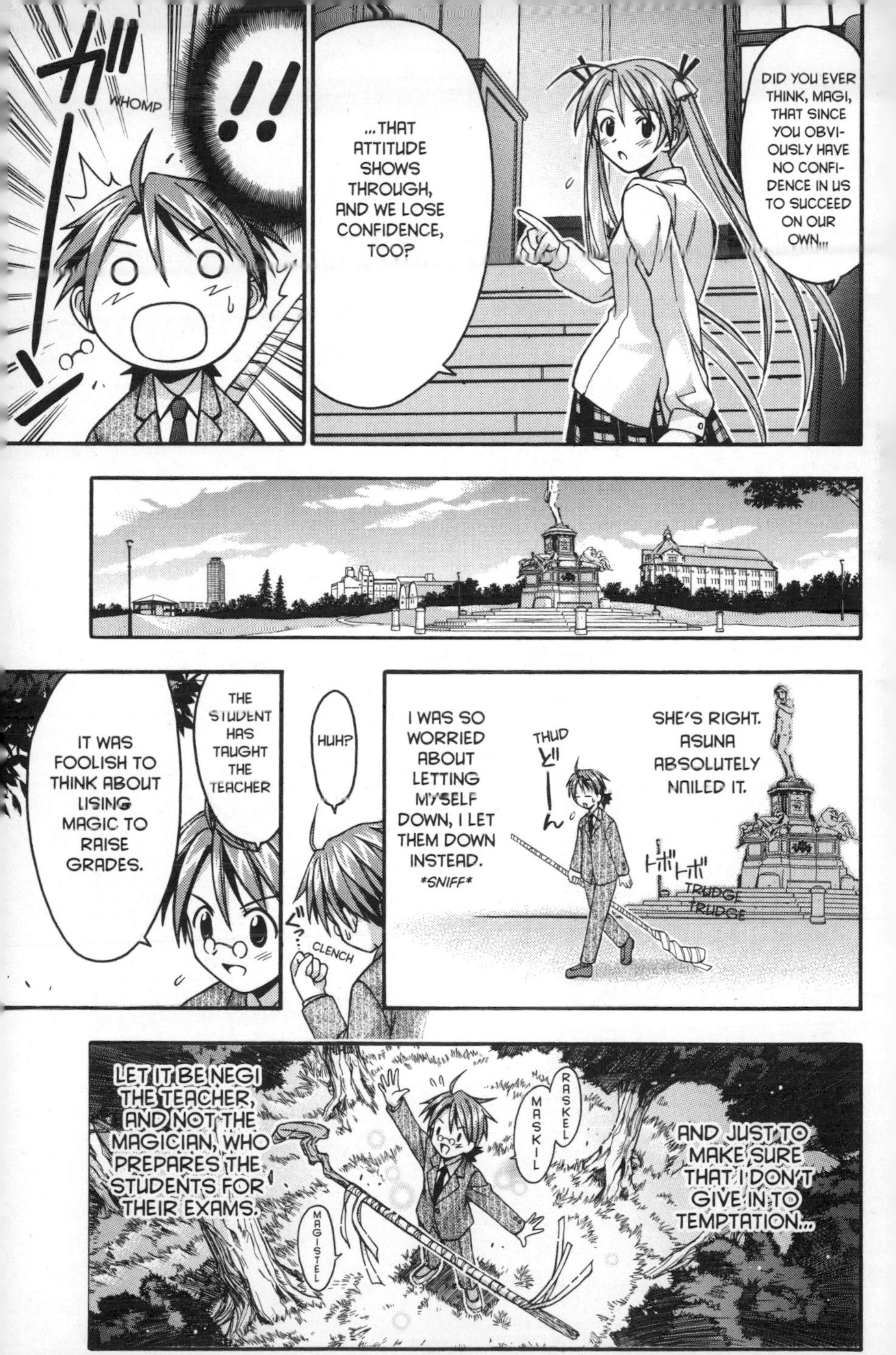
DID YOU EVER THINK, MAGI, THAT SINCE YOU OBVIOUSLY HAVE NO CONFIDENCE IN US TO SUCCEED ON OUR OWN...
...THAT ATTITUDE SHOWS THROUGH, AND WE LOSE CONFIDENCE, TOO?
ガ
WHOMP
!!
SHE'S RIGHT. ASUNA ABSOLUTELY NAILED IT.
トボトボ
TRUDGE TRUDGE
THUD
ど
ーん
I WAS SO WORRIED ABOUT LETTING MYSELF DOWN, I LET THEM DOWN INSTEAD.
SNIFF
HUH?
CLENCH
THE STUDENT HAS TAUGHT THE TEACHER
IT WAS FOOLISH TO THINK ABOUT USING MAGIC TO RAISE GRADES.
LET IT BE NEGI THE TEACHER, AND NOT THE MAGICIAN, WHO PREPARES THE STUDENTS FOR THEIR EXAMS.
AND JUST TO MAKE SURE THAT I DON'T GIVE IN TO TEMPTATION...
RASKEL MASKIL
MAGISTEL

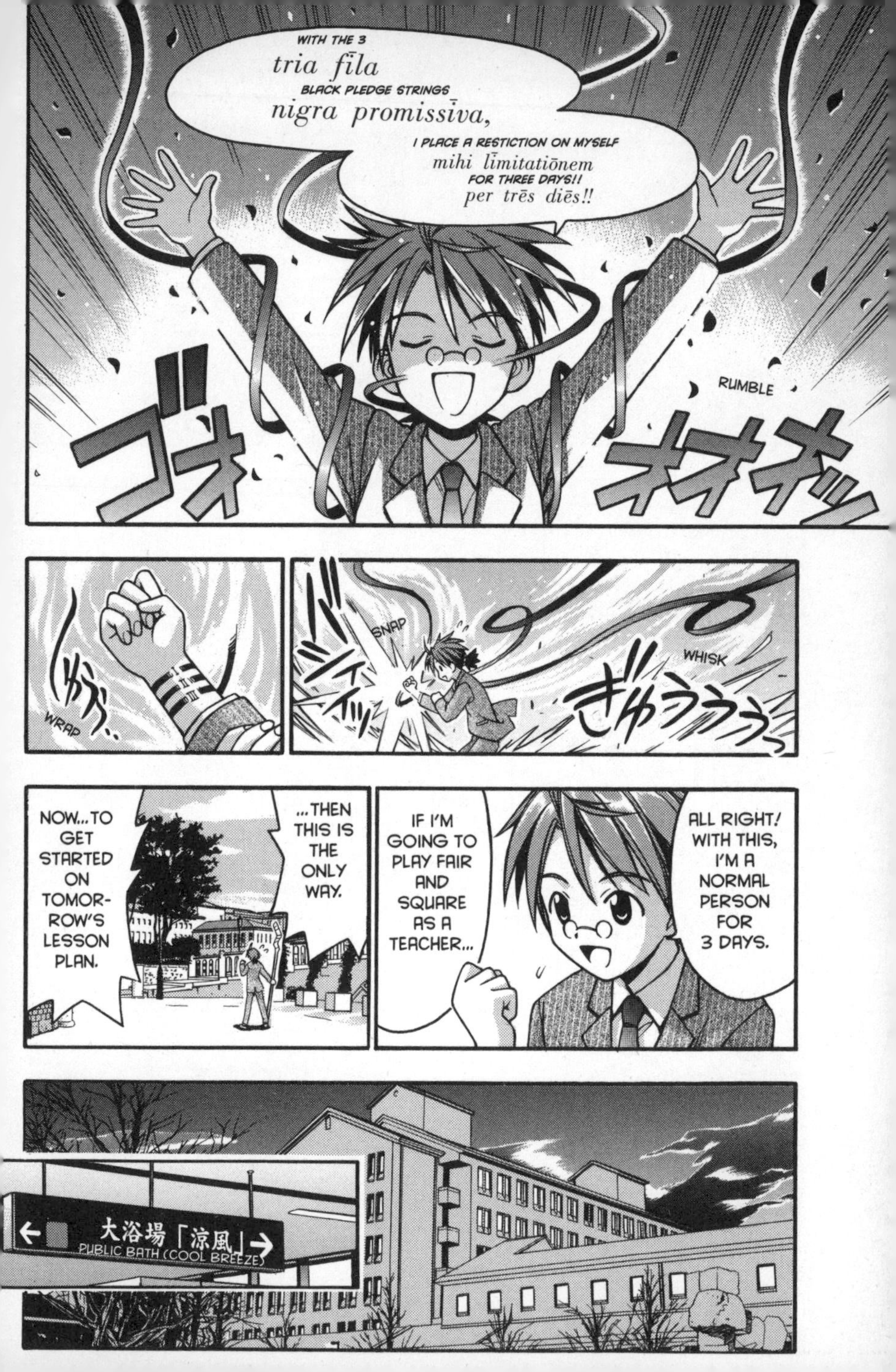
WITH THE 3
tria fīla
BLACK PLEDGE STRINGS
nigra promissīva,
I PLACE A RESTICTION ON MYSELF
mihi līmitatiōnem
FOR THREE DAYS!!
per trēs diēs!!
RUMBLE
SNAP
WHISK
WRAP
ALL RIGHT! WITH THIS, I'M A NORMAL PERSON FOR 3 DAYS.
IF I'M GOING TO PLAY FAIR AND SQUARE AS A TEACHER...
...THEN THIS IS THE ONLY WAY.
NOW...TO GET STARTED ON TOMORROW'S LESSON PLAN.
大浴場「涼風」
PUBLIC BATH (COOL BREEZE)

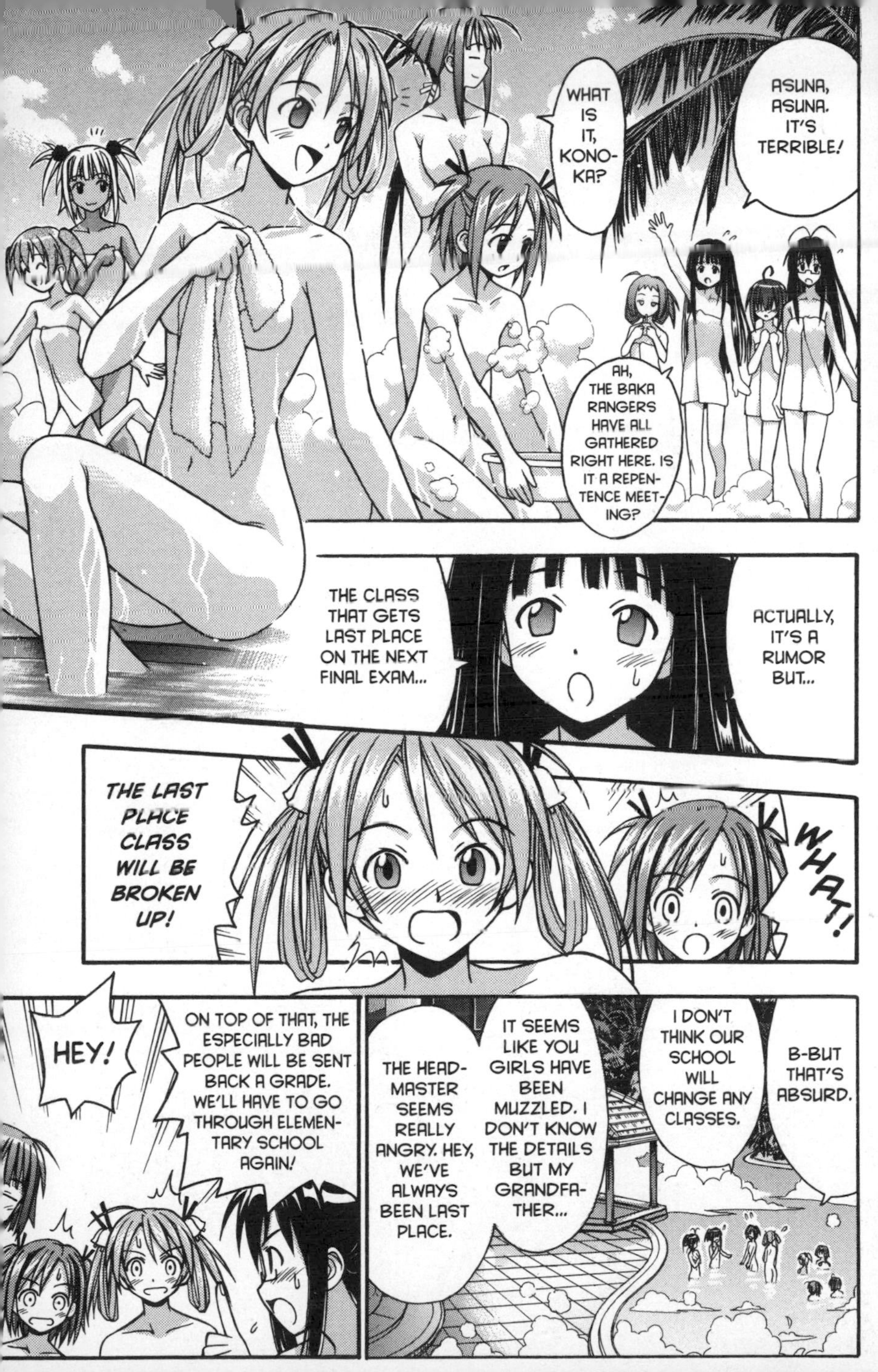
ASUNA, ASUNA. IT'S TERRIBLE!
WHAT IS IT, KONO-KA?
AH, THE BAKA RANGERS HAVE ALL GATHERED RIGHT HERE. IS IT A REPENTENCE MEET-ING?
ACTUALLY, IT'S A RUMOR BUT...
THE CLASS THAT GETS LAST PLACE ON THE NEXT FINAL EXAM...
WHAT!
THE LAST PLACE CLASS WILL BE BROKEN UP!
B-BUT THAT'S ABSURD.
I DON'T THINK OUR SCHOOL WILL CHANGE ANY CLASSES.
IT SEEMS LIKE YOU GIRLS HAVE BEEN MUZZLED. I DON'T KNOW THE DETAILS BUT MY GRANDFA-THER...
THE HEAD-MASTER SEEMS REALLY ANGRY. HEY, WE'VE ALWAYS BEEN LAST PLACE.
ON TOP OF THAT, THE ESPECIALLY BAD PEOPLE WILL BE SENT BACK A GRADE. WE'LL HAVE TO GO THROUGH ELEMEN-TARY SCHOOL AGAIN!
HEY!

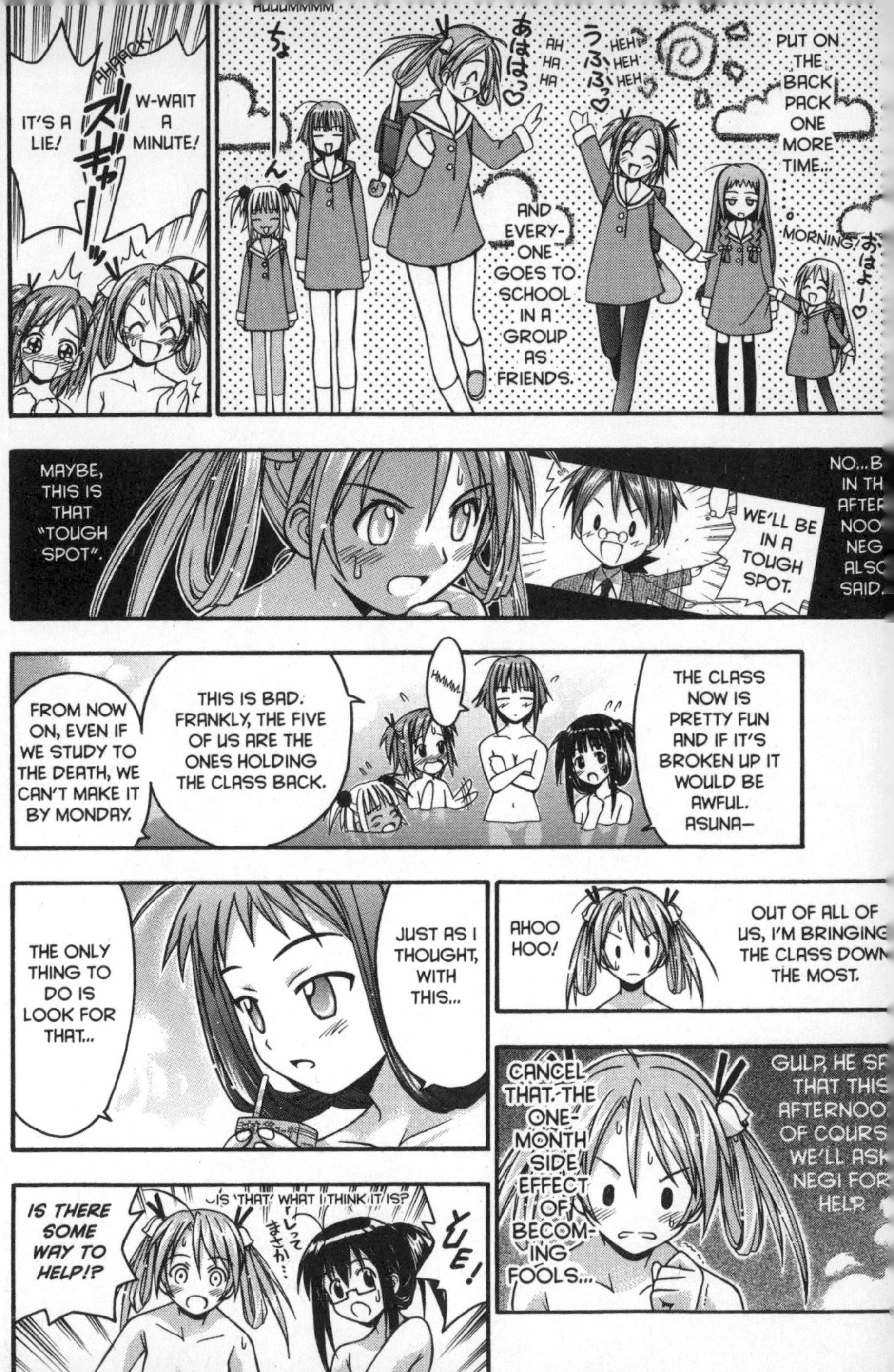
PUT ON THE BACK PACK ONE MORE TIME...
MORNING!
おはよー♡
AND EVERYONE GOES TO SCHOOL IN A GROUP AS FRIENDS.
HEH HEH HEH
うふふっ♡
AH HA HA
あははっ♡
ちょーーん
W-WAIT A MINUTE!
IT'S A LIE!
AHAAACK!
ズギャーーッ
WE'LL BE IN A TOUGH SPOT.
MAYBE, THIS IS THAT "TOUGH SPOT".
THE CLASS NOW IS PRETTY FUN AND IF IT'S BROKEN UP IT WOULD BE AWFUL. ASUNA—
HMMM.
THIS IS BAD. FRANKLY, THE FIVE OF US ARE THE ONES HOLDING THE CLASS BACK.
FROM NOW ON, EVEN IF WE STUDY TO THE DEATH, WE CAN'T MAKE IT BY MONDAY.
OUT OF ALL OF US, I'M BRINGING THE CLASS DOWN THE MOST.
AHOO HOO!
CANCEL THAT. THE ONE-MONTH SIDE EFFECT OF BECOMING FOOLS...
JUST AS I THOUGHT, WITH THIS...
THE ONLY THING TO DO IS LOOK FOR THAT...
IS 'THAT' WHAT I THINK IT IS?
それって まさか…
IS THERE SOME WAY TO HELP!?

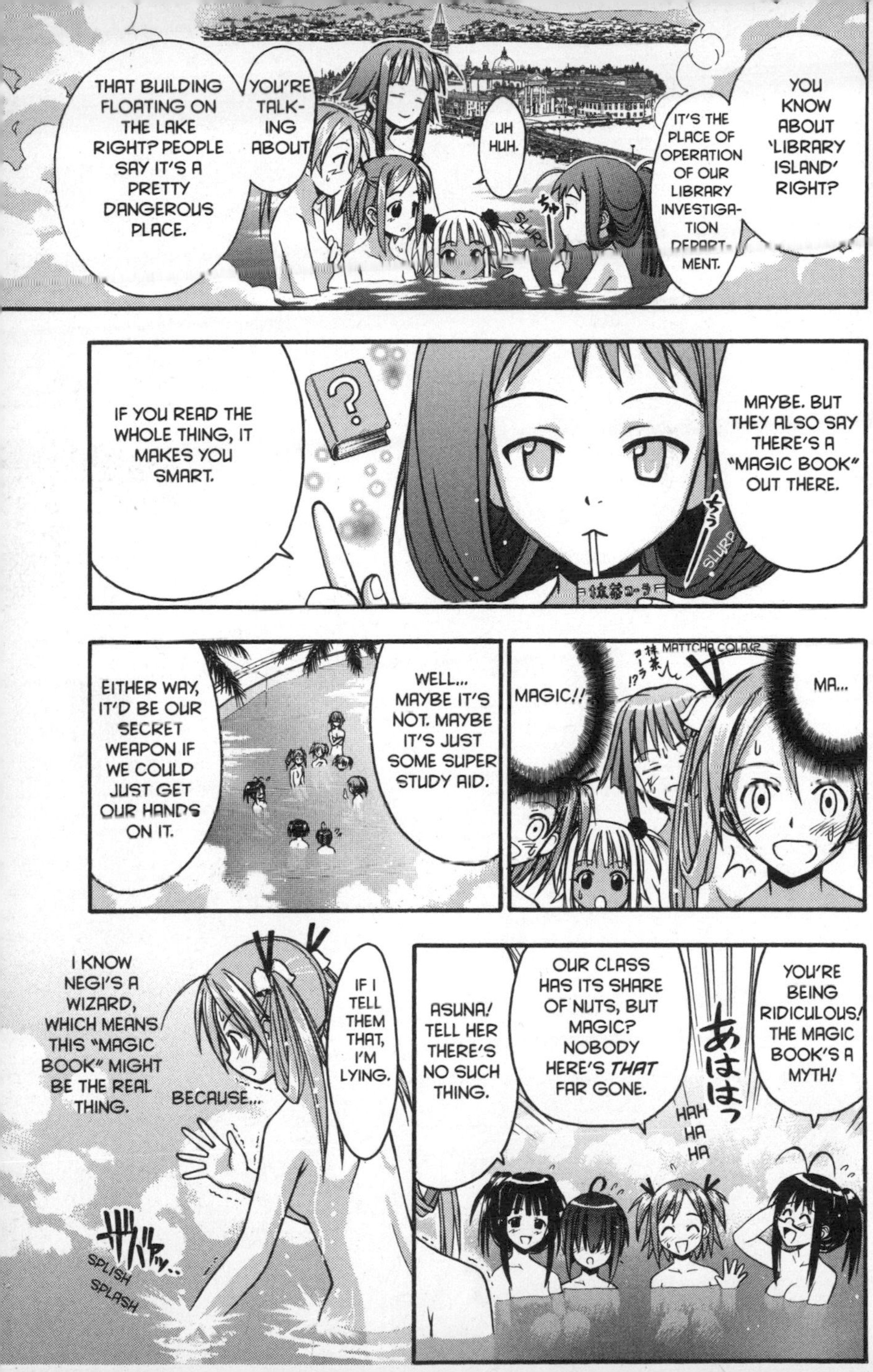
YOU KNOW ABOUT 'LIBRARY ISLAND' RIGHT?
IT'S THE PLACE OF OPERATION OF OUR LIBRARY INVESTIGATION DEPARTMENT.
SLURP
UH HUH.
YOU'RE TALKING ABOUT
THAT BUILDING FLOATING ON THE LAKE RIGHT? PEOPLE SAY IT'S A PRETTY DANGEROUS PLACE.
MAYBE. BUT THEY ALSO SAY THERE'S A "MAGIC BOOK" OUT THERE.
SLURP
IF YOU READ THE WHOLE THING, IT MAKES YOU SMART.
MA...
MATTCHA COLA!?
MAGIC!!
WELL... MAYBE IT'S NOT. MAYBE IT'S JUST SOME SUPER STUDY AID.
EITHER WAY, IT'D BE OUR SECRET WEAPON IF WE COULD JUST GET OUR HANDS ON IT.
YOU'RE BEING RIDICULOUS! THE MAGIC BOOK'S A MYTH!
OUR CLASS HAS ITS SHARE OF NUTS, BUT MAGIC? NOBODY HERE'S *THAT* FAR GONE.
あははっ
HAH HA HA
ASUNA! TELL HER THERE'S NO SUCH THING.
IF I TELL THEM THAT, I'M LYING.
BECAUSE...
I KNOW NEGI'S A WIZARD, WHICH MEANS THIS "MAGIC BOOK" MIGHT BE THE REAL THING.
SPLISH SPLASH

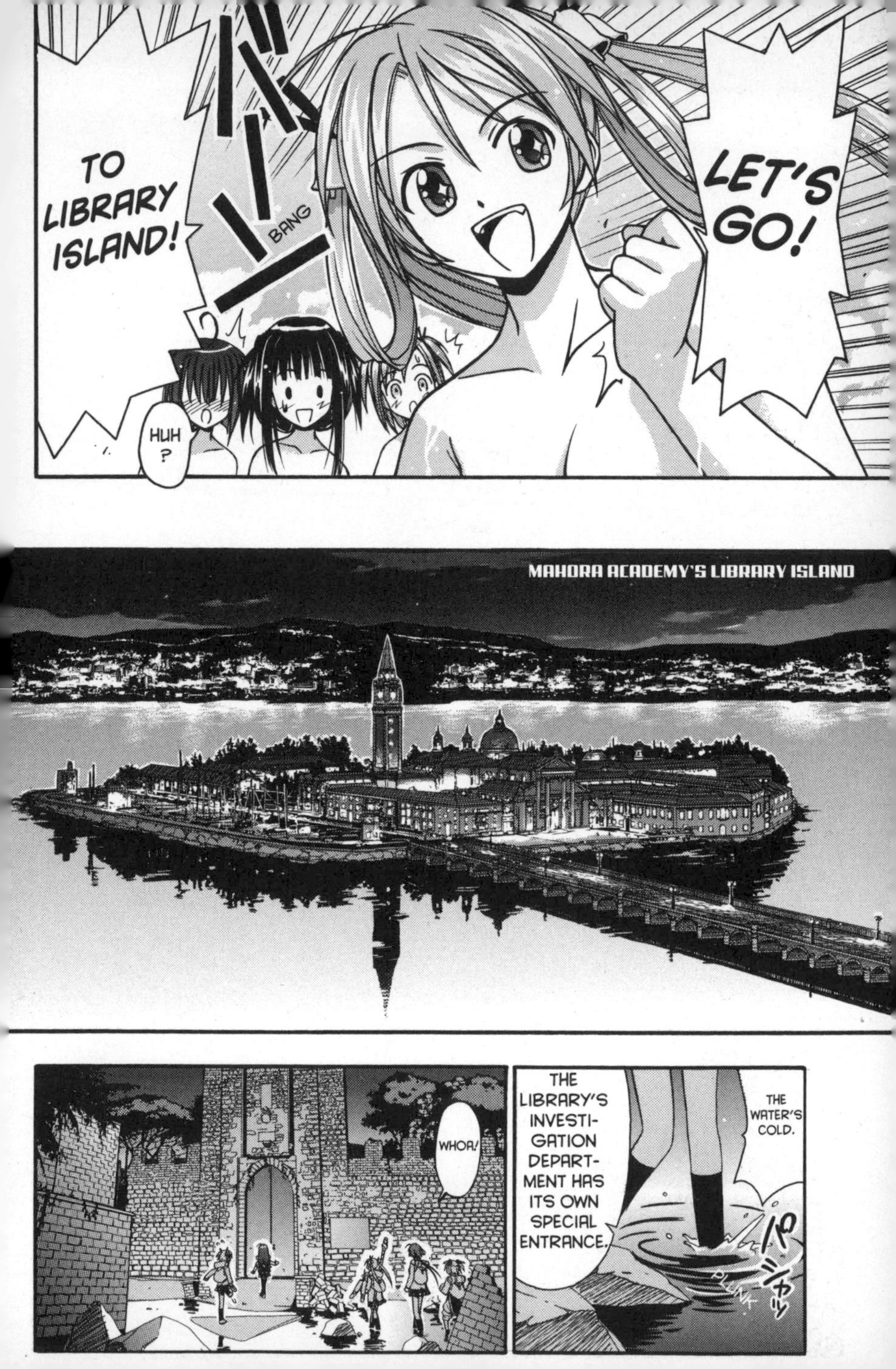
LET'S GO!
TO LIBRARY ISLAND!
BANG
HUH?
MAHORA ACADEMY'S LIBRARY ISLAND
THE WATER'S COLD.
THE LIBRARY'S INVESTIGATION DEPARTMENT HAS ITS OWN SPECIAL ENTRANCE.
WHOA!

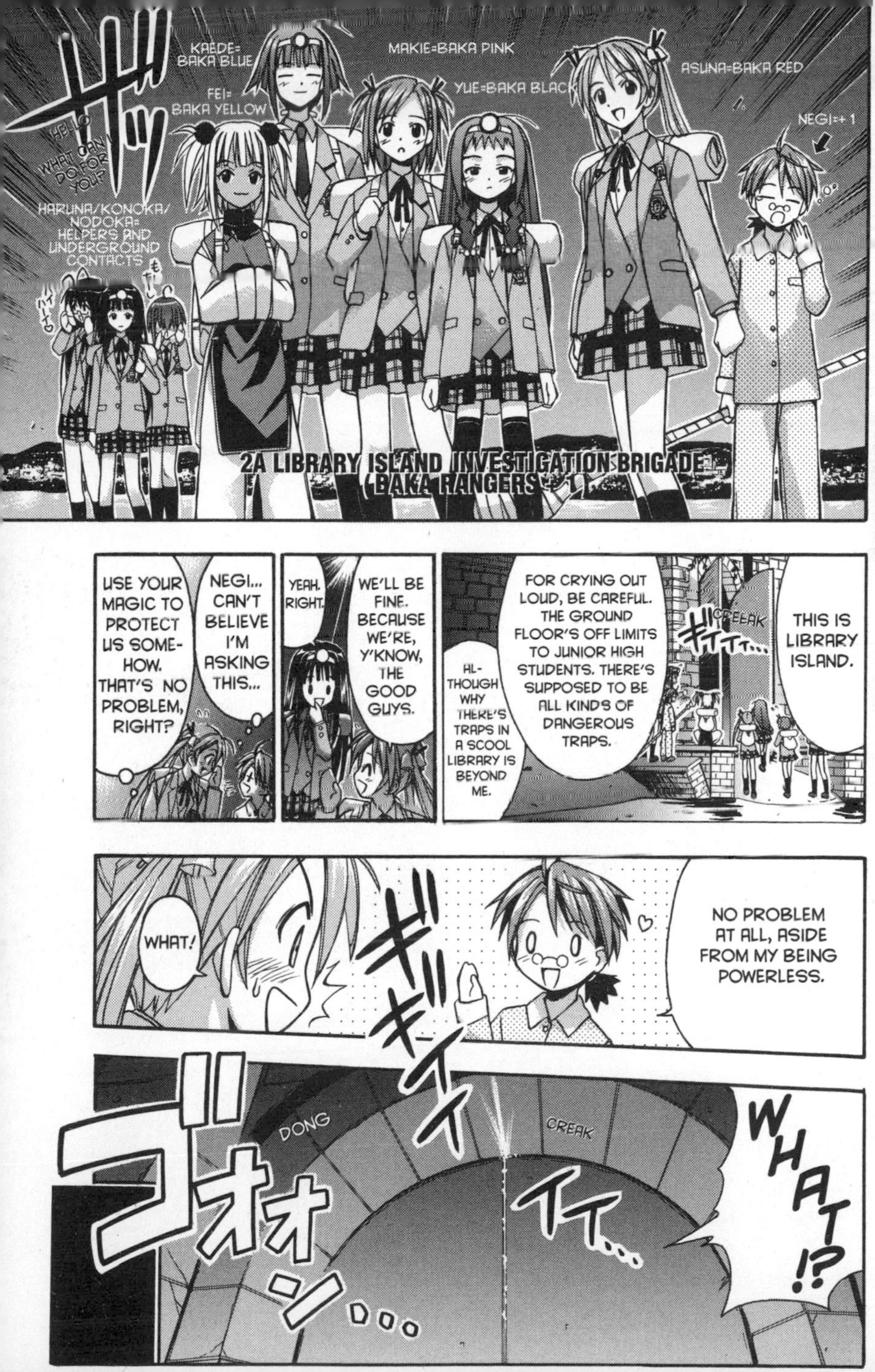
KAEDE= BAKA BLUE
MAKIE=BAKA PINK
ASUNA=BAKA RED
FEI= BAKA YELLOW
YUE=BAKA BLACK
NEGI=+1
HELLO WHAT CAN I DO FOR YOU?
HARUNA/KONOKA/ NODOKA= HELPERS AND UNDERGROUND CONTACTS
2A LIBRARY ISLAND INVESTIGATION BRIGADE (BAKA RANGERS +1)
THIS IS LIBRARY ISLAND.
CREEAK
FOR CRYING OUT LOUD, BE CAREFUL. THE GROUND FLOOR'S OFF LIMITS TO JUNIOR HIGH STUDENTS. THERE'S SUPPOSED TO BE ALL KINDS OF DANGEROUS TRAPS.
AL-THOUGH WHY THERE'S TRAPS IN A SCOOL LIBRARY IS BEYOND ME.
WE'LL BE FINE. BECAUSE WE'RE, Y'KNOW, THE GOOD GUYS.
YEAH. RIGHT.
NEGI... CAN'T BELIEVE I'M ASKING THIS...
USE YOUR MAGIC TO PROTECT US SOME-HOW. THAT'S NO PROBLEM, RIGHT?
NO PROBLEM AT ALL, ASIDE FROM MY BEING POWERLESS.
WHAT!
DONG
CREAK
WHAT!?

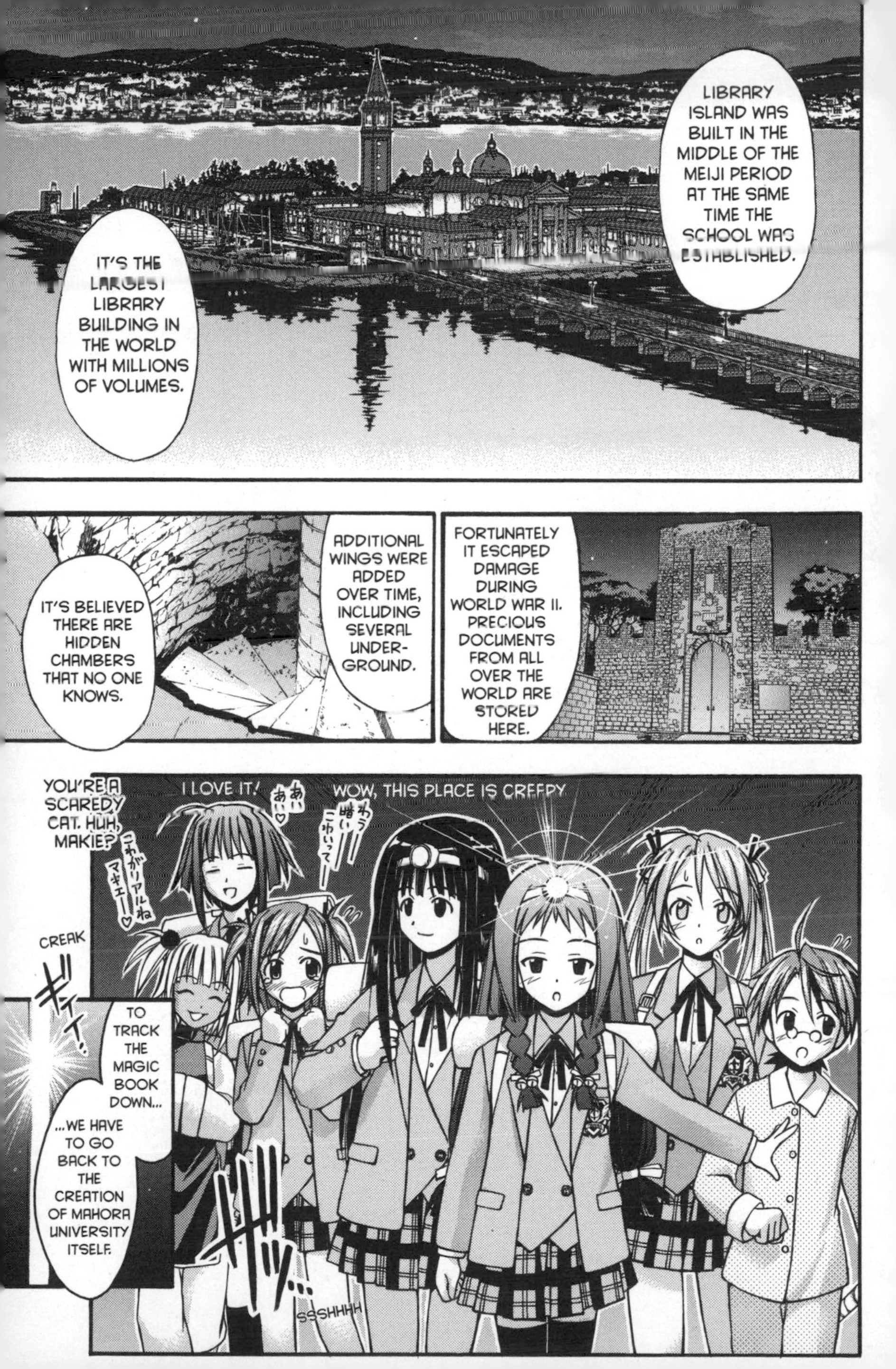
LIBRARY ISLAND WAS BUILT IN THE MIDDLE OF THE MEIJI PERIOD AT THE SAME TIME THE SCHOOL WAS ESTABLISHED.
IT'S THE LARGEST LIBRARY BUILDING IN THE WORLD WITH MILLIONS OF VOLUMES.
FORTUNATELY IT ESCAPED DAMAGE DURING WORLD WAR II. PRECIOUS DOCUMENTS FROM ALL OVER THE WORLD ARE STORED HERE.
ADDITIONAL WINGS WERE ADDED OVER TIME, INCLUDING SEVERAL UNDER-GROUND.
IT'S BELIEVED THERE ARE HIDDEN CHAMBERS THAT NO ONE KNOWS.
WOW, THIS PLACE IS CREEPY
わっ 暗い こわいって
I LOVE IT!
あ、あい♡
YOU'RE A SCAREDY CAT, HUH, MAKIE?
こわがりアルね マキエー♡
CREAK
ギィィ
TO TRACK THE MAGIC BOOK DOWN...
...WE HAVE TO GO BACK TO THE CREATION OF MAHORA UNIVERSITY ITSELF.
SSSHHHH

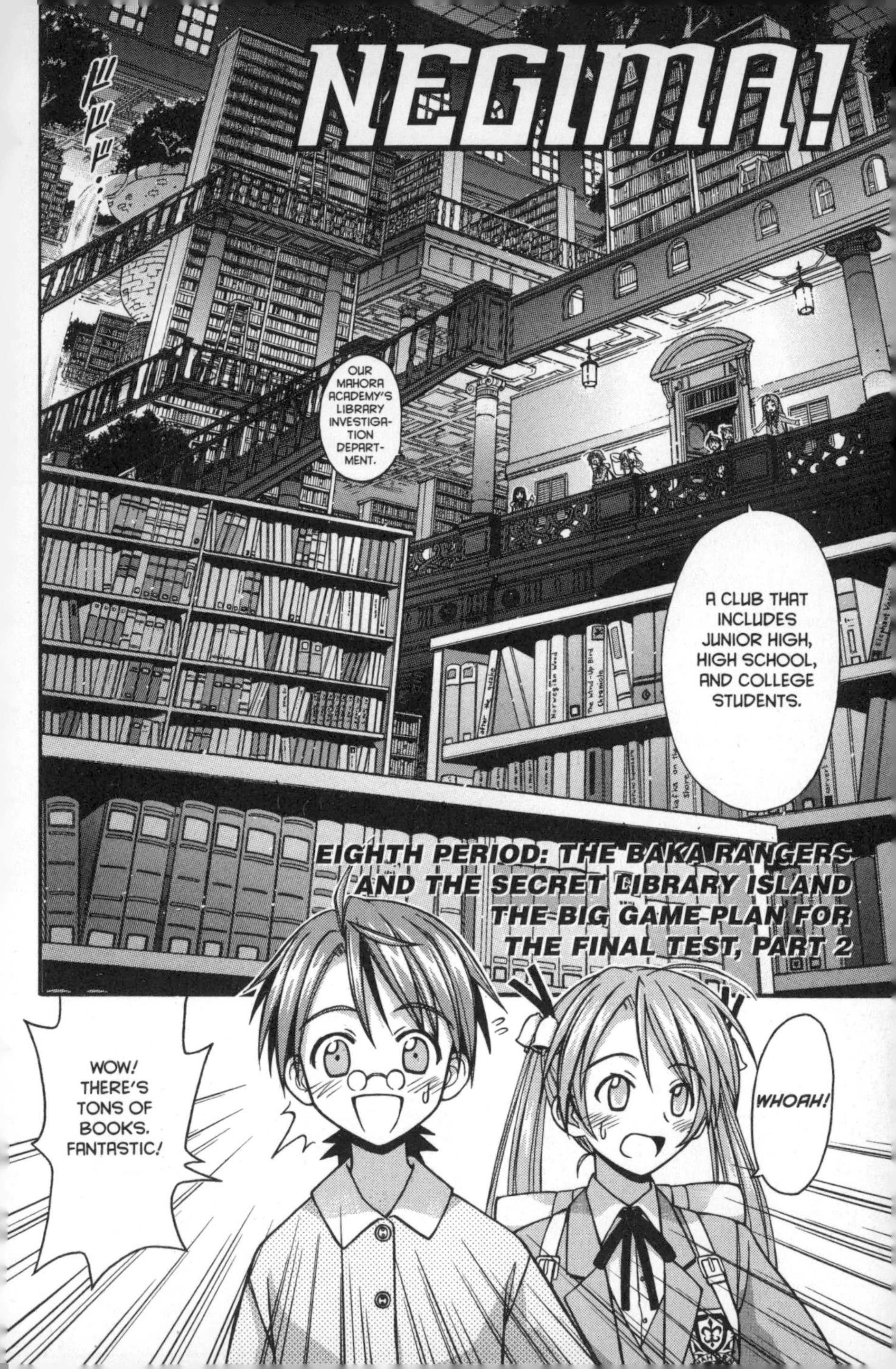
NEGIMA!
OUR MAHORA ACADEMY'S LIBRARY INVESTIGATION DEPARTMENT.
A CLUB THAT INCLUDES JUNIOR HIGH, HIGH SCHOOL, AND COLLEGE STUDENTS.
EIGHTH PERIOD: THE BAKA RANGERS AND THE SECRET LIBRARY ISLAND THE BIG GAME PLAN FOR THE FINAL TEST, PART 2
WHOAH!
WOW! THERE'S TONS OF BOOKS. FANTASTIC!

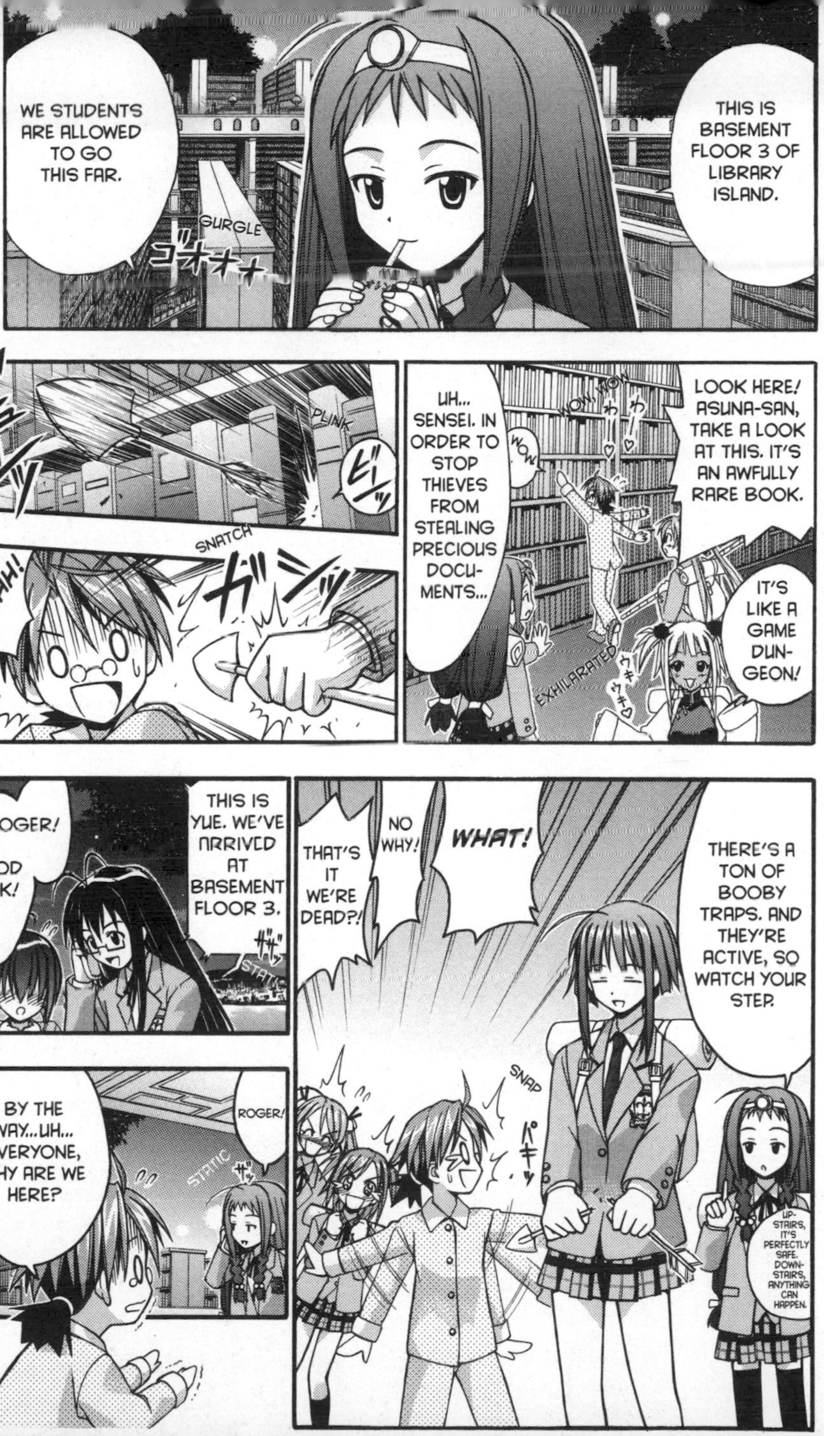
THIS IS BASEMENT FLOOR 3 OF LIBRARY ISLAND.
WE STUDENTS ARE ALLOWED TO GO THIS FAR.
GURGLE
ゴオオオ
LOOK HERE! ASUNA-SAN, TAKE A LOOK AT THIS. IT'S AN AWFULLY RARE BOOK.
WOW WOW
わーわー
WOW
IT'S LIKE A GAME DUN-GEON!
EXHILARATED
ウキウキ
UH... SENSEI. IN ORDER TO STOP THIEVES FROM STEALING PRECIOUS DOCU-MENTS...
WHIZ
ビューッ
PLINK
ビーッ
SNATCH
ガシッ
EEYAH!
THERE'S A TON OF BOOBY TRAPS. AND THEY'RE ACTIVE, SO WATCH YOUR STEP.
WHAT!
NO WHY!
THAT'S IT WE'RE DEAD?!
SNAP
パキッ
UP-STAIRS, IT'S PERFECTLY SAFE. DOWN-STAIRS, ANYTHING CAN HAPPEN.
THIS IS YUE. WE'VE ARRIVED AT BASEMENT FLOOR 3.
STATIC
ザザッ
ROGER!
GOOD LUCK!
ROGER!
STATIC
ザッ
BY THE WAY...UH... EVERYONE, WHY ARE WE HERE?

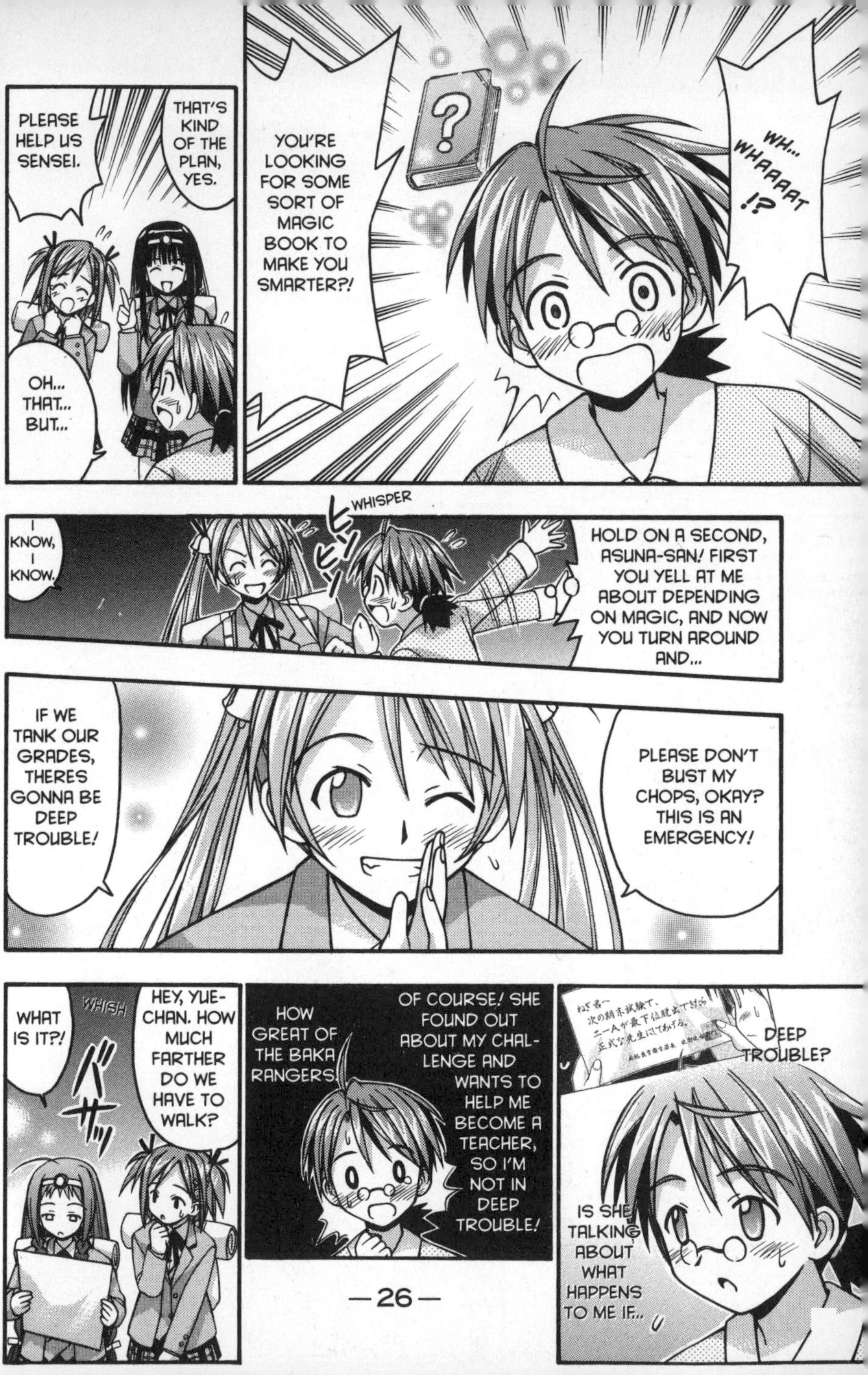
WH... WHAAAAT !?
YOU'RE LOOKING FOR SOME SORT OF MAGIC BOOK TO MAKE YOU SMARTER?!
THAT'S KIND OF THE PLAN, YES.
PLEASE HELP US SENSEI.
OH... THAT... BUT...
WHISPER
HOLD ON A SECOND, ASUNA-SAN! FIRST YOU YELL AT ME ABOUT DEPENDING ON MAGIC, AND NOW YOU TURN AROUND AND...
I KNOW, I KNOW.
PLEASE DON'T BUST MY CHOPS, OKAY? THIS IS AN EMERGENCY!
IF WE TANK OUR GRADES, THERES GONNA BE DEEP TROUBLE!
DEEP TROUBLE?
IS SHE TALKING ABOUT WHAT HAPPENS TO ME IF...
OF COURSE! SHE FOUND OUT ABOUT MY CHALLENGE AND WANTS TO HELP ME BECOME A TEACHER, SO I'M NOT IN DEEP TROUBLE!
HOW GREAT OF THE BAKA RANGERS.
HEY, YUE-CHAN. HOW MUCH FARTHER DO WE HAVE TO WALK?
WHISH
WHAT IS IT?!

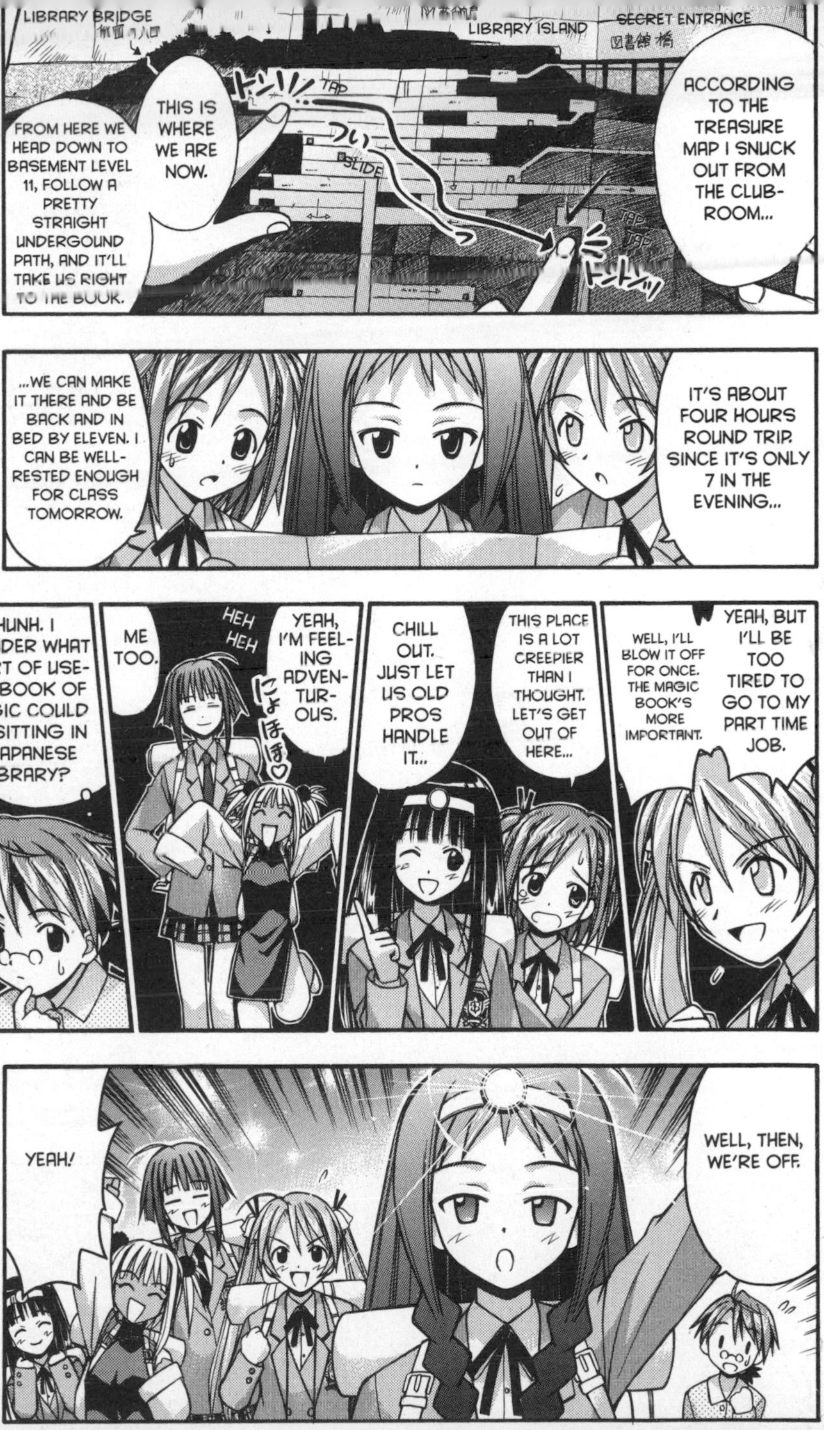
LIBRARY BRIDGE
LIBRARY ISLAND
SECRET ENTRANCE
ACCORDING TO THE TREASURE MAP I SNUCK OUT FROM THE CLUB-ROOM...
TAP
THIS IS WHERE WE ARE NOW.
SLIDE
TAP TAP
FROM HERE WE HEAD DOWN TO BASEMENT LEVEL 11, FOLLOW A PRETTY STRAIGHT UNDERGOUND PATH, AND IT'LL TAKE US RIGHT TO THE BOOK.
IT'S ABOUT FOUR HOURS ROUND TRIP. SINCE IT'S ONLY 7 IN THE EVENING...
...WE CAN MAKE IT THERE AND BE BACK AND IN BED BY ELEVEN. I CAN BE WELL-RESTED ENOUGH FOR CLASS TOMORROW.
YEAH, BUT I'LL BE TOO TIRED TO GO TO MY PART TIME JOB.
WELL, I'LL BLOW IT OFF FOR ONCE. THE MAGIC BOOK'S MORE IMPORTANT.
THIS PLACE IS A LOT CREEPIER THAN I THOUGHT. LET'S GET OUT OF HERE...
CHILL OUT. JUST LET US OLD PROS HANDLE IT...
YEAH, I'M FEEL-ING ADVEN-TUR-OUS.
HEH HEH
ME TOO.
HUNH. I WONDER WHAT SORT OF USE-FUL BOOK OF MAGIC COULD BE SITTING IN A JAPANESE LIBRARY?
WELL, THEN, WE'RE OFF.
YEAH!

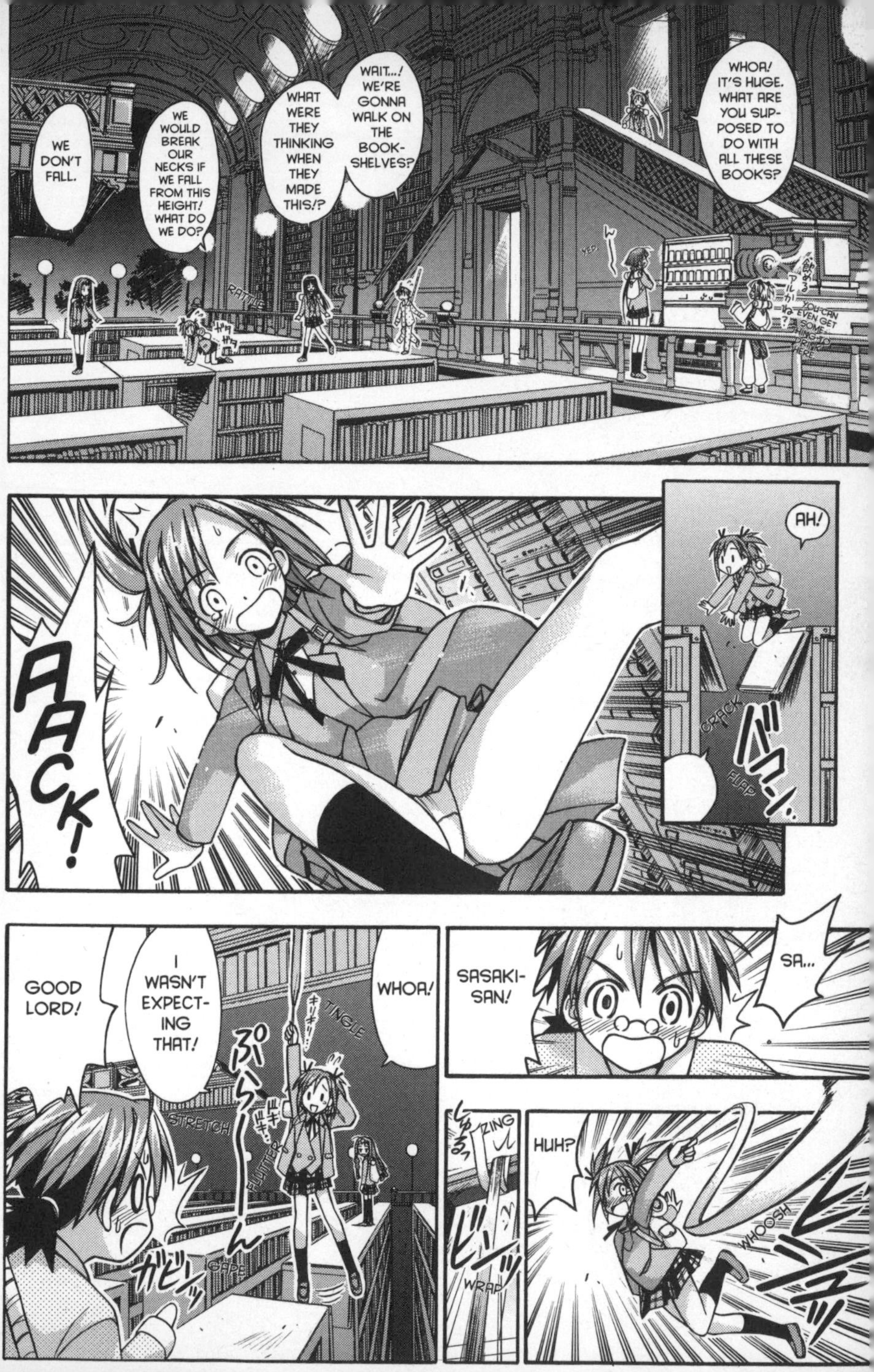
WHOA! IT'S HUGE. WHAT ARE YOU SUP-POSED TO DO WITH ALL THESE BOOKS?
YOU CAN EVEN GET SOME-THING TO DRINK HERE.
YEP.
WAIT...! WE'RE GONNA WALK ON THE BOOK-SHELVES?
WHAT WERE THEY THINKING WHEN THEY MADE THIS!?
WE WOULD BREAK OUR NECKS IF WE FALL FROM THIS HEIGHT! WHAT DO WE DO?
WE DON'T FALL.
RATTLE
AH!
CRACK
FLAP
AACK!
SA...
SASAKI-SAN!
WHOA!
TINGLE
I WASN'T EXPECT-ING THAT!
GOOD LORD!
STRETCH
FLUTTER
GAPE
HUH?
ZING
WRAP
WHOOSH

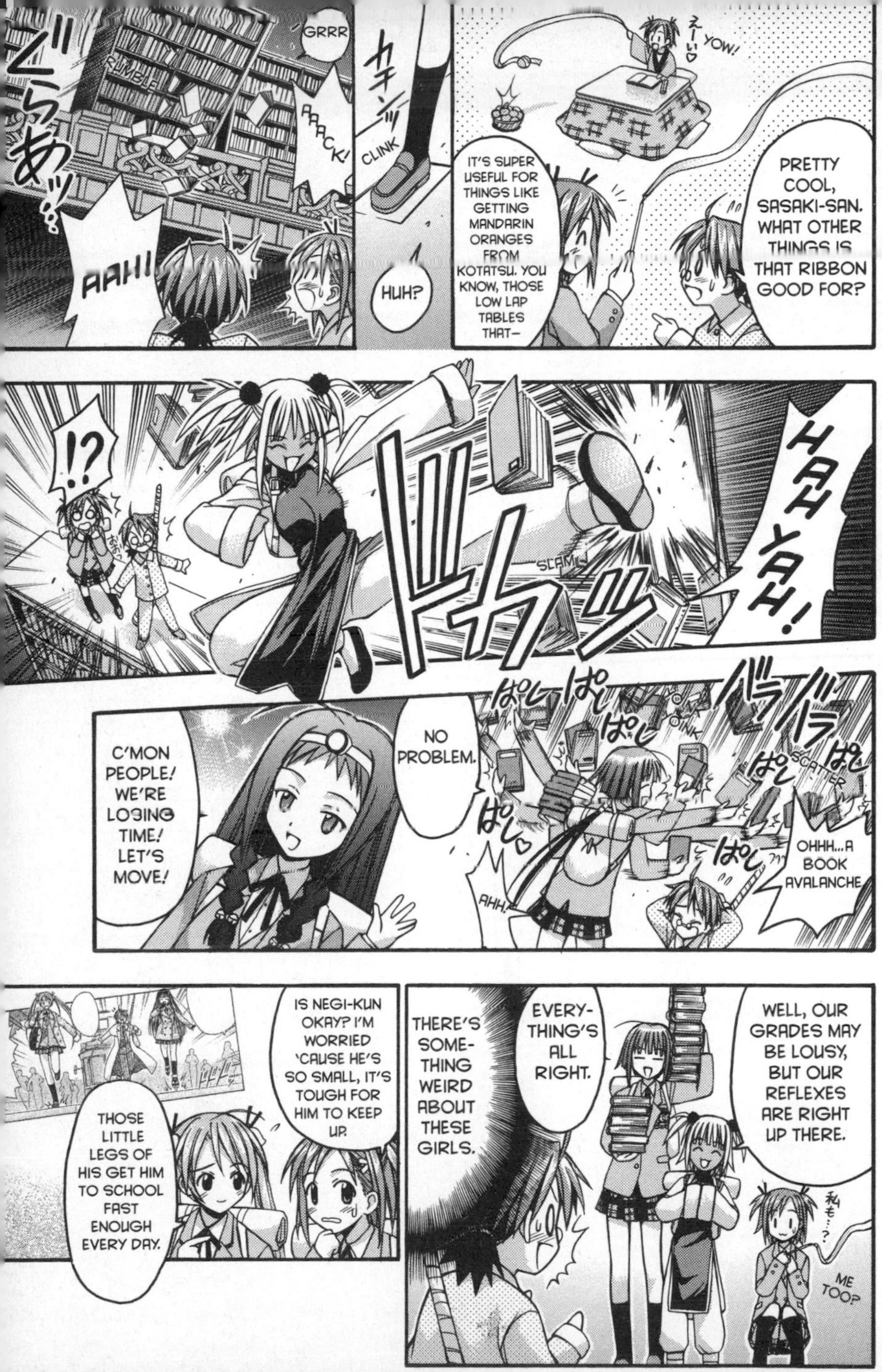
えーい♡
YOW!
PRETTY COOL, SASAKI-SAN. WHAT OTHER THINGS IS THAT RIBBON GOOD FOR?
IT'S SUPER USEFUL FOR THINGS LIKE GETTING MANDARIN ORANGES FROM KOTATSU. YOU KNOW, THOSE LOW LAP TABLES THAT—
CLINK
HUH?
GRRR
RUMBLE
ARRACK!
AAH!
HAH YAH!
SLAM
ドカッ
!?
NO PROBLEM.
C'MON PEOPLE! WE'RE LOSING TIME! LET'S MOVE!
OHHH...A BOOK AVALANCHE
SCATTER
AHH.
WELL, OUR GRADES MAY BE LOUSY, BUT OUR REFLEXES ARE RIGHT UP THERE.
EVERY-THING'S ALL RIGHT.
私も…?
ME TOO?
THERE'S SOME-THING WEIRD ABOUT THESE GIRLS.
IS NEGI-KUN OKAY? I'M WORRIED 'CAUSE HE'S SO SMALL, IT'S TOUGH FOR HIM TO KEEP UP.
THOSE LITTLE LEGS OF HIS GET HIM TO SCHOOL FAST ENOUGH EVERY DAY.

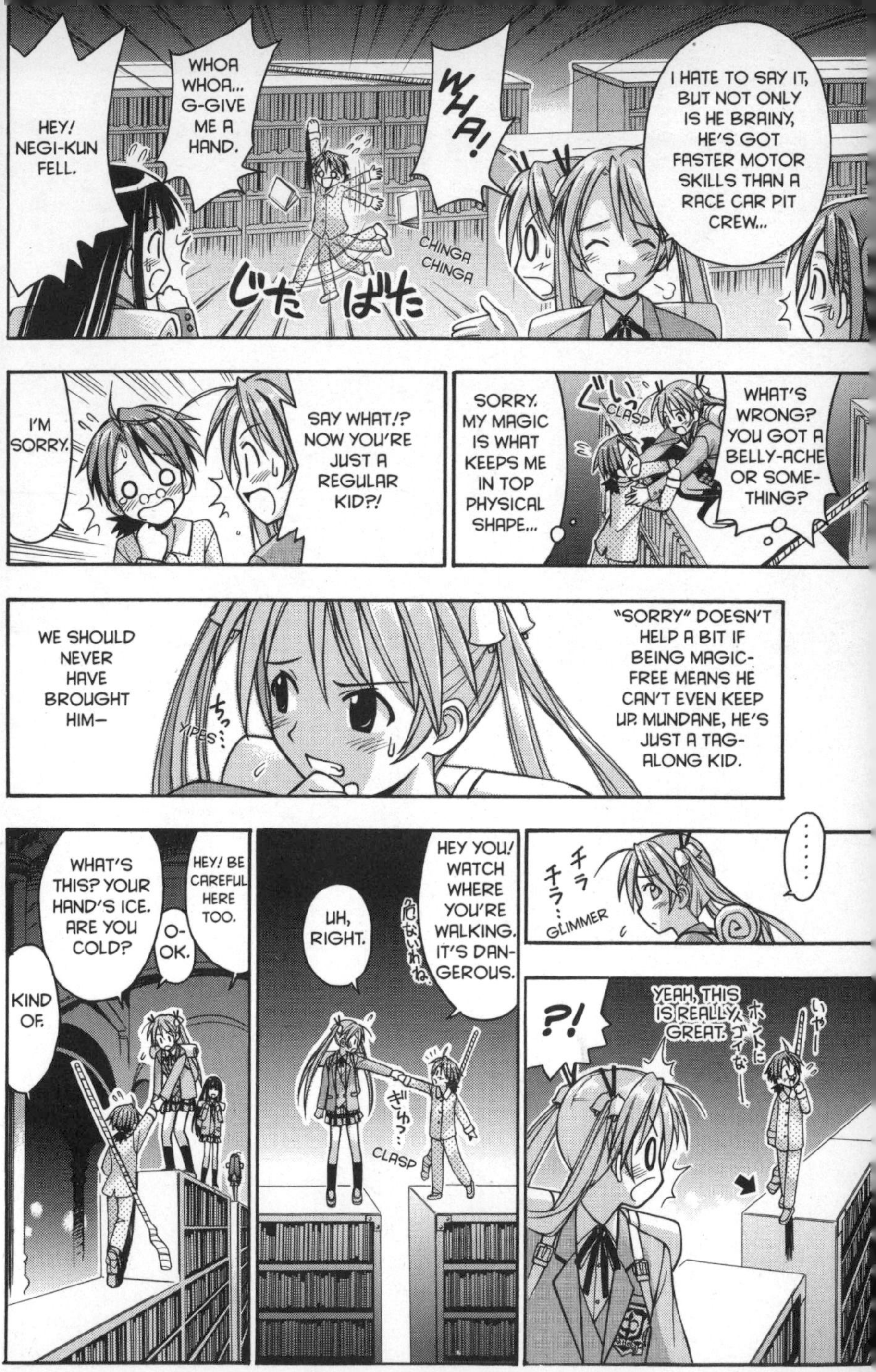

I HATE TO SAY IT, BUT NOT ONLY IS HE BRAINY, HE'S GOT FASTER MOTOR SKILLS THAN A RACE CAR PIT CREW...
WHA!
WHOA WHOA... G-GIVE ME A HAND.
HEY! NEGI-KUN FELL.
CHINGA CHINGA
じた ばた
WHAT'S WRONG? YOU GOT A BELLY-ACHE OR SOME-THING?
CLASP
SORRY. MY MAGIC IS WHAT KEEPS ME IN TOP PHYSICAL SHAPE...
SAY WHAT!? NOW YOU'RE JUST A REGULAR KID?!
I'M SORRY.
"SORRY" DOESN'T HELP A BIT IF BEING MAGIC-FREE MEANS HE CAN'T EVEN KEEP UP. MUNDANE, HE'S JUST A TAG-ALONG KID.
YIPES...
WE SHOULD NEVER HAVE BROUGHT HIM—
......
チラ チラ... GLIMMER
YEAH, THIS IS REALLY GREAT.
ホントにスゴイなー
いやー
?!
HEY YOU! WATCH WHERE YOU'RE WALKING. IT'S DAN-GEROUS.
危ないわね。
UH, RIGHT.
ぎゅっ... CLASP
HEY! BE CAREFUL HERE TOO.
O-OK.
WHAT'S THIS? YOUR HAND'S ICE. ARE YOU COLD?
KIND OF.

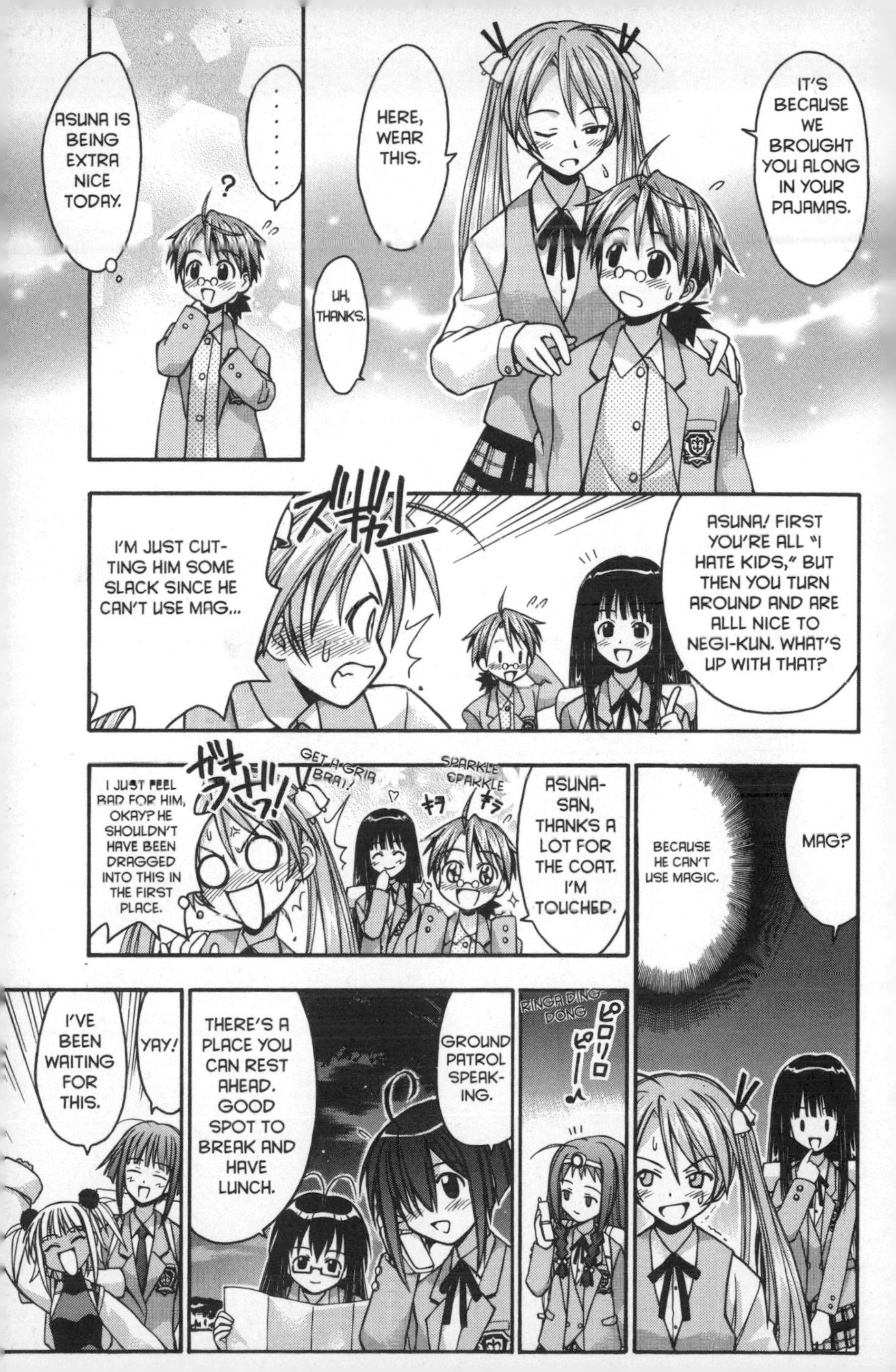

IT'S BECAUSE WE BROUGHT YOU ALONG IN YOUR PAJAMAS.
HERE, WEAR THIS.
UH, THANKS.
. . . . . .
?
ASUNA IS BEING EXTRA NICE TODAY.
ASUNA! FIRST YOU'RE ALL "I HATE KIDS," BUT THEN YOU TURN AROUND AND ARE ALLL NICE TO NEGI-KUN. WHAT'S UP WITH THAT?
I'M JUST CUT-TING HIM SOME SLACK SINCE HE CAN'T USE MAG...
MAG?
BECAUSE HE CAN'T USE MAGIC.
ASUNA-SAN, THANKS A LOT FOR THE COAT. I'M TOUCHED.
SPARKLE SPARKLE
GET A GRIP BRAT!
I JUST FEEL BAD FOR HIM, OKAY? HE SHOULDN'T HAVE BEEN DRAGGED INTO THIS IN THE FIRST PLACE.
RINGA DING-DONG
GROUND PATROL SPEAK-ING.
THERE'S A PLACE YOU CAN REST AHEAD. GOOD SPOT TO BREAK AND HAVE LUNCH.
YAY!
I'VE BEEN WAITING FOR THIS.

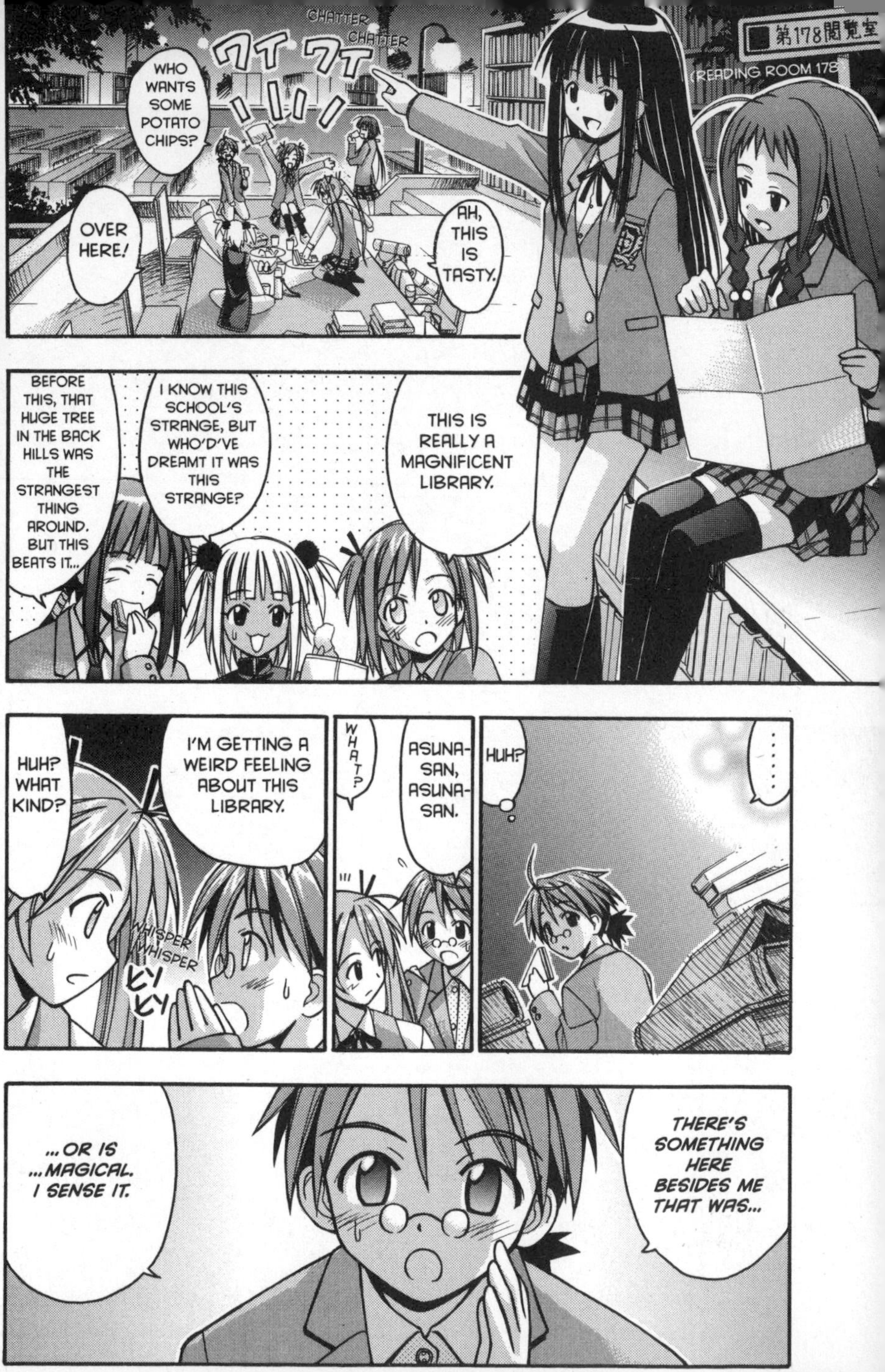

第178閲覧室
READING ROOM 178
CHATTER CHATTER
ワイ ワイ
WHO WANTS SOME POTATO CHIPS?
OVER HERE!
AH, THIS IS TASTY.
THIS IS REALLY A MAGNIFICENT LIBRARY.
I KNOW THIS SCHOOL'S STRANGE, BUT WHO'D'VE DREAMT IT WAS THIS STRANGE?
BEFORE THIS, THAT HUGE TREE IN THE BACK HILLS WAS THE STRANGEST THING AROUND. BUT THIS BEATS IT...
......
HUH?
ASUNA-SAN, ASUNA-SAN.
WHAT?
I'M GETTING A WEIRD FEELING ABOUT THIS LIBRARY.
HUH? WHAT KIND?
WHISPER WHISPER
ヒソ ヒソ
THERE'S SOMETHING HERE BESIDES ME THAT WAS...
...OR IS ...MAGICAL. I SENSE IT.

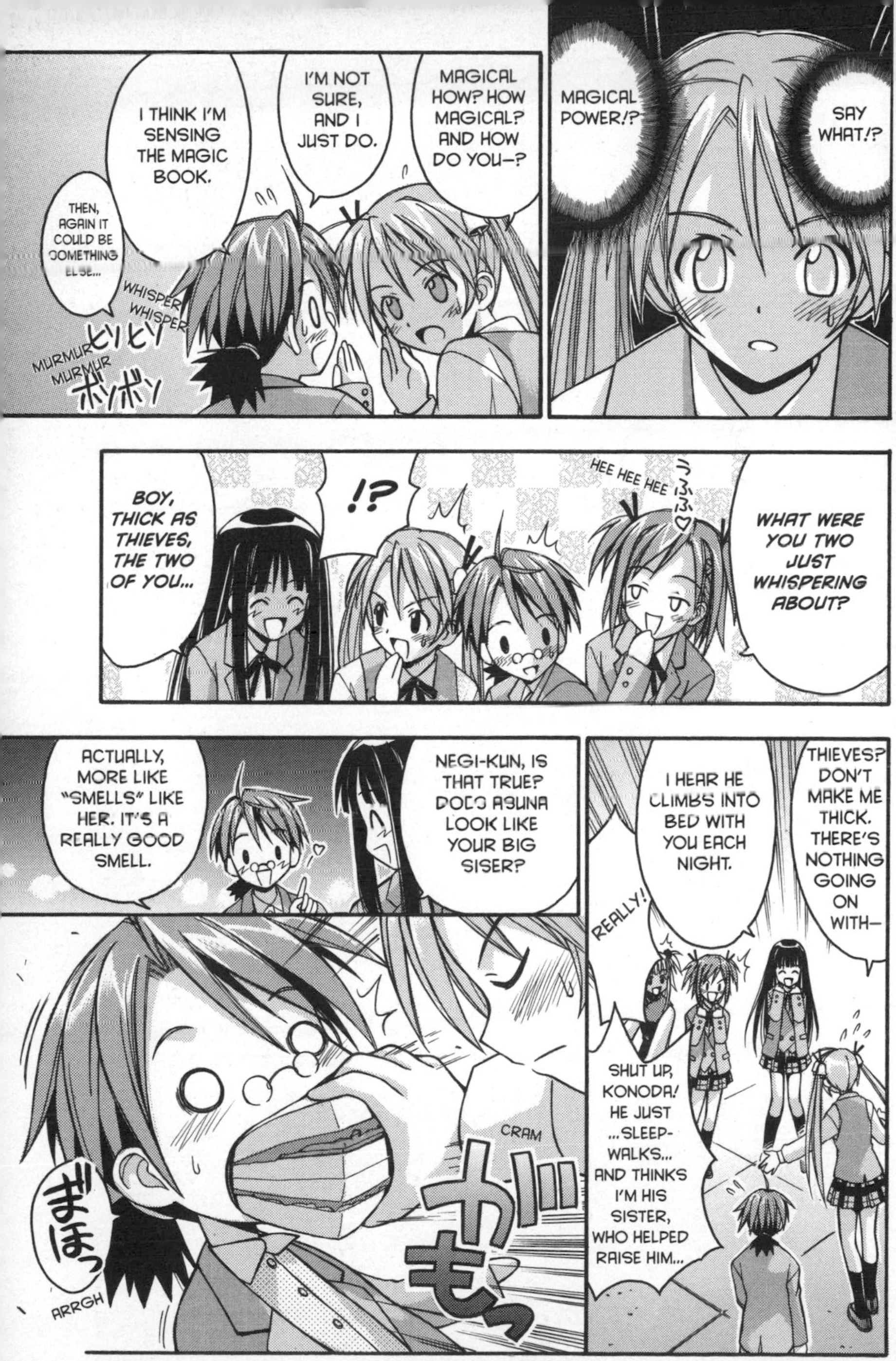
SAY WHAT!?
MAGICAL POWER!?
MAGICAL HOW? HOW MAGICAL? AND HOW DO YOU–?
I'M NOT SURE, AND I JUST DO.
I THINK I'M SENSING THE MAGIC BOOK.
THEN, AGAIN IT COULD BE SOMETHING ELSE...
WHISPER WHISPER
ヒソヒソ
MURMUR MURMUR
ボソボソ
WHAT WERE YOU TWO JUST WHISPERING ABOUT?
HEE HEE HEE
うふふ♡
!?
BOY, THICK AS THIEVES, THE TWO OF YOU...
THIEVES? DON'T MAKE ME THICK. THERE'S NOTHING GOING ON WITH–
I HEAR HE CLIMBS INTO BED WITH YOU EACH NIGHT.
REALLY!
SHUT UP, KONODA! HE JUST ...SLEEP-WALKS... AND THINKS I'M HIS SISTER, WHO HELPED RAISE HIM...
NEGI-KUN, IS THAT TRUE? DOES ASUNA LOOK LIKE YOUR BIG SISER?
ACTUALLY, MORE LIKE "SMELLS" LIKE HER. IT'S A REALLY GOOD SMELL.
CRAM
わっもっ
ARRGH
まほっ

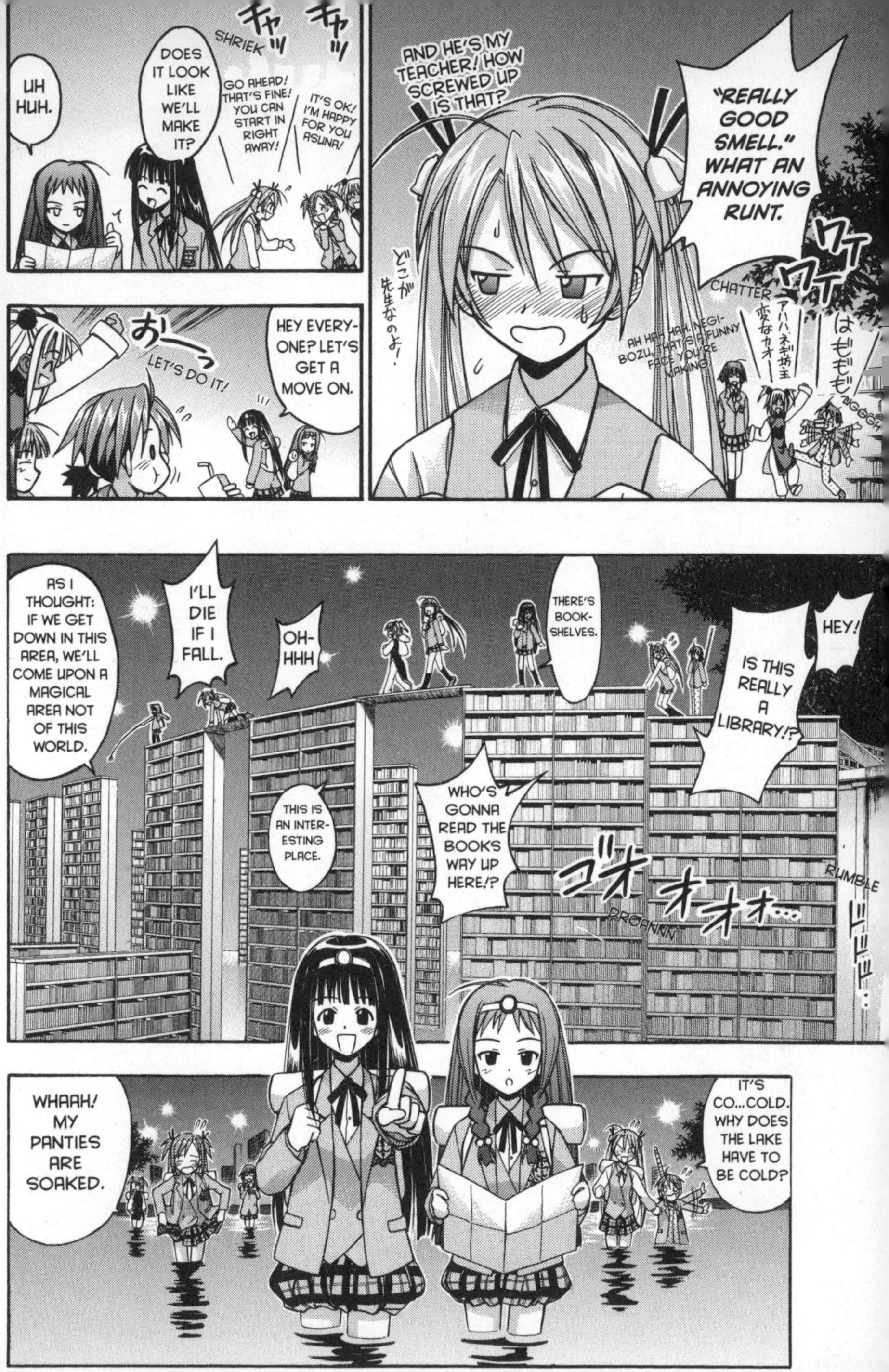
"REALLY GOOD SMELL." WHAT AN ANNOYING RUNT.
AND HE'S MY TEACHER! HOW SCREWED UP IS THAT?
どこが先生なのよ!
ワイワイ
CHATTER
アハハ、ネギ坊主変なカオー
AH HAH HAH. NEGI-BOZU, THAT'S A FUNNY FACE YOU'RE MAKING
はもももも
キャッ キャッ
SHRIEK
IT'S OK! I'M HAPPY FOR YOU ASUNA!
GO AHEAD! THAT'S FINE! YOU CAN START IN RIGHT AWAY!
DOES IT LOOK LIKE WE'LL MAKE IT?
UH HUH.
HEY EVERY-ONE? LET'S GET A MOVE ON.
おーっ
LET'S DO IT!
HEY!
IS THIS REALLY A LIBRARY!?
THERE'S BOOK-SHELVES.
OH-HHH
I'LL DIE IF I FALL.
AS I THOUGHT: IF WE GET DOWN IN THIS AREA, WE'LL COME UPON A MAGICAL AREA NOT OF THIS WORLD.
WHO'S GONNA READ THE BOOKS WAY UP HERE!?
THIS IS AN INTER-ESTING PLACE.
ゴオオオオ…
DROANNN
RUMBLE
ドドドド…
IT'S CO...COLD. WHY DOES THE LAKE HAVE TO BE COLD?
WHAAH! MY PANTIES ARE SOAKED.

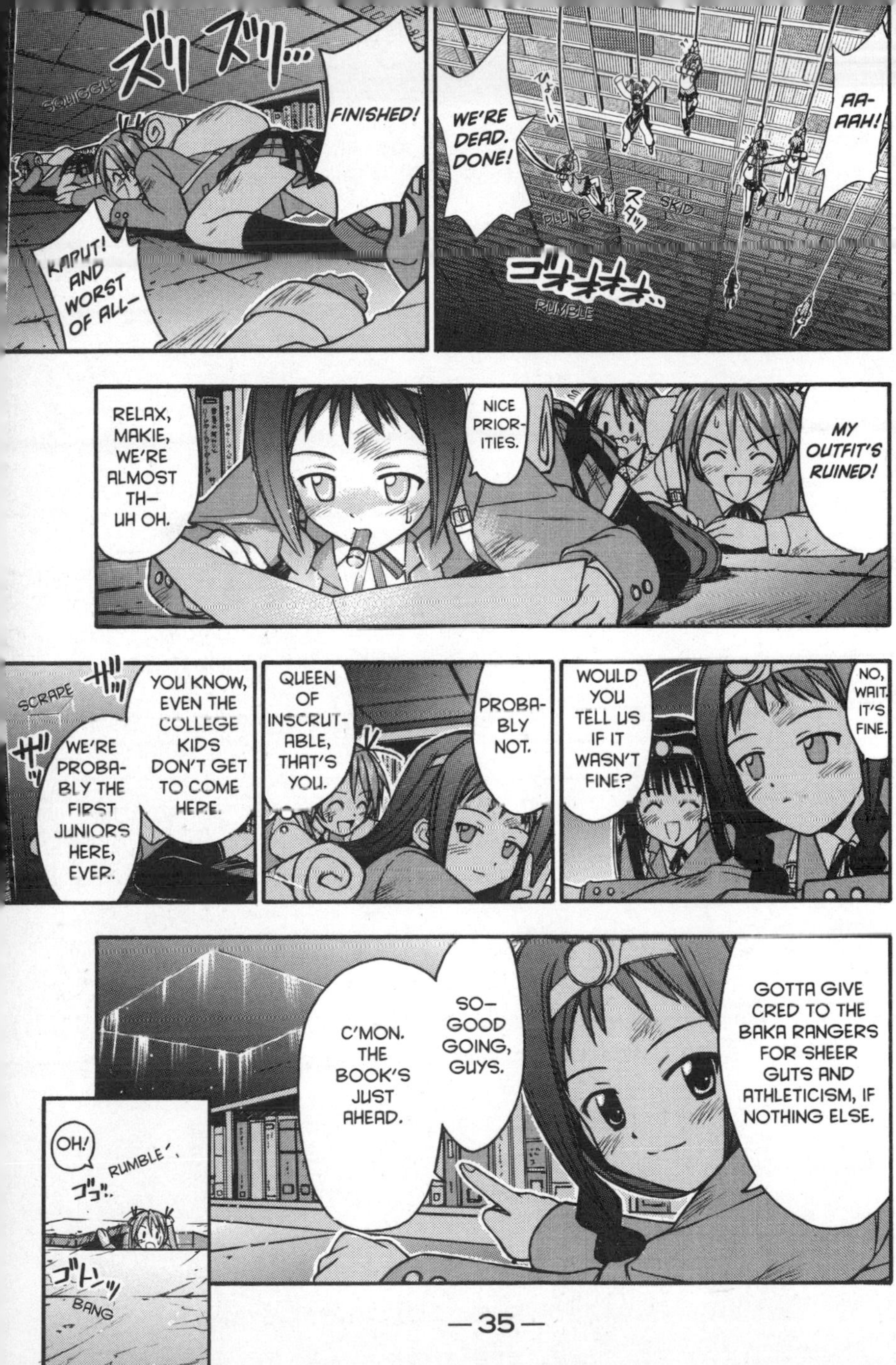
AA-AAH!
WE'RE DEAD. DONE!
ひょーい
スタッ
PLUNG
SKID
ゴオオオオオ
RUMBLE
ズリズリ
SQUIGGLE
FINISHED!
KAPUT! AND WORST OF ALL—
MY OUTFIT'S RUINED!
NICE PRIORITIES.
RELAX, MAKIE, WE'RE ALMOST TH— UH OH.
NO, WAIT. IT'S FINE.
WOULD YOU TELL US IF IT WASN'T FINE?
PROBABLY NOT.
QUEEN OF INSCRUTABLE, THAT'S YOU.
YOU KNOW, EVEN THE COLLEGE KIDS DON'T GET TO COME HERE.
WE'RE PROBABLY THE FIRST JUNIORS HERE, EVER.
ザッ
ザッ
SCRAPE
GOTTA GIVE CRED TO THE BAKA RANGERS FOR SHEER GUTS AND ATHLETICISM, IF NOTHING ELSE.
SO— GOOD GOING, GUYS.
C'MON. THE BOOK'S JUST AHEAD.
OH!
ゴゴ
RUMBLE
ゴトンッ
BANG

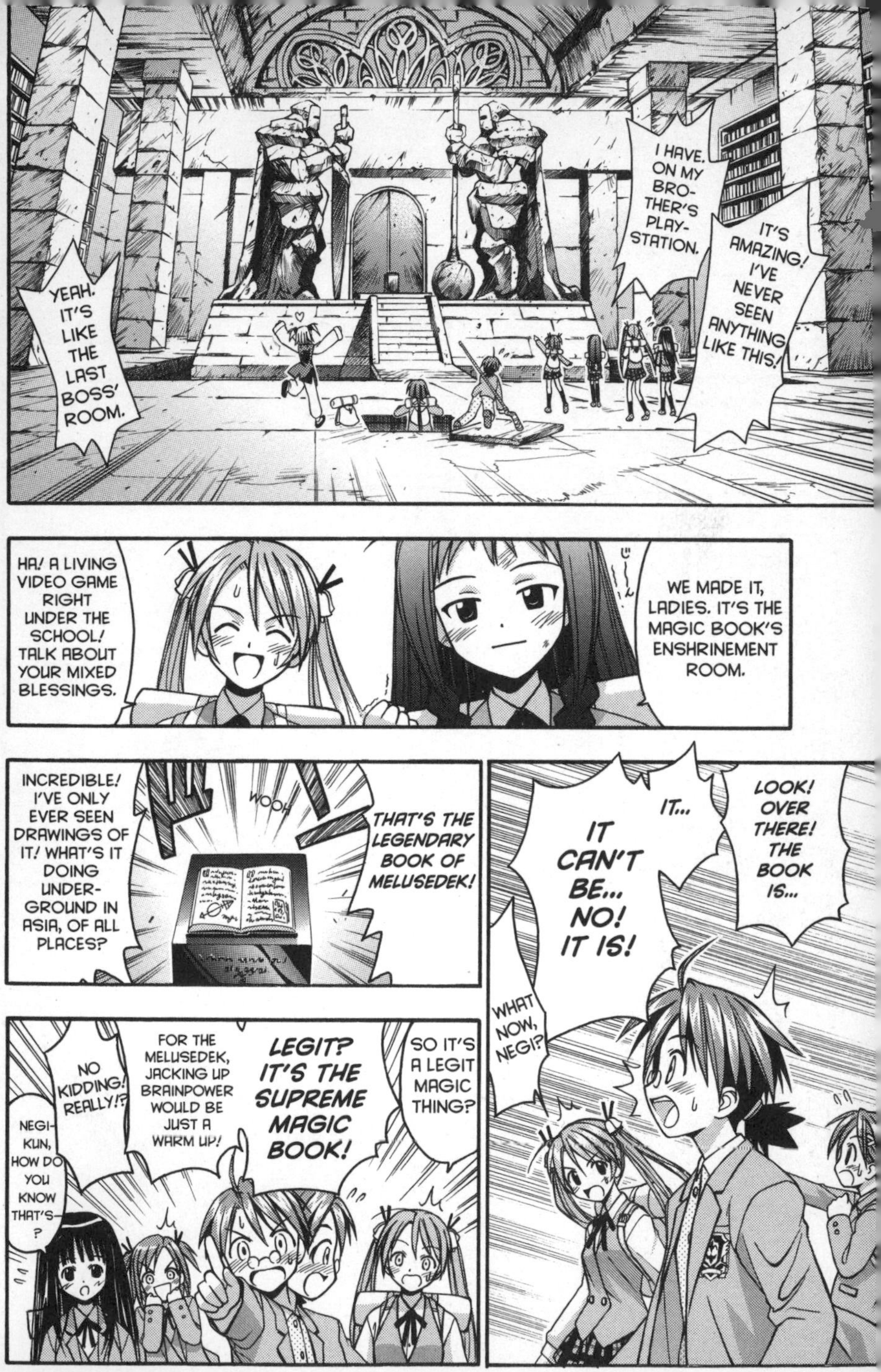
IT'S AMAZING! I'VE NEVER SEEN ANYTHING LIKE THIS!
I HAVE. ON MY BROTHER'S PLAYSTATION.
YEAH. IT'S LIKE THE LAST BOSS' ROOM.
WE MADE IT, LADIES. IT'S THE MAGIC BOOK'S ENSHRINEMENT ROOM.
HA! A LIVING VIDEO GAME RIGHT UNDER THE SCHOOL! TALK ABOUT YOUR MIXED BLESSINGS.
LOOK! OVER THERE! THE BOOK IS...
IT...
IT CAN'T BE... NO! IT IS!
WHAT NOW, NEGI?
THAT'S THE LEGENDARY BOOK OF MELUSEDEK!
WOOH
INCREDIBLE! I'VE ONLY EVER SEEN DRAWINGS OF IT! WHAT'S IT DOING UNDERGROUND IN ASIA, OF ALL PLACES?
SO IT'S A LEGIT MAGIC THING?
LEGIT? IT'S THE SUPREME MAGIC BOOK!
FOR THE MELUSEDEK, JACKING UP BRAINPOWER WOULD BE JUST A WARM UP!
NO KIDDING! REALLY!?
NEGI-KUN, HOW DO YOU KNOW THAT'S—?

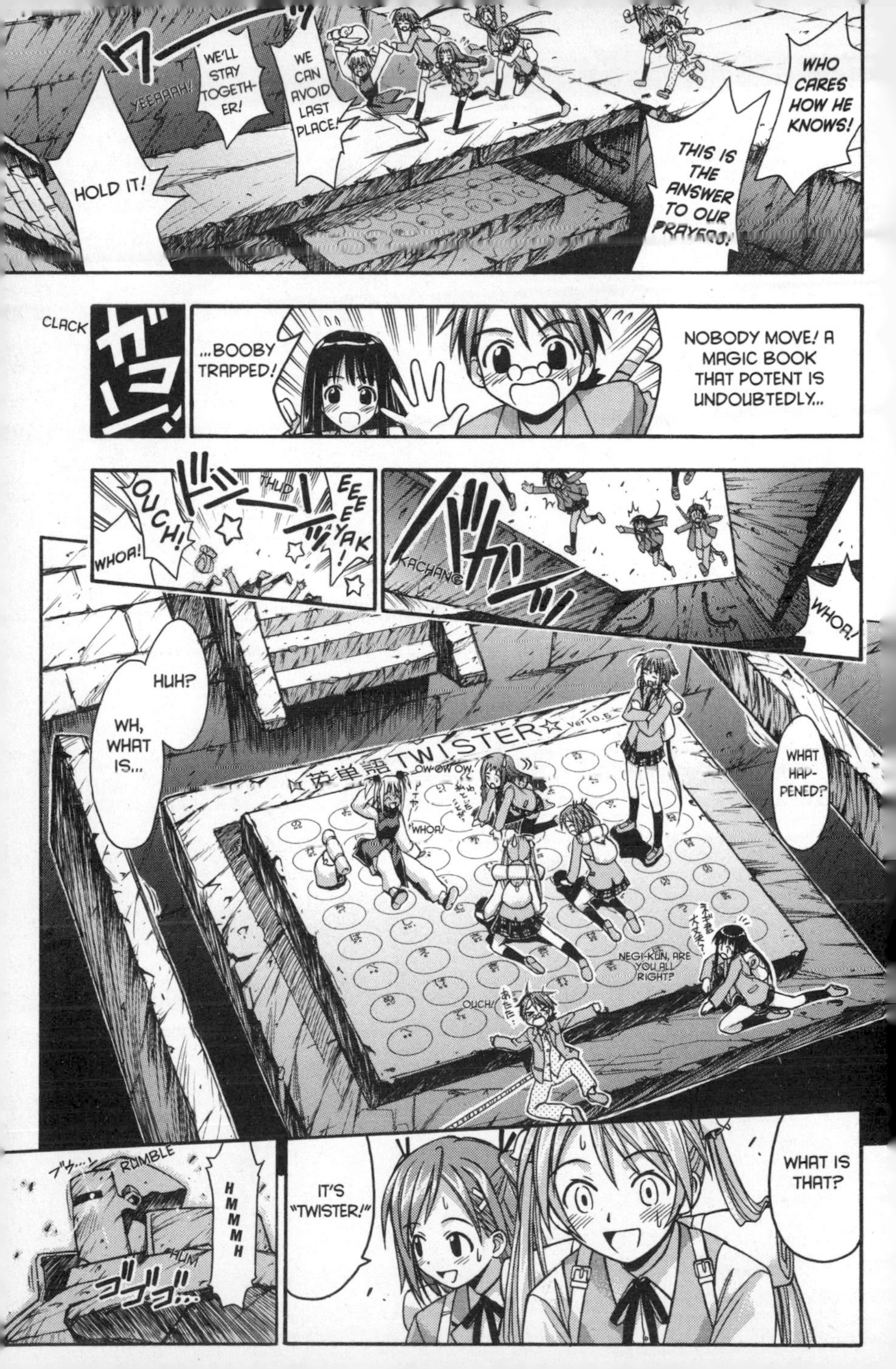

WHO CARES HOW HE KNOWS!
THIS IS THE ANSWER TO OUR PRAYERS!
WE CAN AVOID LAST PLACE!
WE'LL STAY TOGETHER!
YEEAAAH!
HOLD IT!
NOBODY MOVE! A MAGIC BOOK THAT POTENT IS UNDOUBTEDLY...
...BOOBY TRAPPED!
CLACK
KACHANG
WHOA!
EEEEEYAK!
THUD
OUCH!!
WHOA!
WHAT HAPPENED?
OW-OW OW
WHOA!
HUH?
WH, WHAT IS...
NEGI-KUN, ARE YOU ALL RIGHT?
OUCH!
TWISTER
Ver 10.5
WHAT IS THAT?
IT'S "TWISTER!"
RUMBLE
HMMMH
HUM

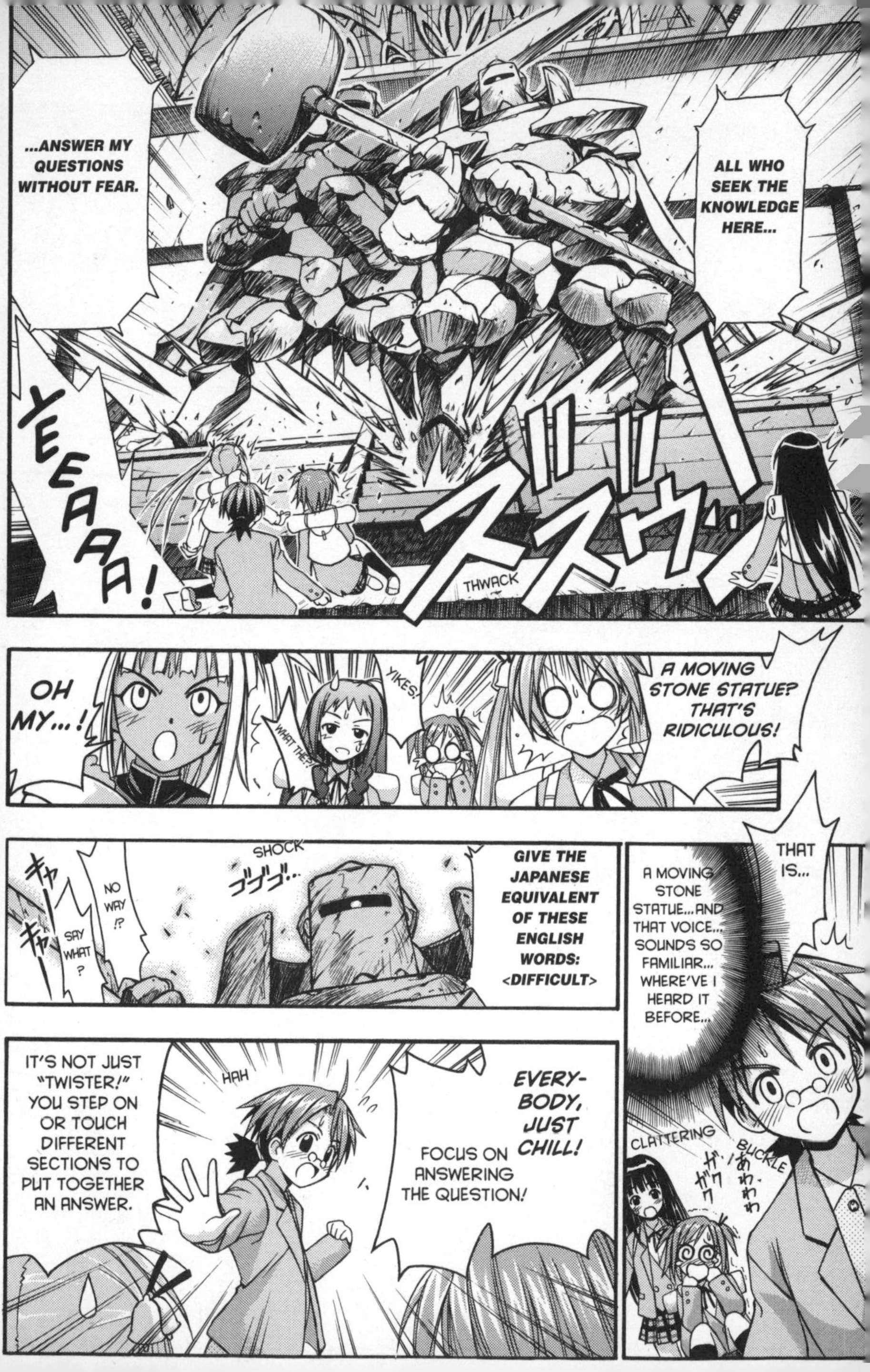
ALL WHO SEEK THE KNOWLEDGE HERE...
...ANSWER MY QUESTIONS WITHOUT FEAR.
ズゥ
THWACK
YEEAAAA!
A MOVING STONE STATUE? THAT'S RIDICULOUS!
YIKES!
WHAT THE?!
OH MY...!
THAT IS...
A MOVING STONE STATUE...AND THAT VOICE... SOUNDS SO FAMILIAR... WHERE'VE I HEARD IT BEFORE...
CLATTERING
ガクガク
BUCKLE
あわわわ
GIVE THE JAPANESE EQUIVALENT OF THESE ENGLISH WORDS: <DIFFICULT>
SHOCK
ゴゴゴ...
NO WAY!?
SAY WHAT?
キャーキャー
EVERY-BODY, JUST CHILL!
FOCUS ON ANSWERING THE QUESTION!
HAH
IT'S NOT JUST "TWISTER!" YOU STEP ON OR TOUCH DIFFERENT SECTIONS TO PUT TOGETHER AN ANSWER.

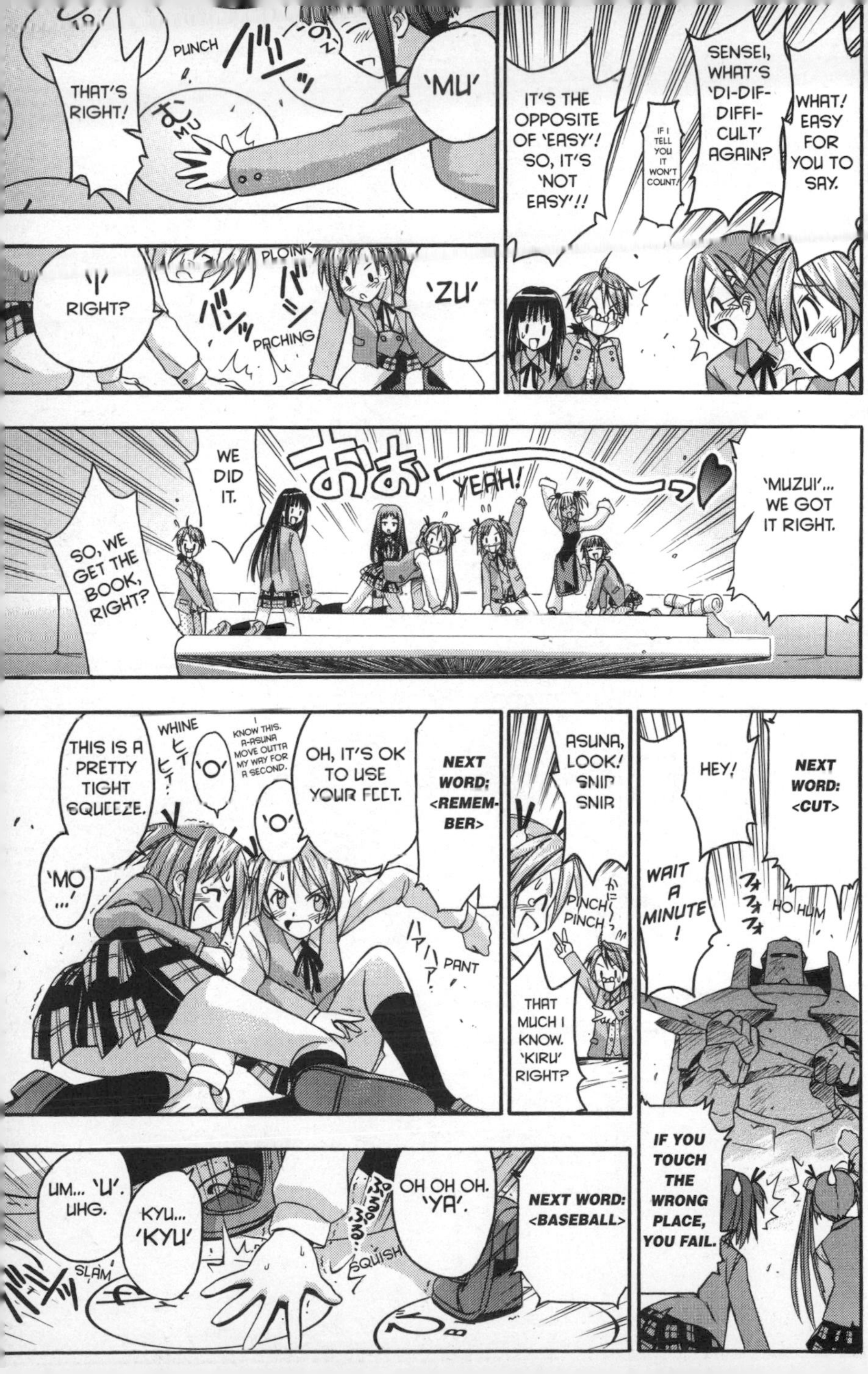
SENSEI, WHAT'S 'DI-DIF-DIFFI-CULT' AGAIN?
WHAT! EASY FOR YOU TO SAY.
IT'S THE OPPOSITE OF 'EASY'! SO, IT'S 'NOT EASY'!!
IF I TELL YOU IT WON'T COUNT!
'MU'
PUNCH
THAT'S RIGHT!
MU
'ZU'
PLOINK
PACHING
RIGHT?
'MUZUI'... WE GOT IT RIGHT.
YEAH!
WE DID IT.
SO, WE GET THE BOOK, RIGHT?
NEXT WORD: <CUT>
HEY!
WAIT A MINUTE!
HO HUM
IF YOU TOUCH THE WRONG PLACE, YOU FAIL.
ASUNA, LOOK! SNIP SNIP
PINCH PINCH
THAT MUCH I KNOW. 'KIRU' RIGHT?
NEXT WORD: <REMEMBER>
OH, IT'S OK TO USE YOUR FEET.
'O'
I KNOW THIS. A-ASUNA MOVE OUTTA MY WAY FOR A SECOND.
WHINE
'O'
THIS IS A PRETTY TIGHT SQUEEZE.
'MO'...
PANT
NEXT WORD: <BASEBALL>
OH OH OH. 'YA'.
SQUISH
KYU... 'KYU'
UM... 'U'. UHG.
SLAM

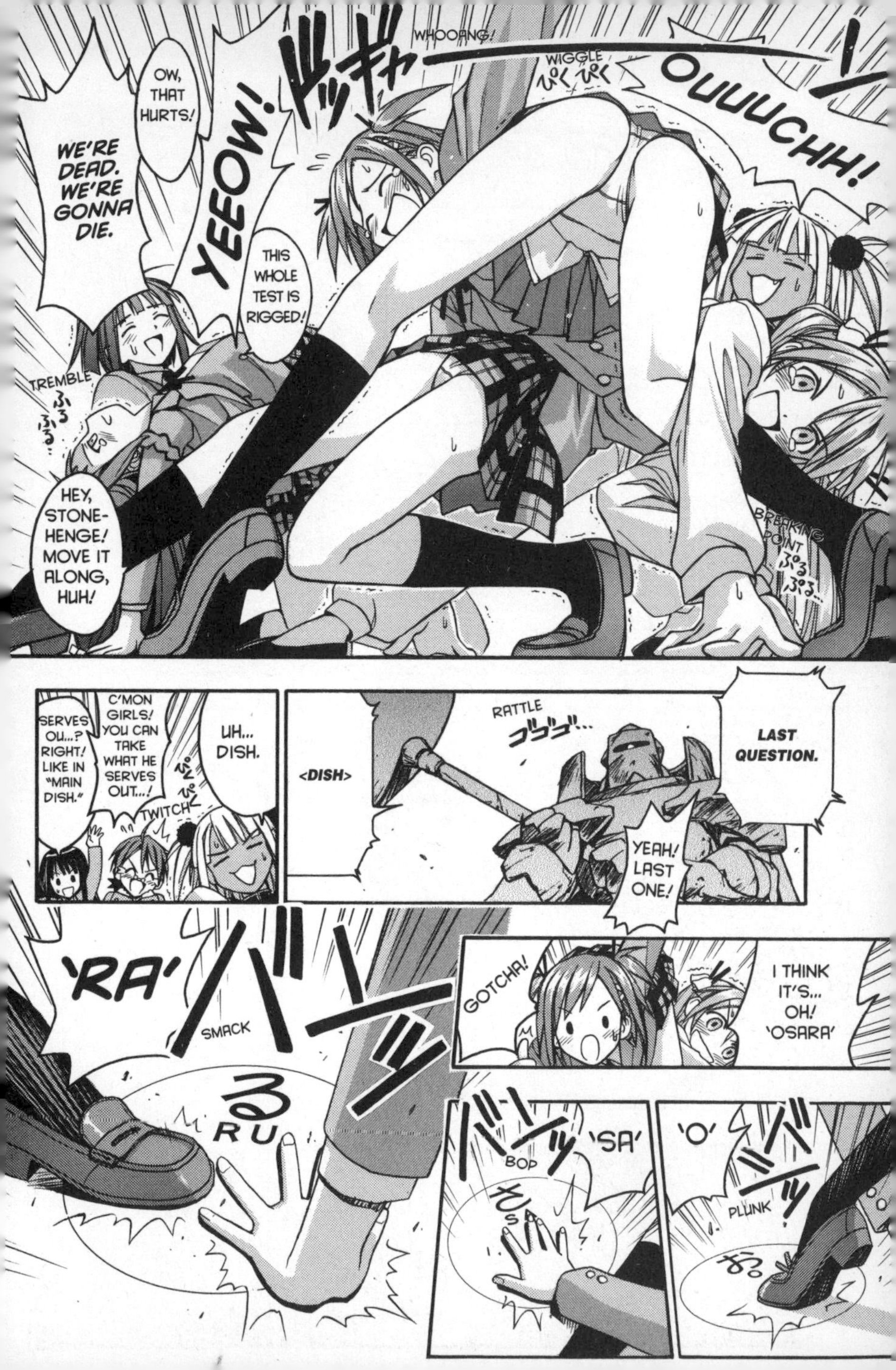
WHOOANG!
ドッギャ
OUUUCHH!
WIGGLE
ぴくぴく
YEEOW!
OW, THAT HURTS!
WE'RE DEAD. WE'RE GONNA DIE.
THIS WHOLE TEST IS RIGGED!
TREMBLE
ふるふる
HEY, STONE-HENGE! MOVE IT ALONG, HUH!
BREAKING POINT
ぷるぷる
LAST QUESTION.
RATTLE
ゴゴゴ…
<DISH>
YEAH! LAST ONE!
UH... DISH.
C'MON GIRLS! YOU CAN TAKE WHAT HE SERVES OUT...!
SERVES OU...? RIGHT! LIKE IN "MAIN DISH."
TWITCH
I THINK IT'S... OH! 'OSARA'
GOTCHA!
'RA'
SMACK
る
RU
'SA'
BOP
さ
SA
'O'
PLUNK
お

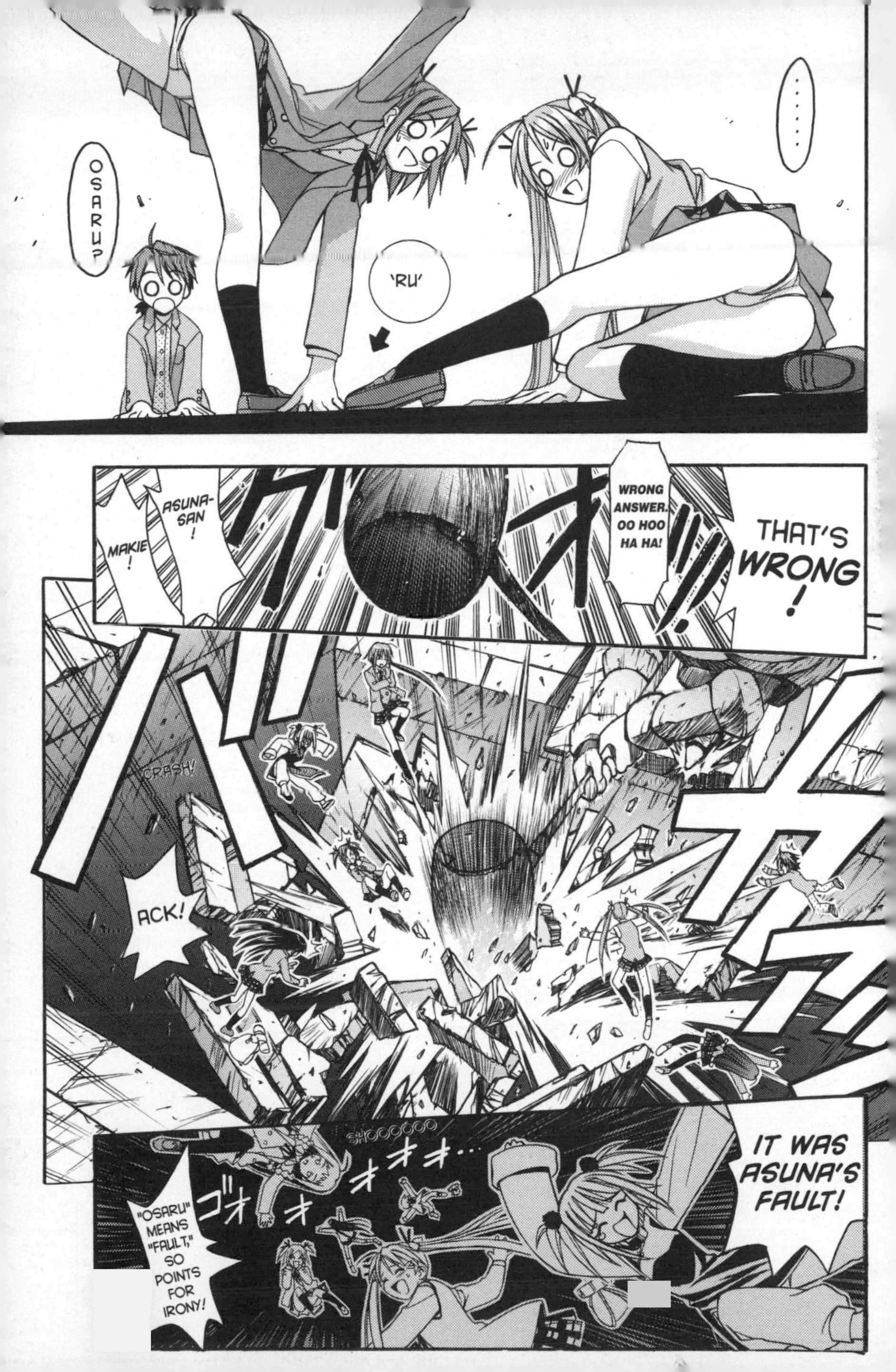
......
'RU'
OSARU?
THAT'S WRONG!
WRONG ANSWER. OO HOO HA HA!
ASUNA-SAN!
MAKIE!
CRASH!
ACK!
IT WAS ASUNA'S FAULT!
SHOOOOOO
"OSARU" MEANS "FAULT," SO POINTS FOR IRONY!

STUDENT NUMBER 12
FEI KU

BORN: MARCH 16, 1989
BLOOD TYPE: A
LIKES: APPRENTICESHIP, STRONG MEN, STICKY
      BUNS
DISLIKES: NEW INVENTIONS IN FOOD AND SWORDS.
AFFILIATIONS: CHINESE WEAPON TECHNOLOGY
      RESEARCH GROUP.

STUDENT NUMBER 20
KAEDE NAGASE

BORN: NOVEMBER, 11 1988
BLOOD TYPE: O
LIKES: PUDDING, RELAXING
DISLIKES: FROGS
AFFILIATIONS: STROLLING CLUB
NOTE: FROM KOUGA (A COUNTY IN SHIGA
      PREFECTURE)

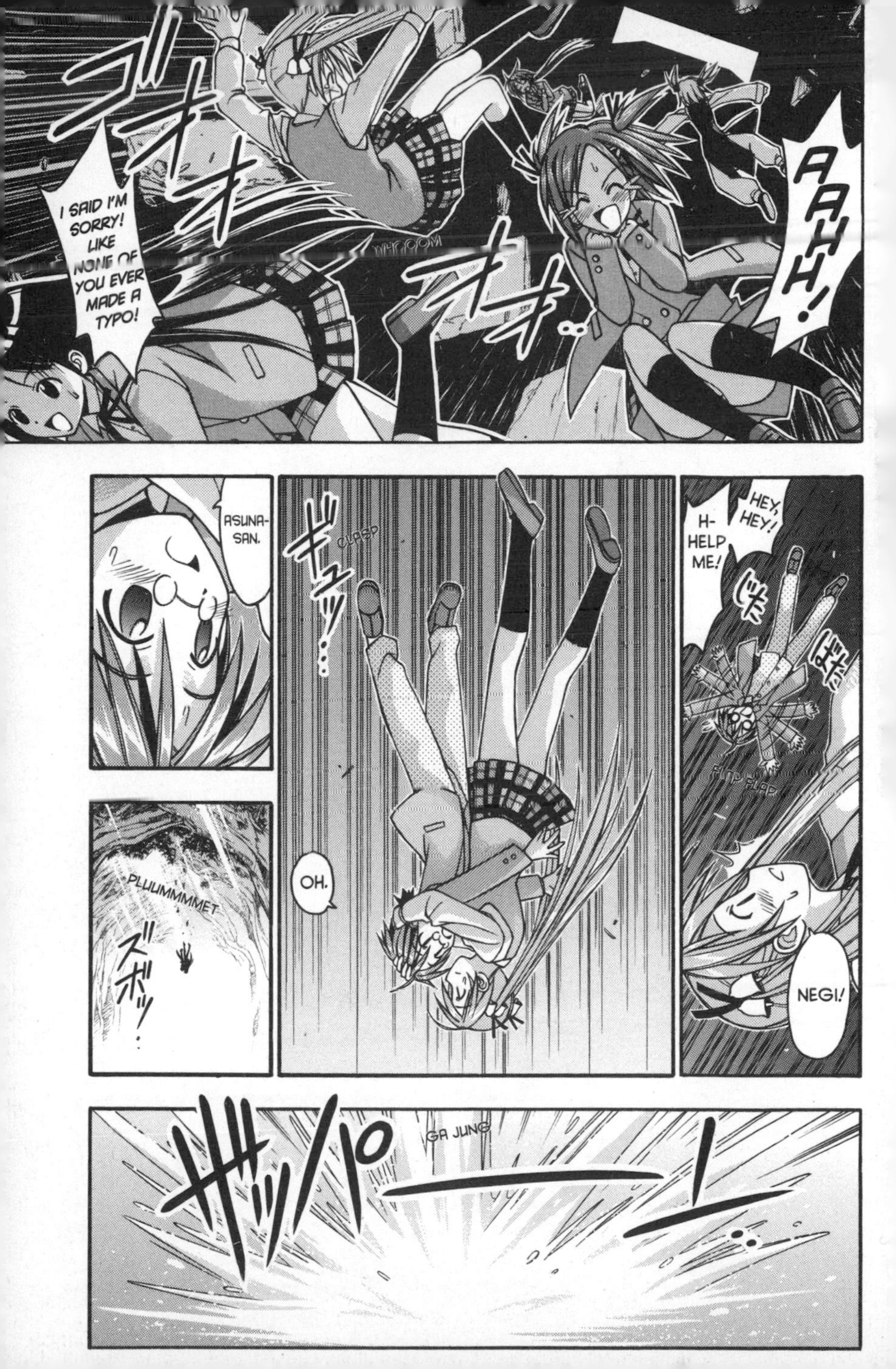
AAHH!
WHOOOM
I SAID I'M SORRY! LIKE NONE OF YOU EVER MADE A TYPO!
HEY, HEY!
H- HELP ME!
FLAP FLAP
NEGI!
CLASP
OH.
ASUNA-SAN.
PLUUMMMMET
GA JUNG

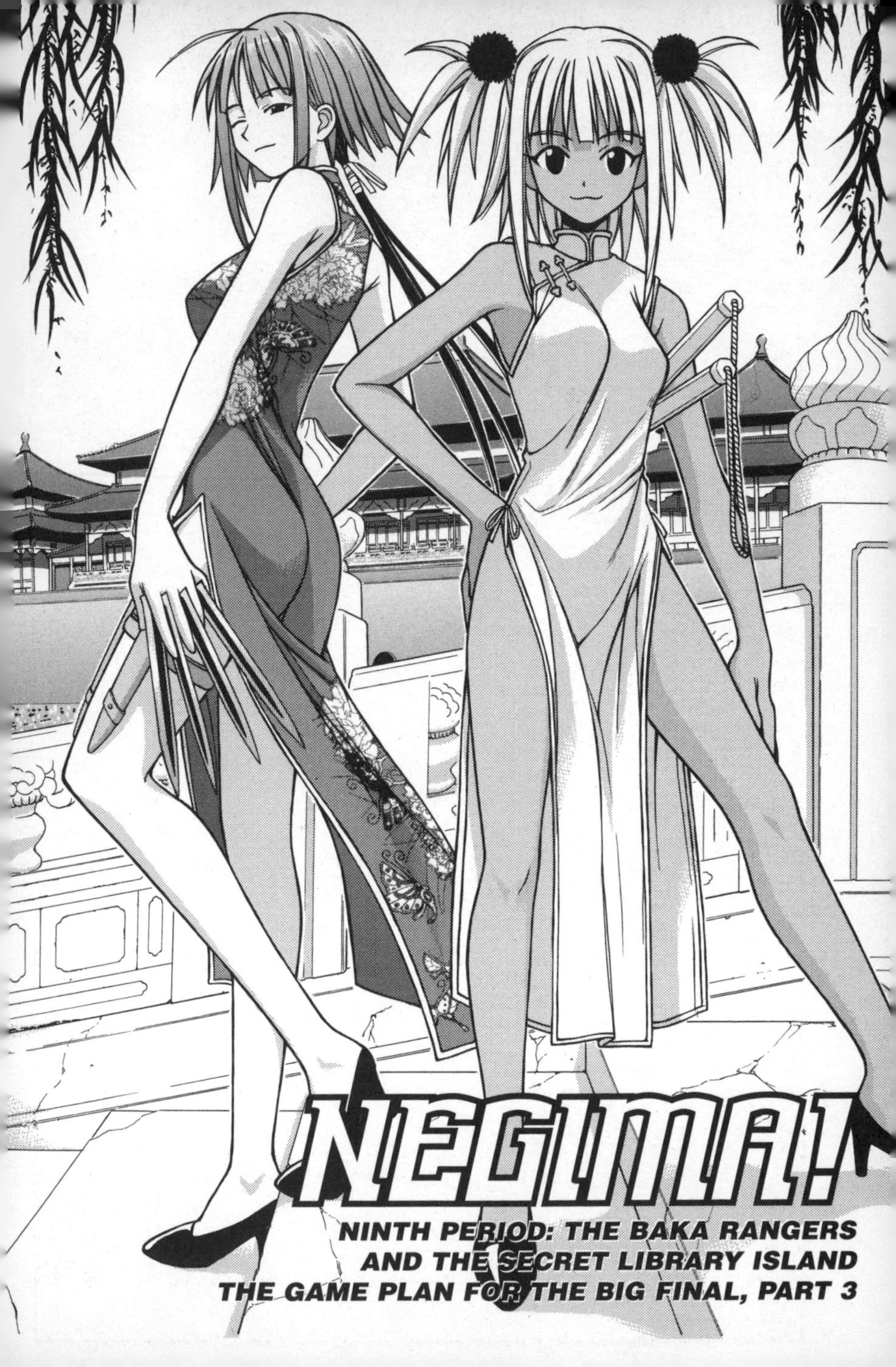
NEGIMA!
NINTH PERIOD: THE BAKA RANGERS
AND THE SECRET LIBRARY ISLAND
THE GAME PLAN FOR THE BIG FINAL, PART 3

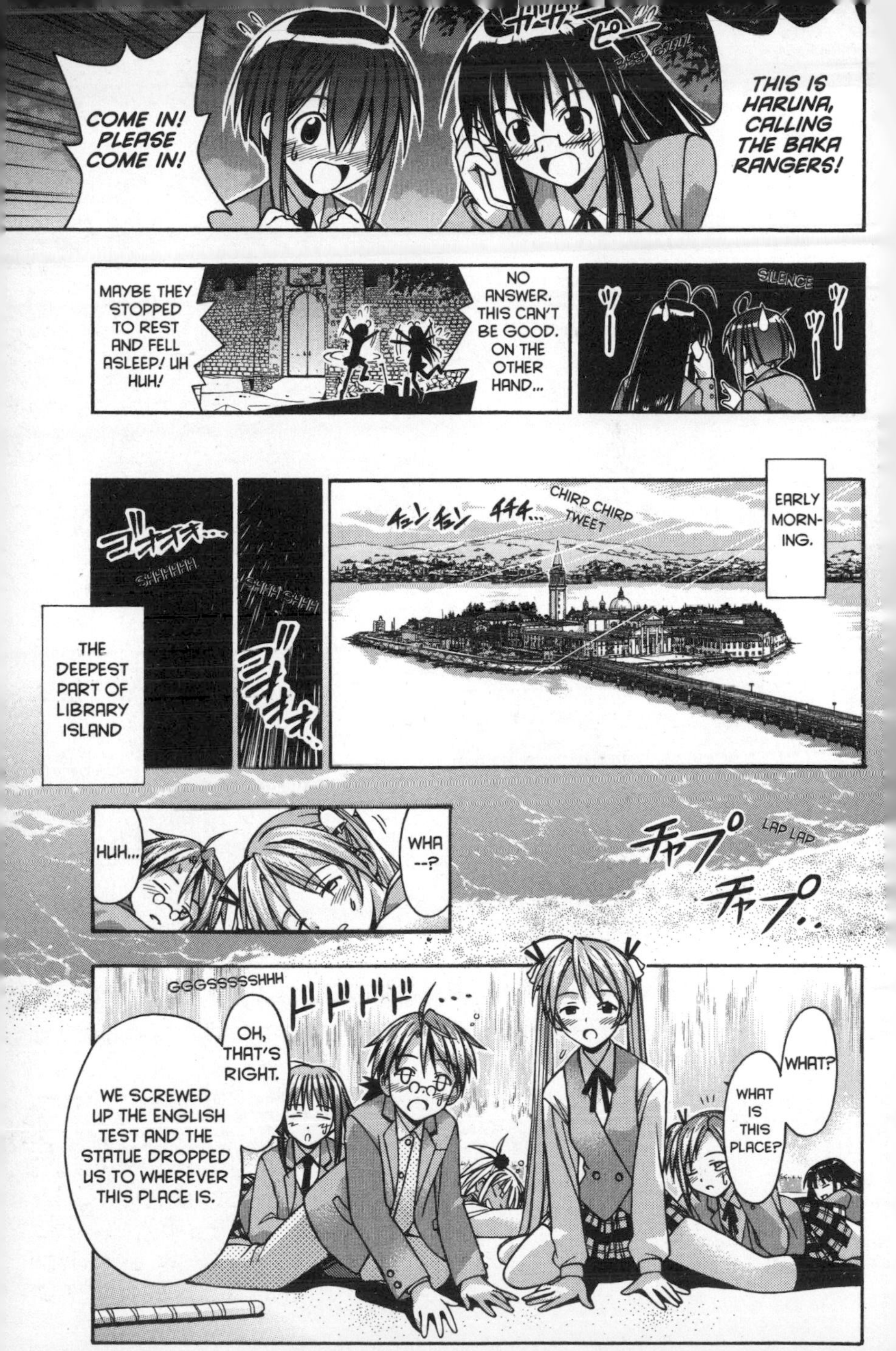
BEEP GZZZ
THIS IS HARUNA, CALLING THE BAKA RANGERS!
COME IN! PLEASE COME IN!
SILENCE
NO ANSWER. THIS CAN'T BE GOOD. ON THE OTHER HAND...
MAYBE THEY STOPPED TO REST AND FELL ASLEEP! UH HUH!
EARLY MORNING.
CHIRP CHIRP TWEET
SHHH SHHH
SHHHHH
THE DEEPEST PART OF LIBRARY ISLAND
LAP LAP
WHA --?
HUH...
WHAT?
WHAT IS THIS PLACE?
GGGSSSSSHHH
OH, THAT'S RIGHT.
WE SCREWED UP THE ENGLISH TEST AND THE STATUE DROPPED US TO WHEREVER THIS PLACE IS.

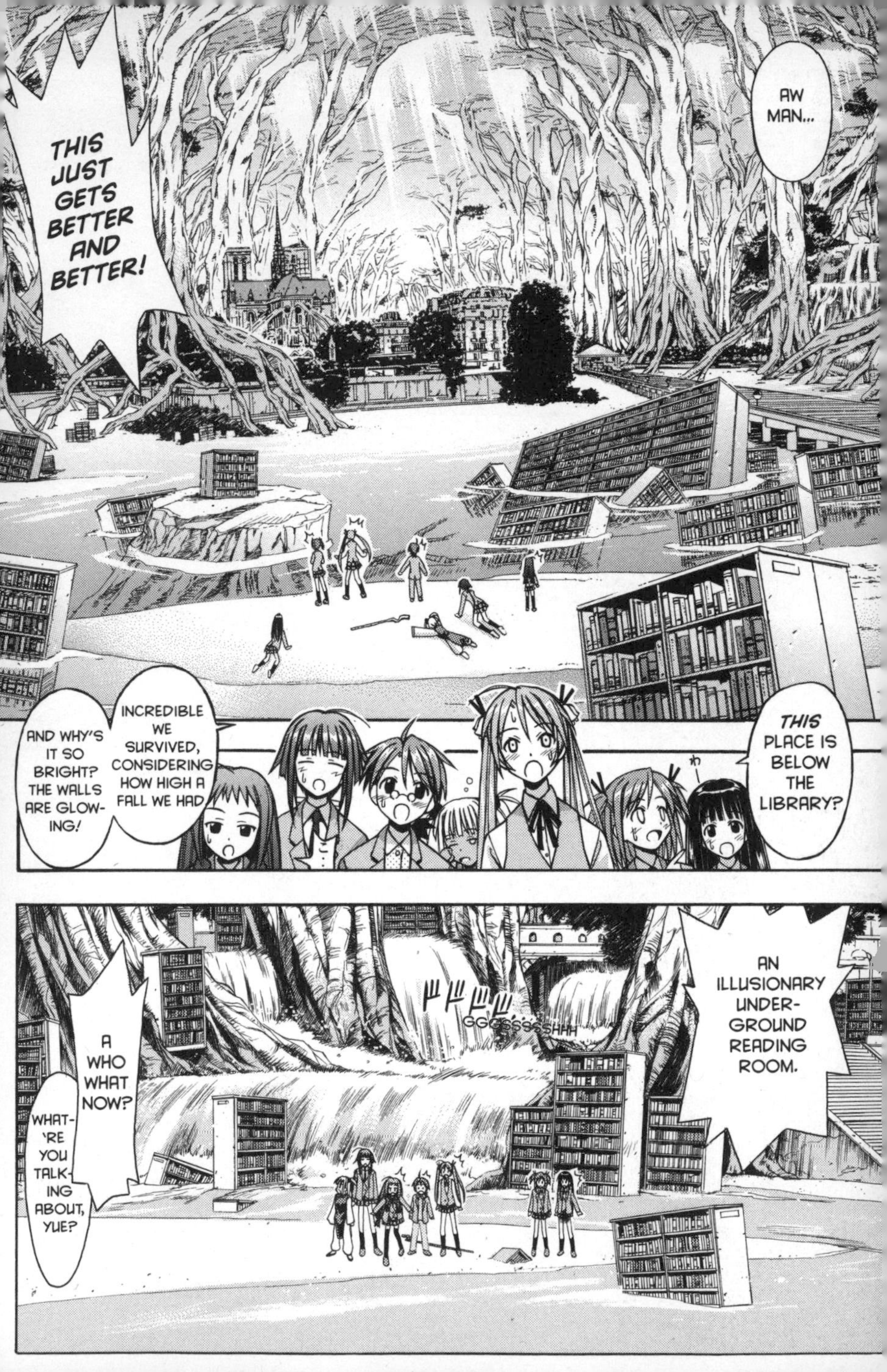
AW MAN...
THIS JUST GETS BETTER AND BETTER!
THIS PLACE IS BELOW THE LIBRARY?
INCREDIBLE WE SURVIVED, CONSIDERING HOW HIGH A FALL WE HAD
AND WHY'S IT SO BRIGHT? THE WALLS ARE GLOWING!
AN ILLUSIONARY UNDERGROUND READING ROOM.
GGGSSSSSSHHH
A WHO WHAT NOW?
WHAT'RE YOU TALKING ABOUT, YUE?

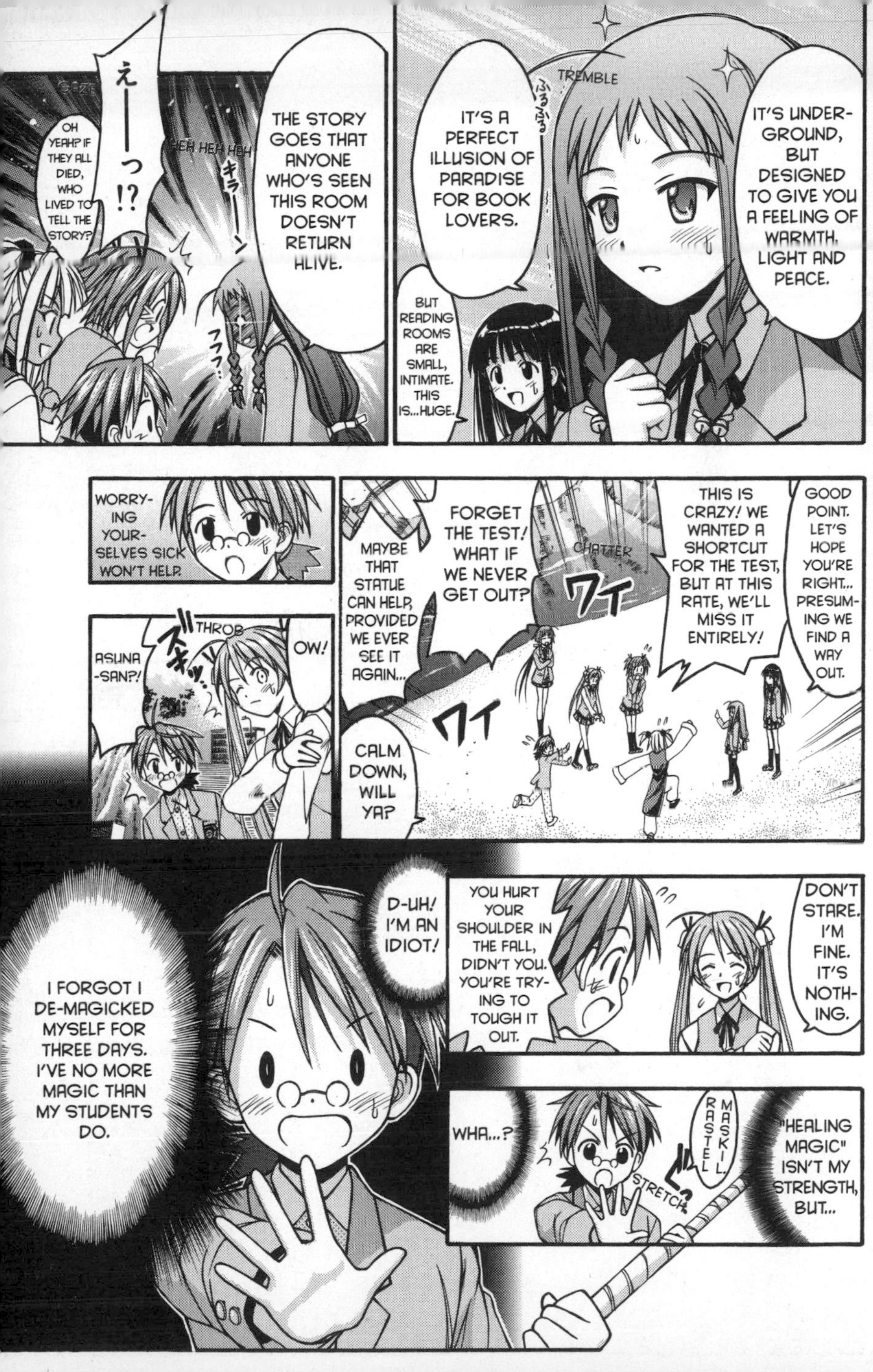
IT'S UNDER-GROUND, BUT DESIGNED TO GIVE YOU A FEELING OF WARMTH, LIGHT AND PEACE.
TREMBLE
ふるふる
IT'S A PERFECT ILLUSION OF PARADISE FOR BOOK LOVERS.
BUT READING ROOMS ARE SMALL, INTIMATE. THIS IS...HUGE.
えーーっ!?
THE STORY GOES THAT ANYONE WHO'S SEEN THIS ROOM DOESN'T RETURN ALIVE.
HEH HEH HEH
キラーーン
フフフ...
OH YEAH? IF THEY ALL DIED, WHO LIVED TO TELL THE STORY?
GOOD POINT. LET'S HOPE YOU'RE RIGHT... PRESUMING WE FIND A WAY OUT.
THIS IS CRAZY! WE WANTED A SHORTCUT FOR THE TEST, BUT AT THIS RATE, WE'LL MISS IT ENTIRELY!
CHATTER
ワイ
FORGET THE TEST! WHAT IF WE NEVER GET OUT?
MAYBE THAT STATUE CAN HELP, PROVIDED WE EVER SEE IT AGAIN...
ワイ
CALM DOWN, WILL YA?
WORRY-ING YOUR-SELVES SICK WON'T HELP.
OW!
THROB
ズキッ
ASUNA-SAN?!
DON'T STARE. I'M FINE. IT'S NOTH-ING.
YOU HURT YOUR SHOULDER IN THE FALL, DIDN'T YOU. YOU'RE TRY-ING TO TOUGH IT OUT.
"HEALING MAGIC" ISN'T MY STRENGTH, BUT...
RASTEL MASKIL.
STRETCH
WHA...?
D-UH! I'M AN IDIOT!
I FORGOT I DE-MAGICKED MYSELF FOR THREE DAYS. I'VE NO MORE MAGIC THAN MY STUDENTS DO.

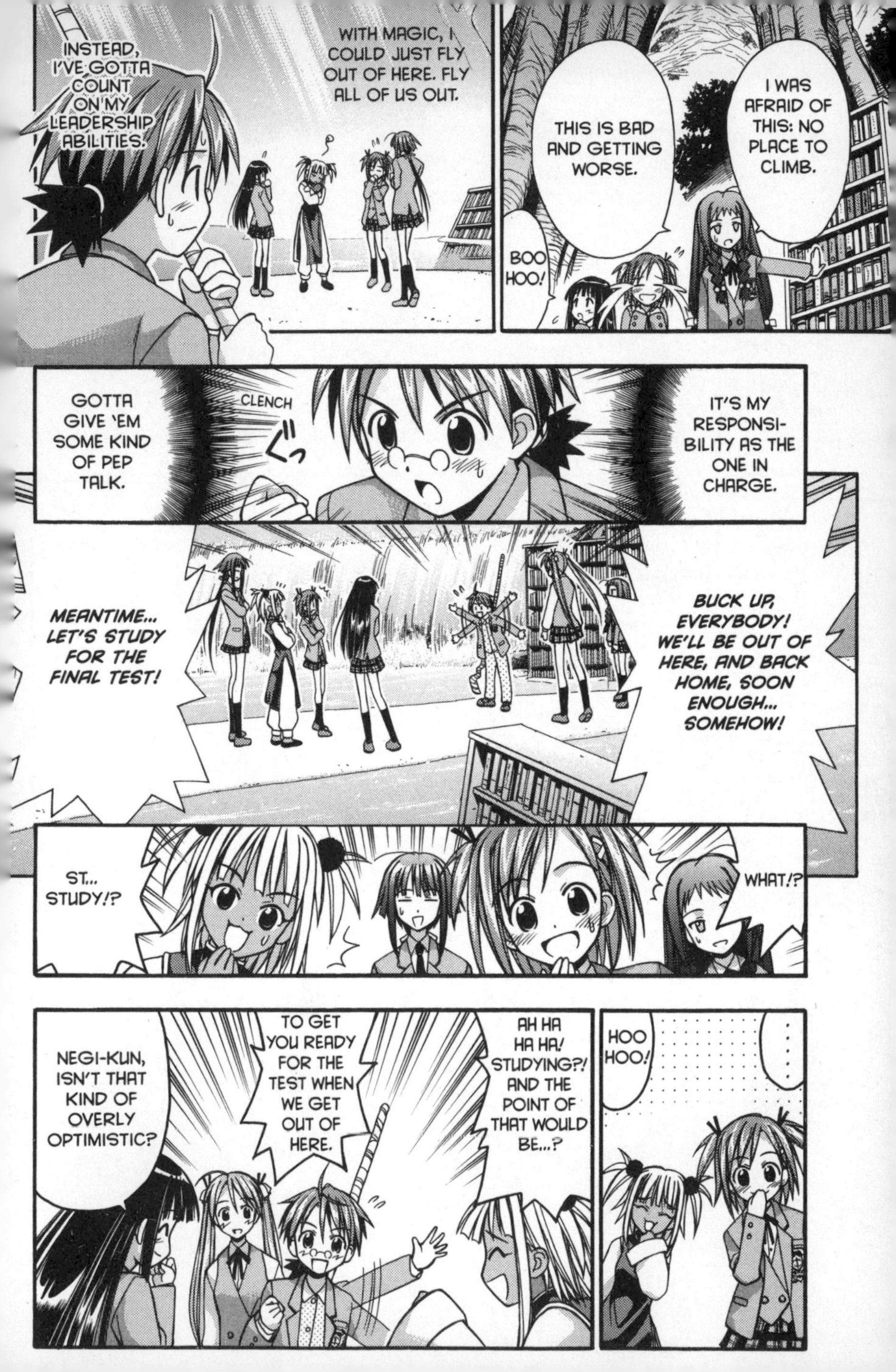
I WAS AFRAID OF THIS: NO PLACE TO CLIMB.
THIS IS BAD AND GETTING WORSE.
BOO HOO!
WITH MAGIC, I COULD JUST FLY OUT OF HERE. FLY ALL OF US OUT.
INSTEAD, I'VE GOTTA COUNT ON MY LEADERSHIP ABILITIES.
IT'S MY RESPONSI-BILITY AS THE ONE IN CHARGE.
CLENCH
GOTTA GIVE 'EM SOME KIND OF PEP TALK.
BUCK UP, EVERYBODY! WE'LL BE OUT OF HERE, AND BACK HOME, SOON ENOUGH... SOMEHOW!
MEANTIME... LET'S STUDY FOR THE FINAL TEST!
WHAT!?
ST... STUDY!?
...
HOO HOO!
AH HA HA HA! STUDYING?! AND THE POINT OF THAT WOULD BE...?
TO GET YOU READY FOR THE TEST WHEN WE GET OUT OF HERE.
NEGI-KUN, ISN'T THAT KIND OF OVERLY OPTIMISTIC?

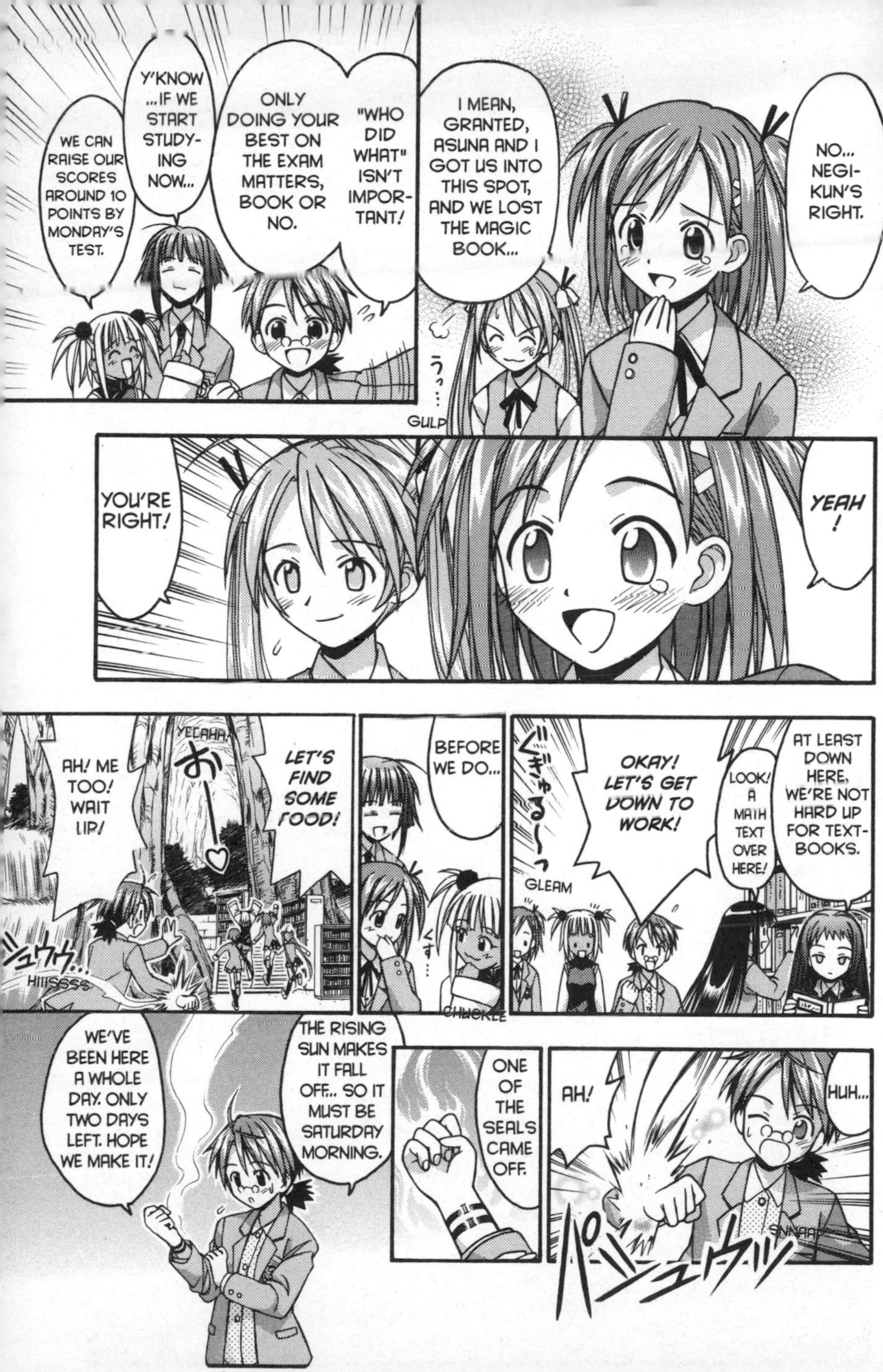
NO... NEGI-KUN'S RIGHT.
I MEAN, GRANTED, ASUNA AND I GOT US INTO THIS SPOT, AND WE LOST THE MAGIC BOOK...
GULP
"WHO DID WHAT" ISN'T IMPORTANT!
ONLY DOING YOUR BEST ON THE EXAM MATTERS, BOOK OR NO.
Y'KNOW ...IF WE START STUDYING NOW...
WE CAN RAISE OUR SCORES AROUND 10 POINTS BY MONDAY'S TEST.
YEAH!
YOU'RE RIGHT!
AT LEAST DOWN HERE, WE'RE NOT HARD UP FOR TEXTBOOKS.
LOOK! A MATH TEXT OVER HERE!
OKAY! LET'S GET DOWN TO WORK!
GLEAM
BEFORE WE DO...
CHUCKLE
LET'S FIND SOME FOOD!
YEEAHH!
AH! ME TOO! WAIT UP!
HIIISSSS
HUH...
AH!
SNAAP
ONE OF THE SEALS CAME OFF.
THE RISING SUN MAKES IT FALL OFF... SO IT MUST BE SATURDAY MORNING.
WE'VE BEEN HERE A WHOLE DAY. ONLY TWO DAYS LEFT. HOPE WE MAKE IT!

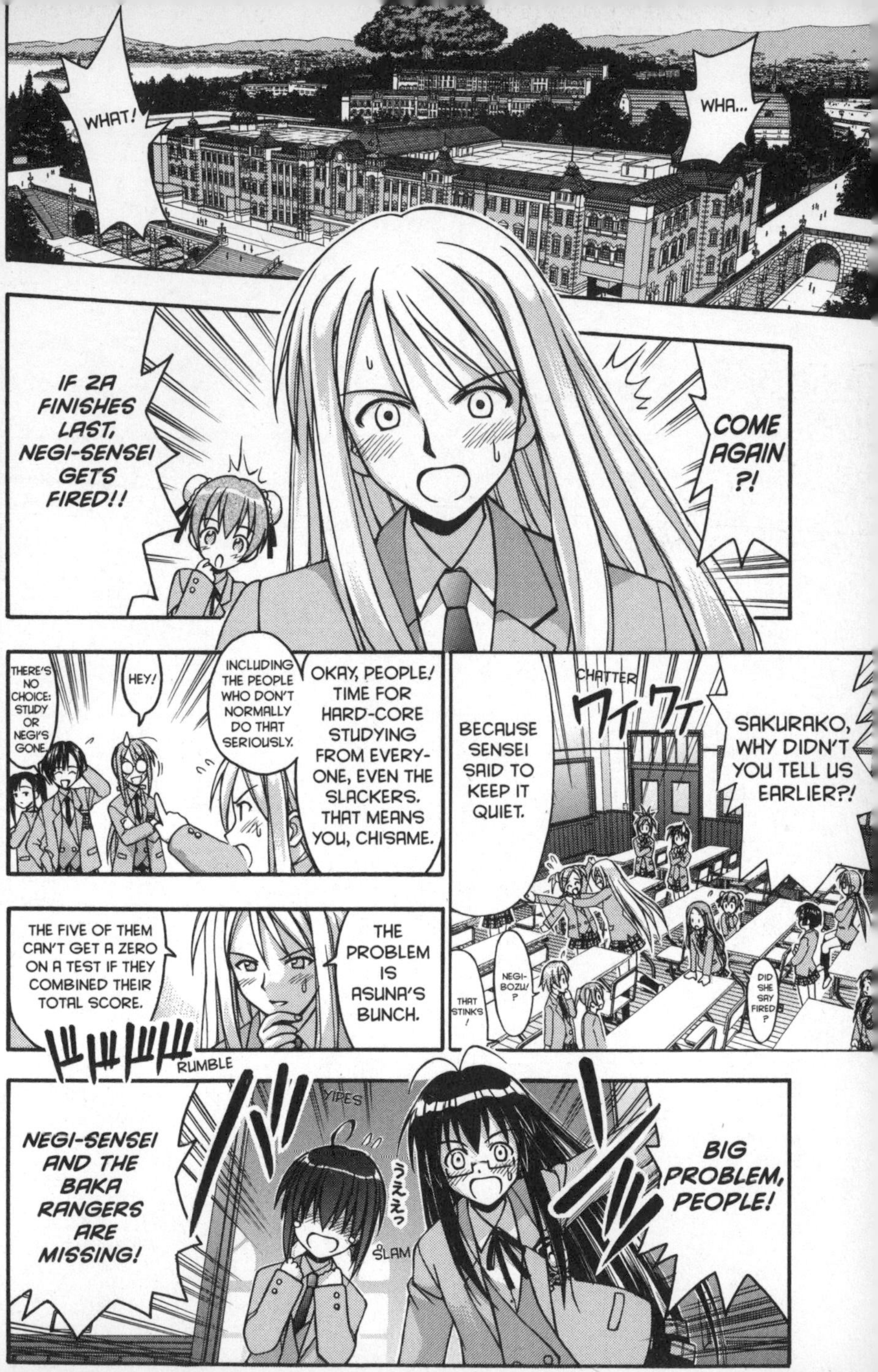
WHA...
WHAT!
COME AGAIN?!
IF 2A FINISHES LAST, NEGI-SENSEI GETS FIRED!!
CHATTER
SAKURAKO, WHY DIDN'T YOU TELL US EARLIER?!
BECAUSE SENSEI SAID TO KEEP IT QUIET.
DID SHE SAY FIRED?
NEGI-BOZU!?
THAT STINKS!
OKAY, PEOPLE! TIME FOR HARD-CORE STUDYING FROM EVERY-ONE, EVEN THE SLACKERS. THAT MEANS YOU, CHISAME.
INCLUDING THE PEOPLE WHO DON'T NORMALLY DO THAT SERIOUSLY.
HEY!
THERE'S NO CHOICE: STUDY OR NEGI'S GONE.
THE PROBLEM IS ASUNA'S BUNCH.
THE FIVE OF THEM CAN'T GET A ZERO ON A TEST IF THEY COMBINED THEIR TOTAL SCORE.
RUMBLE
BIG PROBLEM, PEOPLE!
YIPES
うえぇっ
SLAM
NEGI-SENSEI AND THE BAKA RANGERS ARE MISSING!

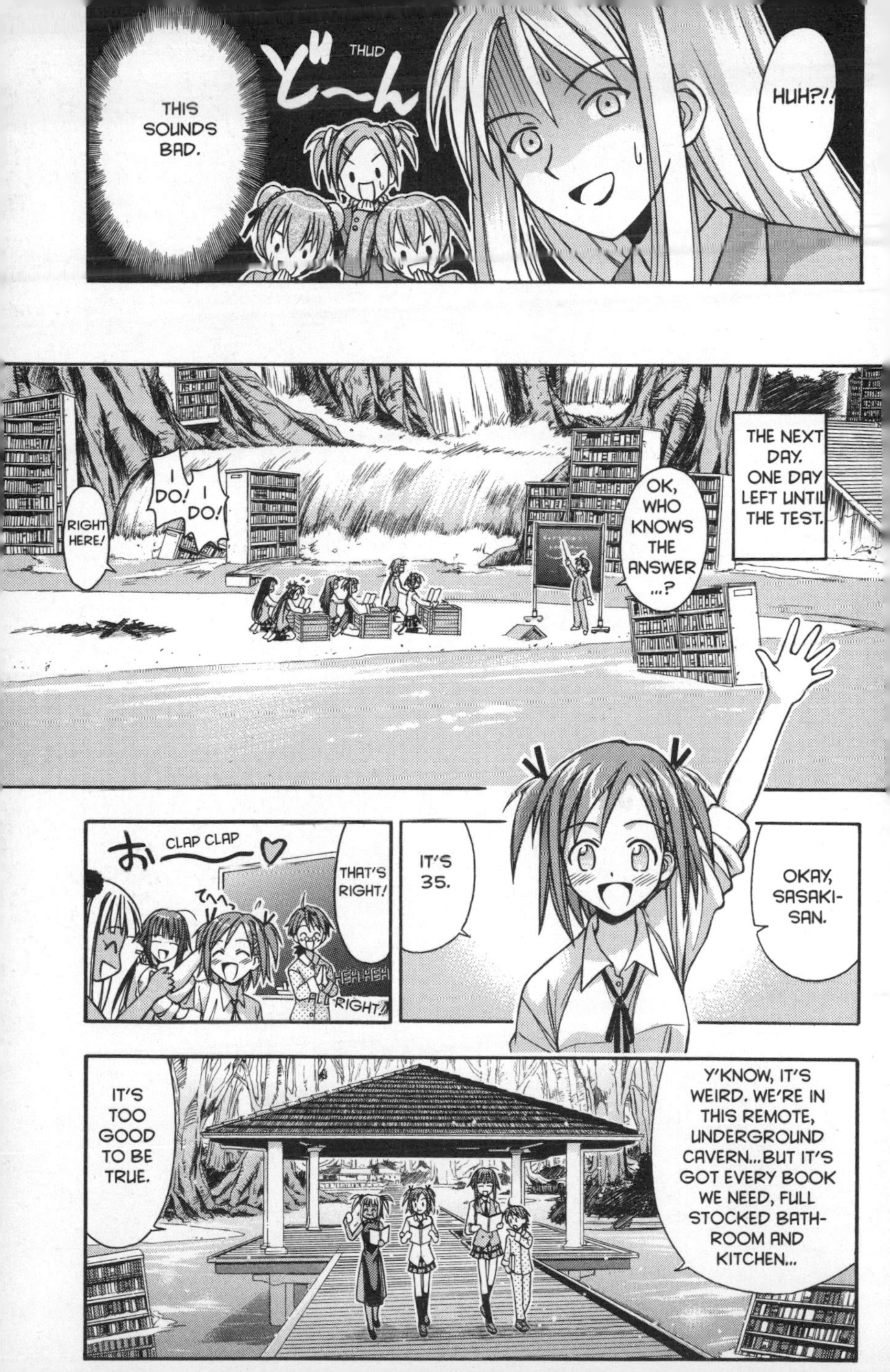

HUH?!!
THUD
THIS SOUNDS BAD.
THE NEXT DAY. ONE DAY LEFT UNTIL THE TEST.
OK, WHO KNOWS THE ANSWER ...?
I DO! I DO!
RIGHT HERE!
OKAY, SASAKI-SAN.
IT'S 35.
THAT'S RIGHT!
CLAP CLAP
HEH HEH
ALL RIGHT.
Y'KNOW, IT'S WEIRD. WE'RE IN THIS REMOTE, UNDERGROUND CAVERN...BUT IT'S GOT EVERY BOOK WE NEED, FULL STOCKED BATH-ROOM AND KITCHEN...
IT'S TOO GOOD TO BE TRUE.

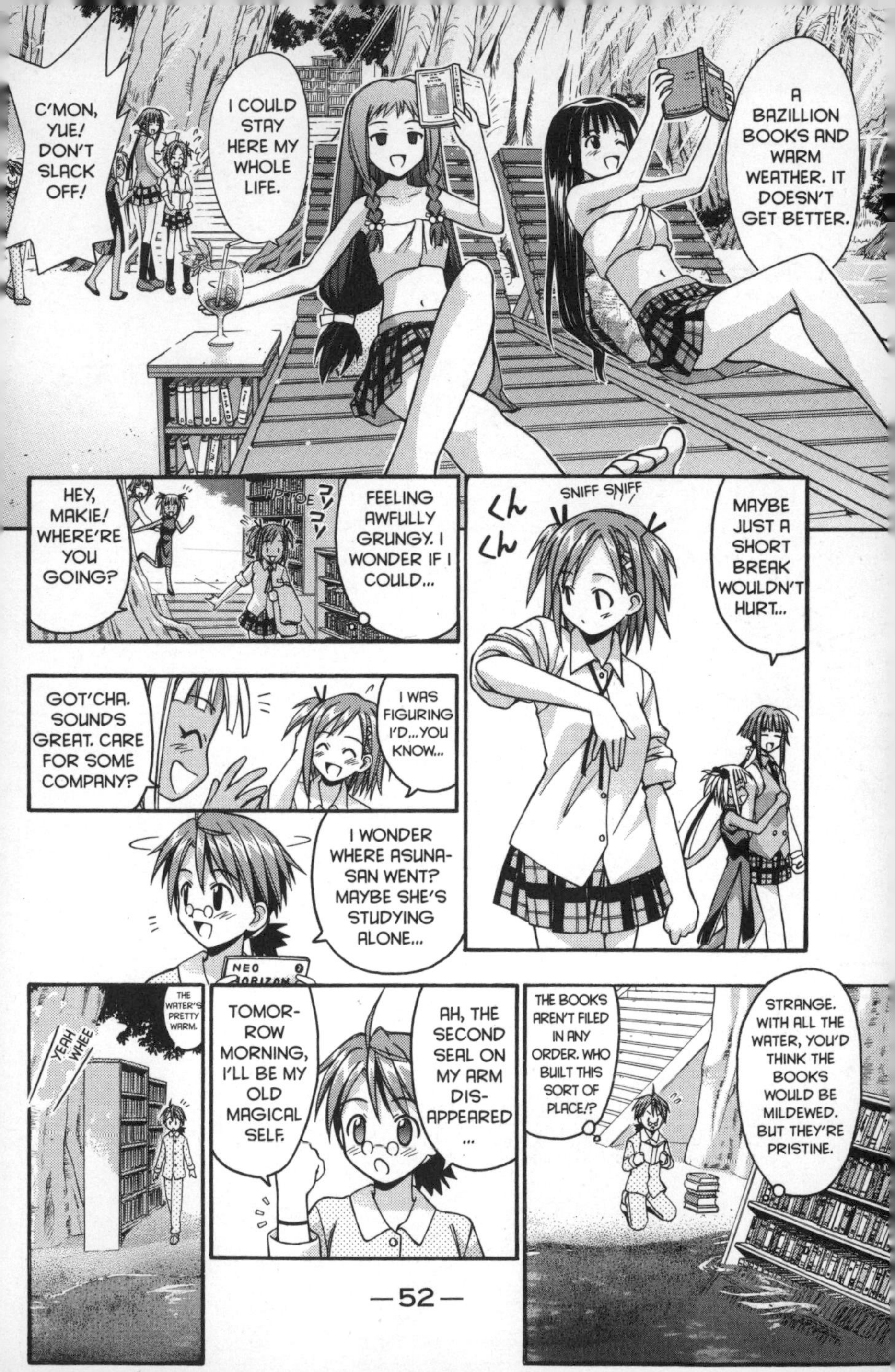
A BAZILLION BOOKS AND WARM WEATHER. IT DOESN'T GET BETTER.
I COULD STAY HERE MY WHOLE LIFE.
C'MON, YUE! DON'T SLACK OFF!
SNIFF SNIFF
くん くん
MAYBE JUST A SHORT BREAK WOULDN'T HURT...
FEELING AWFULLY GRUNGY. I WONDER IF I COULD...
コソコソ
TIPTOE
HEY, MAKIE! WHERE'RE YOU GOING?
I WAS FIGURING I'D...YOU KNOW...
GOT'CHA. SOUNDS GREAT. CARE FOR SOME COMPANY?
I WONDER WHERE ASUNA-SAN WENT? MAYBE SHE'S STUDYING ALONE...
NEO HORIZON
STRANGE. WITH ALL THE WATER, YOU'D THINK THE BOOKS WOULD BE MILDEWED. BUT THEY'RE PRISTINE.
THE BOOKS AREN'T FILED IN ANY ORDER. WHO BUILT THIS SORT OF PLACE!?
AH, THE SECOND SEAL ON MY ARM DIS-APPEARED ...
TOMOR-ROW MORNING, I'LL BE MY OLD MAGICAL SELF.
THE WATER'S PRETTY WARM.
YEAH WHEE

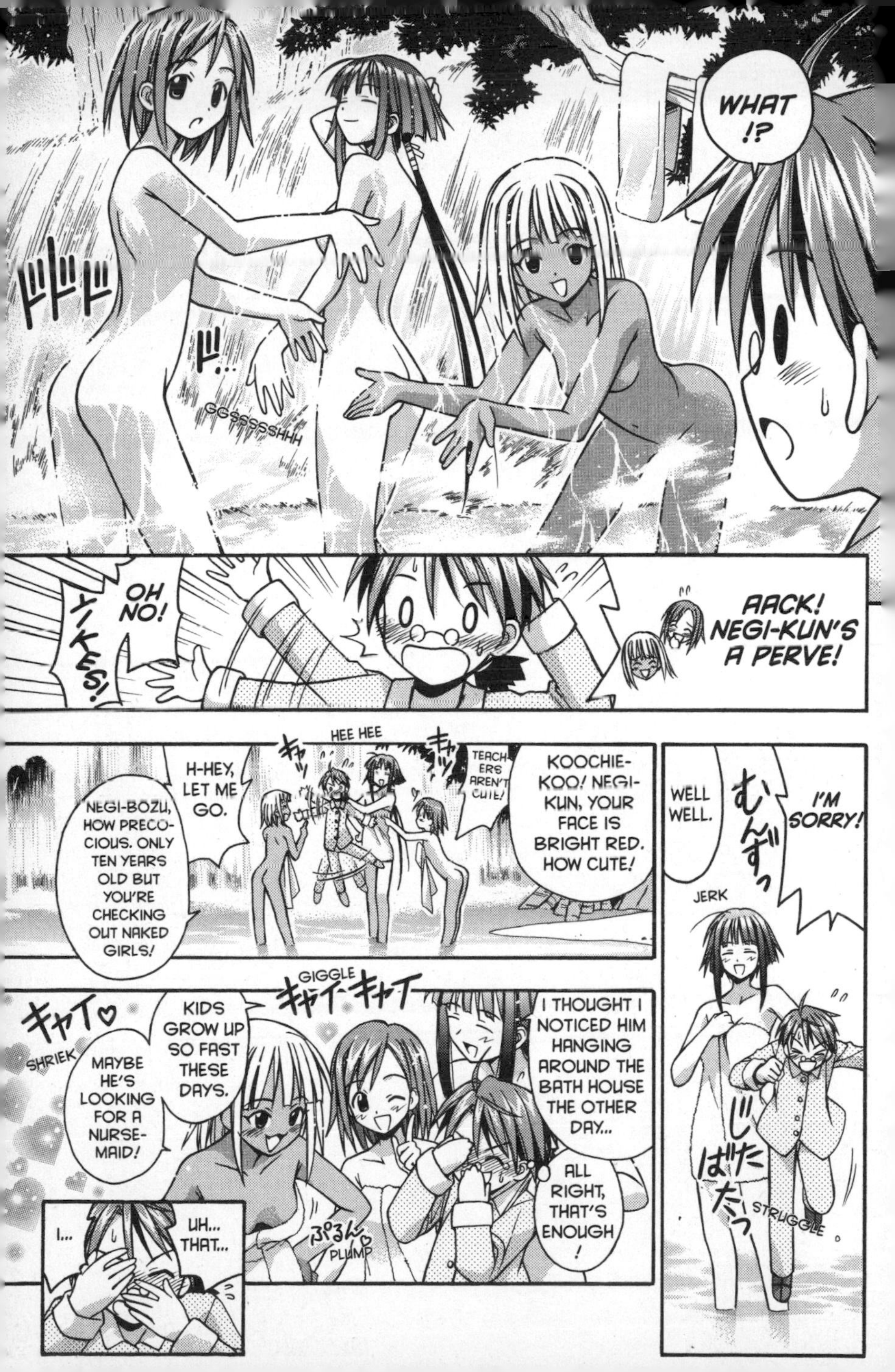
WHAT !?
ドドドド
ド...
GGSSSSSSHHH
AACK! NEGI-KUN'S A PERVE!
OH NO!
YIKES!
I'M SORRY!
むんずっ
WELL WELL.
JERK
じたばたっ
STRUGGLE
KOOCHIE-KOO! NEGI-KUN, YOUR FACE IS BRIGHT RED. HOW CUTE!
TEACHERS AREN'T CUTE!
キャッ
キャッ
HEE HEE
H-HEY, LET ME GO.
NEGI-BOZU, HOW PRECOCIOUS. ONLY TEN YEARS OLD BUT YOU'RE CHECKING OUT NAKED GIRLS!
I THOUGHT I NOTICED HIM HANGING AROUND THE BATH HOUSE THE OTHER DAY...
キャイーキャイー
GIGGLE
KIDS GROW UP SO FAST THESE DAYS.
キャイ♡
SHRIEK
MAYBE HE'S LOOKING FOR A NURSEMAID!
ALL RIGHT, THAT'S ENOUGH!
ぷるん
PLUMP
UH... THAT...
I...

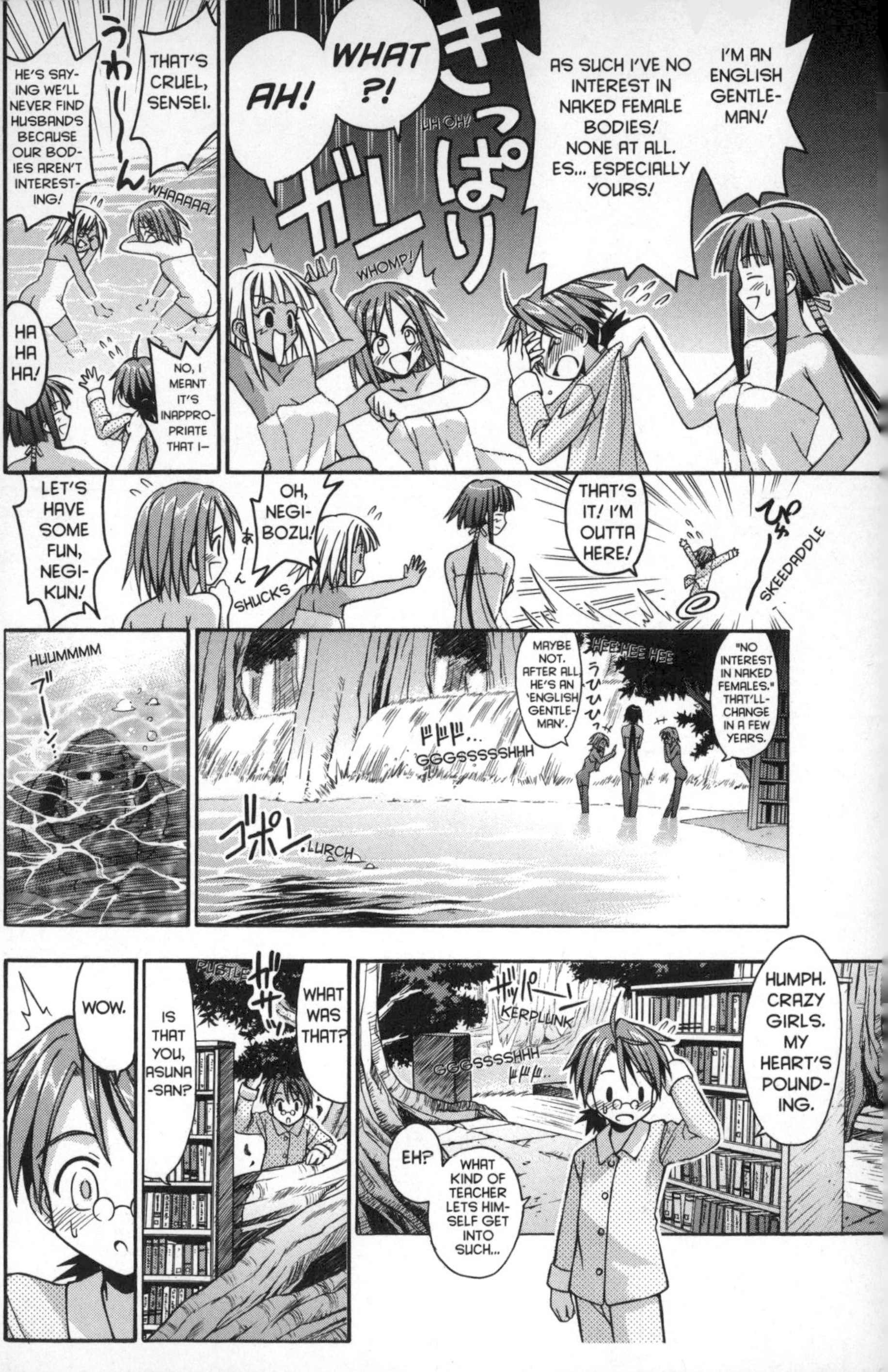

I'M AN ENGLISH GENTLEMAN!
AS SUCH I'VE NO INTEREST IN NAKED FEMALE BODIES! NONE AT ALL. ES... ESPECIALLY YOURS!
きっぱり
WHAT ?!
AH!
ガーン
WHOMP!
THAT'S CRUEL, SENSEI.
うわーーん
HE'S SAYING WE'LL NEVER FIND HUSBANDS BECAUSE OUR BODIES AREN'T INTERESTING!
WHAAAAA!
NO, I MEANT IT'S INAPPROPRIATE THAT I—
HA HA HA!
ぴゅー
SKEEDADDLE
THAT'S IT! I'M OUTTA HERE!
OH, NEGI-BOZU!
あーん
SHUCKS
LET'S HAVE SOME FUN, NEGI-KUN!
"NO INTEREST IN NAKED FEMALES." THAT'LL CHANGE IN A FEW YEARS.
うひひひ
HEE HEE HEE
MAYBE NOT. AFTER ALL, HE'S AN 'ENGLISH GENTLEMAN'.
ドドド...
GGGSSSSSHHH
ゴポン
LURCH
ブーン
HUUMMMM
HUMPH. CRAZY GIRLS. MY HEART'S POUNDING.
WHAT KIND OF TEACHER LETS HIMSELF GET INTO SUCH...
ザッパーン
KERPLUNK
GGGSSSSSHHH
ドドド...
EH?
WHAT WAS THAT?
ガサッ
RUSTLE
IS THAT YOU, ASUNA-SAN?
WOW.

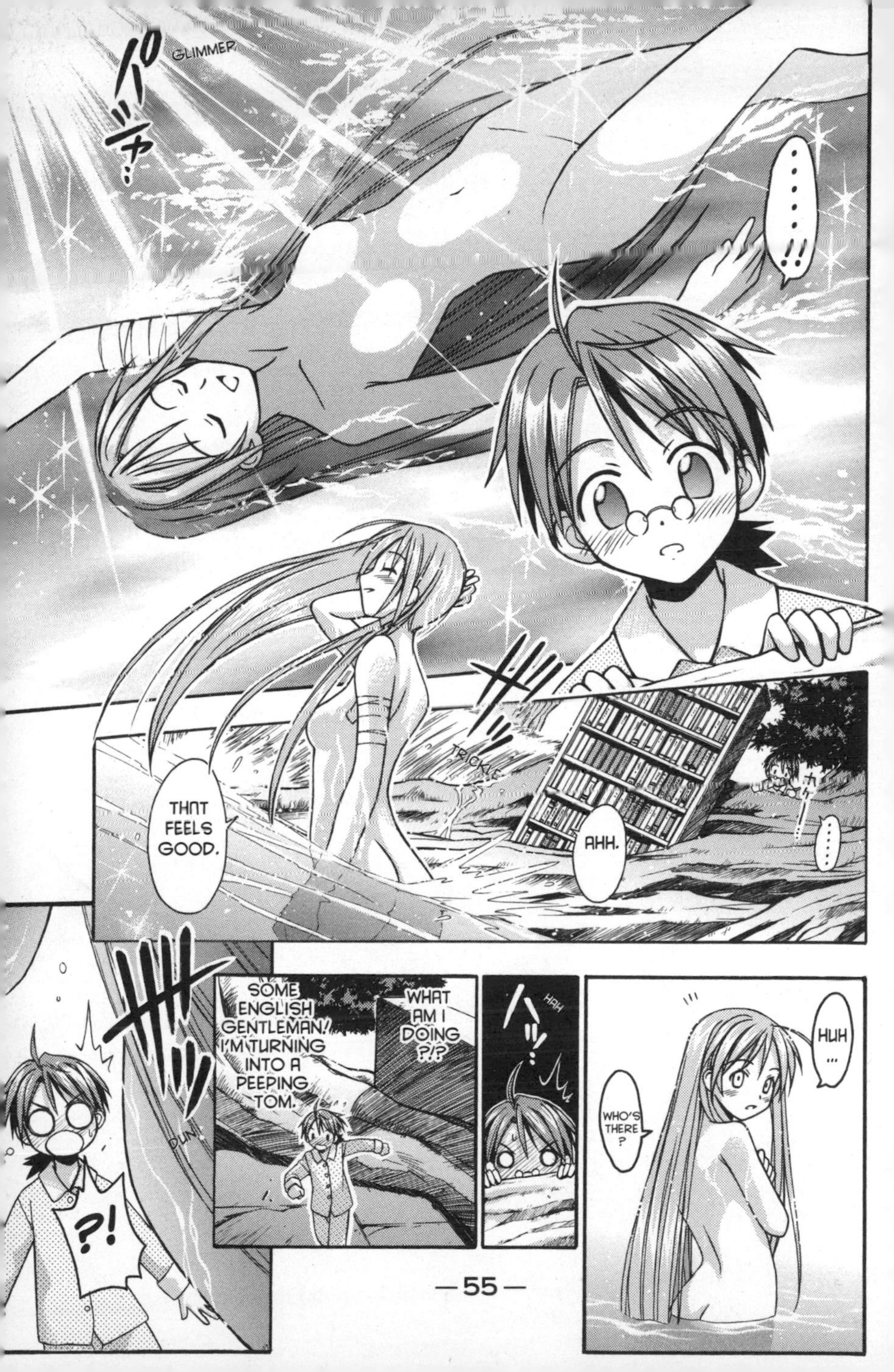
GLIMMER
......!!
AHH.
THAT FEELS GOOD.
TRICKLE
......
HUH ...
WHO'S THERE ?
HAH
WHAT AM I DOING ?!?
SOME ENGLISH GENTLEMAN! I'M TURNING INTO A PEEPING TOM.
DUN
?!

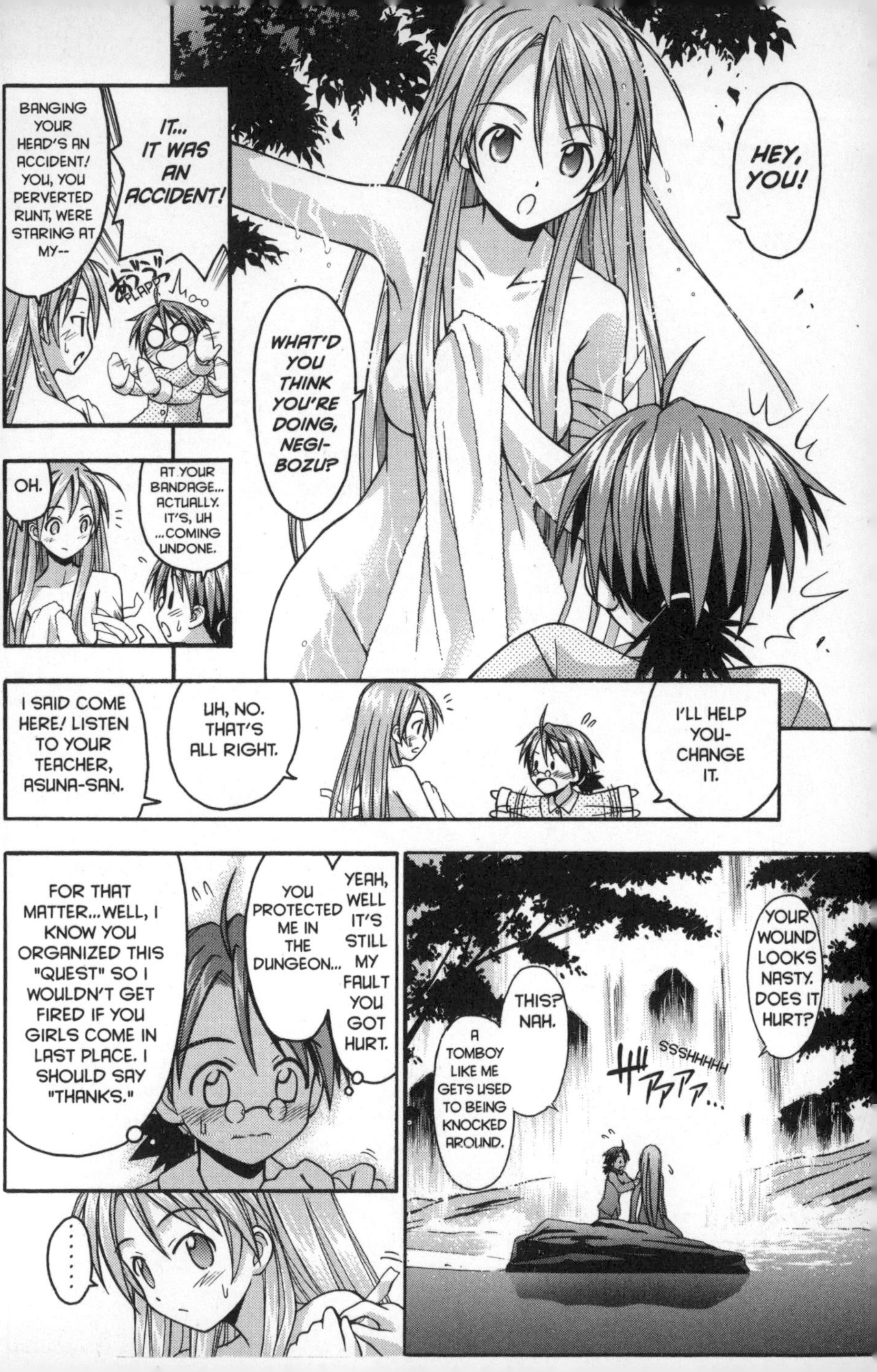
HEY, YOU!
WHAT'D YOU THINK YOU'RE DOING, NEGI-BOZU?
IT... IT WAS AN ACCIDENT!
BANGING YOUR HEAD'S AN ACCIDENT! YOU, YOU PERVERTED RUNT, WERE STARING AT MY--
あうう
FLAPP
AT YOUR BANDAGE... ACTUALLY. IT'S, UH ...COMING UNDONE.
OH.
I'LL HELP YOU- CHANGE IT.
UH, NO. THAT'S ALL RIGHT.
I SAID COME HERE! LISTEN TO YOUR TEACHER, ASUNA-SAN.
YOUR WOUND LOOKS NASTY. DOES IT HURT?
THIS? NAH.
A TOMBOY LIKE ME GETS USED TO BEING KNOCKED AROUND.
ザアアア...
SSSHHHHH
YEAH, WELL IT'S STILL MY FAULT YOU GOT HURT.
YOU PROTECTED ME IN THE DUNGEON...
FOR THAT MATTER...WELL, I KNOW YOU ORGANIZED THIS "QUEST" SO I WOULDN'T GET FIRED IF YOU GIRLS COME IN LAST PLACE. I SHOULD SAY "THANKS."
......

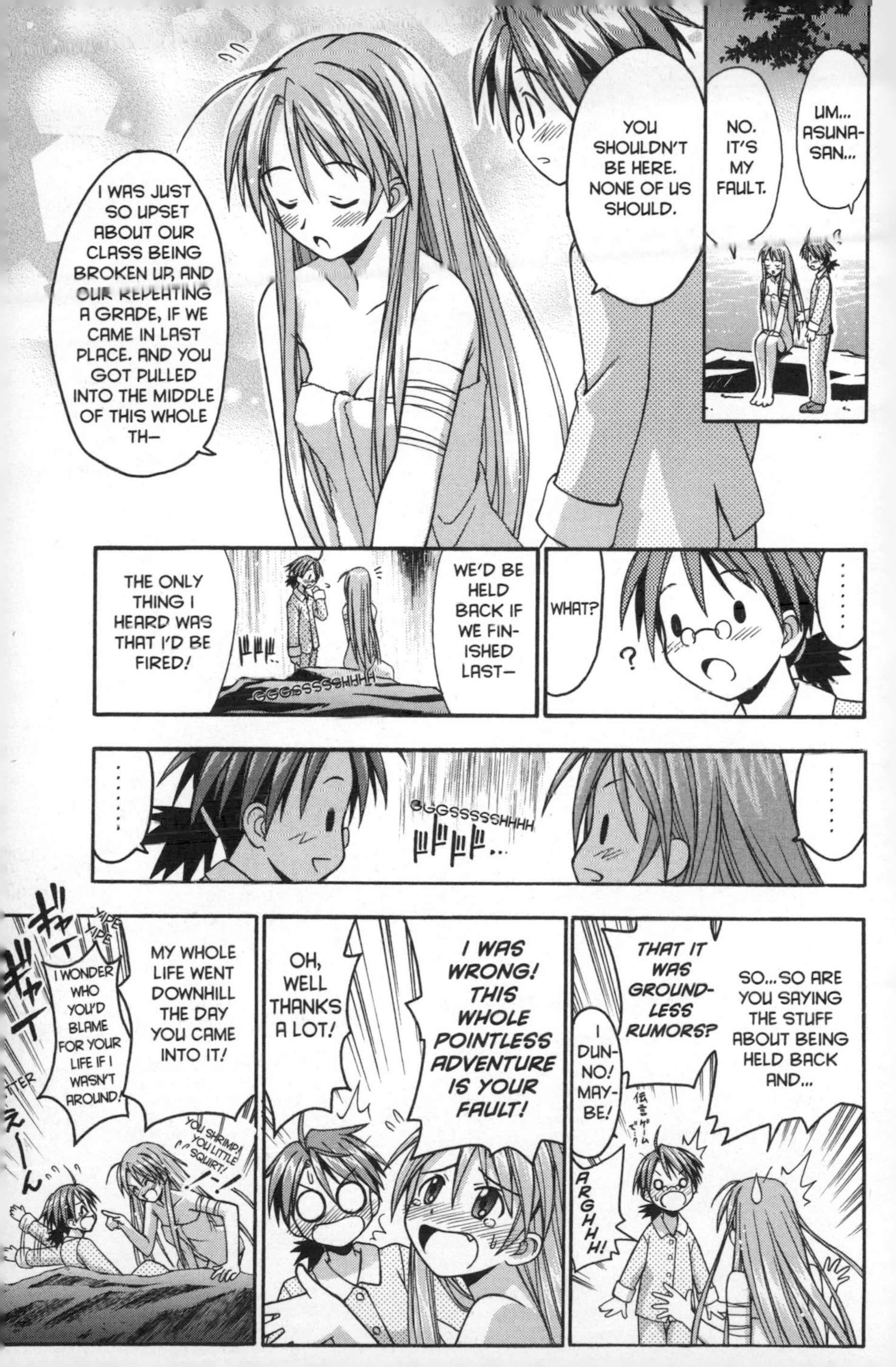
UM... ASUNA-SAN...
NO. IT'S MY FAULT.
YOU SHOULDN'T BE HERE. NONE OF US SHOULD.
I WAS JUST SO UPSET ABOUT OUR CLASS BEING BROKEN UP, AND OUR REPEATING A GRADE, IF WE CAME IN LAST PLACE. AND YOU GOT PULLED INTO THE MIDDLE OF THIS WHOLE TH—
......
WHAT?
WE'D BE HELD BACK IF WE FIN-ISHED LAST—
THE ONLY THING I HEARD WAS THAT I'D BE FIRED!
GGGSSSSSHHHH
......
GGGSSSSSHHHH
......
SO...SO ARE YOU SAYING THE STUFF ABOUT BEING HELD BACK AND...
THAT IT WAS GROUND-LESS RUMORS?
I DUN-NO! MAY-BE!
ARGHHH!
I WAS WRONG! THIS WHOLE POINTLESS ADVENTURE IS YOUR FAULT!
OH, WELL THANKS A LOT!
MY WHOLE LIFE WENT DOWNHILL THE DAY YOU CAME INTO IT!
I WONDER WHO YOU'D BLAME FOR YOUR LIFE IF I WASN'T AROUND!
YOU SHRIMP! YOU LITTLE SQUIRT!
YIPE YIPE

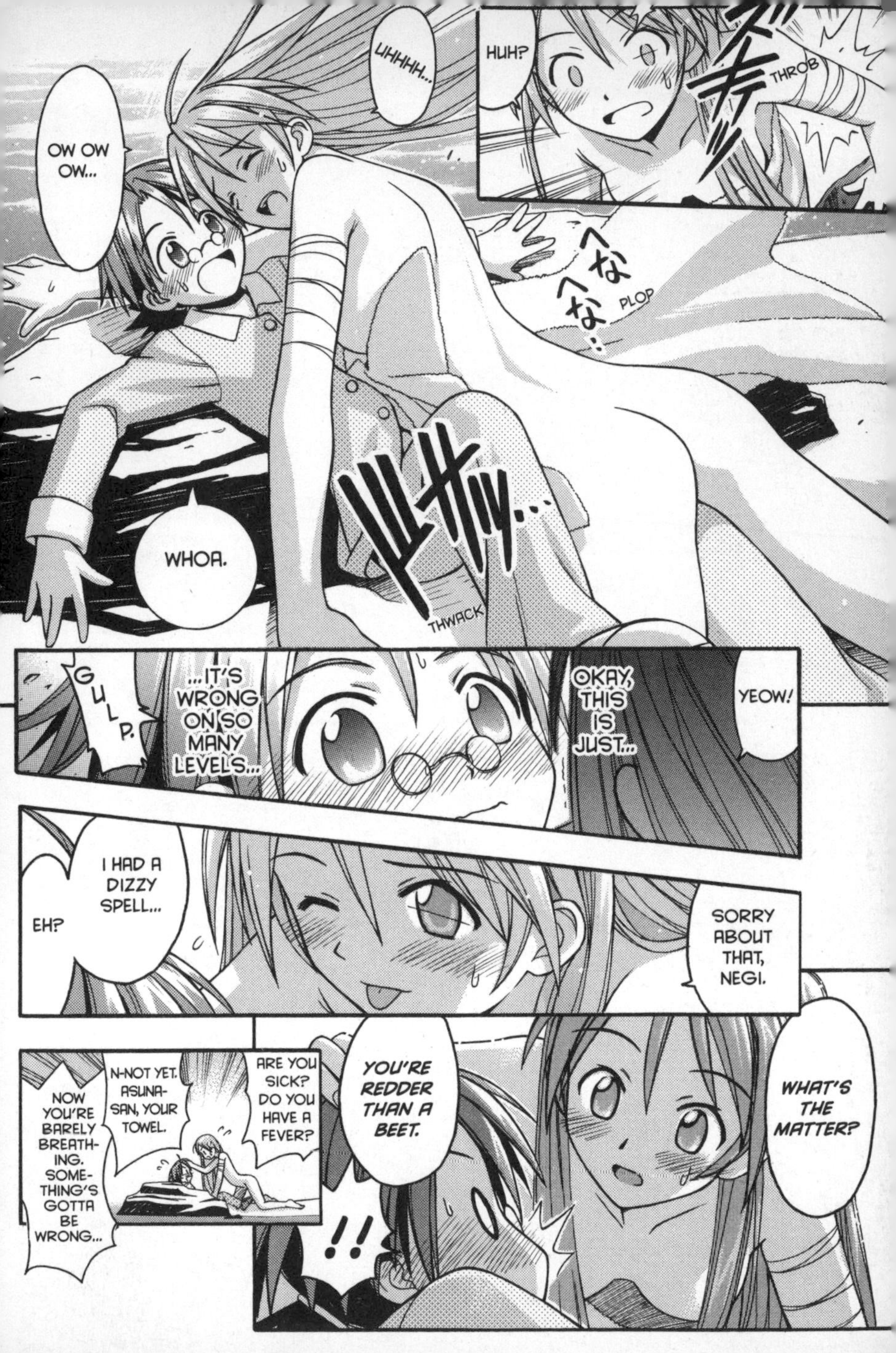
HUH?
THROB
UHHHH...
OW OW OW...
へな へな‥
PLOP
THWACK
WHOA.
YEOW!
OKAY, THIS IS JUST...
...IT'S WRONG ON SO MANY LEVELS...
GULP.
SORRY ABOUT THAT, NEGI.
I HAD A DIZZY SPELL...
EH?
WHAT'S THE MATTER?
YOU'RE REDDER THAN A BEET.
!!
ARE YOU SICK? DO YOU HAVE A FEVER?
N-NOT YET. ASUNA-SAN, YOUR TOWEL.
NOW YOU'RE BARELY BREATHING. SOMETHING'S GOTTA BE WRONG...

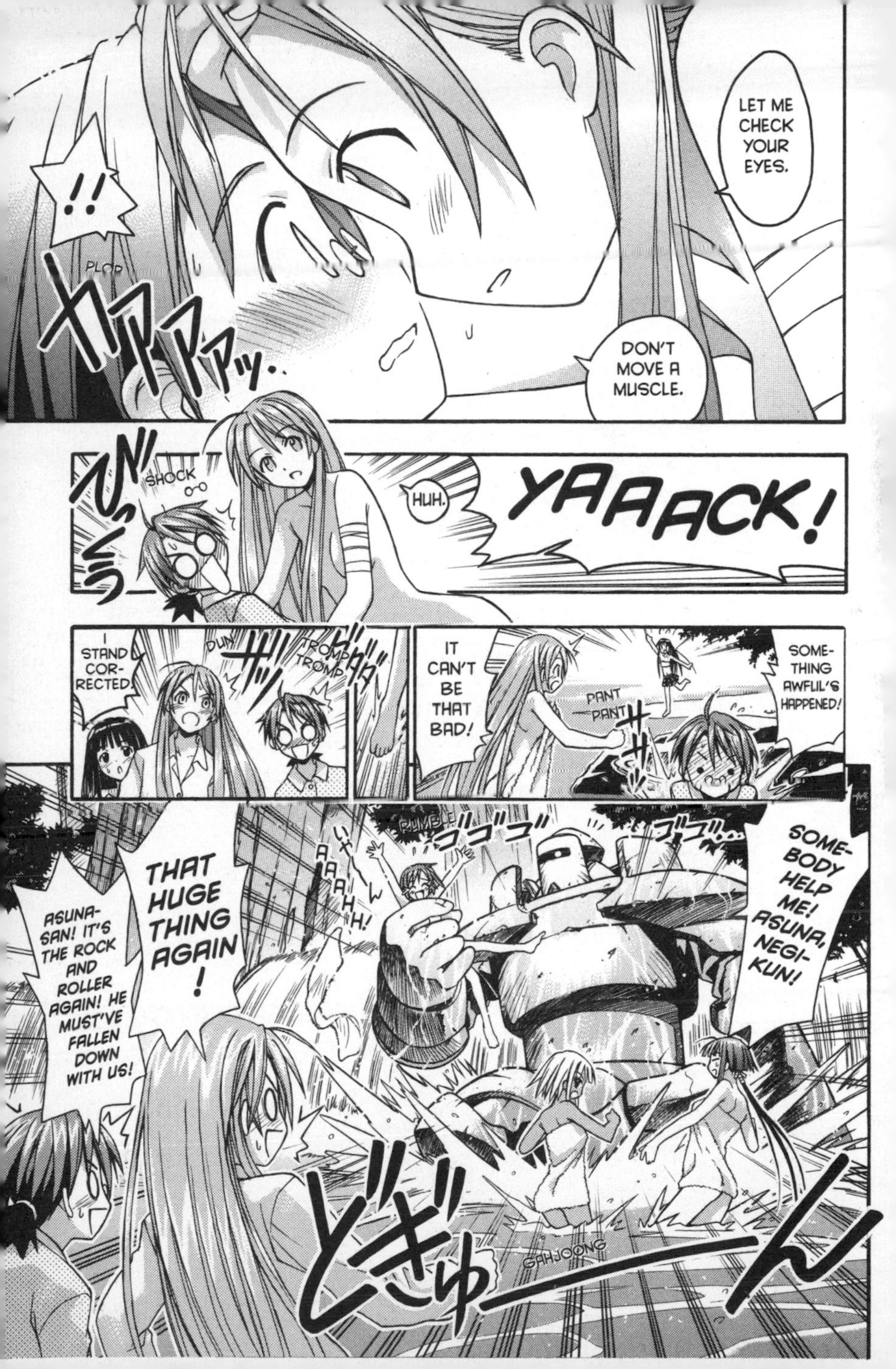
LET ME CHECK YOUR EYES.
DON'T MOVE A MUSCLE.
!!
PLOP
YAAACK!
HUH.
SHOCK
SOME-THING AWFUL'S HAPPENED!
PANT PANT
IT CAN'T BE THAT BAD!
TROMP TROMP
DUN
I STAND COR-RECTED.
SOME-BODY HELP ME! ASUNA, NEGI-KUN!
RUMBLE
AAAHH!
THAT HUGE THING AGAIN!
ASUNA-SAN! IT'S THE ROCK AND ROLLER AGAIN! HE MUST'VE FALLEN DOWN WITH US!
GAHJOONG

2A STUDENT PROFILE
(TEACHER EDITION)

NEGI SPRINGFIELD

BORN: 1994
BLOOD TYPE: AB
LIKES: OLDER SISTER (GIRLS IN GENERAL), HERBAL TEA, ANTIQUES (WANDS)
DISLIKES: BATHS, SLEEPING ALONE
AFFILIATIONS: A PROBATIONARY INSTRUCTOR AT THE JUNIOR HIGH DEPARTMENT OF MAHORA ACADEMY.
NOTE: MELDIANA SCHOOL OF MAGIC, TOP CLASS FOR THE ACADEMIC YEAR 2002.

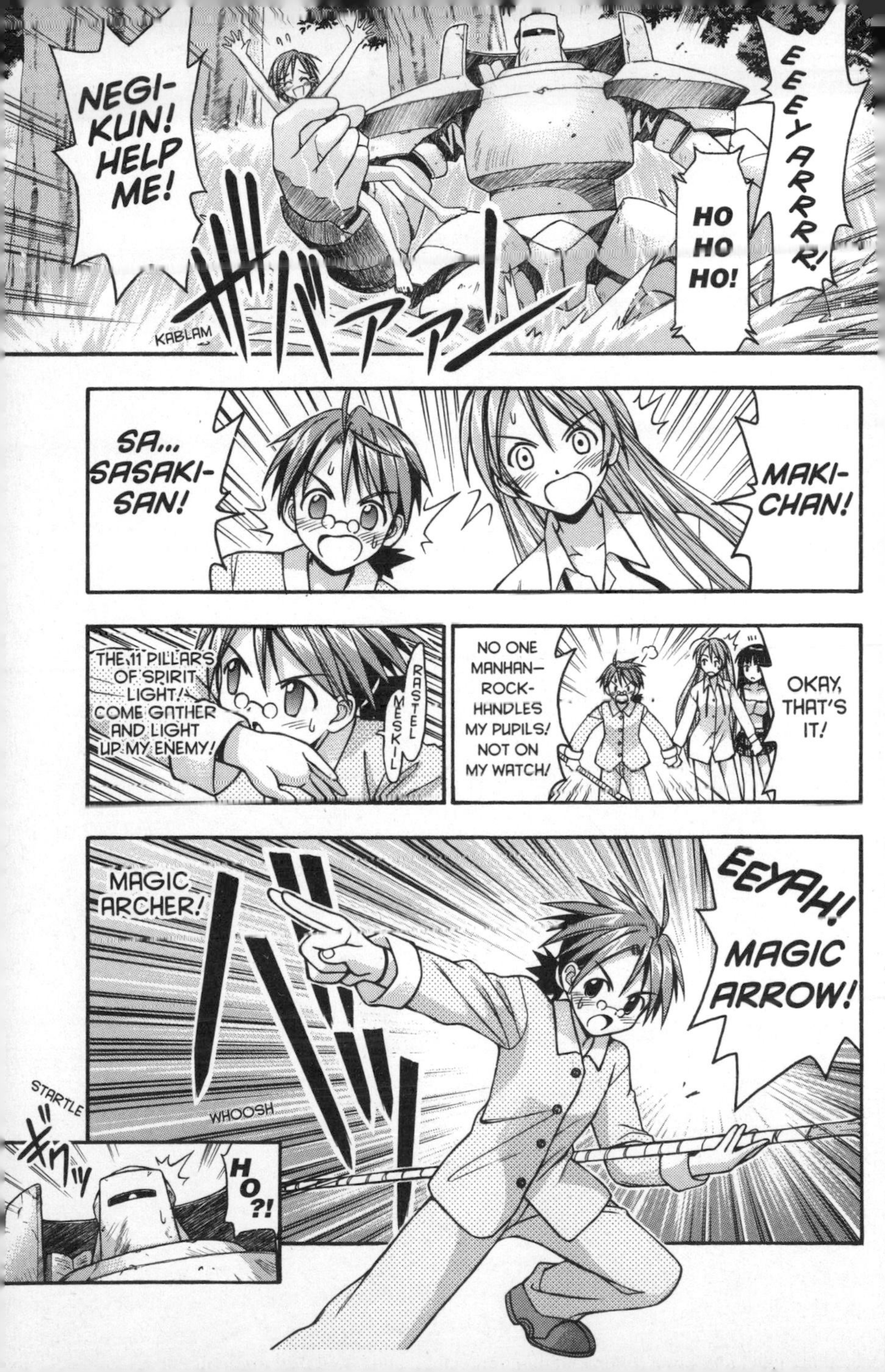
EEEYARRRR!
HO HO HO!
NEGI-KUN! HELP ME!
KABLAM
MAKI-CHAN!
SA... SASAKI-SAN!
OKAY, THAT'S IT!
NO ONE MANHAN-ROCK-HANDLES MY PUPILS! NOT ON MY WATCH!
RASTEL MESKIL
THE 11 PILLARS OF SPIRIT LIGHT! COME GATHER AND LIGHT UP MY ENEMY!
EEYAH! MAGIC ARROW!
MAGIC ARCHER!
WHOOSH
STARTLE
HO?!

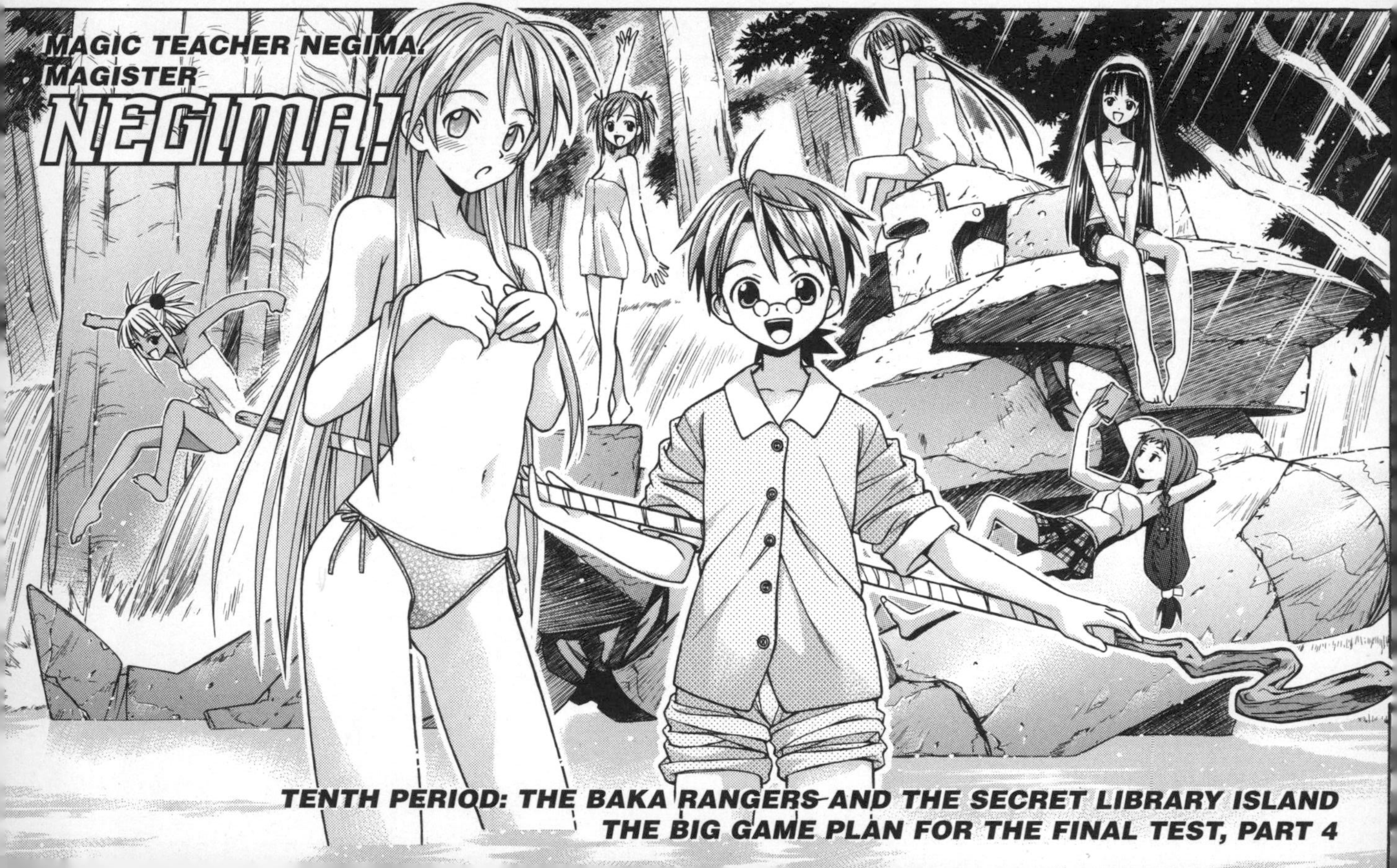
MAGIC TEACHER NEGIMA.
MAGISTER
NEGIMA!
TENTH PERIOD: THE BAKA RANGERS AND THE SECRET LIBRARY ISLAND
THE BIG GAME PLAN FOR THE FINAL TEST, PART 4

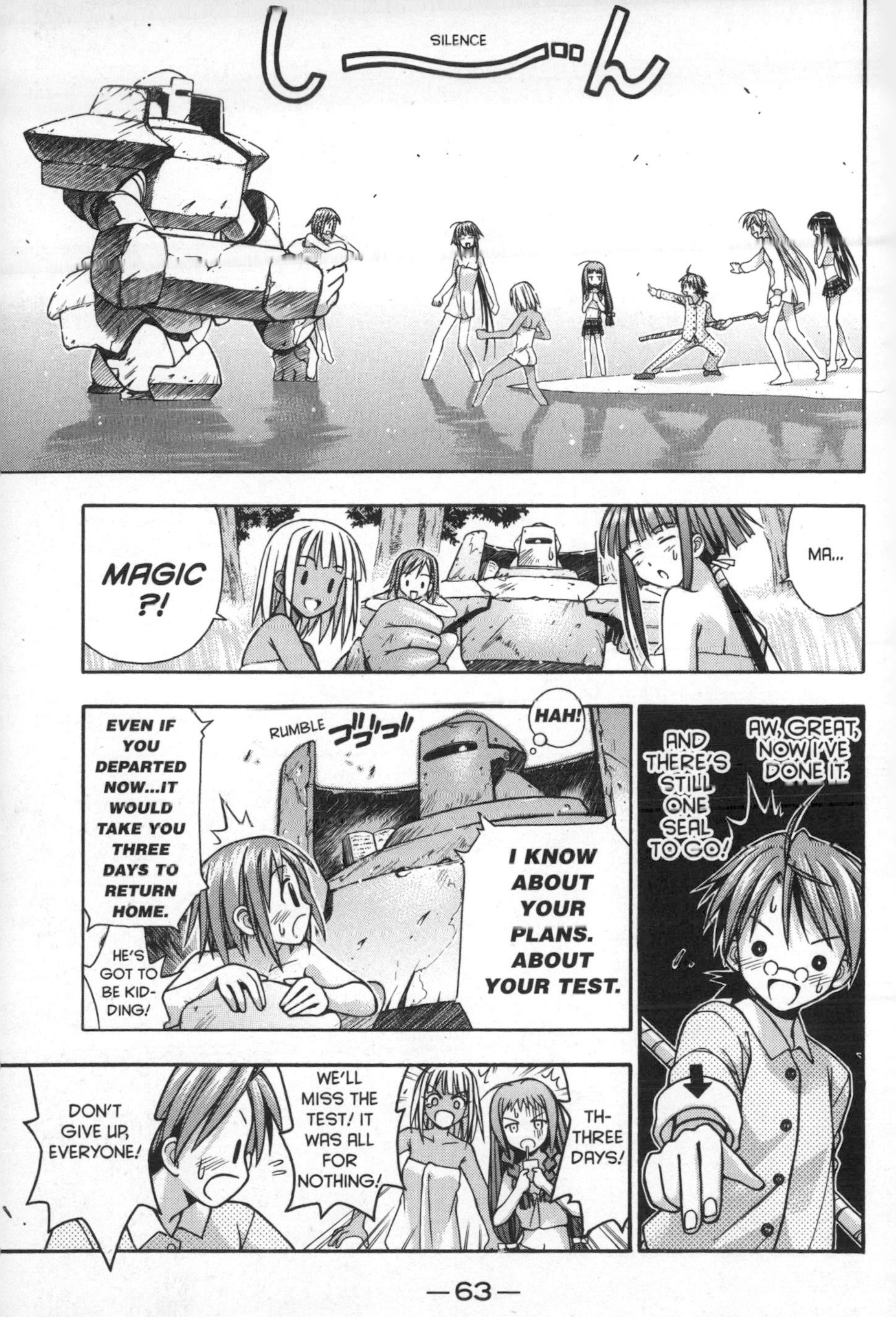

しーーん
SILENCE
MA...
MAGIC ?!
AW, GREAT, NOW I'VE DONE IT.
AND THERE'S STILL ONE SEAL TO GO!
HAH!
RUMBLE
ゴゴゴ
I KNOW ABOUT YOUR PLANS. ABOUT YOUR TEST.
EVEN IF YOU DEPARTED NOW...IT WOULD TAKE YOU THREE DAYS TO RETURN HOME.
HE'S GOT TO BE KID-DING!
TH-THREE DAYS!
WE'LL MISS THE TEST! IT WAS ALL FOR NOTHING!
DON'T GIVE UP, EVERYONE!

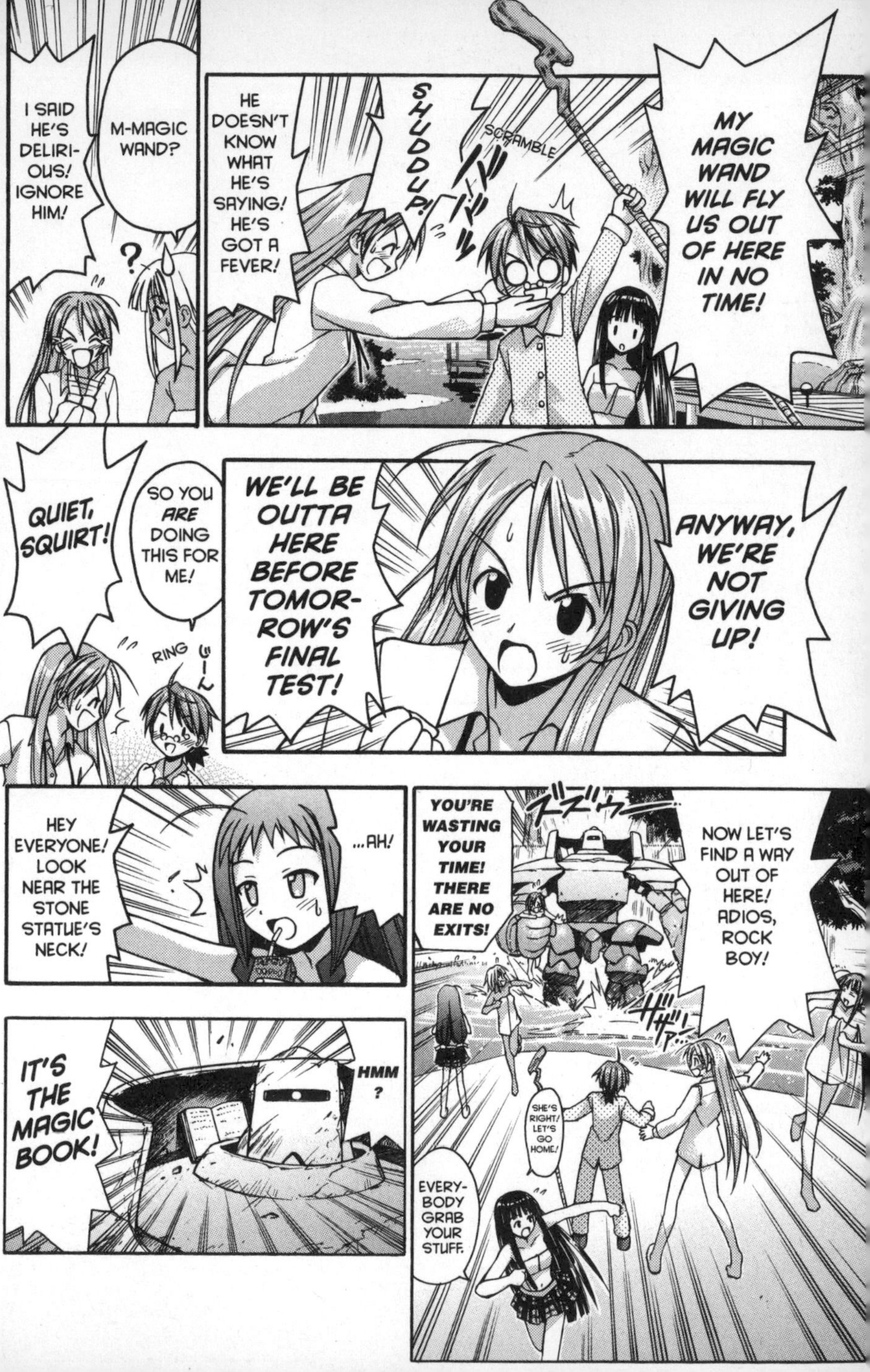
MY MAGIC WAND WILL FLY US OUT OF HERE IN NO TIME!
SCRAMBLE
SHUDDUP!
HE DOESN'T KNOW WHAT HE'S SAYING! HE'S GOT A FEVER!
M-MAGIC WAND?
I SAID HE'S DELIRI-OUS! IGNORE HIM!
ANYWAY, WE'RE NOT GIVING UP!
WE'LL BE OUTTA HERE BEFORE TOMOR-ROW'S FINAL TEST!
SO YOU ARE DOING THIS FOR ME!
QUIET, SQUIRT!
RING
NOW LET'S FIND A WAY OUT OF HERE! ADIOS, ROCK BOY!
YOU'RE WASTING YOUR TIME! THERE ARE NO EXITS!
SHE'S RIGHT! LET'S GO HOME!
EVERY-BODY GRAB YOUR STUFF.
...AH!
HEY EVERYONE! LOOK NEAR THE STONE STATUE'S NECK!
HMM?
IT'S THE MAGIC BOOK!

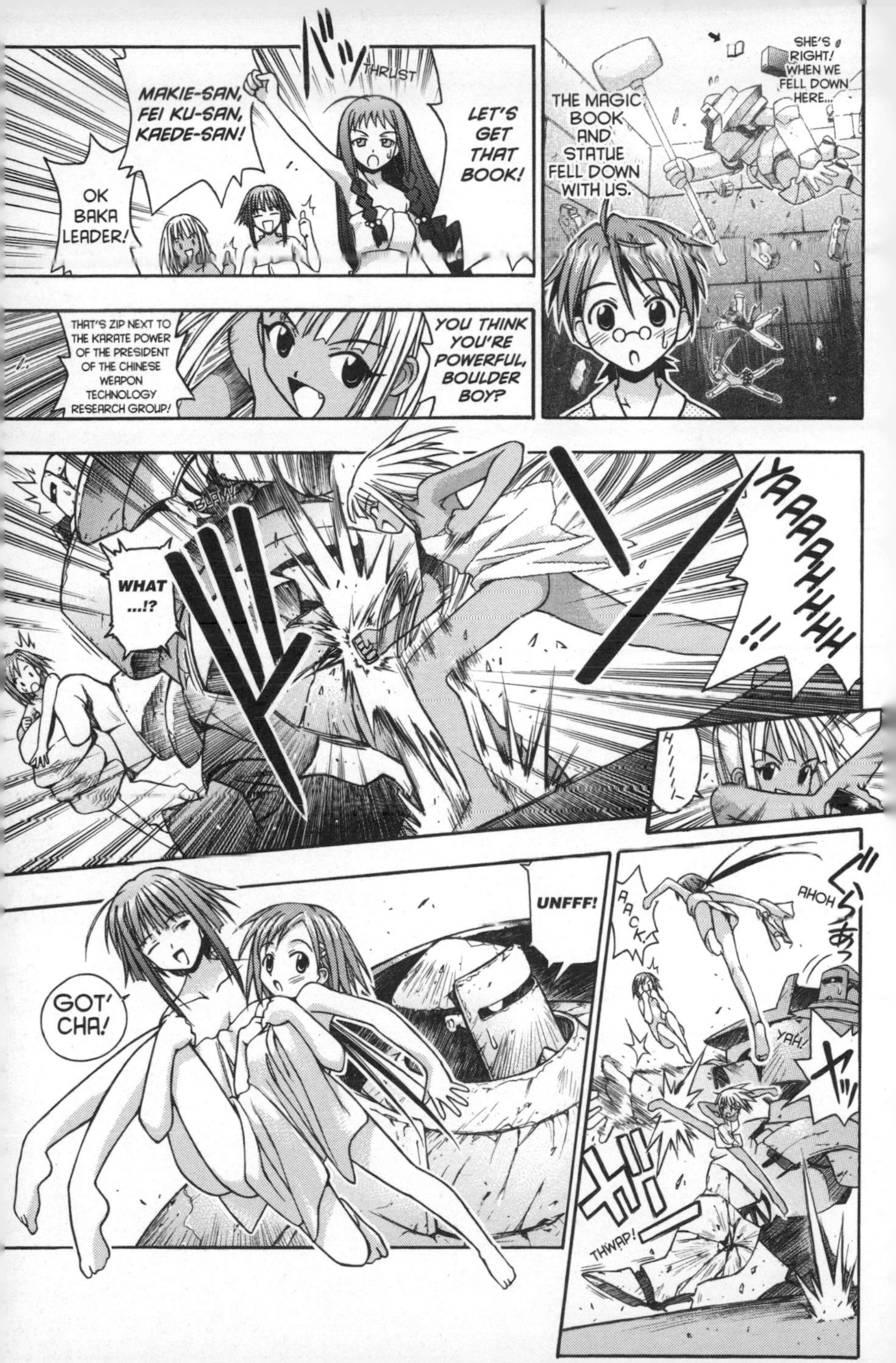
SHE'S RIGHT! WHEN WE FELL DOWN HERE...
THE MAGIC BOOK AND STATUE FELL DOWN WITH US.
THRUST
LET'S GET THAT BOOK!
MAKIE-SAN, FEI KU-SAN, KAEDE-SAN!
OK BAKA LEADER!
YOU THINK YOU'RE POWERFUL, BOULDER BOY?
THAT'S ZIP NEXT TO THE KARATE POWER OF THE PRESIDENT OF THE CHINESE WEAPON TECHNOLOGY RESEARCH GROUP!
YAAAAHHHHH!!
BLAM!
WHAT ...!?
AHOH
AACK!
YAH!
THWAP!
UNFFF!
GOT'CHA!

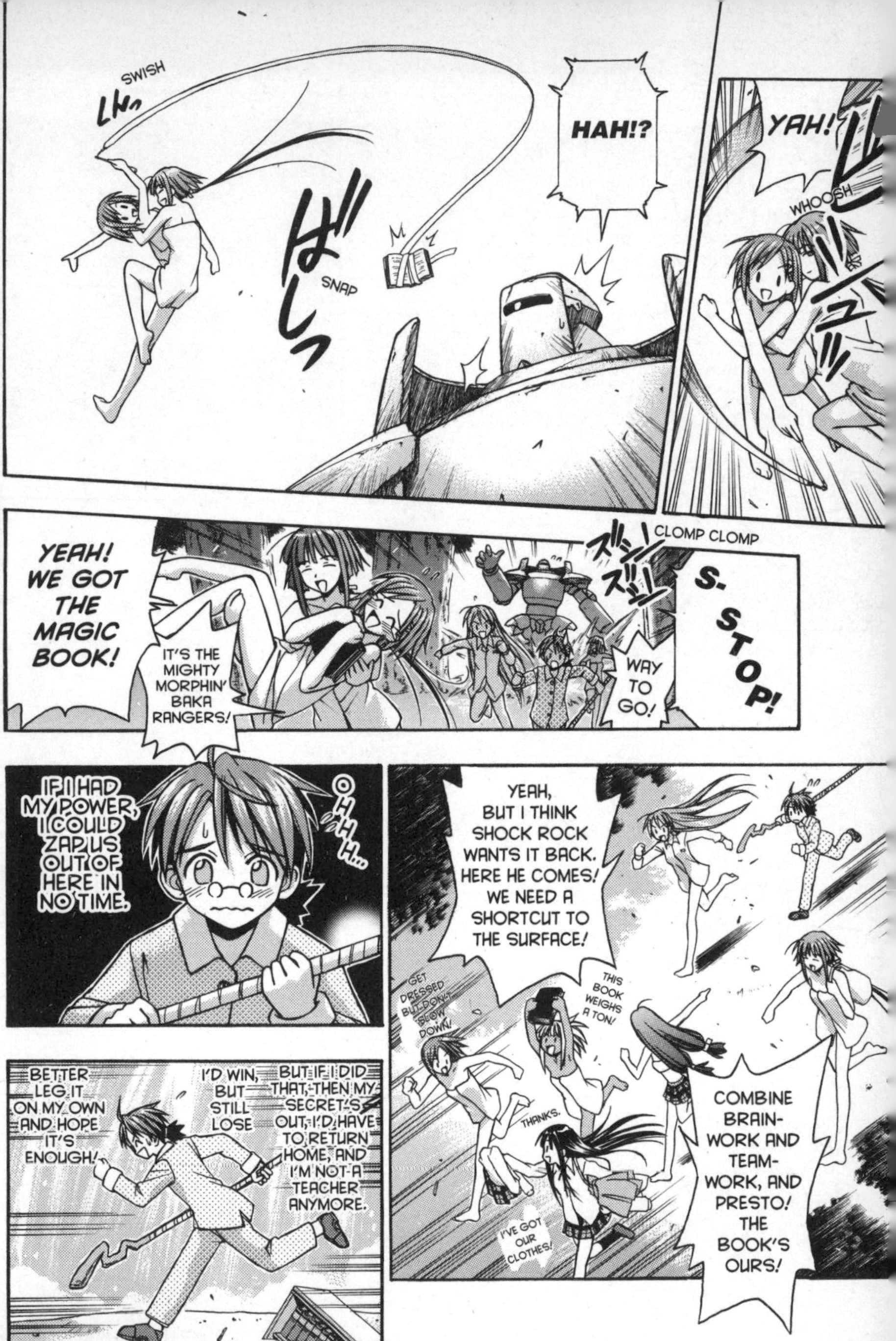
YAH!
WHOOSH
HAH!?
SWISH
SNAP
S-STOP!
CLOMP CLOMP
WAY TO GO!
YEAH! WE GOT THE MAGIC BOOK!
IT'S THE MIGHTY MORPHIN' BAKA RANGERS!
YEAH, BUT I THINK SHOCK ROCK WANTS IT BACK. HERE HE COMES! WE NEED A SHORTCUT TO THE SURFACE!
THIS BOOK WEIGHS A TON!
GET DRESSED BUT DON'T SLOW DOWN!
THANKS.
I'VE GOT OUR CLOTHES!
COMBINE BRAIN-WORK AND TEAM-WORK, AND PRESTO! THE BOOK'S OURS!
OHHHH...
IF I HAD MY POWER, I COULD ZAP US OUT OF HERE IN NO TIME.
BUT IF I DID THAT, THEN MY SECRET'S OUT, I'D HAVE TO RETURN HOME, AND I'M NOT A TEACHER ANYMORE.
I'D WIN, BUT STILL LOSE
BETTER LEG IT ON MY OWN AND HOPE IT'S ENOUGH!

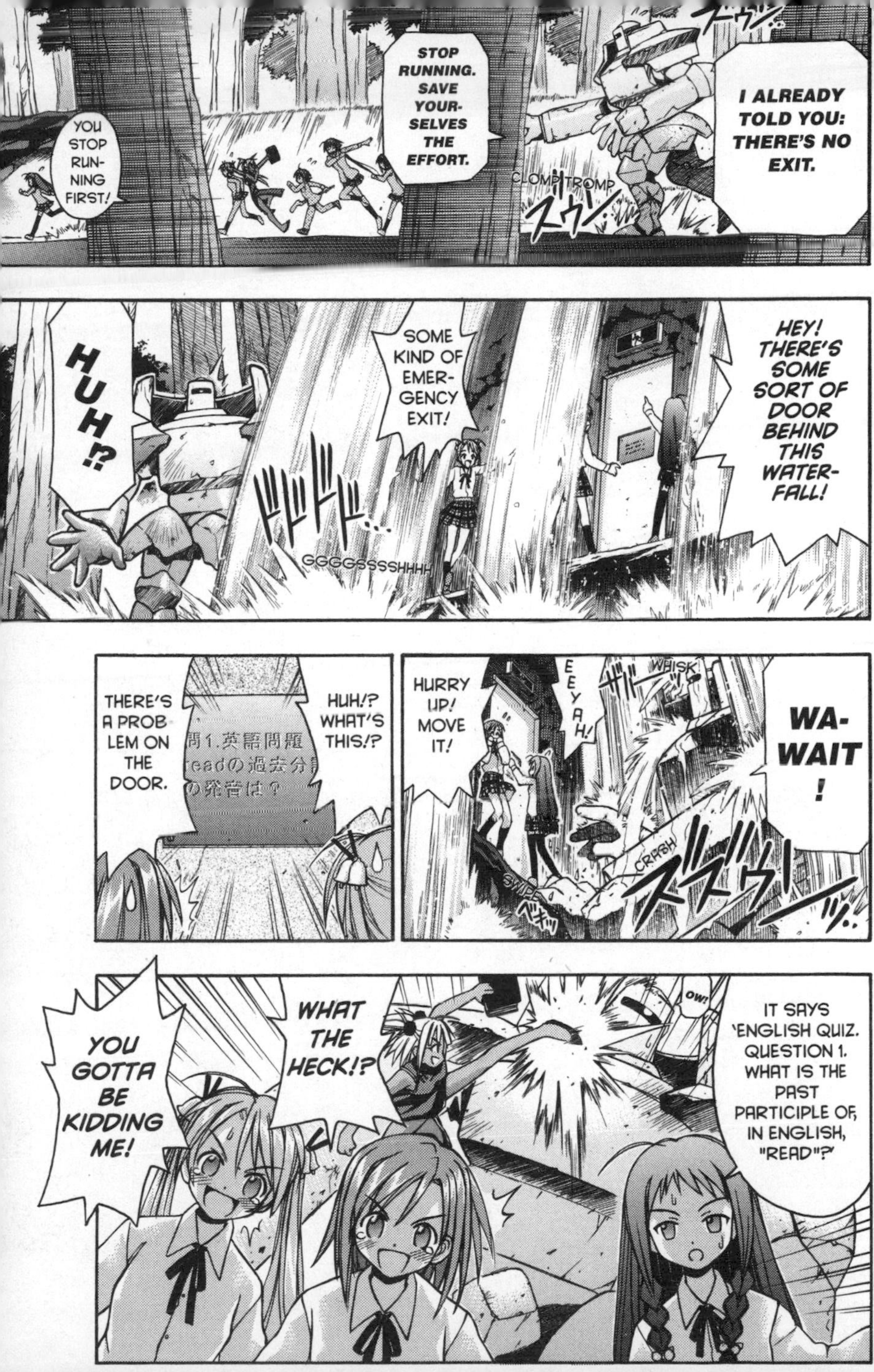
I ALREADY TOLD YOU: THERE'S NO EXIT.
CLOMP TROMP
STOP RUNNING. SAVE YOURSELVES THE EFFORT.
YOU STOP RUNNING FIRST!
HEY! THERE'S SOME SORT OF DOOR BEHIND THIS WATERFALL!
SOME KIND OF EMERGENCY EXIT!
GGGGSSSSHHHH
HUH!?
WA-WAIT!
WHISK
EEYAH!
HURRY UP! MOVE IT!
CRASH
SWIPE
HUH!? WHAT'S THIS!?
THERE'S A PROBLEM ON THE DOOR.
IT SAYS 'ENGLISH QUIZ. QUESTION 1. WHAT IS THE PAST PARTICIPLE OF, IN ENGLISH, "READ"?'
OW!
WHAT THE HECK!?
YOU GOTTA BE KIDDING ME!

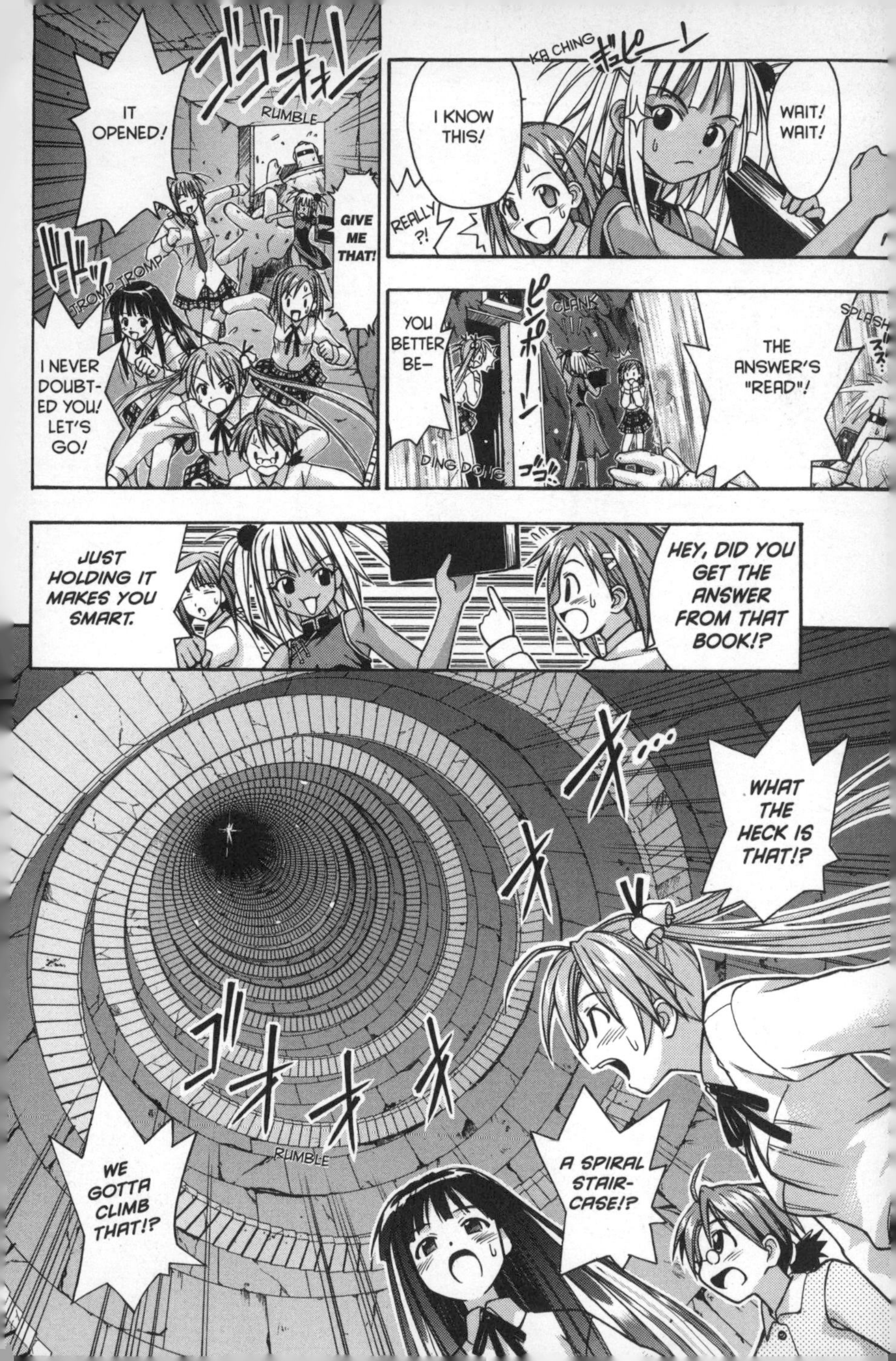
KA CHING
WAIT! WAIT!
I KNOW THIS!
REALLY ?!
SPLASH
THE ANSWER'S "READ"!
CLANK
YOU BETTER BE—
DING DONG
IT OPENED!
RUMBLE
GIVE ME THAT!
TROMP TROMP
I NEVER DOUBTED YOU! LET'S GO!
HEY, DID YOU GET THE ANSWER FROM THAT BOOK!?
JUST HOLDING IT MAKES YOU SMART.
WHAT THE HECK IS THAT!?
A SPIRAL STAIRCASE!?
WE GOTTA CLIMB THAT!?
RUMBLE

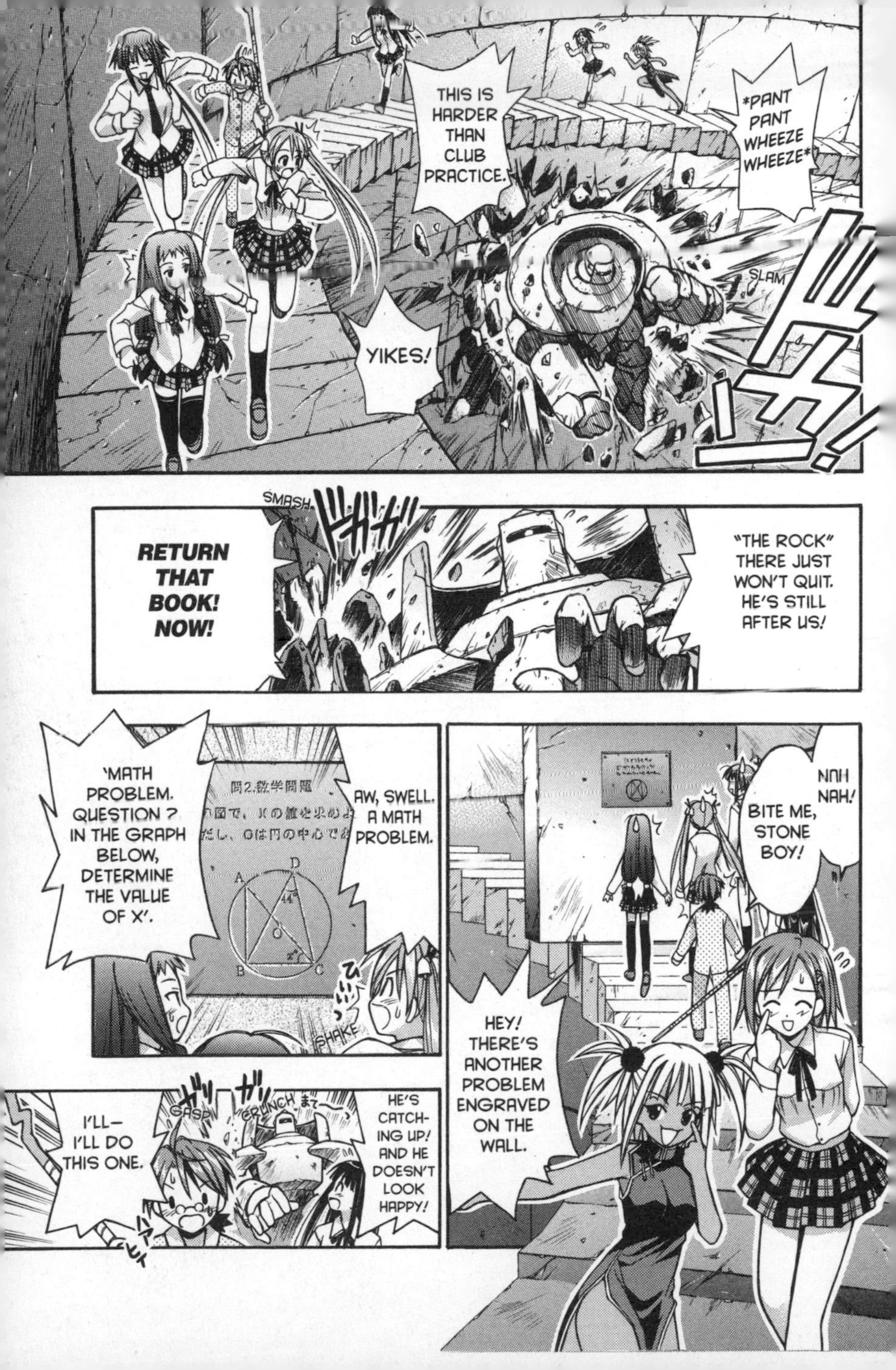
PANT PANT WHEEZE WHEEZE
THIS IS HARDER THAN CLUB PRACTICE.
SLAM
YIKES!
"THE ROCK" THERE JUST WON'T QUIT. HE'S STILL AFTER US!
SMASH
RETURN THAT BOOK! NOW!
NAH NAH!
BITE ME, STONE BOY!
HEY! THERE'S ANOTHER PROBLEM ENGRAVED ON THE WALL.
AW, SWELL. A MATH PROBLEM.
問2.数学問題
'MATH PROBLEM. QUESTION 7 IN THE GRAPH BELOW, DETERMINE THE VALUE OF X'.
SHAKE
HE'S CATCHING UP! AND HE DOESN'T LOOK HAPPY!
CRUNCH まて～
GASP
I'LL— I'LL DO THIS ONE.

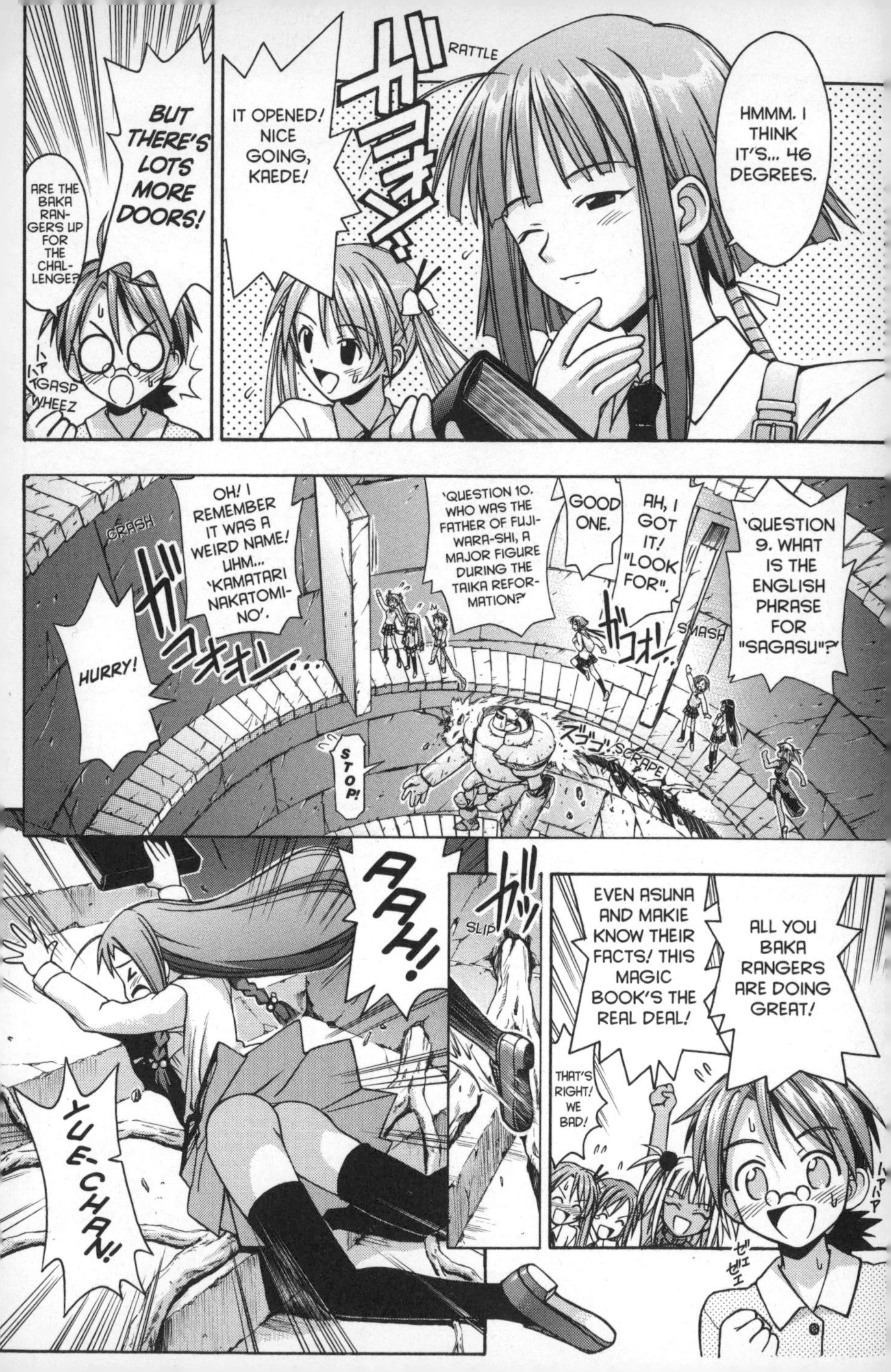
HMMM. I THINK IT'S... 46 DEGREES.
RATTLE
IT OPENED! NICE GOING, KAEDE!
BUT THERE'S LOTS MORE DOORS!
ARE THE BAKA RANGERS UP FOR THE CHALLENGE?
GASP WHEEZ
'QUESTION 9. WHAT IS THE ENGLISH PHRASE FOR "SAGASU"?'
AH, I GOT IT! "LOOK FOR".
SMASH
GOOD ONE.
'QUESTION 10. WHO WAS THE FATHER OF FUJIWARA-SHI, A MAJOR FIGURE DURING THE TAIKA REFORMATION?'
OH! I REMEMBER IT WAS A WEIRD NAME! UHM... 'KAMATARI NAKATOMI-NO'.
CRASH
HURRY!
SCRAPE
STOP!
ALL YOU BAKA RANGERS ARE DOING GREAT!
EVEN ASUNA AND MAKIE KNOW THEIR FACTS! THIS MAGIC BOOK'S THE REAL DEAL!
THAT'S RIGHT! WE BAD!
SLIP
AAH!
YUE-CHAN!

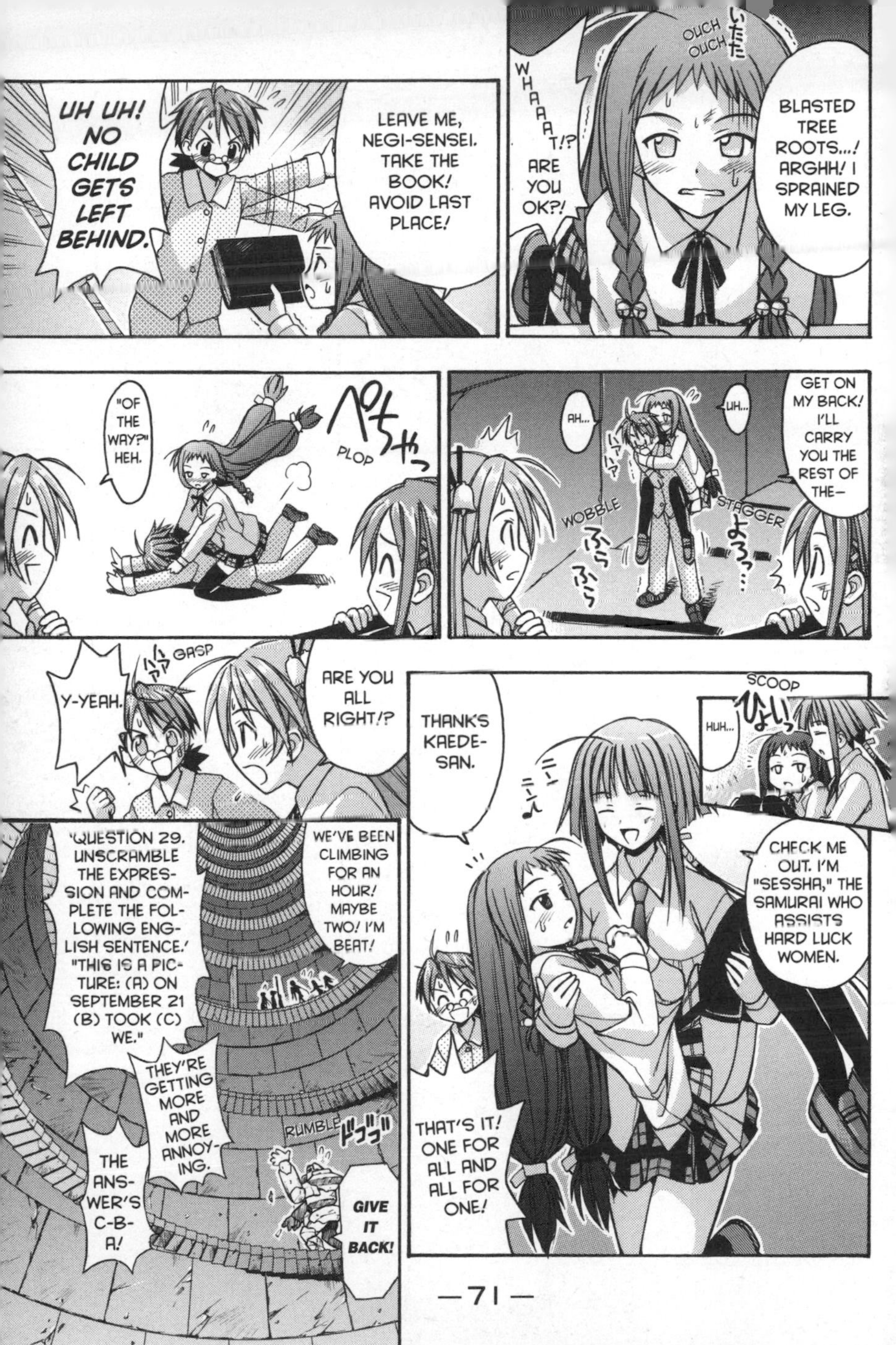
OUCH OUCH いたた
WHAAAAT!?
ARE YOU OK?!
BLASTED TREE ROOTS...! ARGHH! I SPRAINED MY LEG.
LEAVE ME, NEGI-SENSEI. TAKE THE BOOK! AVOID LAST PLACE!
UH UH! NO CHILD GETS LEFT BEHIND.
GET ON MY BACK! I'LL CARRY YOU THE REST OF THE—
UH...
AH...
STAGGER よろっ…
WOBBLE ふらふら
ぺちゃっ PLOP
"OF THE WAY?" HEH.
SCOOP ひょいっ
HUH...
THANKS KAEDE-SAN.
CHECK ME OUT. I'M "SESSHA," THE SAMURAI WHO ASSISTS HARD LUCK WOMEN.
THAT'S IT! ONE FOR ALL AND ALL FOR ONE!
ARE YOU ALL RIGHT!?
GASP
Y-YEAH.
WE'VE BEEN CLIMBING FOR AN HOUR! MAYBE TWO! I'M BEAT!
'QUESTION 29. UNSCRAMBLE THE EXPRESSION AND COMPLETE THE FOLLOWING ENGLISH SENTENCE.' "THIS IS A PICTURE: (A) ON SEPTEMBER 21 (B) TOOK (C) WE."
THEY'RE GETTING MORE AND MORE ANNOYING.
RUMBLE ドゴゴ
GIVE IT BACK!
THE ANSWER'S C-B-A!

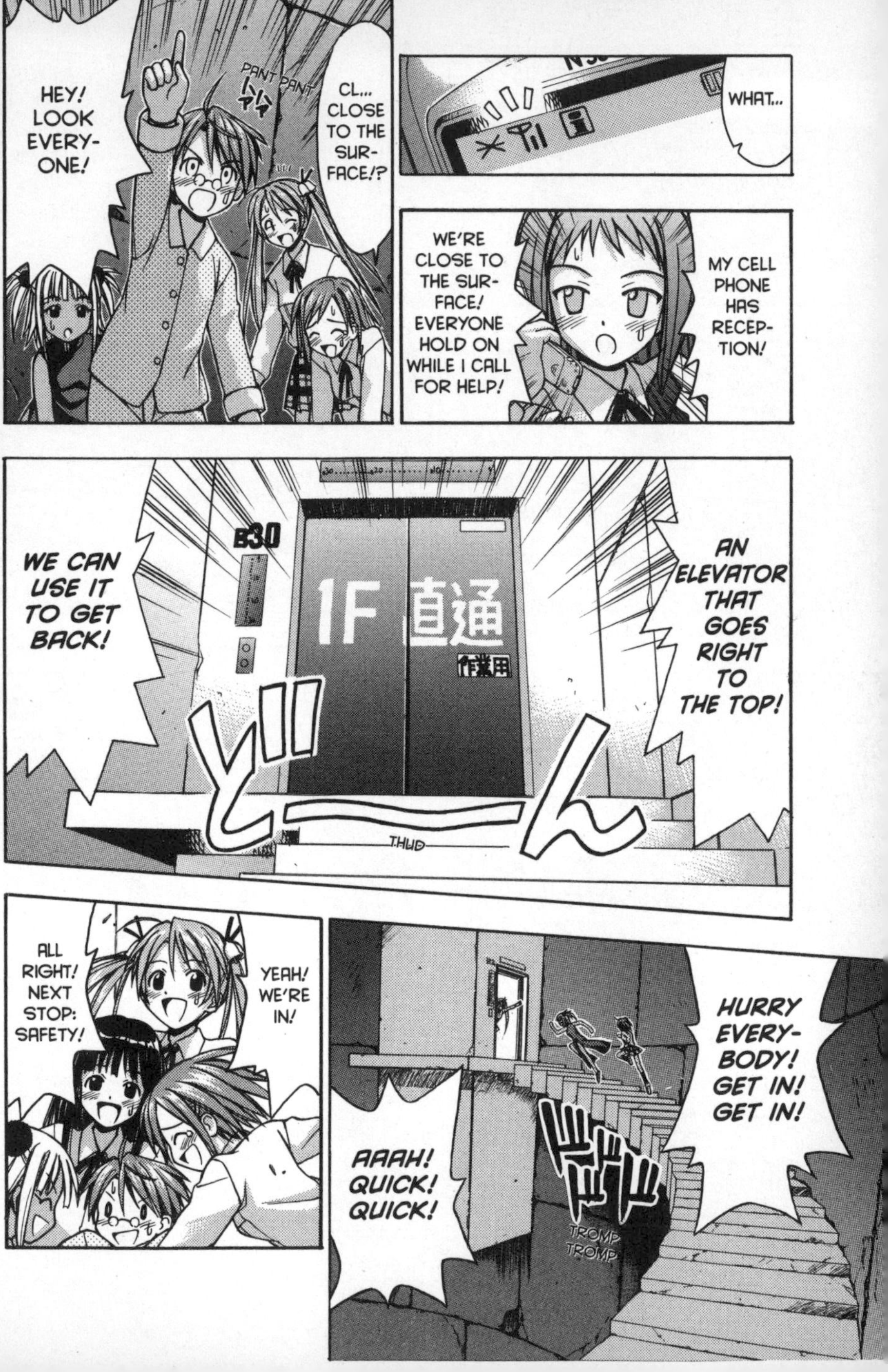
WHAT...
MY CELL PHONE HAS RECEPTION!
WE'RE CLOSE TO THE SUR-FACE! EVERYONE HOLD ON WHILE I CALL FOR HELP!
CL... CLOSE TO THE SUR-FACE!?
PANT PANT
HEY! LOOK EVERY-ONE!
AN ELEVATOR THAT GOES RIGHT TO THE TOP!
1F 直通
作業用
B30
WE CAN USE IT TO GET BACK!
THUD
HURRY EVERY-BODY! GET IN! GET IN!
AAAH! QUICK! QUICK!
TROMP TROMP
YEAH! WE'RE IN!
ALL RIGHT! NEXT STOP: SAFETY!

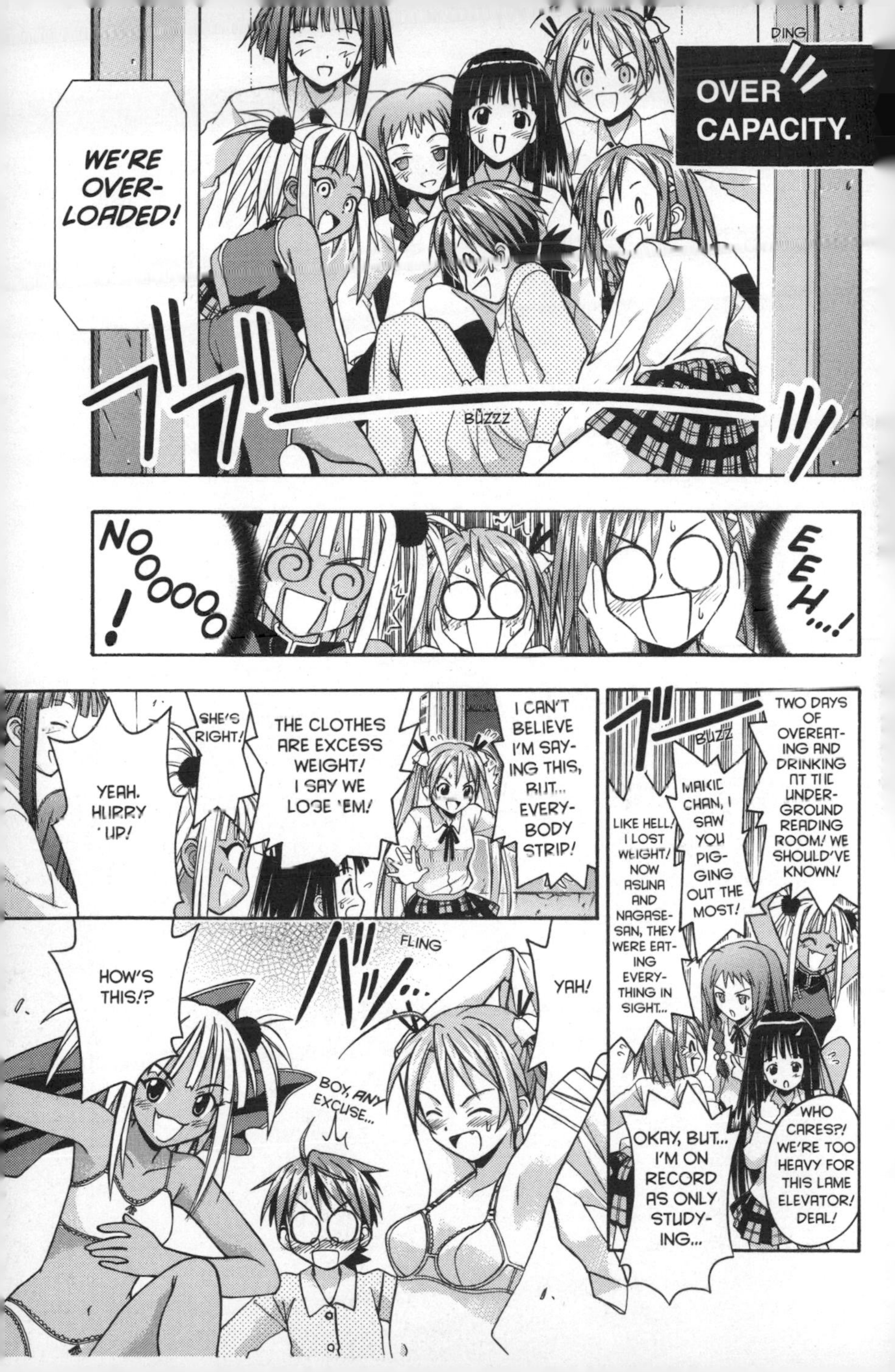
DING
OVER CAPACITY.
WE'RE OVER-LOADED!
BUZZZ
EEEH...!
NOOOOOO!
TWO DAYS OF OVEREATING AND DRINKING AT THE UNDERGROUND READING ROOM! WE SHOULD'VE KNOWN!
BUZZ
MAKIE-CHAN, I SAW YOU PIGGING OUT THE MOST!
LIKE HELL! I LOST WEIGHT! NOW ASUNA AND NAGASE-SAN, THEY WERE EATING EVERYTHING IN SIGHT...
WHO CARES?! WE'RE TOO HEAVY FOR THIS LAME ELEVATOR! DEAL!
OKAY, BUT... I'M ON RECORD AS ONLY STUDYING...
I CAN'T BELIEVE I'M SAYING THIS, BUT... EVERYBODY STRIP!
THE CLOTHES ARE EXCESS WEIGHT! I SAY WE LOSE 'EM!
SHE'S RIGHT!
YEAH. HURRY UP!
YAH!
FLING
BOY, ANY EXCUSE...
HOW'S THIS!?

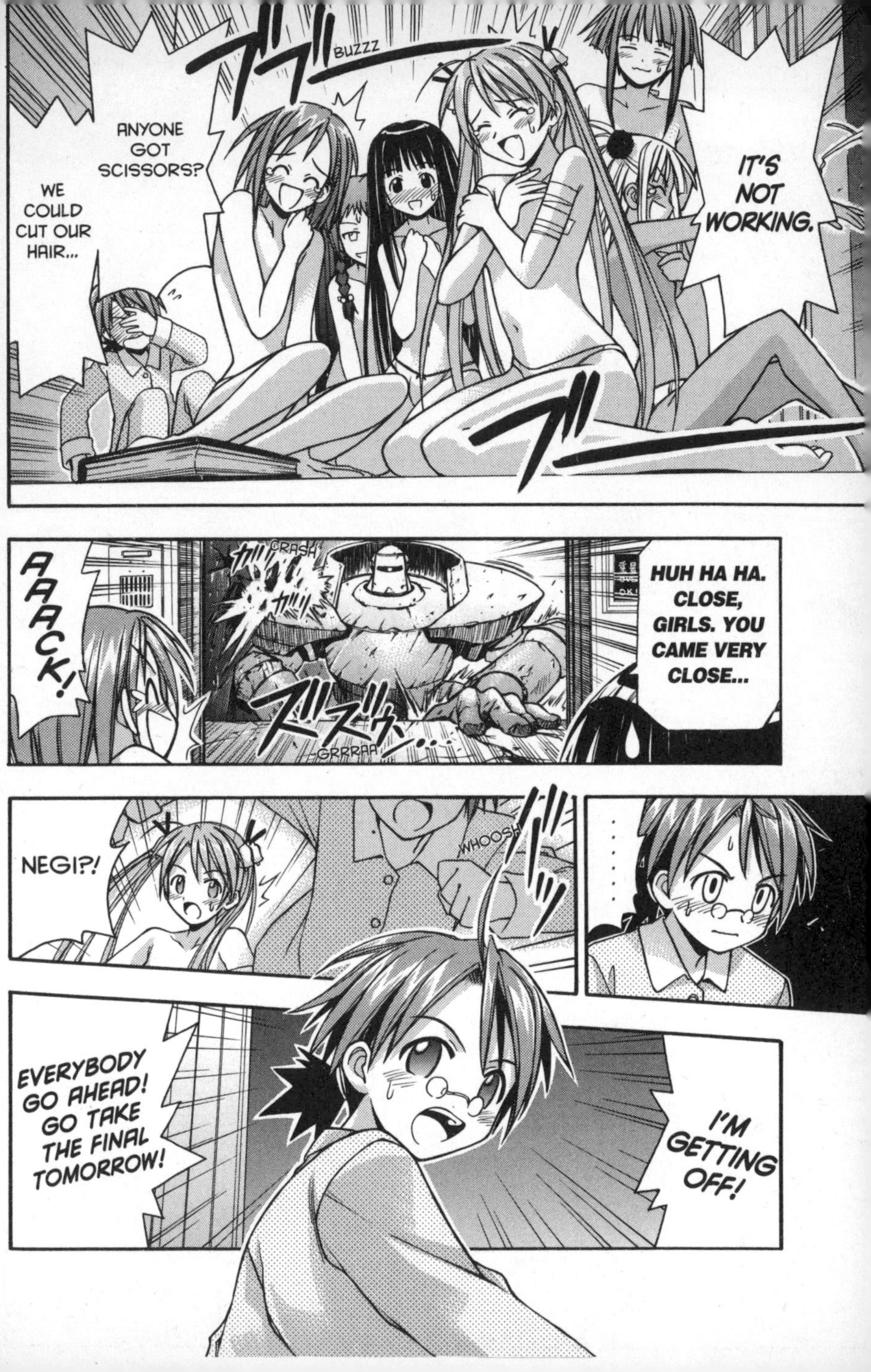
BUZZZ
IT'S NOT WORKING.
ANYONE GOT SCISSORS?
WE COULD CUT OUR HAIR...
HUH HA HA. CLOSE, GIRLS. YOU CAME VERY CLOSE...
CRASH
GRRRAA
AAAACK!
......
WHOOSH
NEGI?!
I'M GETTING OFF!
EVERYBODY GO AHEAD! GO TAKE THE FINAL TOMORROW!

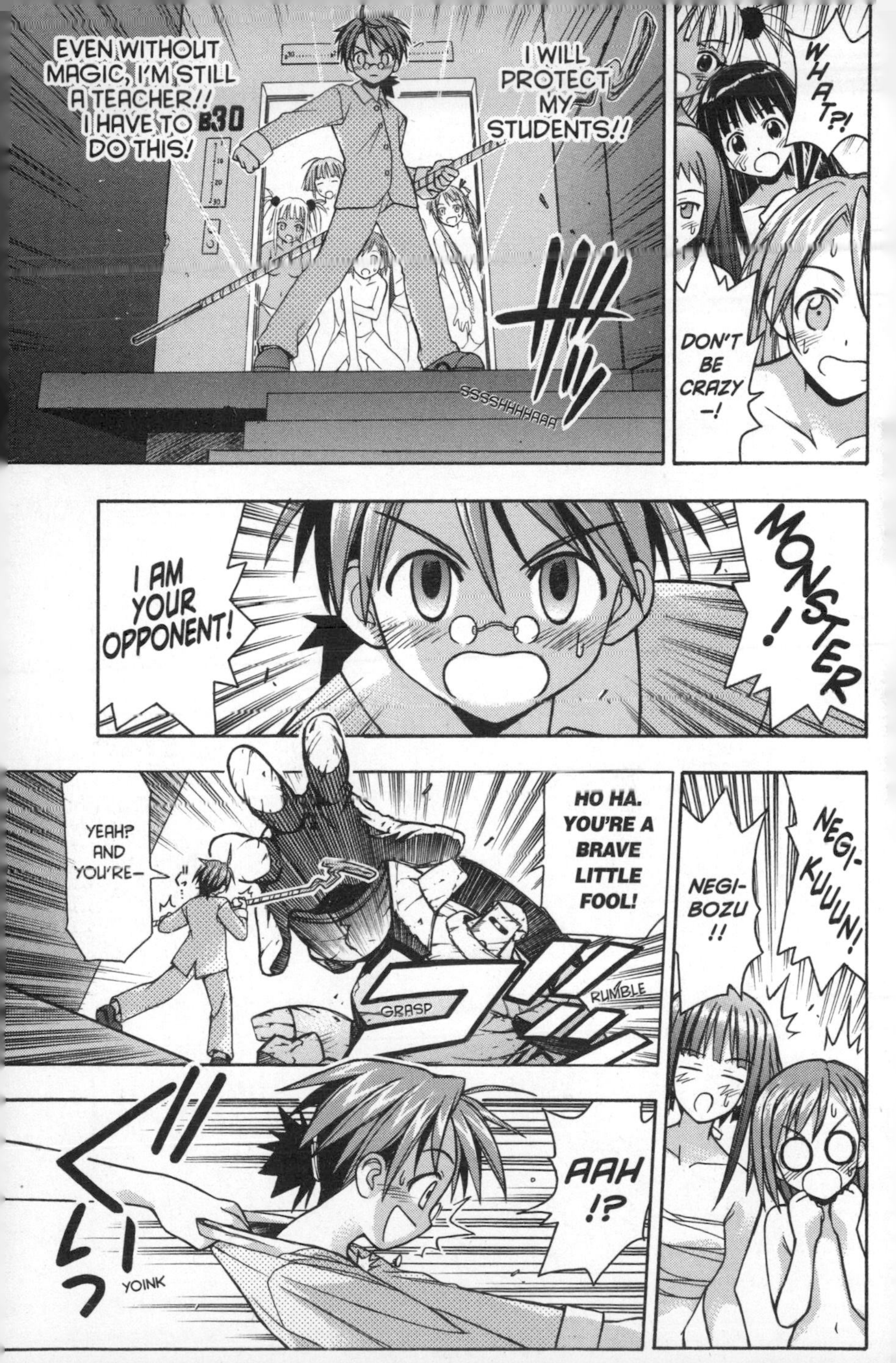
WHAT?!
DON'T BE CRAZY—!
EVEN WITHOUT MAGIC, I'M STILL A TEACHER!! I HAVE TO DO THIS!
I WILL PROTECT MY STUDENTS!!
SSSSHHHHAAAA
MONSTER!
I AM YOUR OPPONENT!
NEGI-KUUUN!
NEGI-BOZU!!
HO HA. YOU'RE A BRAVE LITTLE FOOL!
YEAH? AND YOU'RE—
GRASP
RUMBLE
AAH!?
YOINK

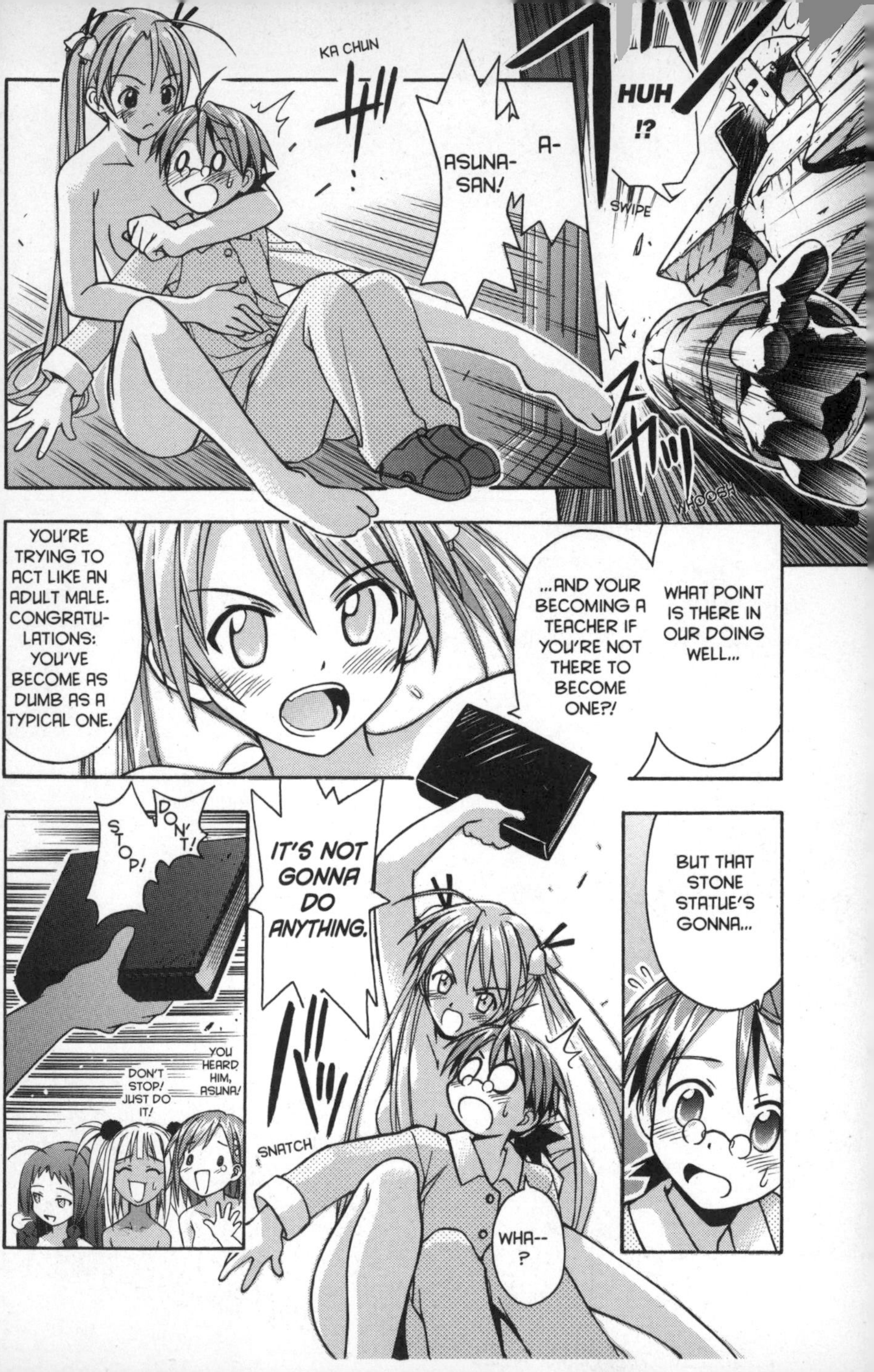
HUH !?
SWIPE
WHOOSH
A- ASUNA-SAN!
KA CHUN
WHAT POINT IS THERE IN OUR DOING WELL...
...AND YOUR BECOMING A TEACHER IF YOU'RE NOT THERE TO BECOME ONE?!
YOU'RE TRYING TO ACT LIKE AN ADULT MALE. CONGRATU-LATIONS: YOU'VE BECOME AS DUMB AS A TYPICAL ONE.
BUT THAT STONE STATUE'S GONNA...
IT'S NOT GONNA DO ANYTHING.
SNATCH
WHA-- ?
DON'T!
STOP!
YOU HEARD HIM, ASUNA!
DON'T STOP! JUST DO IT!

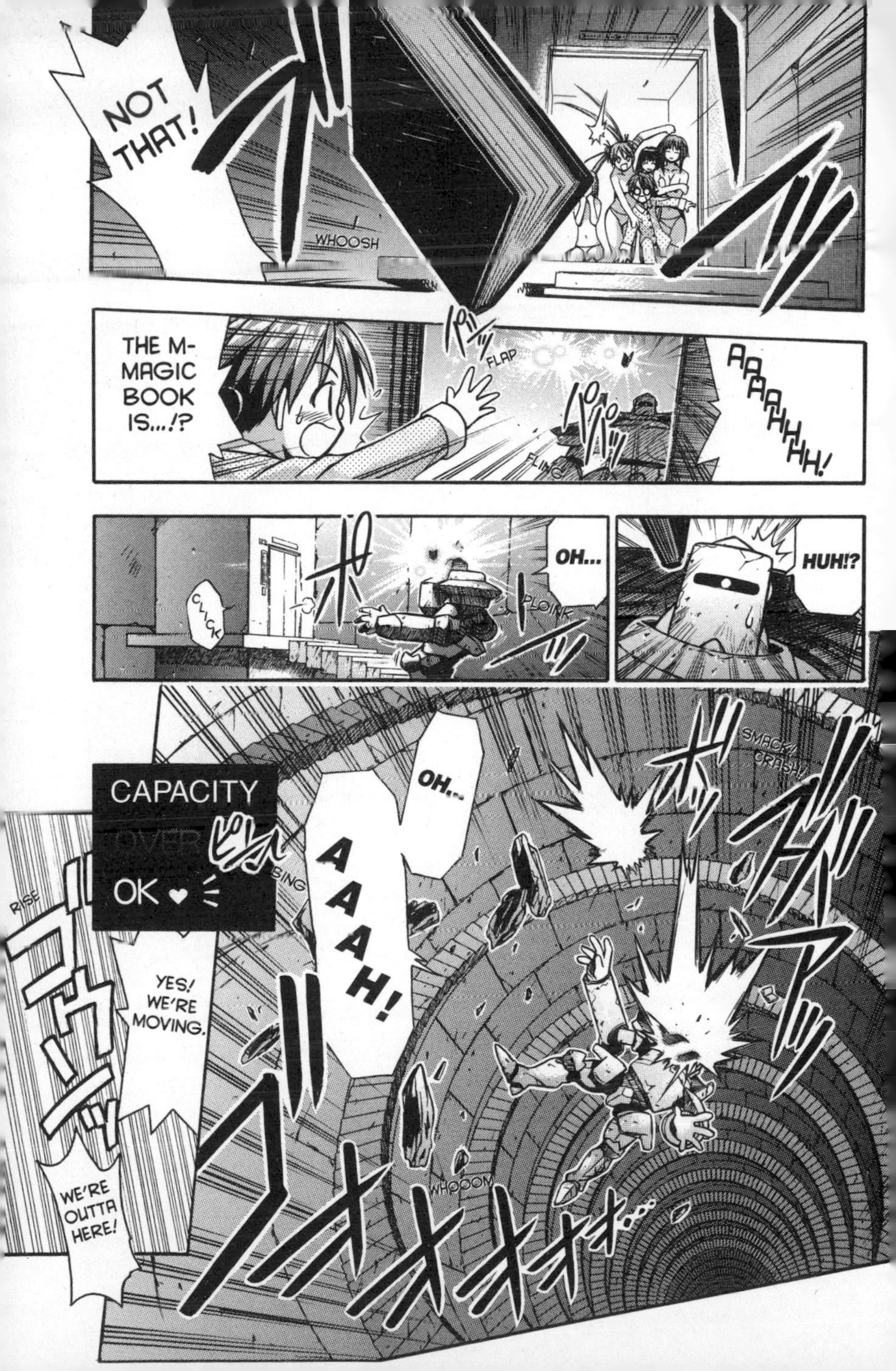
NOT THAT!
WHOOSH
AAAAHHHHH!
FLAP
FLING
THE M-MAGIC BOOK IS...!?
HUH!?
OH...
PLOINK
CLICK
SMACK! CRASH!
OH...
AAAAH!
SING
CAPACITY
OVER
OK
YES! WE'RE MOVING.
RISE
WE'RE OUTTA HERE!
WHOOOM

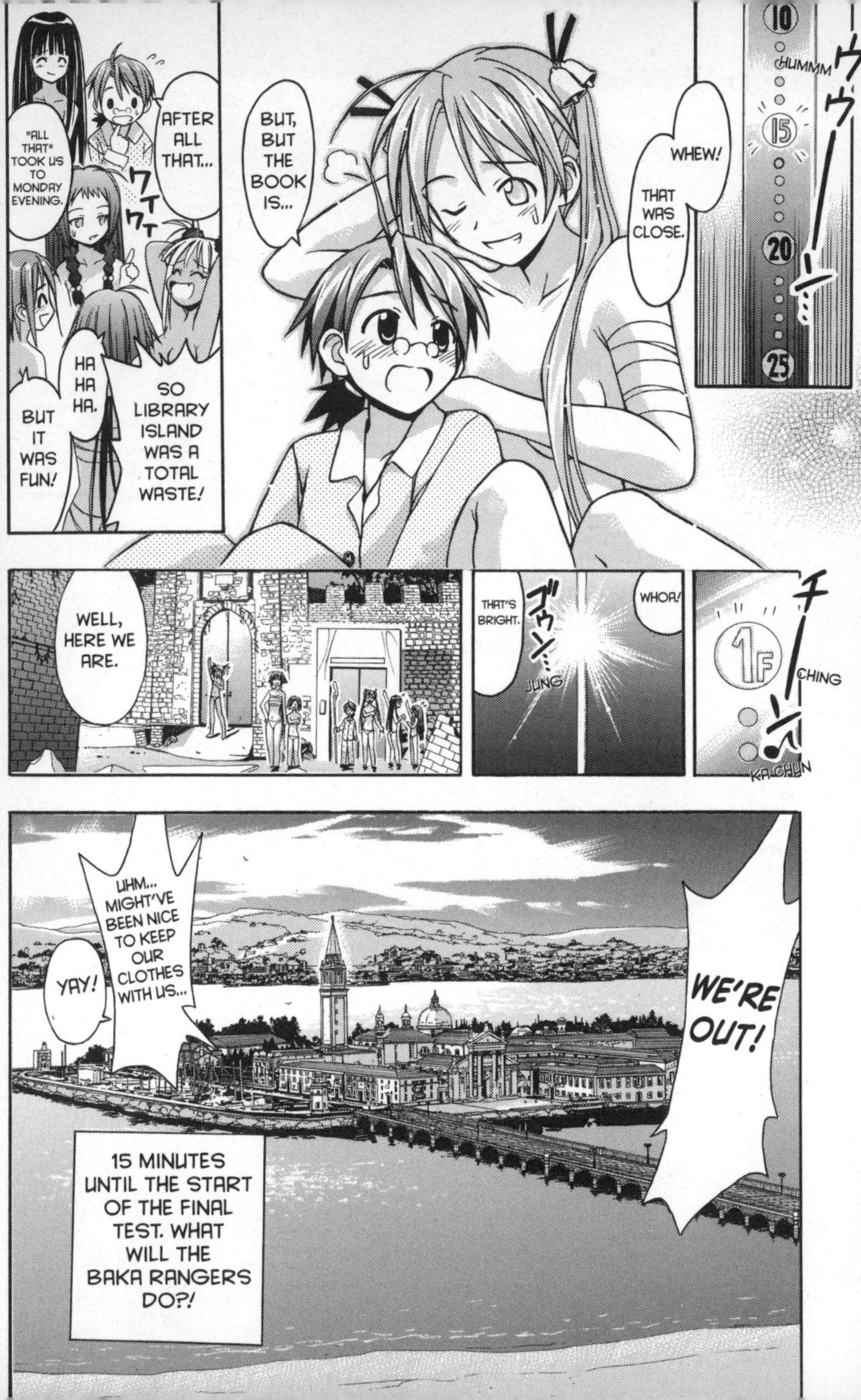
10
HUMMM
15
20
25
WHEW!
THAT WAS CLOSE.
BUT, BUT THE BOOK IS...
AFTER ALL THAT...
"ALL THAT" TOOK US TO MONDAY EVENING.
SO LIBRARY ISLAND WAS A TOTAL WASTE!
HA HA HA.
BUT IT WAS FUN!
1F
CHING
KA-CHUN
WHOA!
THAT'S BRIGHT.
JUNG
WELL, HERE WE ARE.
WE'RE OUT!
UHM... MIGHT'VE BEEN NICE TO KEEP OUR CLOTHES WITH US...
YAY!
15 MINUTES UNTIL THE START OF THE FINAL TEST. WHAT WILL THE BAKA RANGERS DO?!

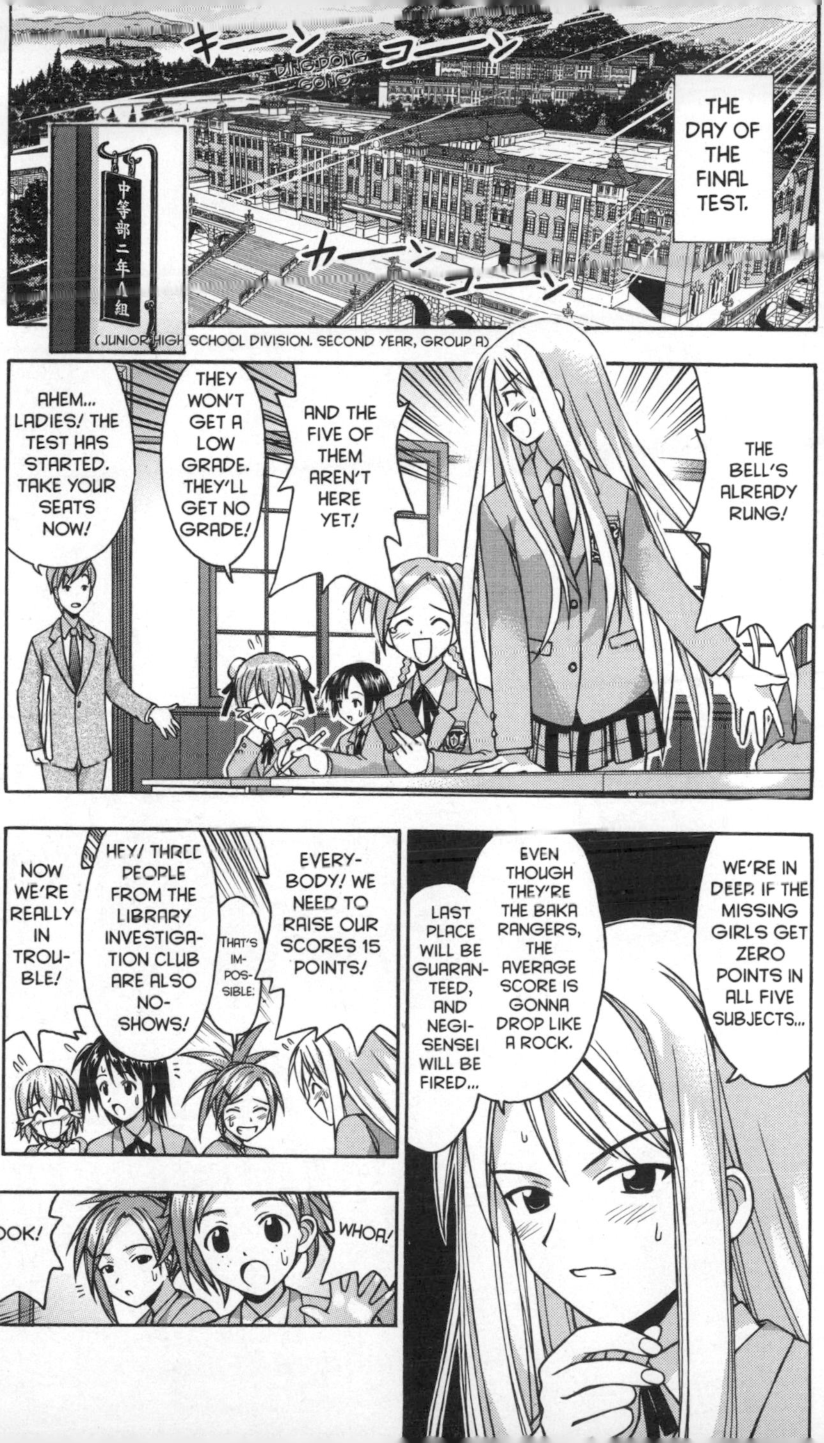
キーン コーン
DING DONG GONG
THE DAY OF THE FINAL TEST.
中等部二年A組
(JUNIOR HIGH SCHOOL DIVISION. SECOND YEAR, GROUP A)
カーン コーン
THE BELL'S ALREADY RUNG!
AND THE FIVE OF THEM AREN'T HERE YET!
THEY WON'T GET A LOW GRADE. THEY'LL GET NO GRADE!
AHEM... LADIES! THE TEST HAS STARTED. TAKE YOUR SEATS NOW!
WE'RE IN DEEP. IF THE MISSING GIRLS GET ZERO POINTS IN ALL FIVE SUBJECTS...
EVEN THOUGH THEY'RE THE BAKA RANGERS, THE AVERAGE SCORE IS GONNA DROP LIKE A ROCK.
LAST PLACE WILL BE GUARANTEED, AND NEGI-SENSEI WILL BE FIRED...
EVERYBODY! WE NEED TO RAISE OUR SCORES 15 POINTS!
THAT'S IMPOSSIBLE.
HEY! THREE PEOPLE FROM THE LIBRARY INVESTIGATION CLUB ARE ALSO NO-SHOWS!
NOW WE'RE REALLY IN TROUBLE!
WHOA!
LOOK!

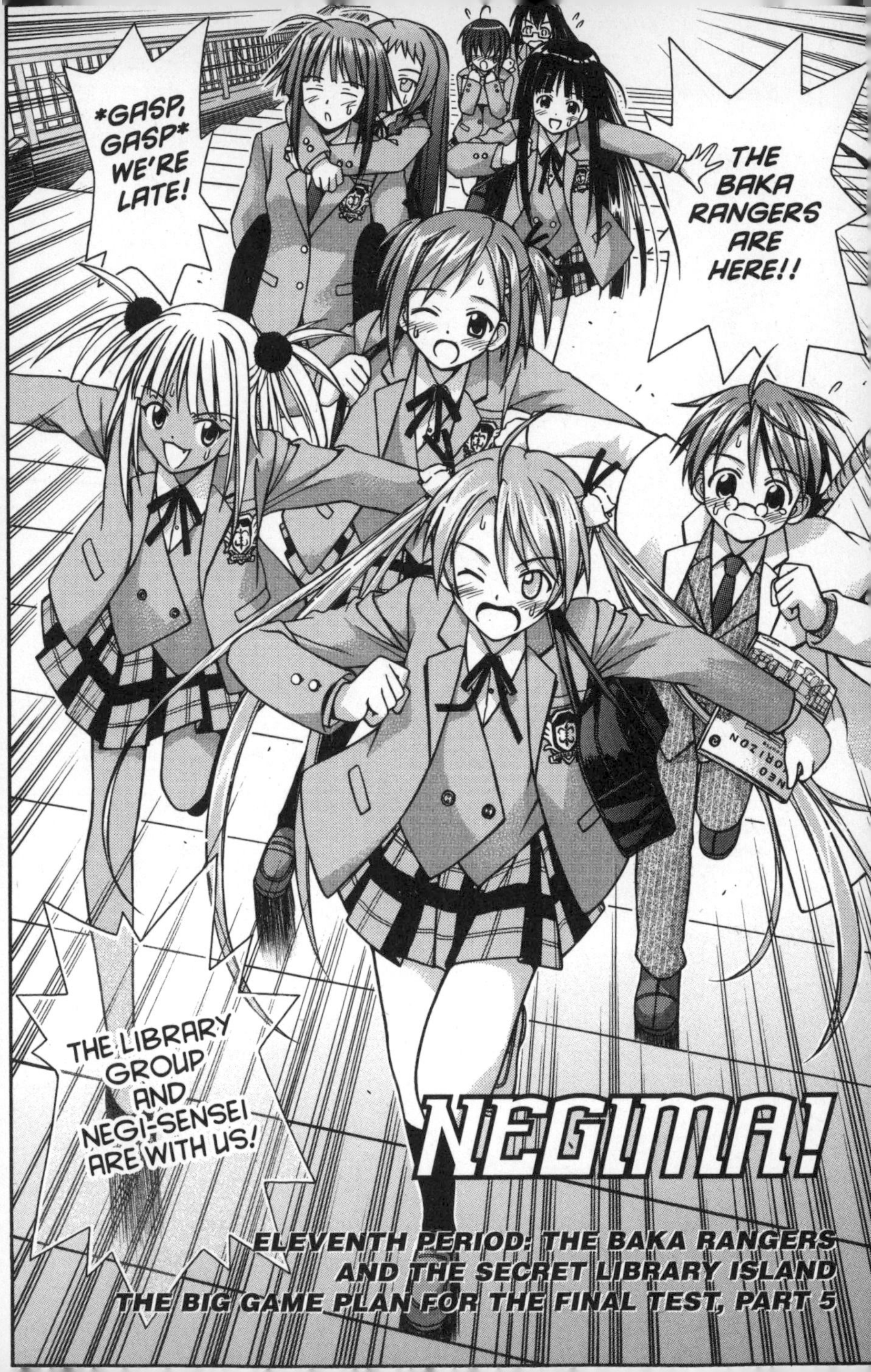
THE BAKA RANGERS ARE HERE!!
GASP, GASP WE'RE LATE!
THE LIBRARY GROUP AND NEGI-SENSEI ARE WITH US!
NEGIMA!
ELEVENTH PERIOD: THE BAKA RANGERS AND THE SECRET LIBRARY ISLAND
THE BIG GAME PLAN FOR THE FINAL TEST, PART 5

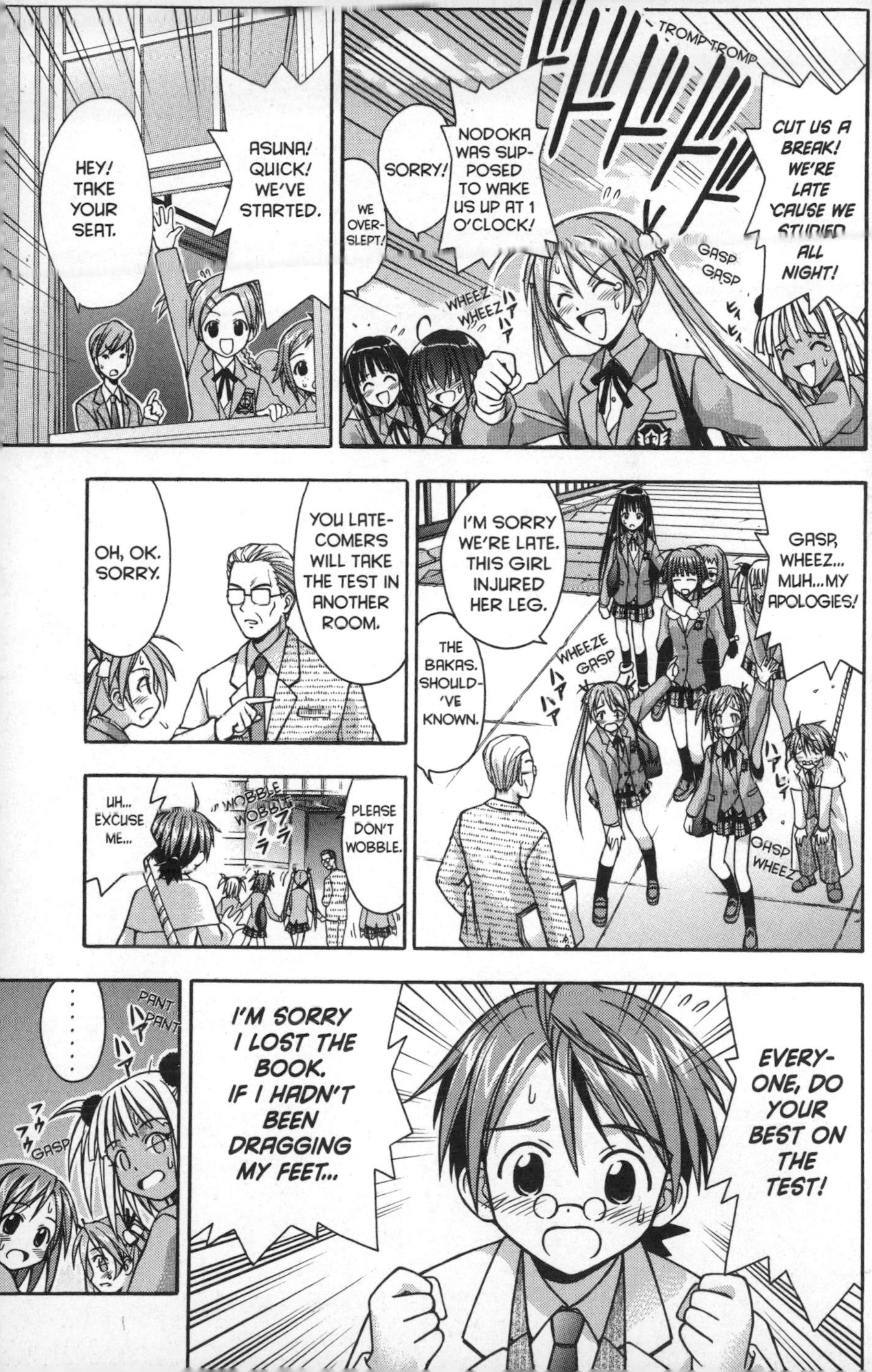
TROMP TROMP
CUT US A BREAK! WE'RE LATE 'CAUSE WE STUDIED ALL NIGHT!
GASP GASP
NODOKA WAS SUP-POSED TO WAKE US UP AT 1 O'CLOCK!
SORRY!
WE OVER-SLEPT!
WHEEZ WHEEZ
ASUNA! QUICK! WE'VE STARTED.
HEY! TAKE YOUR SEAT.
GASP, WHEEZ... MUH...MY APOLOGIES!
I'M SORRY WE'RE LATE. THIS GIRL INJURED HER LEG.
THE BAKAS. SHOULD-'VE KNOWN.
WHEEZE GASP
GASP WHEEZ
YOU LATE-COMERS WILL TAKE THE TEST IN ANOTHER ROOM.
OH, OK. SORRY.
PLEASE DON'T WOBBLE.
WOBBLE WOBBLE
UH... EXCUSE ME...
EVERY-ONE, DO YOUR BEST ON THE TEST!
I'M SORRY I LOST THE BOOK. IF I HADN'T BEEN DRAGGING MY FEET...
......
PANT PANT
GASP

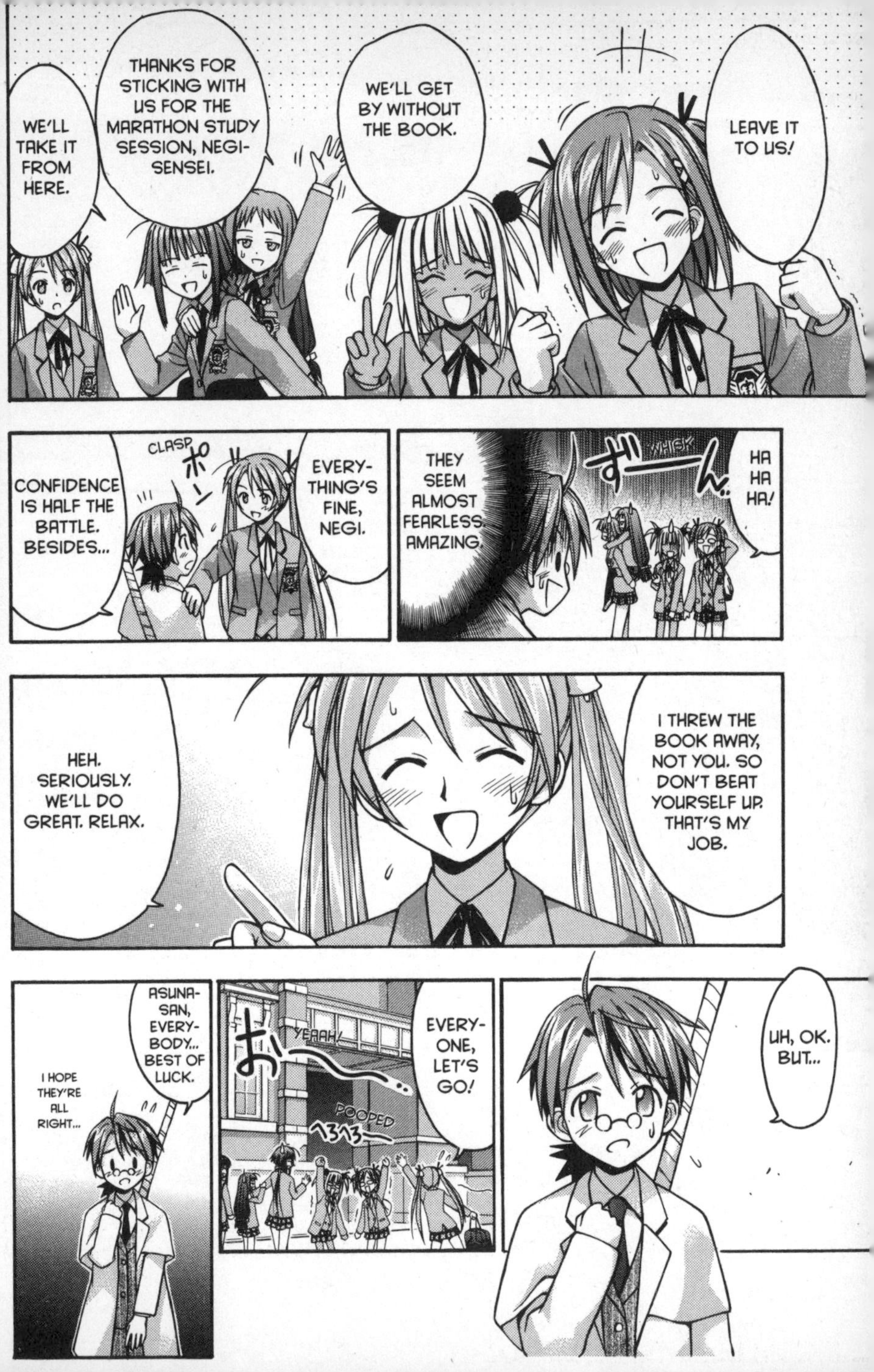
LEAVE IT TO US!
WE'LL GET BY WITHOUT THE BOOK.
THANKS FOR STICKING WITH US FOR THE MARATHON STUDY SESSION, NEGI-SENSEI.
WE'LL TAKE IT FROM HERE.
HA HA HA!
ずーん
WHISK
THEY SEEM ALMOST FEARLESS. AMAZING.
EVERY-THING'S FINE, NEGI.
ポン
CLASP
CONFIDENCE IS HALF THE BATTLE. BESIDES...
I THREW THE BOOK AWAY, NOT YOU. SO DON'T BEAT YOURSELF UP. THAT'S MY JOB.
HEH. SERIOUSLY. WE'LL DO GREAT. RELAX.
UH, OK. BUT...
EVERY-ONE, LET'S GO!
お〜
YEAAH!
へろへろ〜
POOPED
ASUNA-SAN, EVERY-BODY... BEST OF LUCK.
I HOPE THEY'RE ALL RIGHT...

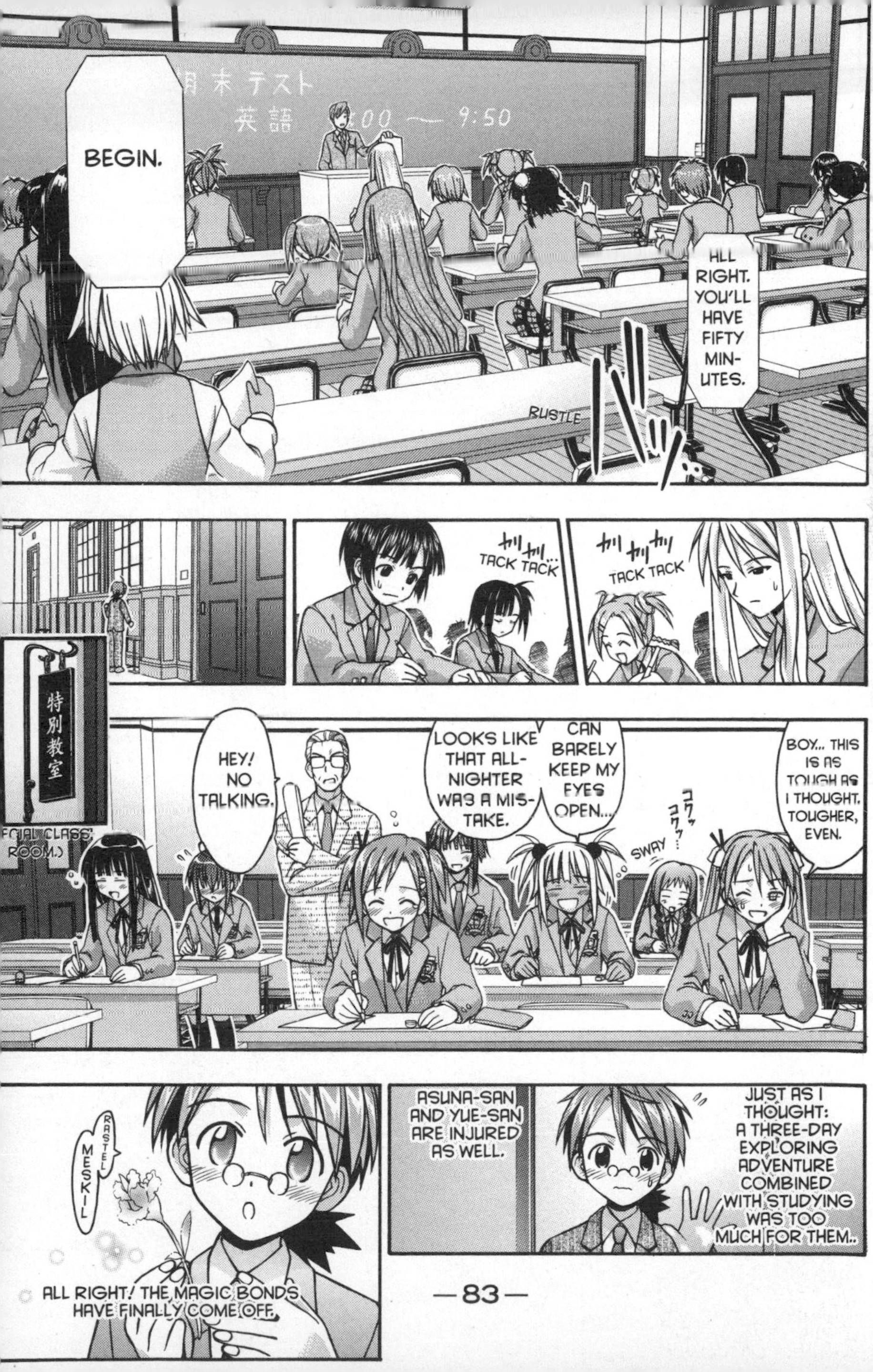

ALL RIGHT. YOU'LL HAVE FIFTY MIN-UTES.
BEGIN.
RUSTLE
TACK TACK
TACK TACK...
BOY... THIS IS AS TOUGH AS I THOUGHT. TOUGHER, EVEN.
SWAY
CAN BARELY KEEP MY EYES OPEN...
LOOKS LIKE THAT ALL-NIGHTER WAS A MIS-TAKE.
HEY! NO TALKING.
JUST AS I THOUGHT: A THREE-DAY EXPLORING ADVENTURE COMBINED WITH STUDYING WAS TOO MUCH FOR THEM..
ASUNA-SAN AND YUE-SAN ARE INJURED AS WELL.
RASTEL MESKIL
ALL RIGHT! THE MAGIC BONDS HAVE FINALLY COME OFF.

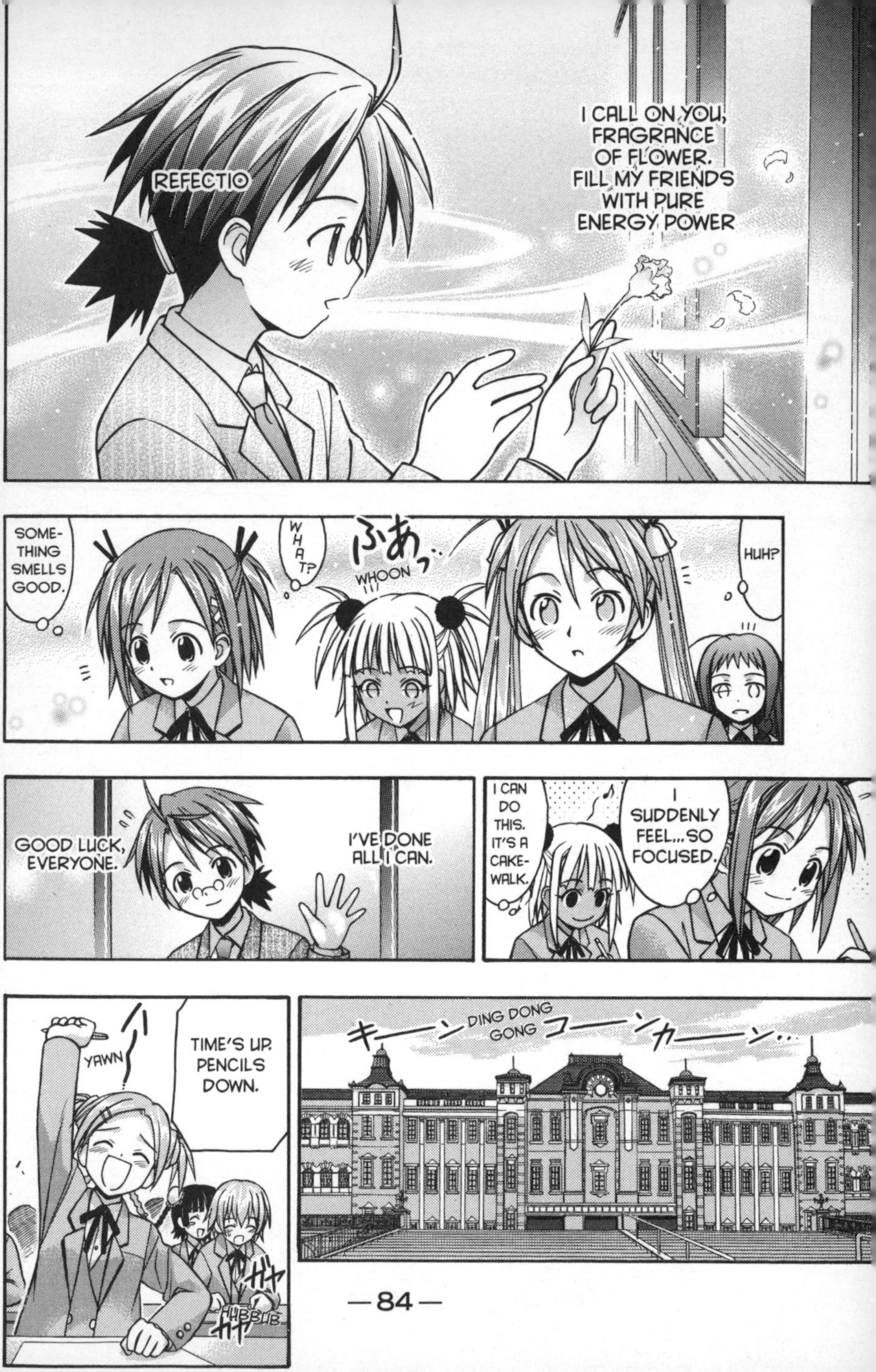
I CALL ON YOU, FRAGRANCE OF FLOWER. FILL MY FRIENDS WITH PURE ENERGY POWER
REFECTIO
HUH?
ふあっ
WHOON
WHAT?
SOMETHING SMELLS GOOD.
I SUDDENLY FEEL...SO FOCUSED.
I CAN DO THIS. IT'S A CAKEWALK.
I'VE DONE ALL I CAN.
GOOD LUCK, EVERYONE.
キーーン コーーン カーーン…
DING DONG GONG
TIME'S UP. PENCILS DOWN.
YAWN
HUBBUB

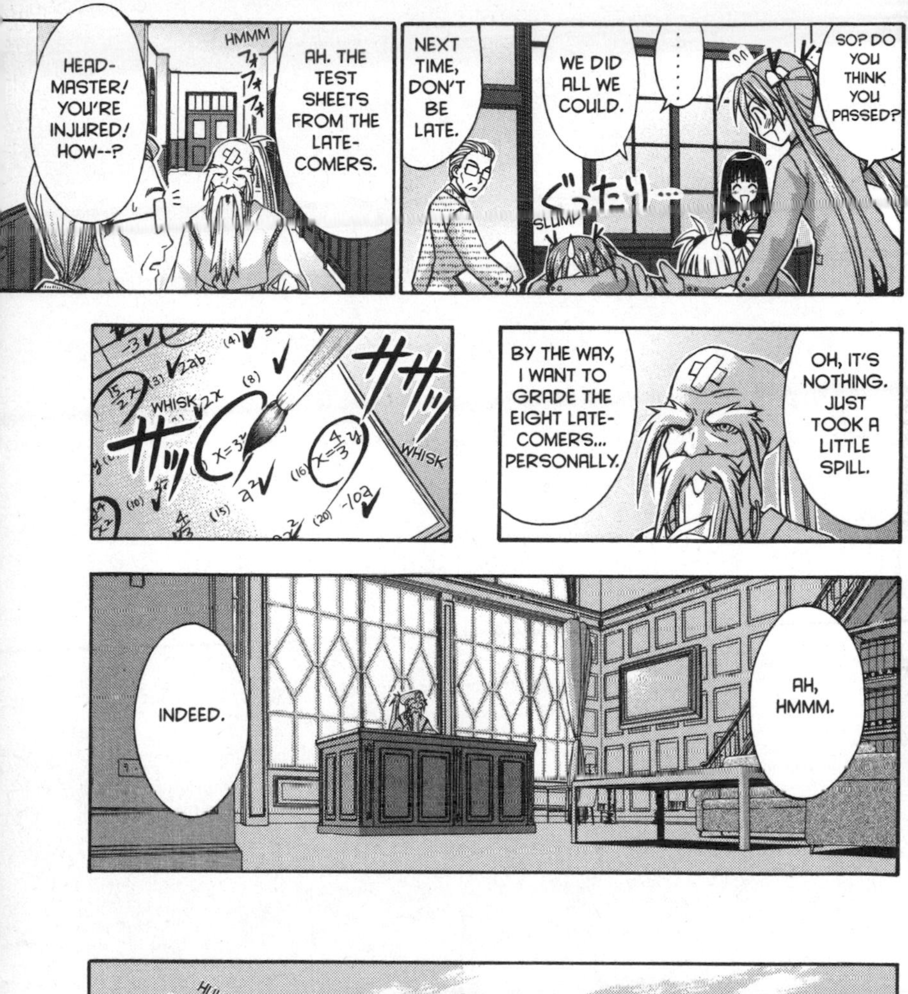
SO? DO YOU THINK YOU PASSED?
. . . . .
WE DID ALL WE COULD.
ぐったり…
SLUMP
NEXT TIME, DON'T BE LATE.
AH. THE TEST SHEETS FROM THE LATE-COMERS.
HMMM
フォフォフォ
HEAD-MASTER! YOU'RE INJURED! HOW--?
OH, IT'S NOTHING. JUST TOOK A LITTLE SPILL.
BY THE WAY, I WANT TO GRADE THE EIGHT LATE-COMERS... PERSONALLY.
ササッ
WHISK
サッ
WHISK
AH, HMMM.
INDEED.
THE ANNOUNCEMENT DAY OF CLASS GRADES.
ワイワイ
ガヤガヤ
HULLABALOO

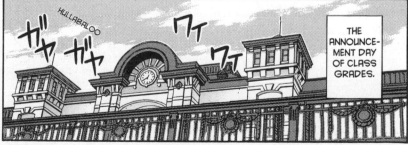

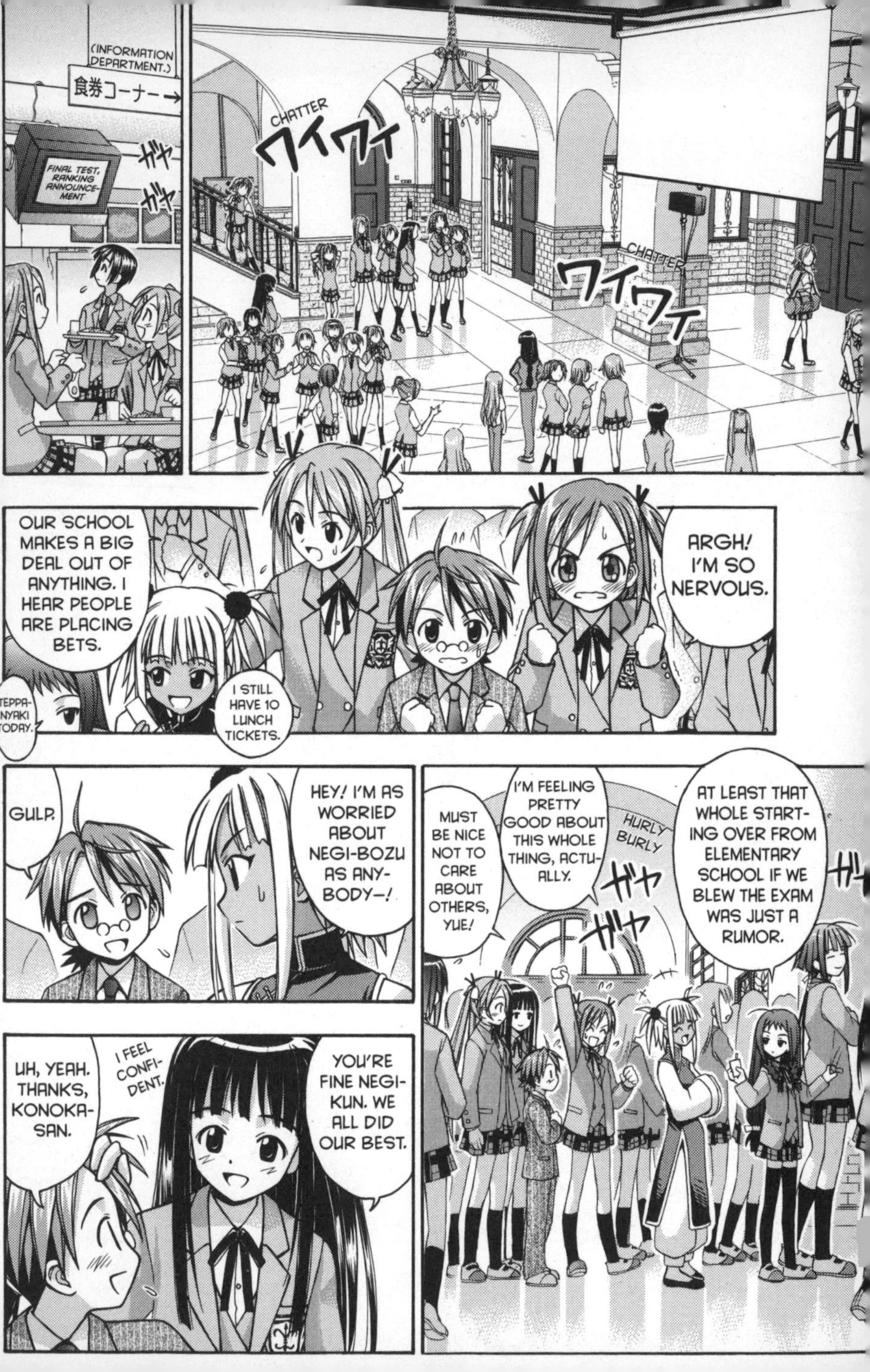

(INFORMATION DEPARTMENT.)
食券コーナー→
FINAL TEST, RANKING ANNOUNCEMENT
ガヤ ガヤ
CHATTER
ワイワイ
CHATTER
ワイワイ
ARGH! I'M SO NERVOUS.
OUR SCHOOL MAKES A BIG DEAL OUT OF ANYTHING. I HEAR PEOPLE ARE PLACING BETS.
I STILL HAVE 10 LUNCH TICKETS.
TEPPANYAKI TODAY.
AT LEAST THAT WHOLE STARTING OVER FROM ELEMENTARY SCHOOL IF WE BLEW THE EXAM WAS JUST A RUMOR.
I'M FEELING PRETTY GOOD ABOUT THIS WHOLE THING, ACTUALLY.
MUST BE NICE NOT TO CARE ABOUT OTHERS, YUE!
HURLY BURLY
ガヤ ガヤ
HEY! I'M AS WORRIED ABOUT NEGI-BOZU AS ANYBODY—!
GULP.
YOU'RE FINE NEGI-KUN. WE ALL DID OUR BEST.
I FEEL CONFIDENT.
UH, YEAH. THANKS, KONOKA-SAN.

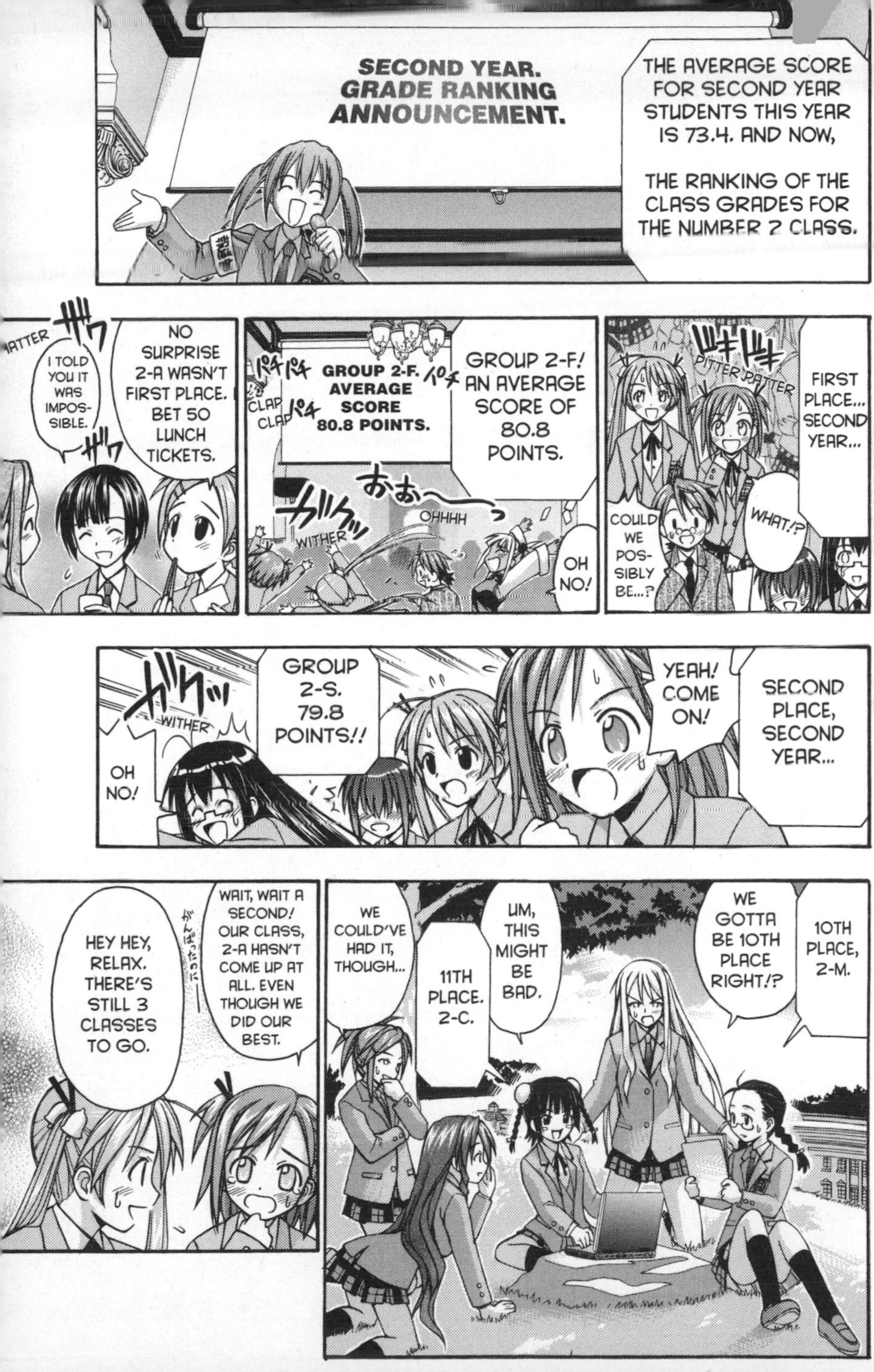

SECOND YEAR. GRADE RANKING ANNOUNCEMENT.
THE AVERAGE SCORE FOR SECOND YEAR STUDENTS THIS YEAR IS 73.4. AND NOW,
THE RANKING OF THE CLASS GRADES FOR THE NUMBER 2 CLASS.
FIRST PLACE... SECOND YEAR...
ドキドキ
PITTER PATTER
WHAT!?
COULD WE POSSIBLY BE...?
GROUP 2-F! AN AVERAGE SCORE OF 80.8 POINTS.
GROUP 2-F. AVERAGE SCORE 80.8 POINTS.
パチパチ
CLAP CLAP
おおー
OHHHH
WITHER
OH NO!
NO SURPRISE 2-A WASN'T FIRST PLACE. BET 50 LUNCH TICKETS.
I TOLD YOU IT WAS IMPOSSIBLE.
ザワ
SECOND PLACE, SECOND YEAR...
YEAH! COME ON!
GROUP 2-S. 79.8 POINTS!!
WITHER
OH NO!
10TH PLACE, 2-M.
WE GOTTA BE 10TH PLACE RIGHT!?
UM, THIS MIGHT BE BAD.
11TH PLACE. 2-C.
WE COULD'VE HAD IT, THOUGH...
WAIT, WAIT A SECOND! OUR CLASS, 2-A HASN'T COME UP AT ALL. EVEN THOUGH WE DID OUR BEST.
がんばったのに
HEY HEY, RELAX. THERE'S STILL 3 CLASSES TO GO.

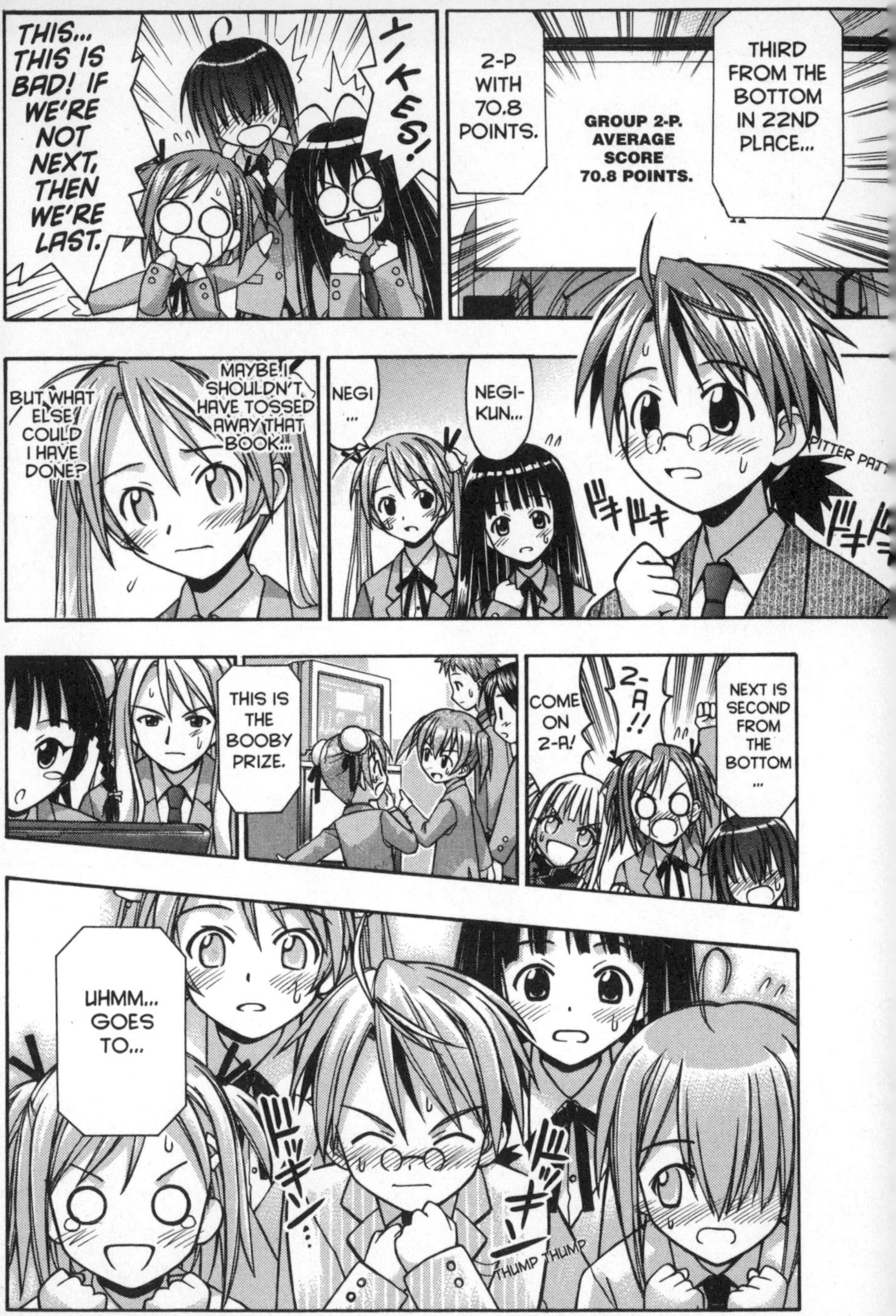
THIRD FROM THE BOTTOM IN 22ND PLACE...
GROUP 2-P. AVERAGE SCORE 70.8 POINTS.
2-P WITH 70.8 POINTS.
YIKES!
THIS... THIS IS BAD! IF WE'RE NOT NEXT, THEN WE'RE LAST.
PITTER PATT
ドキドキ
NEGI-KUN...
NEGI ...
MAYBE I SHOULDN'T HAVE TOSSED AWAY THAT BOOK...
BUT WHAT ELSE COULD I HAVE DONE?
NEXT IS SECOND FROM THE BOTTOM ...
2-A!!
COME ON 2-A!
THIS IS THE BOOBY PRIZE.
UHMM... GOES TO...
THUMP THUMP

GROUP 2-K.
AVERAGE
SCORE
69.5 POINTS.

2-K. AN AVERAGE SCORE OF 69.5. NEXT TIME TRY HARDER.

THAT MEANS...

UH...

SIGH

CHATTER

GHASP

...IS ALL OURS?!

...LAST PLACE...

UH? WHAT WAS THAT?

DASH

OH DEAR. THE STUDENTS TOOK IT UPON THEMSELVES TO START THE ANNOUNCEMENT MEETING.

SHOCK

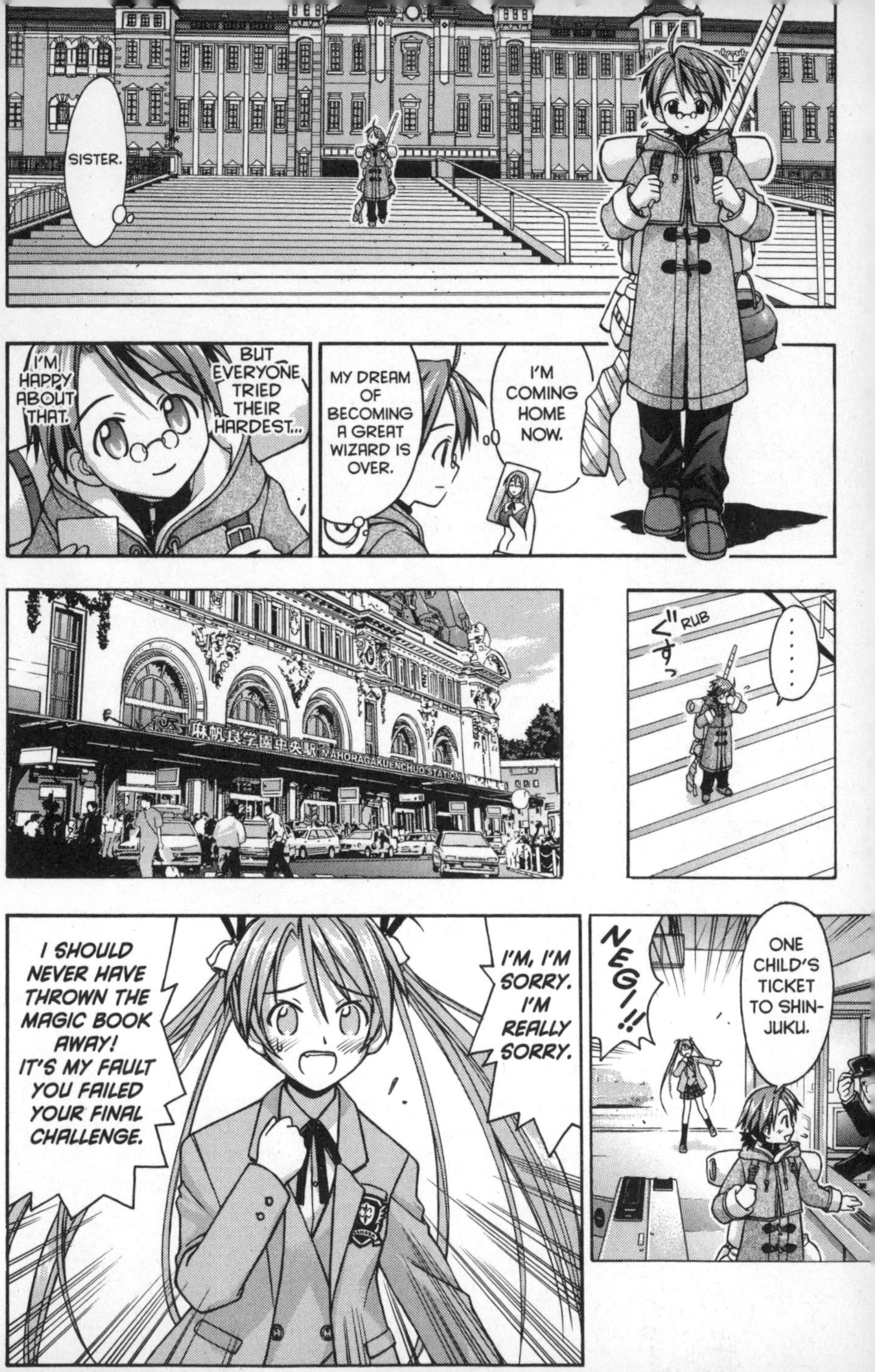
SISTER.
I'M COMING HOME NOW.
MY DREAM OF BECOMING A GREAT WIZARD IS OVER.
BUT EVERYONE TRIED THEIR HARDEST...
I'M HAPPY ABOUT THAT.
ぐすっ RUB
......
麻帆良学園中央駅
MAHORAGAKUENCHUO STATION
ONE CHILD'S TICKET TO SHIN-JUKU.
NEGI!!
I'M, I'M SORRY. I'M REALLY SORRY.
I SHOULD NEVER HAVE THROWN THE MAGIC BOOK AWAY! IT'S MY FAULT YOU FAILED YOUR FINAL CHALLENGE.

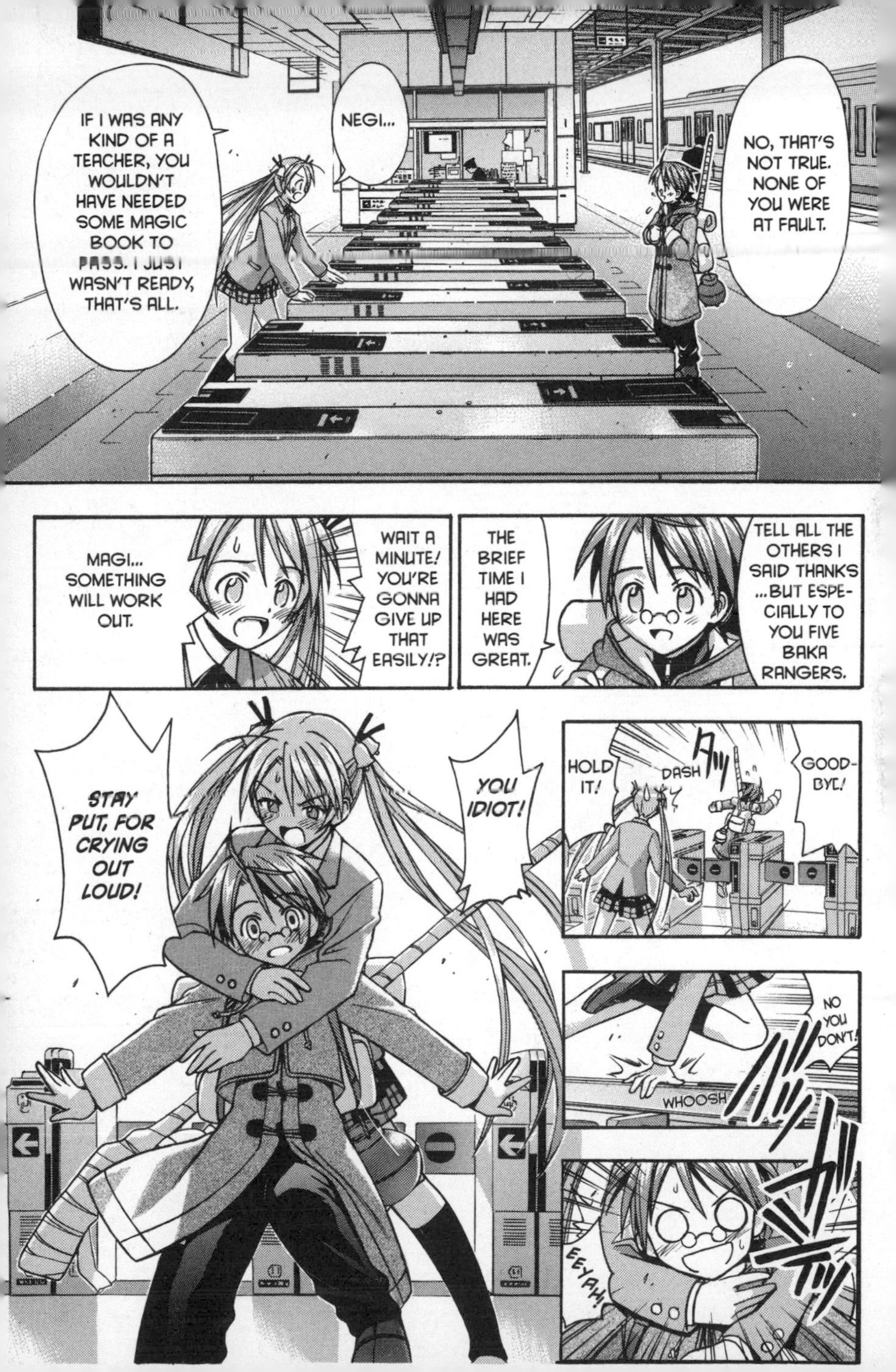

NO, THAT'S NOT TRUE. NONE OF YOU WERE AT FAULT.
NEGI...
IF I WAS ANY KIND OF A TEACHER, YOU WOULDN'T HAVE NEEDED SOME MAGIC BOOK TO PASS. I JUST WASN'T READY, THAT'S ALL.
TELL ALL THE OTHERS I SAID THANKS ...BUT ESPECIALLY TO YOU FIVE BAKA RANGERS.
THE BRIEF TIME I HAD HERE WAS GREAT.
WAIT A MINUTE! YOU'RE GONNA GIVE UP THAT EASILY!?
MAGI... SOMETHING WILL WORK OUT.
GOOD-BYE!
DASH
HOLD IT!
NO YOU DON'T!
WHOOSH
EEYAH!
YOU IDIOT!
STAY PUT, FOR CRYING OUT LOUD!

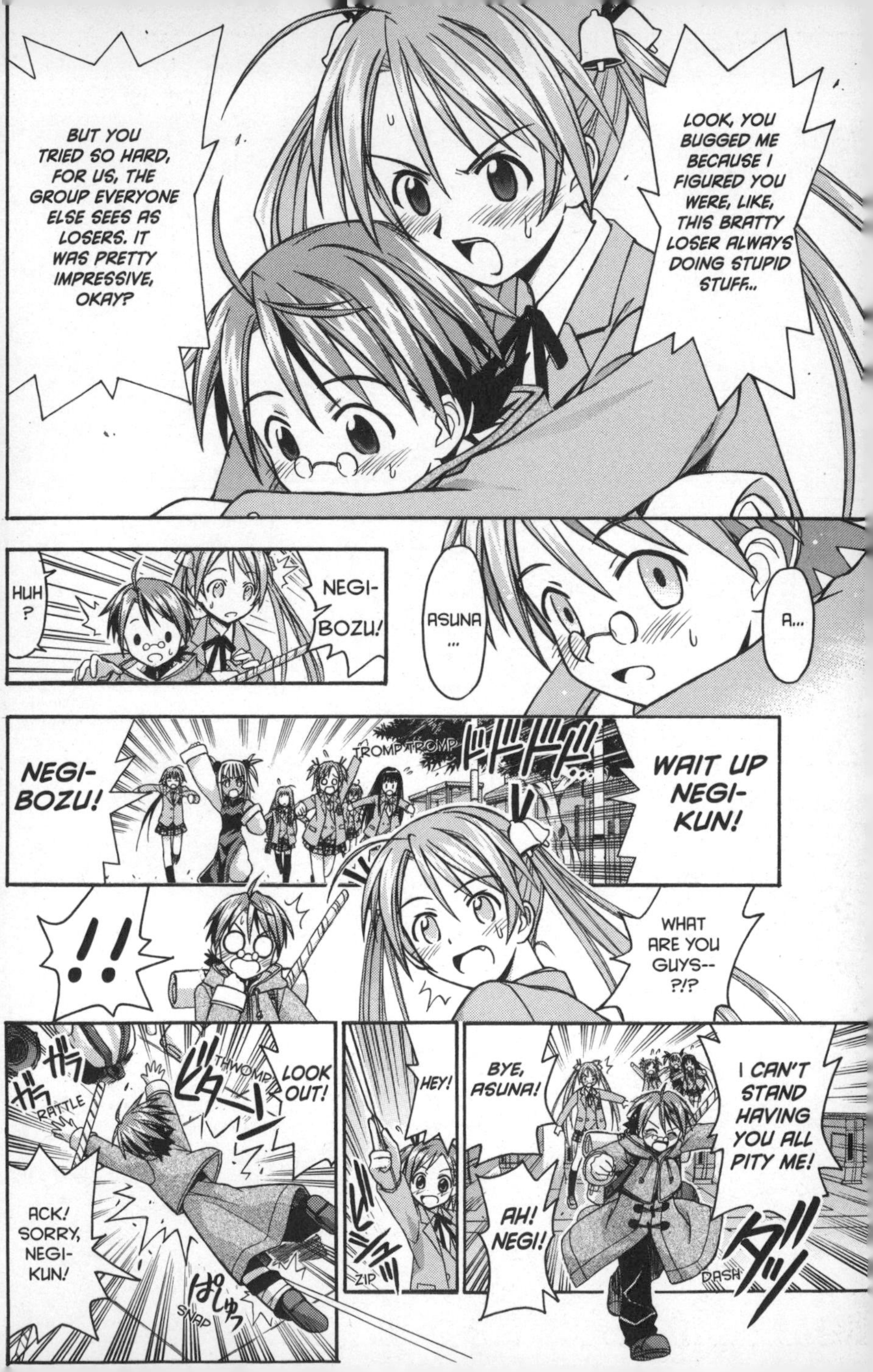

LOOK, YOU BUGGED ME BECAUSE I FIGURED YOU WERE, LIKE, THIS BRATTY LOSER ALWAYS DOING STUPID STUFF...
BUT YOU TRIED SO HARD, FOR US, THE GROUP EVERYONE ELSE SEES AS LOSERS. IT WAS PRETTY IMPRESSIVE, OKAY?
A...
ASUNA ...
NEGI-BOZU!
HUH ?
WAIT UP NEGI-KUN!
TROMP TROMP
NEGI-BOZU!
WHAT ARE YOU GUYS--?!?
!!
I CAN'T STAND HAVING YOU ALL PITY ME!
BYE, ASUNA!
AH! NEGI!
DASH
HEY!
ZIP
LOOK OUT!
THWOMP
RATTLE
ACK! SORRY, NEGI-KUN!
SNAP

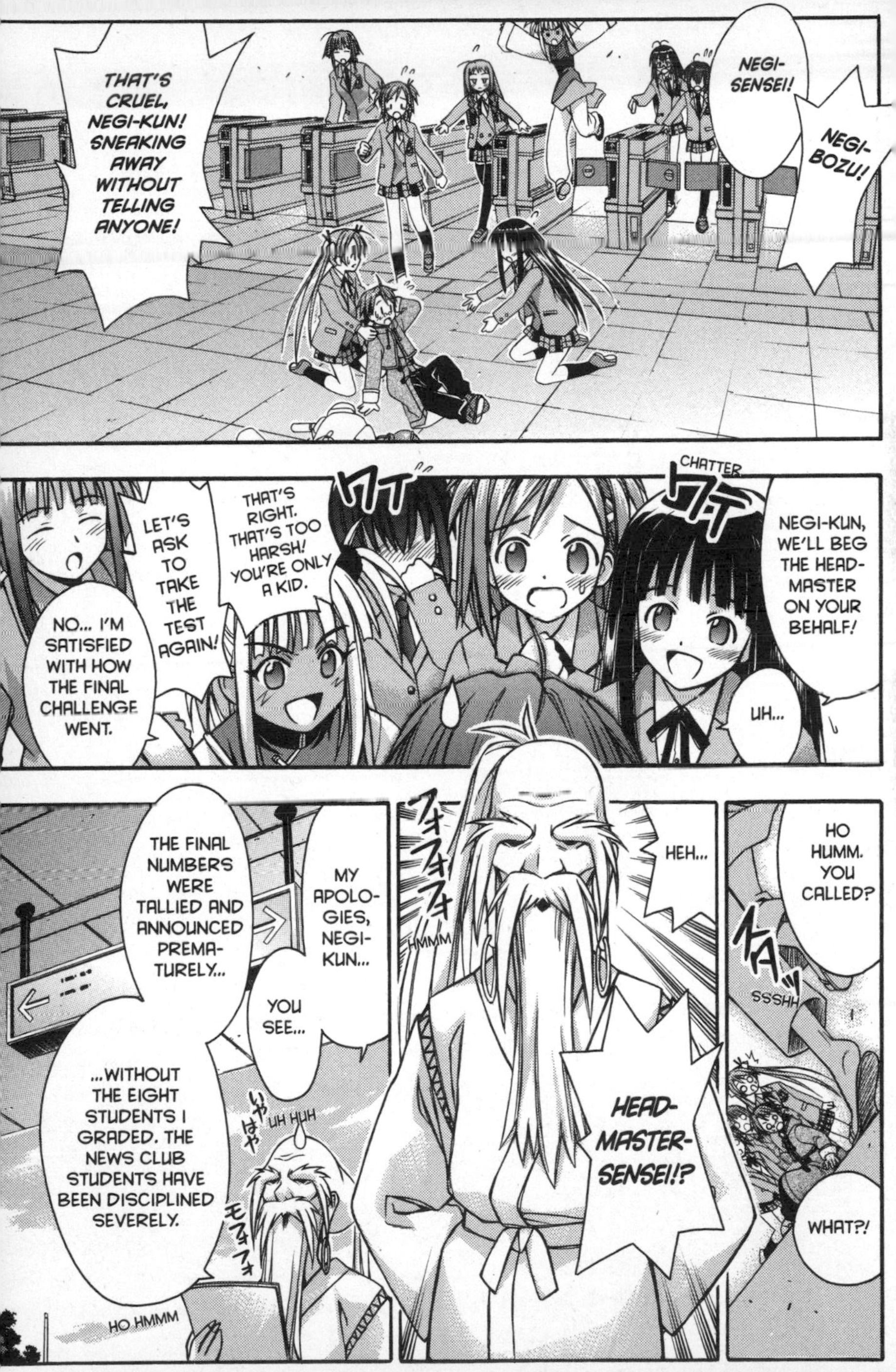
NEGI-SENSEI!
NEGI-BOZU!
THAT'S CRUEL, NEGI-KUN! SNEAKING AWAY WITHOUT TELLING ANYONE!
CHATTER
NEGI-KUN, WE'LL BEG THE HEAD-MASTER ON YOUR BEHALF!
THAT'S RIGHT. THAT'S TOO HARSH! YOU'RE ONLY A KID.
LET'S ASK TO TAKE THE TEST AGAIN!
UH...
NO... I'M SATISFIED WITH HOW THE FINAL CHALLENGE WENT.
HO HUMM. YOU CALLED?
SSSHH
WHAT?!
HEH...
HMMM
HEAD-MASTER-SENSEI!!?
MY APOLOGIES, NEGI-KUN...
YOU SEE...
THE FINAL NUMBERS WERE TALLIED AND ANNOUNCED PREMATURELY...
...WITHOUT THE EIGHT STUDENTS I GRADED. THE NEWS CLUB STUDENTS HAVE BEEN DISCIPLINED SEVERELY.
UH HUH
HO HMMM

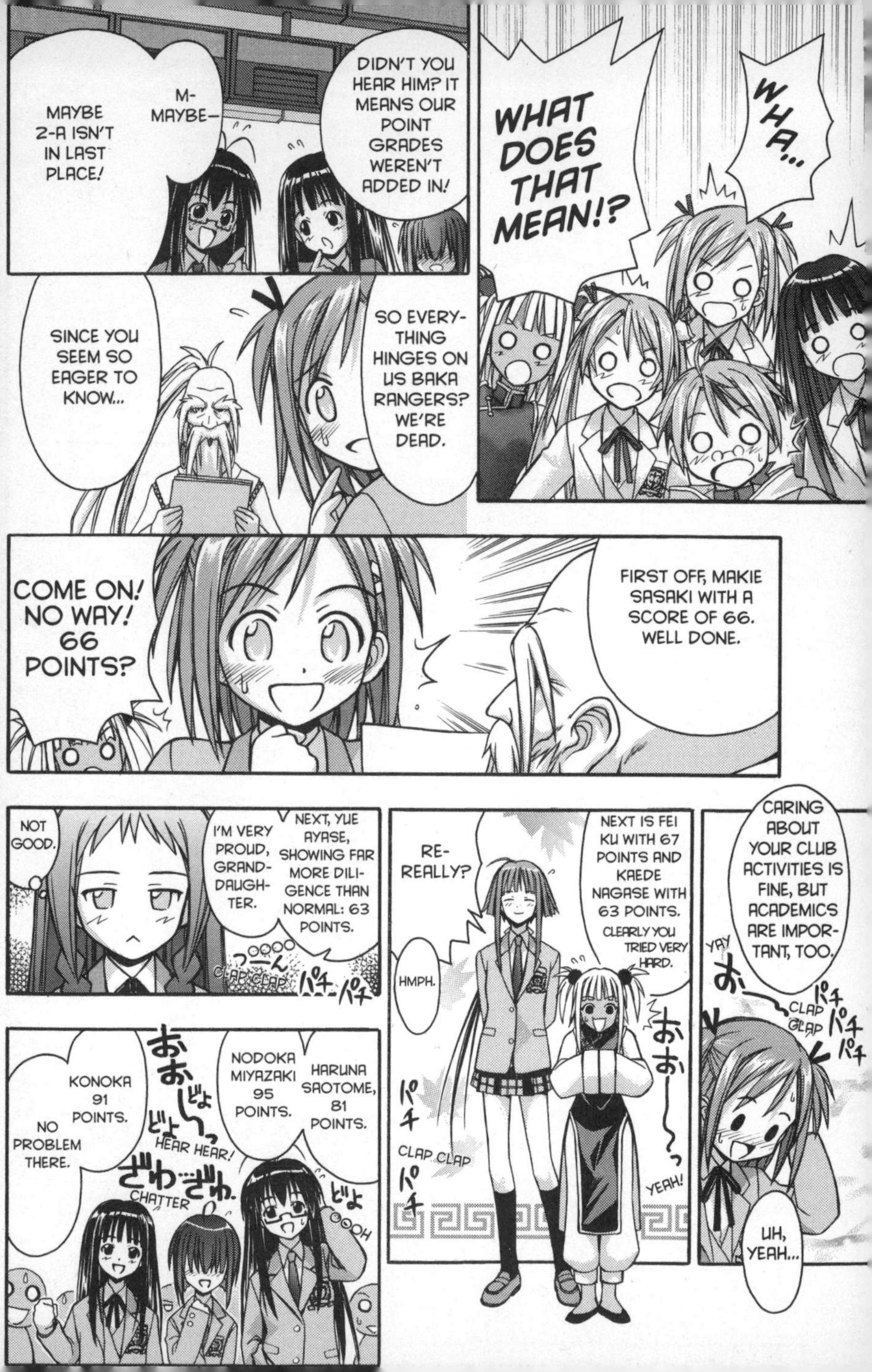
WHA...
WHAT DOES THAT MEAN!?
DIDN'T YOU HEAR HIM? IT MEANS OUR POINT GRADES WEREN'T ADDED IN!
M-MAYBE—
MAYBE 2-A ISN'T IN LAST PLACE!
SO EVERYTHING HINGES ON US BAKA RANGERS? WE'RE DEAD.
SINCE YOU SEEM SO EAGER TO KNOW...
FIRST OFF, MAKIE SASAKI WITH A SCORE OF 66. WELL DONE.
COME ON! NO WAY! 66 POINTS?
CARING ABOUT YOUR CLUB ACTIVITIES IS FINE, BUT ACADEMICS ARE IMPORTANT, TOO.
YAY
おー
パチパチ
CLAP CLAP
UH, YEAH...
NEXT IS FEI KU WITH 67 POINTS AND KAEDE NAGASE WITH 63 POINTS.
CLEARLY YOU TRIED VERY HARD.
RE-REALLY?
HMPH.
おお～っ
YEAH!
パチパチ
CLAP CLAP
NEXT, YUE AYASE, SHOWING FAR MORE DILIGENCE THAN NORMAL: 63 POINTS.
I'M VERY PROUD, GRANDDAUGHTER.
NOT GOOD.
つーん
OOOO
パチーパチ
CLAP CLAP
HARUNA SAOTOME, 81 POINTS.
NODOKA MIYAZAKI 95 POINTS.
KONOKA 91 POINTS.
NO PROBLEM THERE.
おお どよどよっ
HEAR HEAR!
ざわざわ
CHATTER
どよ
OOOH

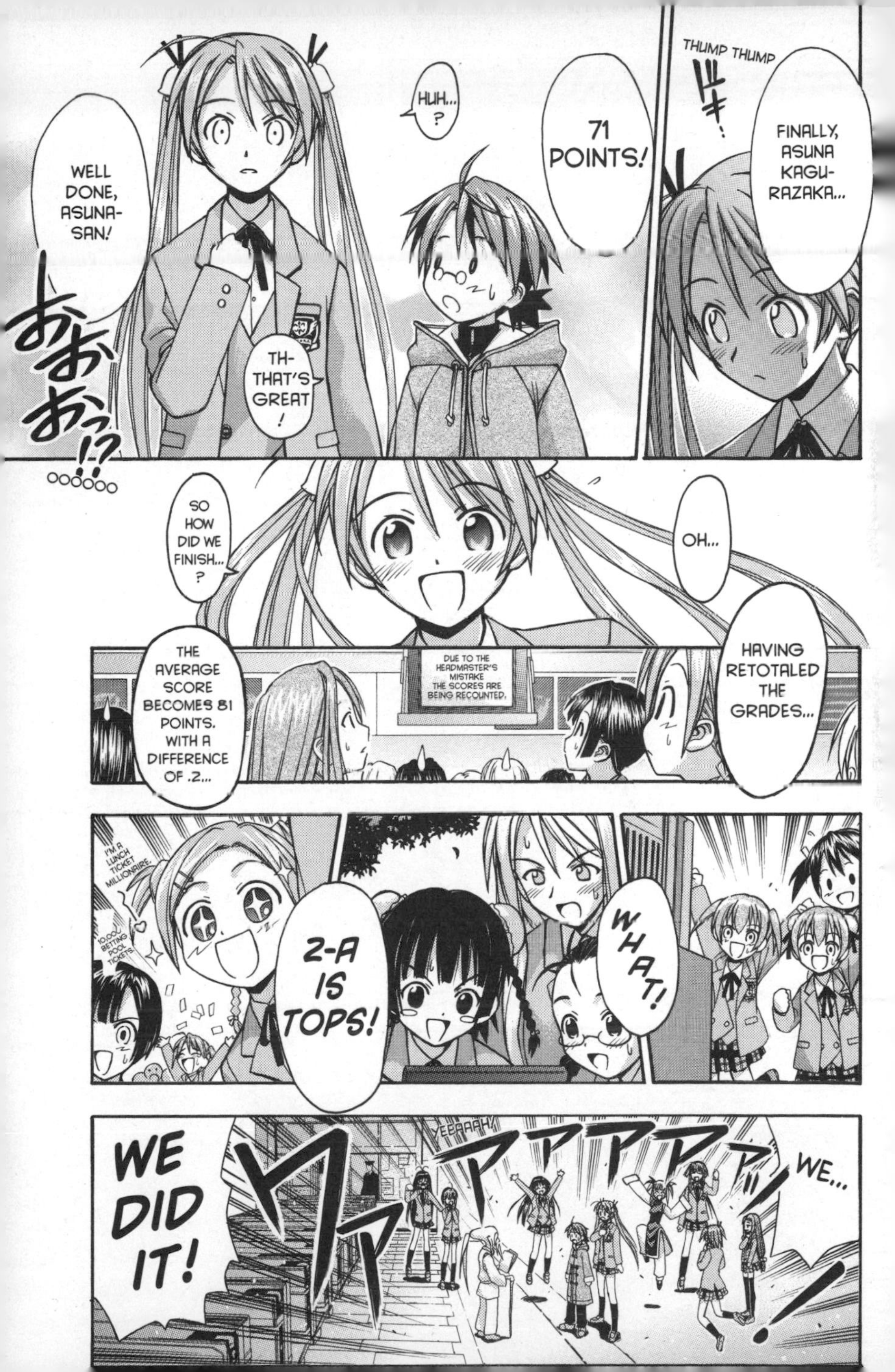
THUMP THUMP
ドキ
FINALLY, ASUNA KAGURAZAKA...
71 POINTS!
HUH... ?
WELL DONE, ASUNA-SAN!
TH-THAT'S GREAT!
おおおっ!?
OOOOOO
OH...
SO HOW DID WE FINISH... ?
HAVING RETOTALED THE GRADES...
DUE TO THE HEADMASTER'S MISTAKE THE SCORES ARE BEING RECOUNTED.
THE AVERAGE SCORE BECOMES 81 POINTS. WITH A DIFFERENCE OF .2...
WHAT!
2-A IS TOPS!
I'M A LUNCH TICKET MILLIONAIRE.
10,000 BETTING POOL TICKETS.
WE...
YEAAAAH
WE DID IT!

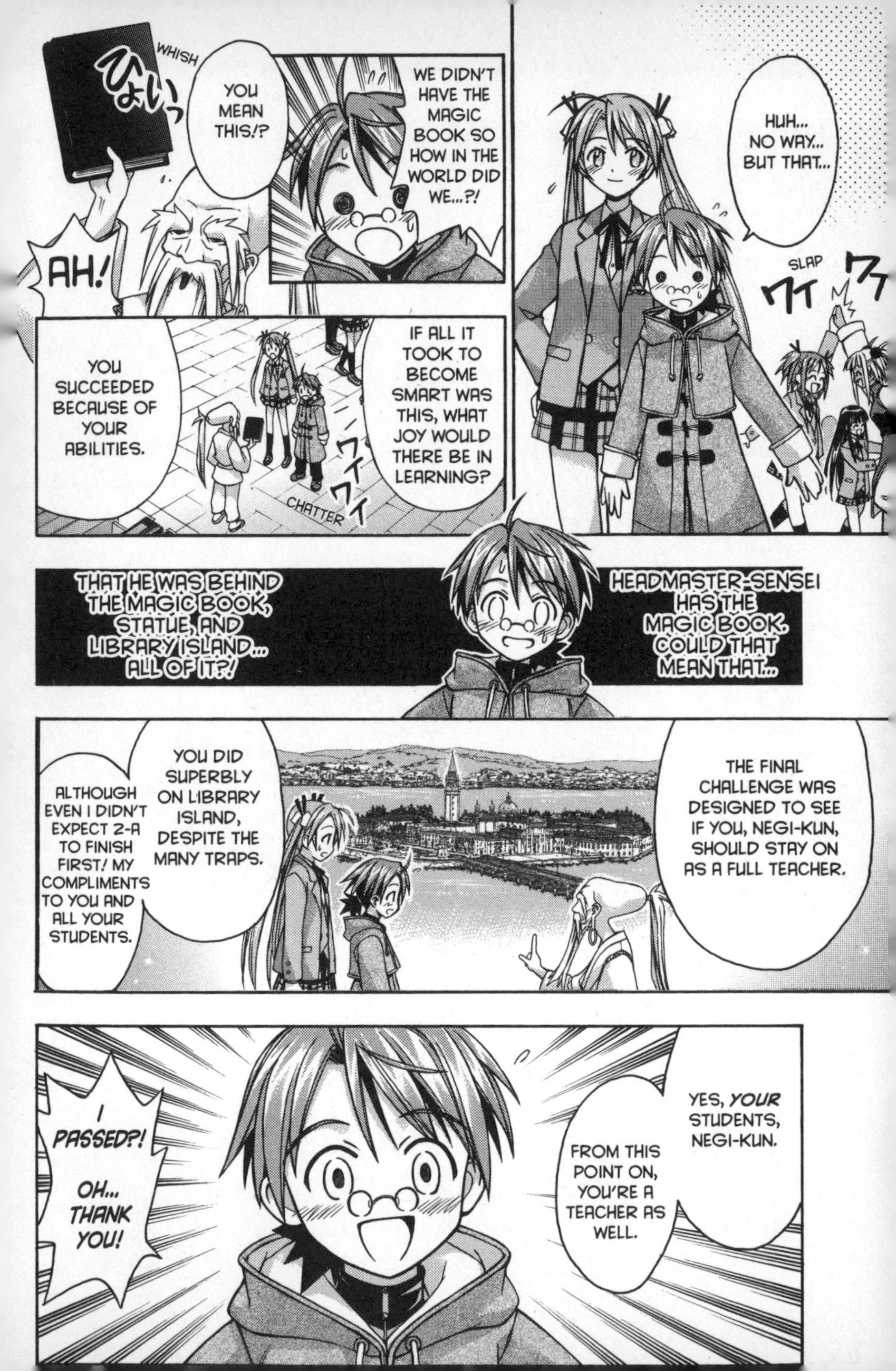

HUH... NO WAY... BUT THAT...
SLAP
WE DIDN'T HAVE THE MAGIC BOOK SO HOW IN THE WORLD DID WE...?!
YOU MEAN THIS!?
WHISH
AH!
IF ALL IT TOOK TO BECOME SMART WAS THIS, WHAT JOY WOULD THERE BE IN LEARNING?
YOU SUCCEEDED BECAUSE OF YOUR ABILITIES.
CHATTER
HEADMASTER-SENSEI HAS THE MAGIC BOOK. COULD THAT MEAN THAT...
THAT HE WAS BEHIND THE MAGIC BOOK, STATUE, AND LIBRARY ISLAND... ALL OF IT?!
THE FINAL CHALLENGE WAS DESIGNED TO SEE IF YOU, NEGI-KUN, SHOULD STAY ON AS A FULL TEACHER.
YOU DID SUPERBLY ON LIBRARY ISLAND, DESPITE THE MANY TRAPS.
ALTHOUGH EVEN I DIDN'T EXPECT 2-A TO FINISH FIRST! MY COMPLIMENTS TO YOU AND ALL YOUR STUDENTS.
YES, *YOUR* STUDENTS, NEGI-KUN.
FROM THIS POINT ON, YOU'RE A TEACHER AS WELL.
I *PASSED?!*
OH... THANK YOU!

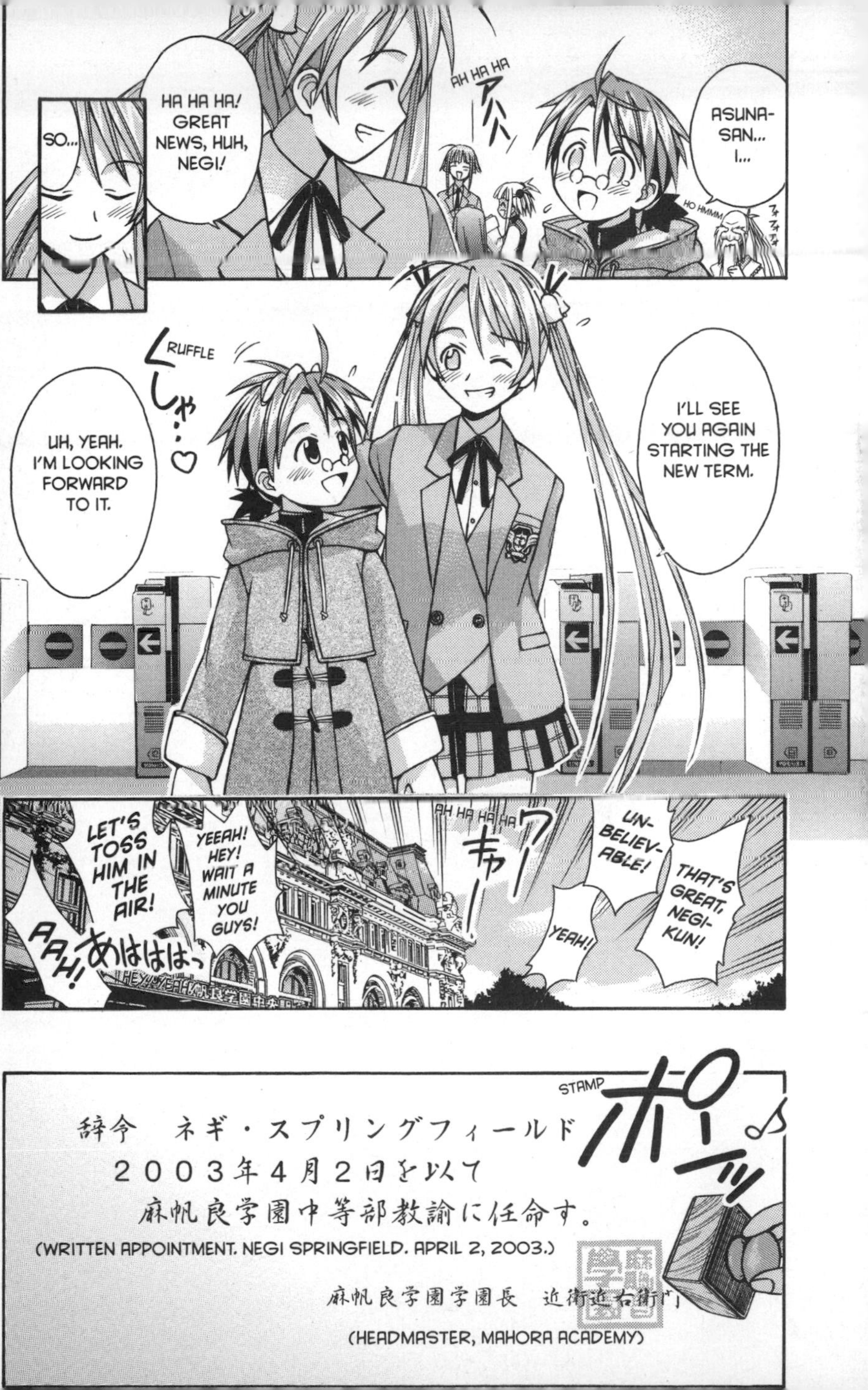
ASUNA-SAN... I...
HO HMMM
AH HA HA
アハハ
HA HA HA! GREAT NEWS, HUH, NEGI!
SO...
I'LL SEE YOU AGAIN STARTING THE NEW TERM.
RUFFLE
くしゃ・・・♡
UH, YEAH. I'M LOOKING FORWARD TO IT.
THAT'S GREAT, NEGI-KUN!
UN-BELIEV-ABLE!
YEAH!
AH HA HA HA
ワー
キャー
YEEAH! HEY! WAIT A MINUTE YOU GUYS!
LET'S TOSS HIM IN THE AIR!
AAH!
あははは
STAMP
ポンッ
辞令　ネギ・スプリングフィールド
２００３年４月２日を以て
麻帆良学園中等部教諭に任命す。
(WRITTEN APPOINTMENT. NEGI SPRINGFIELD. APRIL 2, 2003.)
麻帆良学園学園長　近衛近右衛門
(HEADMASTER, MAHORA ACADEMY)

STUDENT NUMBER 25
CHISAME HASEGAWA

BORN: FEBRUARY 2, 1989
BLOOD TYPE: B
LIKES: SMALL AND EFFICIENT MACHINES
**   (SUBNOTEBOOK COMPUTERS, ETC.)**
DISLIKES: NEW INVENTIONS IN FOOD AND SWORDS.
AFFILIATIONS: NONE
NOTE: EYESIGHT 1.2

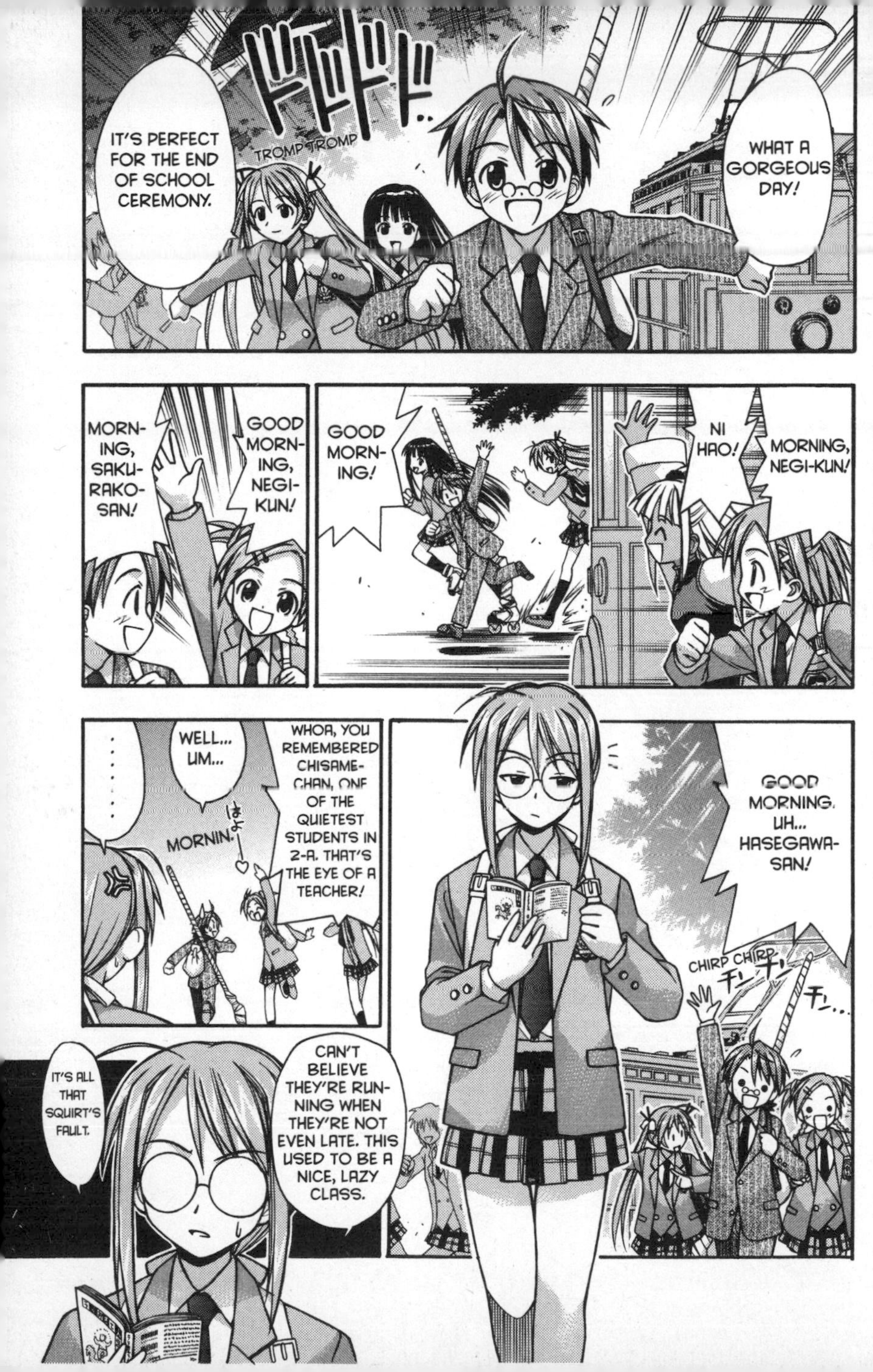
WHAT A GORGEOUS DAY!
TROMP TROMP
IT'S PERFECT FOR THE END OF SCHOOL CEREMONY.
MORNING, NEGI-KUN!
NI HAO!
GOOD MORNING!
GOOD MORNING, NEGI-KUN!
MORNING, SAKURAKO-SAN!
GOOD MORNING. UH... HASEGAWA-SAN!
CHIRP CHIRP
WHOA, YOU REMEMBERED CHISAME-CHAN, ONE OF THE QUIETEST STUDENTS IN 2-A. THAT'S THE EYE OF A TEACHER!
WELL... UM...
MORNIN.
......
CAN'T BELIEVE THEY'RE RUNNING WHEN THEY'RE NOT EVEN LATE. THIS USED TO BE A NICE, LAZY CLASS.
IT'S ALL THAT SQUIRT'S FAULT.

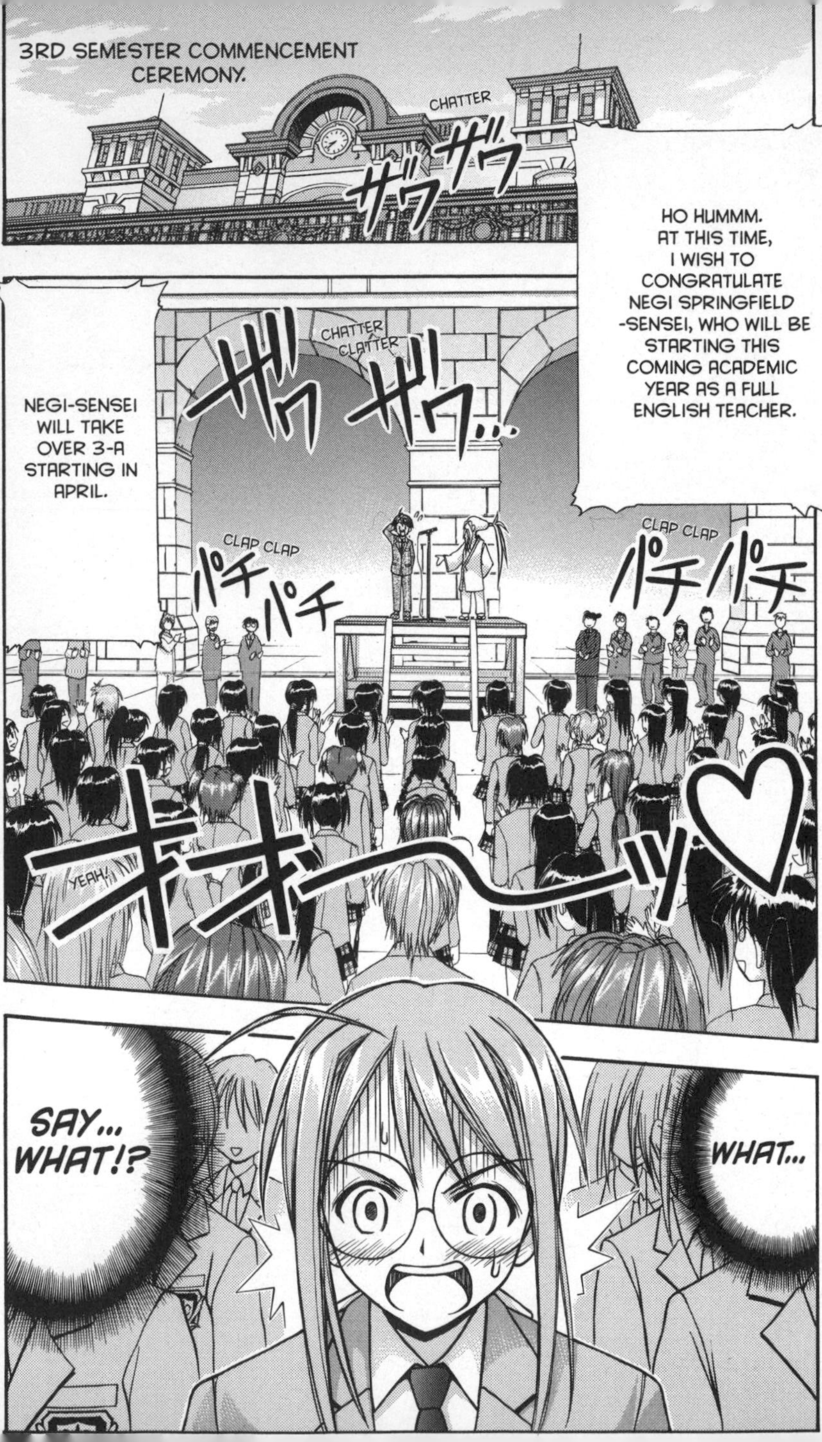
3RD SEMESTER COMMENCEMENT CEREMONY.
CHATTER
ザワザワ
HO HUMMM. AT THIS TIME, I WISH TO CONGRATULATE NEGI SPRINGFIELD -SENSEI, WHO WILL BE STARTING THIS COMING ACADEMIC YEAR AS A FULL ENGLISH TEACHER.
CHATTER CLATTER
ザワ ザワ...
NEGI-SENSEI WILL TAKE OVER 3-A STARTING IN APRIL.
CLAP CLAP
パチ パチ
CLAP CLAP
パチパチ
YEAH!
オオーーッ♡
WHAT...
SAY... WHAT!?

TWELFTH PERIOD: EGIRL LIFE.

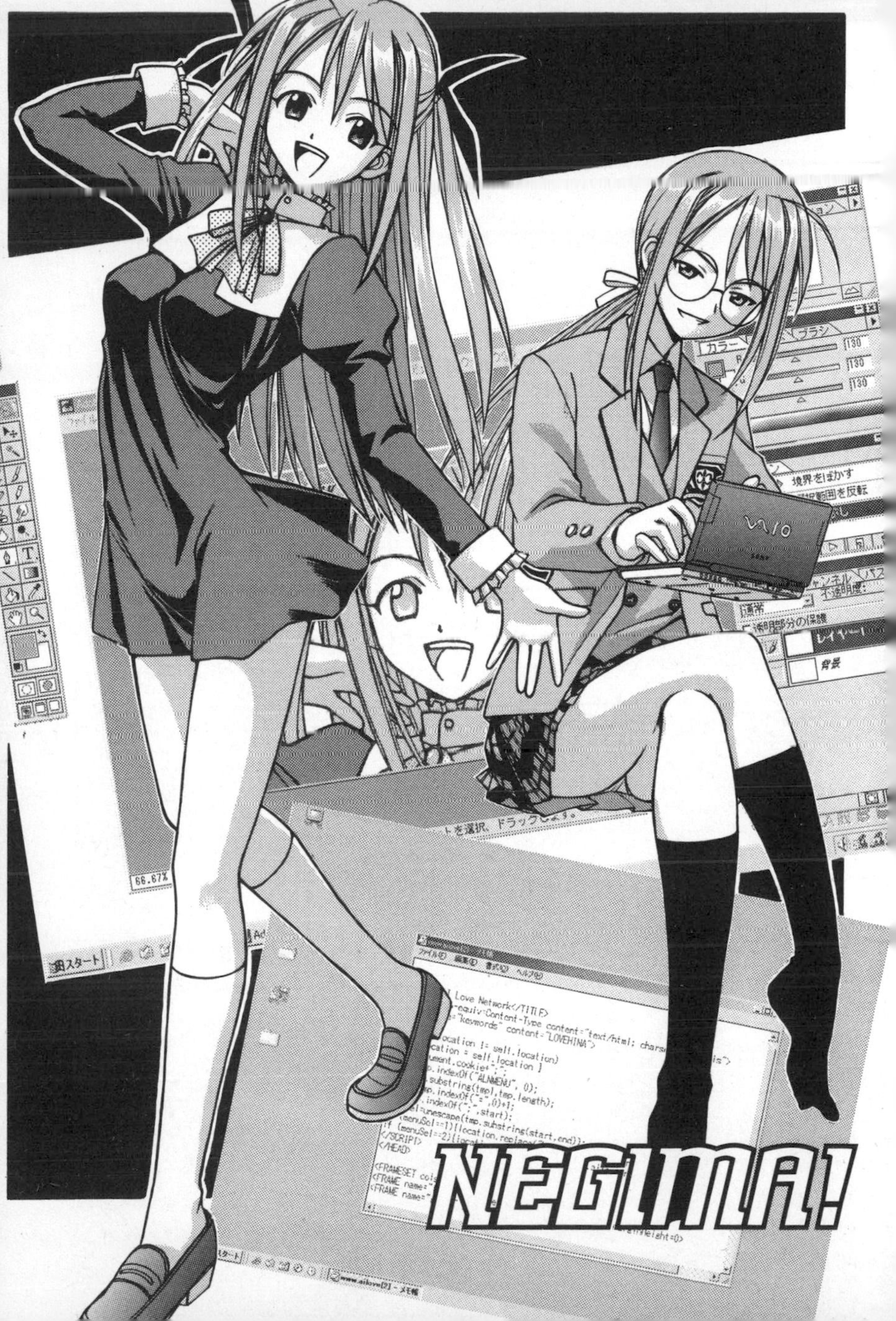
NEGIMA!

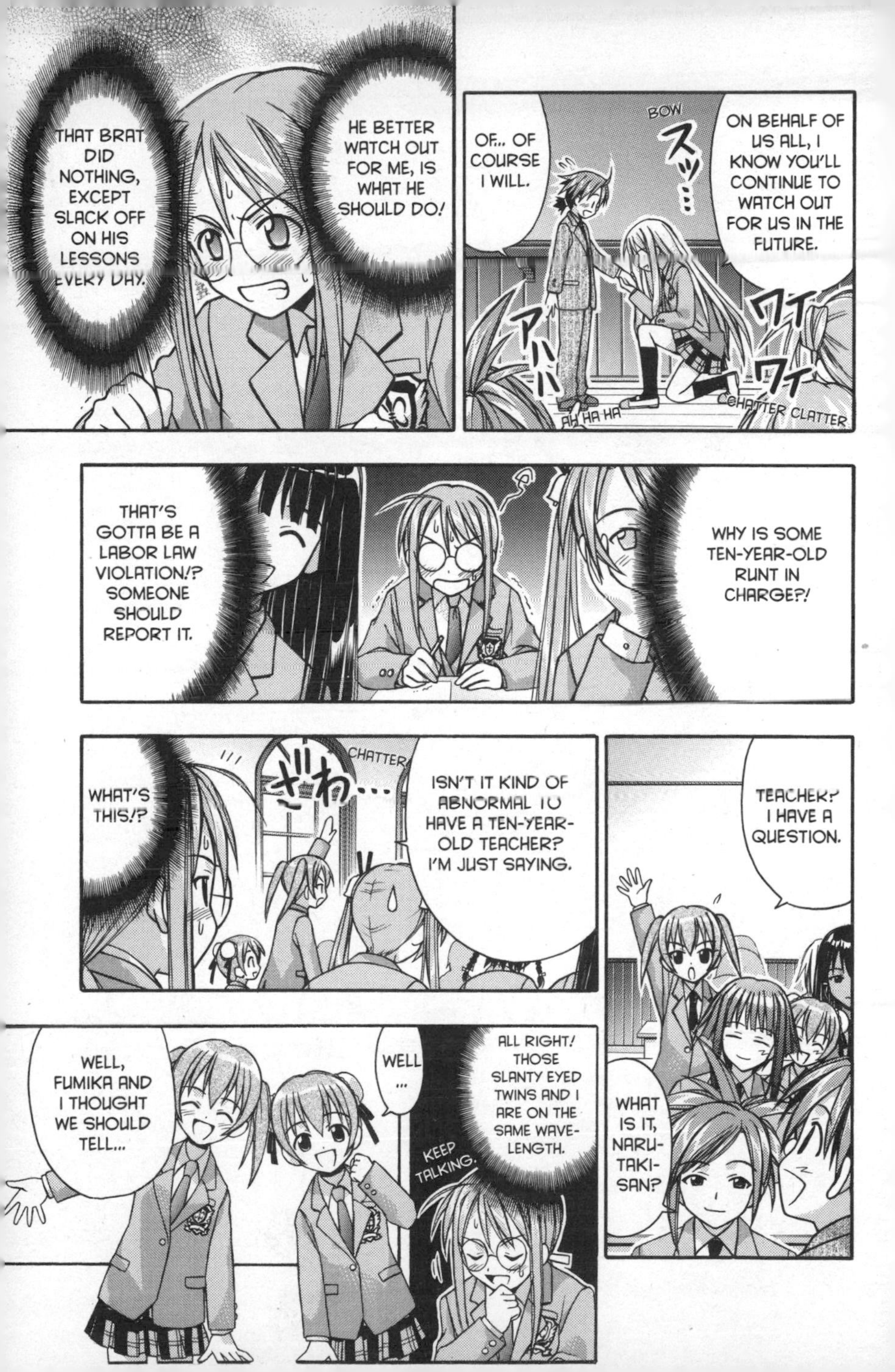

BOW
スッ…
ON BEHALF OF US ALL, I KNOW YOU'LL CONTINUE TO WATCH OUT FOR US IN THE FUTURE.
OF... OF COURSE I WILL.
ワイワイ
CHATTER CLATTER
アハハ
AH HA HA
HE BETTER WATCH OUT FOR ME, IS WHAT HE SHOULD DO!
THAT BRAT DID NOTHING, EXCEPT SLACK OFF ON HIS LESSONS EVERY DAY.
WHY IS SOME TEN-YEAR-OLD RUNT IN CHARGE?!
THAT'S GOTTA BE A LABOR LAW VIOLATION!? SOMEONE SHOULD REPORT IT.
TEACHER? I HAVE A QUESTION.
WHAT IS IT, NARU-TAKI-SAN?
ISN'T IT KIND OF ABNORMAL TO HAVE A TEN-YEAR-OLD TEACHER? I'M JUST SAYING.
CHATTER
ざわ…
WHAT'S THIS!?
ALL RIGHT! THOSE SLANTY EYED TWINS AND I ARE ON THE SAME WAVE-LENGTH.
KEEP TALKING.
WELL ...
WELL, FUMIKA AND I THOUGHT WE SHOULD TELL...

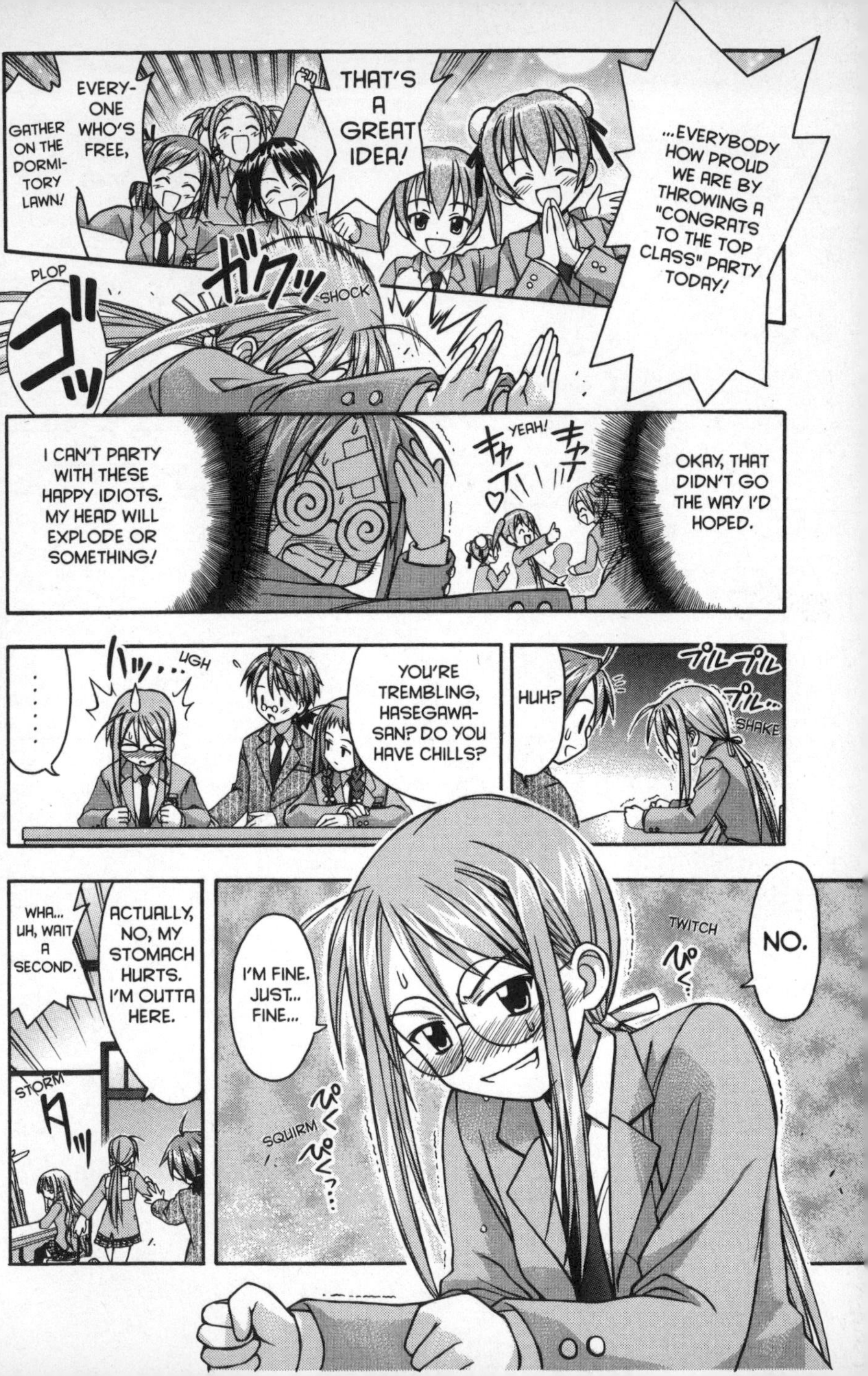
...EVERYBODY HOW PROUD WE ARE BY THROWING A "CONGRATS TO THE TOP CLASS" PARTY TODAY!
THAT'S A GREAT IDEA!
EVERY-ONE WHO'S FREE,
GATHER ON THE DORMITORY LAWN!
SHOCK
PLOP
OKAY, THAT DIDN'T GO THE WAY I'D HOPED.
YEAH!
I CAN'T PARTY WITH THESE HAPPY IDIOTS. MY HEAD WILL EXPLODE OR SOMETHING!
SHAKE
HUH?
YOU'RE TREMBLING, HASEGAWA-SAN? DO YOU HAVE CHILLS?
UGH
......
NO.
TWITCH
I'M FINE. JUST... FINE...
SQUIRM
ACTUALLY, NO, MY STOMACH HURTS. I'M OUTTA HERE.
WHA... UH, WAIT A SECOND.
STORM

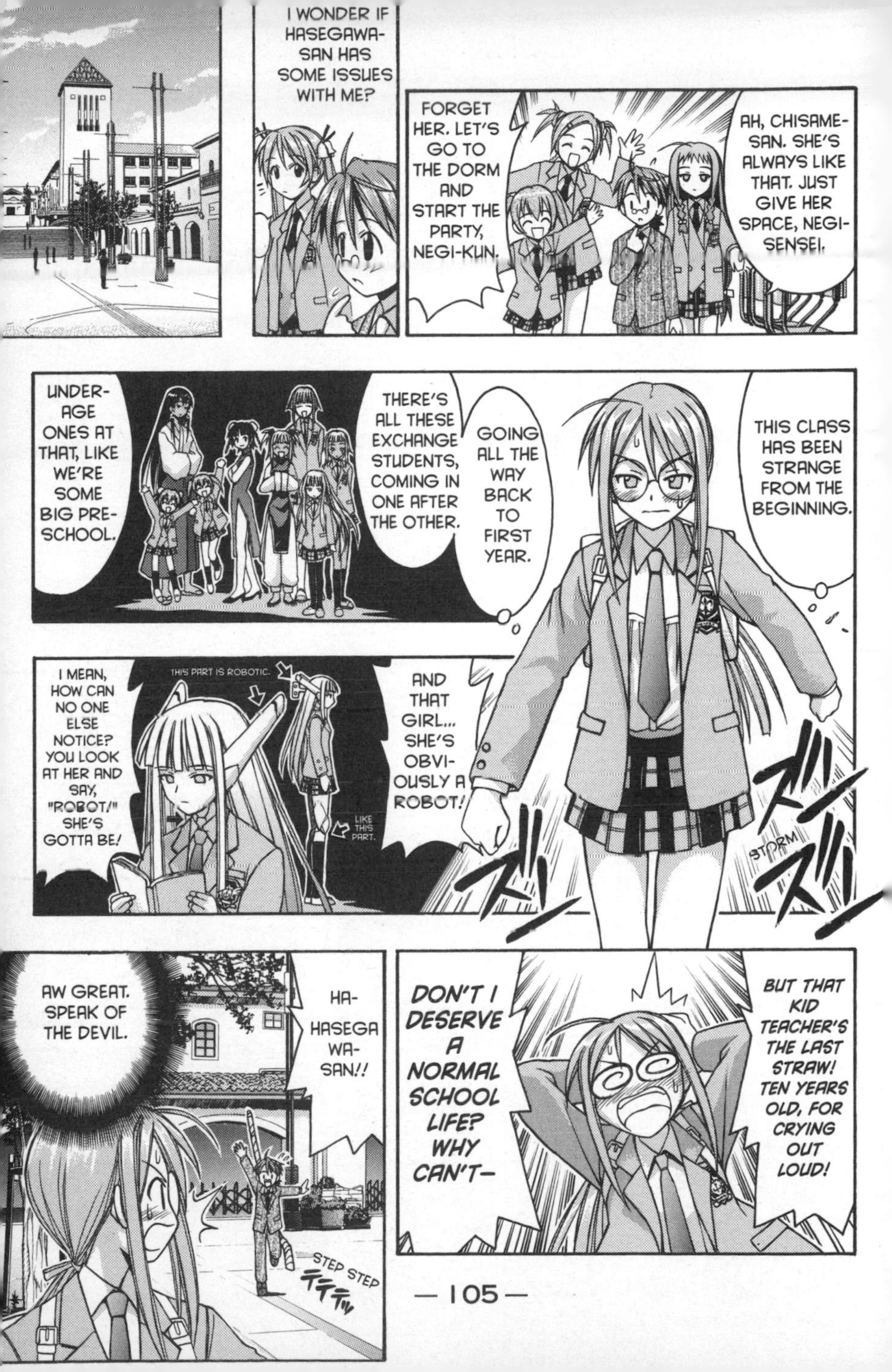
AH, CHISAME-SAN. SHE'S ALWAYS LIKE THAT. JUST GIVE HER SPACE, NEGI-SENSEI.
FORGET HER. LET'S GO TO THE DORM AND START THE PARTY, NEGI-KUN.
I WONDER IF HASEGAWA-SAN HAS SOME ISSUES WITH ME?
THIS CLASS HAS BEEN STRANGE FROM THE BEGINNING.
GOING ALL THE WAY BACK TO FIRST YEAR.
THERE'S ALL THESE EXCHANGE STUDENTS, COMING IN ONE AFTER THE OTHER.
UNDER-AGE ONES AT THAT, LIKE WE'RE SOME BIG PRE-SCHOOL.
STORM
AND THAT GIRL... SHE'S OBVIOUSLY A ROBOT!
THIS PART IS ROBOTIC.
LIKE THIS PART.
I MEAN, HOW CAN NO ONE ELSE NOTICE? YOU LOOK AT HER AND SAY, "ROBOT!" SHE'S GOTTA BE!
BUT THAT KID TEACHER'S THE LAST STRAW! TEN YEARS OLD, FOR CRYING OUT LOUD!
DON'T I DESERVE A NORMAL SCHOOL LIFE? WHY CAN'T—
HA-HASEGAWA-SAN!!
AW GREAT. SPEAK OF THE DEVIL.
STEP STEP

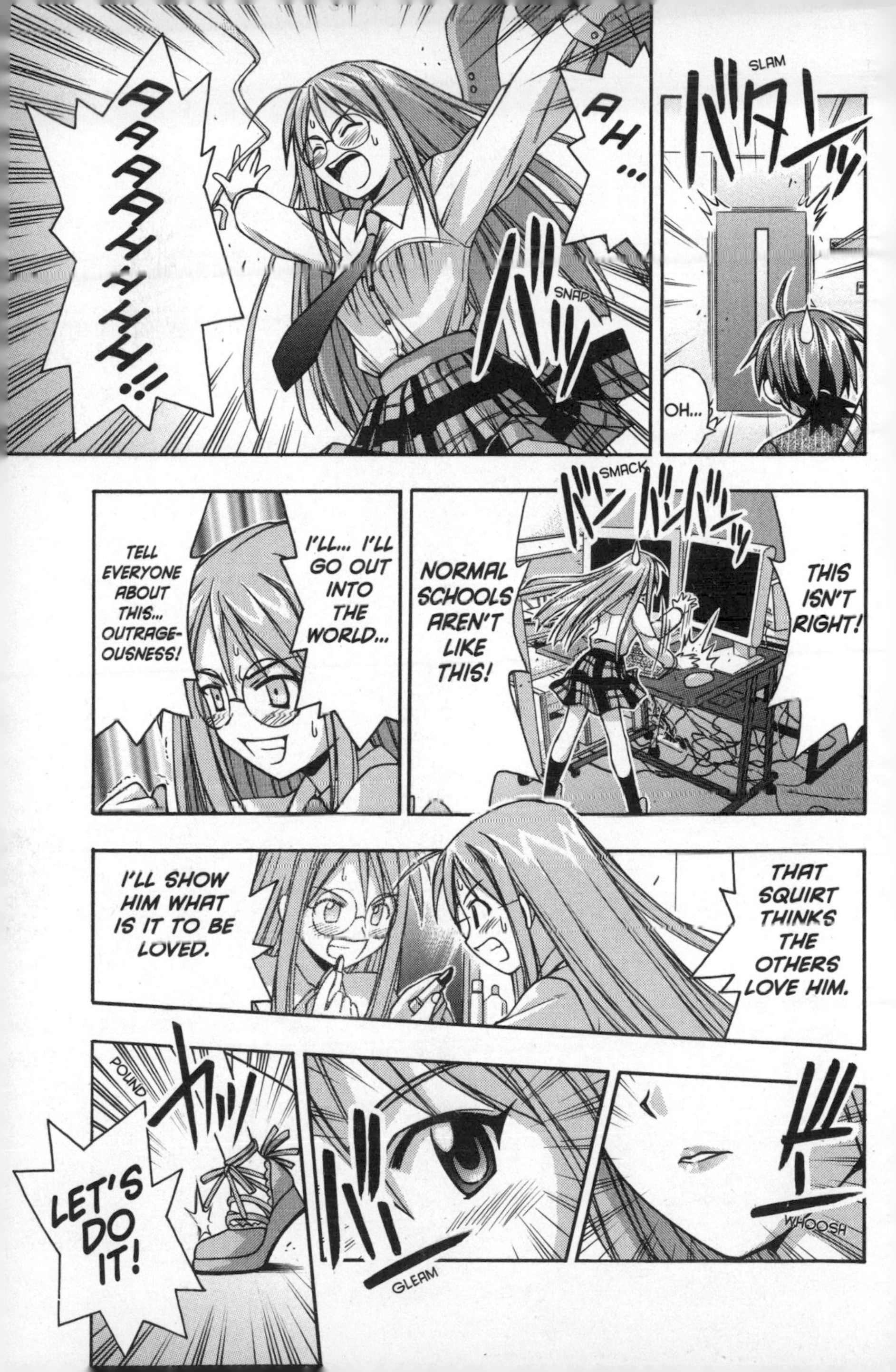
SLAM
OH...
AH...
SNAP
AAAAHHHHHH!!!
SMACK
THIS ISN'T RIGHT!
NORMAL SCHOOLS AREN'T LIKE THIS!
I'LL... I'LL GO OUT INTO THE WORLD...
TELL EVERYONE ABOUT THIS... OUTRAGE-OUSNESS!
THAT SQUIRT THINKS THE OTHERS LOVE HIM.
I'LL SHOW HIM WHAT IS IT TO BE LOVED.
WHOOSH
GLEAM
POUND
LET'S DO IT!

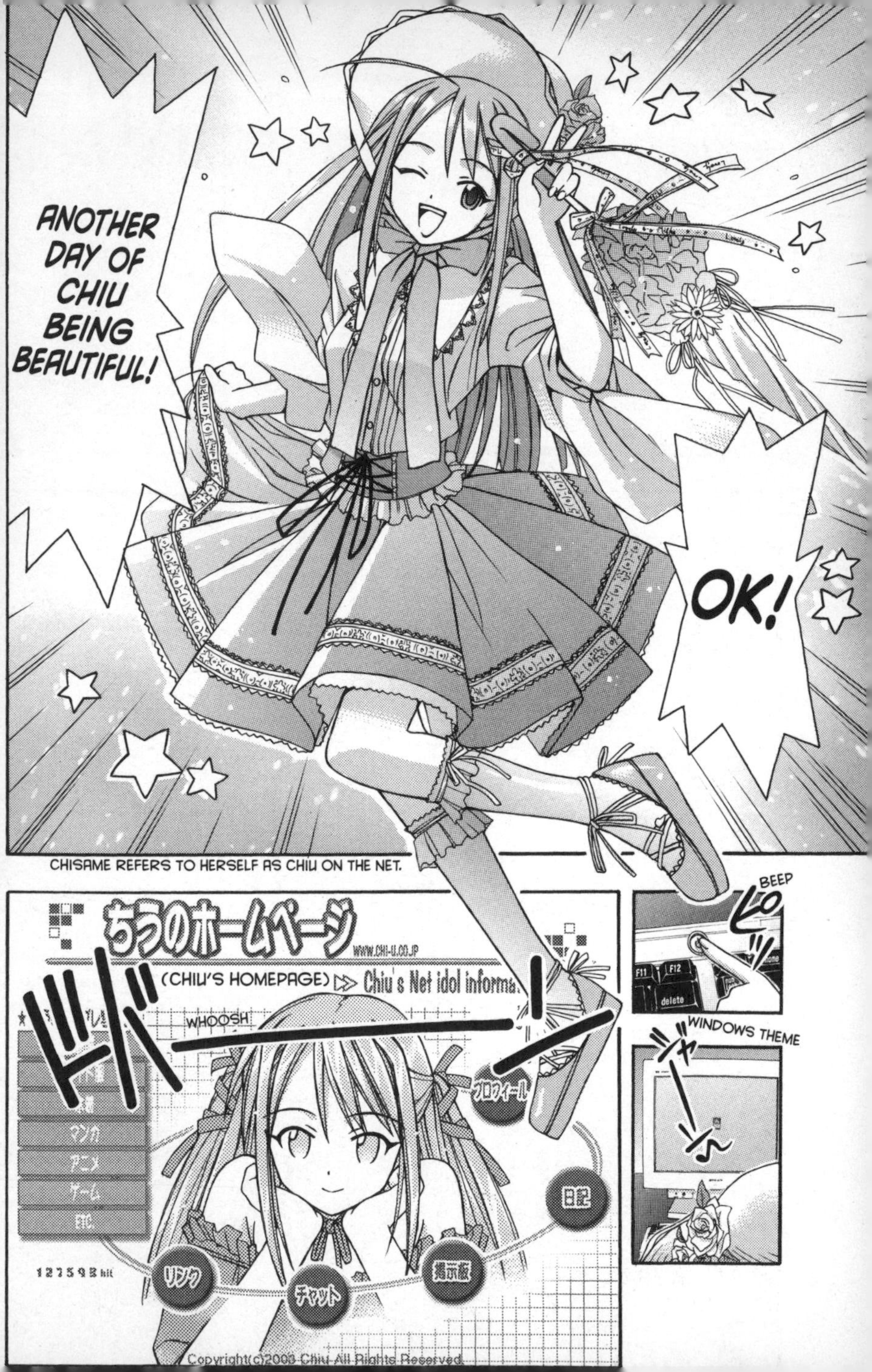

ANOTHER DAY OF CHIU BEING BEAUTIFUL!
OK!
CHISAME REFERS TO HERSELF AS CHIU ON THE NET.
ピ
BEEP
ジャーン♪
WINDOWS THEME
ちうのホームページ
WWW.CHI-U.CO.JP
(CHIU'S HOMEPAGE)
Chiu's Net idol informa
ドバー
WHOOSH
マンガ
アニメ
ゲーム
ETC.
プロフィール
日記
掲示板
チャット
リンク
123598 hit
Copyright(c)2003 Chiu All Rights Reserved.

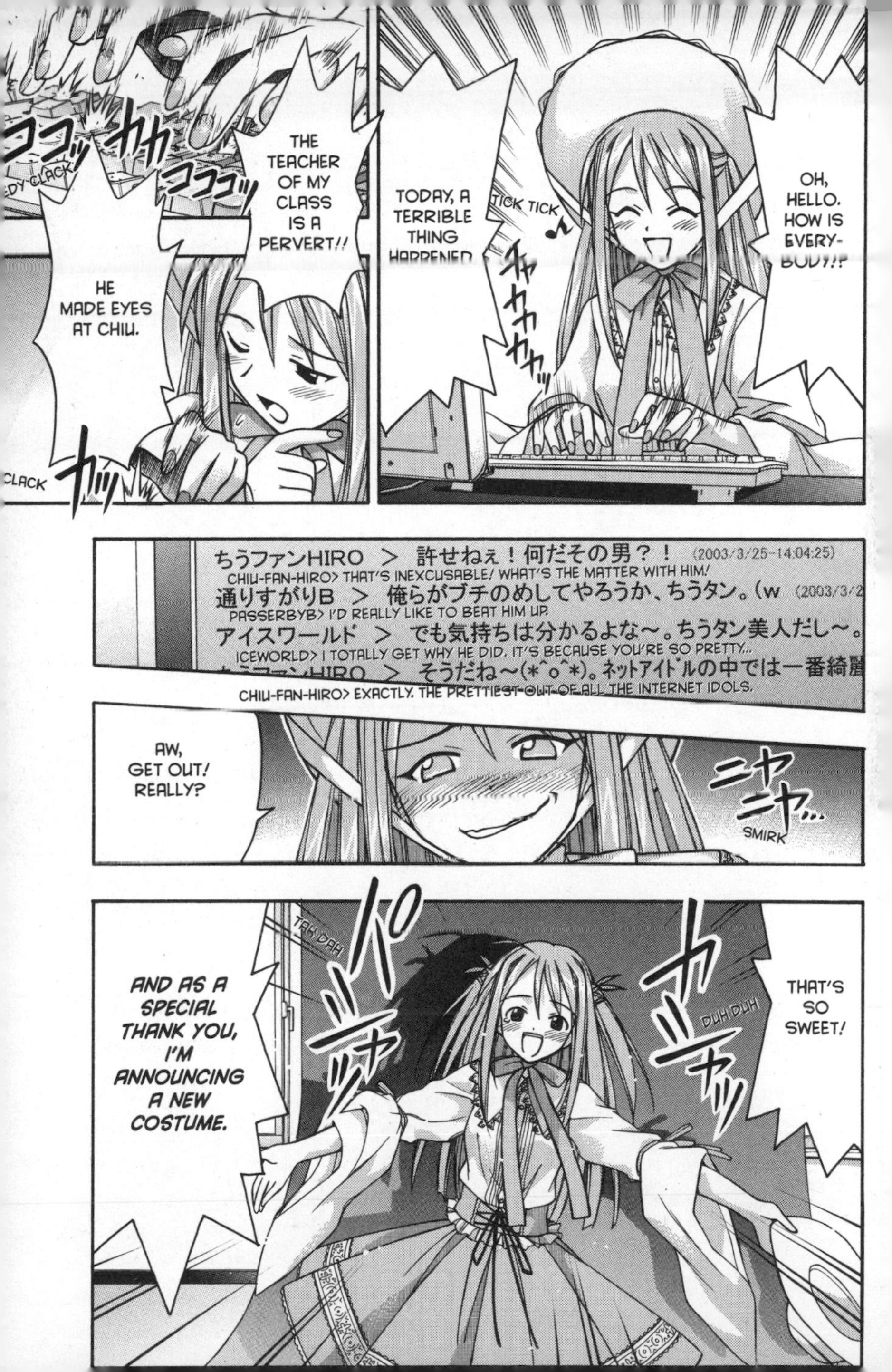
OH, HELLO. HOW IS EVERYBODY!?
TODAY, A TERRIBLE THING HAPPENED
TICK TICK
THE TEACHER OF MY CLASS IS A PERVERT!!
HE MADE EYES AT CHIU.
CLACK
ちうファンHIRO ＞ 許せねぇ！何だその男？！ (2003/3/25-14:04:25)
CHIU-FAN-HIRO> THAT'S INEXCUSABLE! WHAT'S THE MATTER WITH HIM!
通りすがりB ＞ 俺らがブチのめしてやろうか、ちうタン。(w
PASSERBYB> I'D REALLY LIKE TO BEAT HIM UP.
アイスワールド ＞ でも気持ちは分かるよな～。ちうタン美人だし～。
ICEWORLD> I TOTALLY GET WHY HE DID. IT'S BECAUSE YOU'RE SO PRETTY...
そうだね～(*^o^*)。ネットアイドルの中では一番綺麗
CHIU-FAN-HIRO> EXACTLY. THE PRETTIEST OUT OF ALL THE INTERNET IDOLS.
AW, GET OUT! REALLY?
ニヤニヤ…
SMIRK
THAT'S SO SWEET!
DUH DUH
TAH DAH
AND AS A SPECIAL THANK YOU, I'M ANNOUNCING A NEW COSTUME.

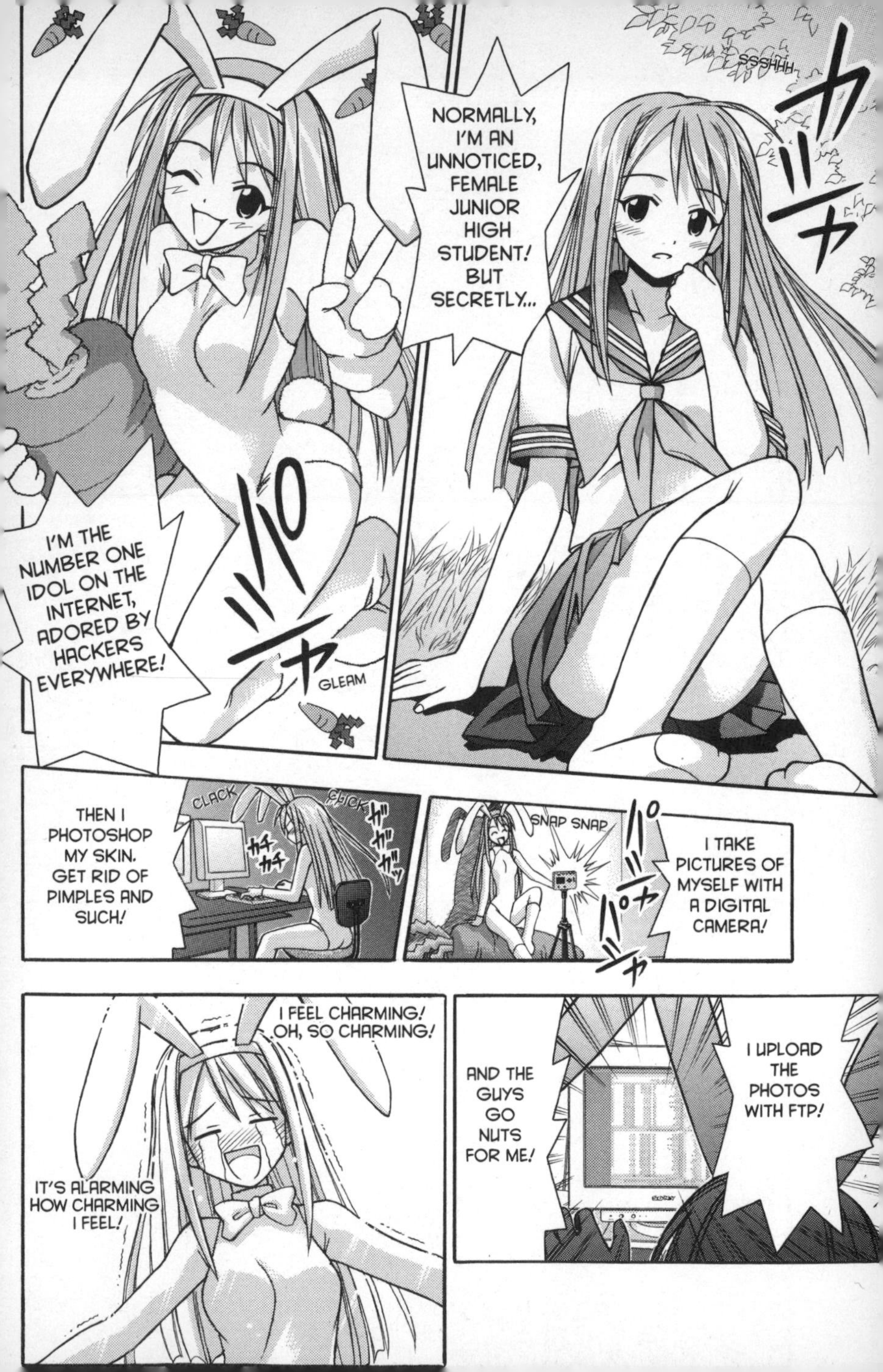
SSSHHH
NORMALLY, I'M AN UNNOTICED, FEMALE JUNIOR HIGH STUDENT! BUT SECRETLY...
I'M THE NUMBER ONE IDOL ON THE INTERNET, ADORED BY HACKERS EVERYWHERE!
GLEAM
SNAP SNAP
I TAKE PICTURES OF MYSELF WITH A DIGITAL CAMERA!
CLACK
CLICK
THEN I PHOTOSHOP MY SKIN. GET RID OF PIMPLES AND SUCH!
I UPLOAD THE PHOTOS WITH FTP!
AND THE GUYS GO NUTS FOR ME!
I FEEL CHARMING! OH, SO CHARMING!
IT'S ALARMING HOW CHARMING I FEEL!

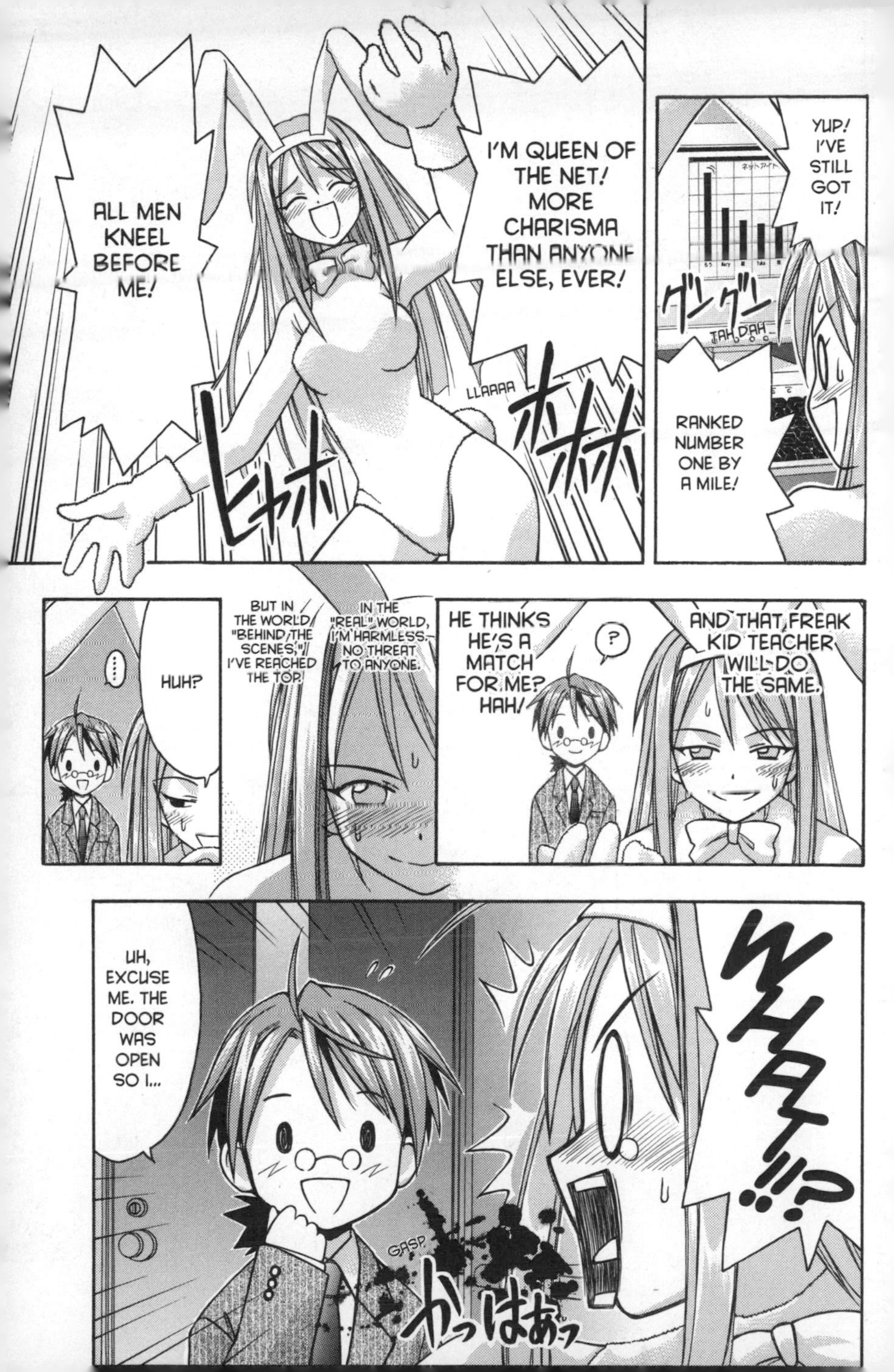
YUP! I'VE STILL GOT IT!
TAH DAH
RANKED NUMBER ONE BY A MILE!
I'M QUEEN OF THE NET! MORE CHARISMA THAN ANYONE ELSE, EVER!
LLAAAA
ALL MEN KNEEL BEFORE ME!
AND THAT FREAK KID TEACHER WILL DO THE SAME.
HE THINKS HE'S A MATCH FOR ME? HAH!
?
IN THE "REAL" WORLD, I'M HARMLESS. NO THREAT TO ANYONE.
BUT IN THE WORLD "BEHIND THE SCENES," I'VE REACHED THE TOP.
HUH?
....
UH, EXCUSE ME. THE DOOR WAS OPEN SO I...
GASP
かっはあっ

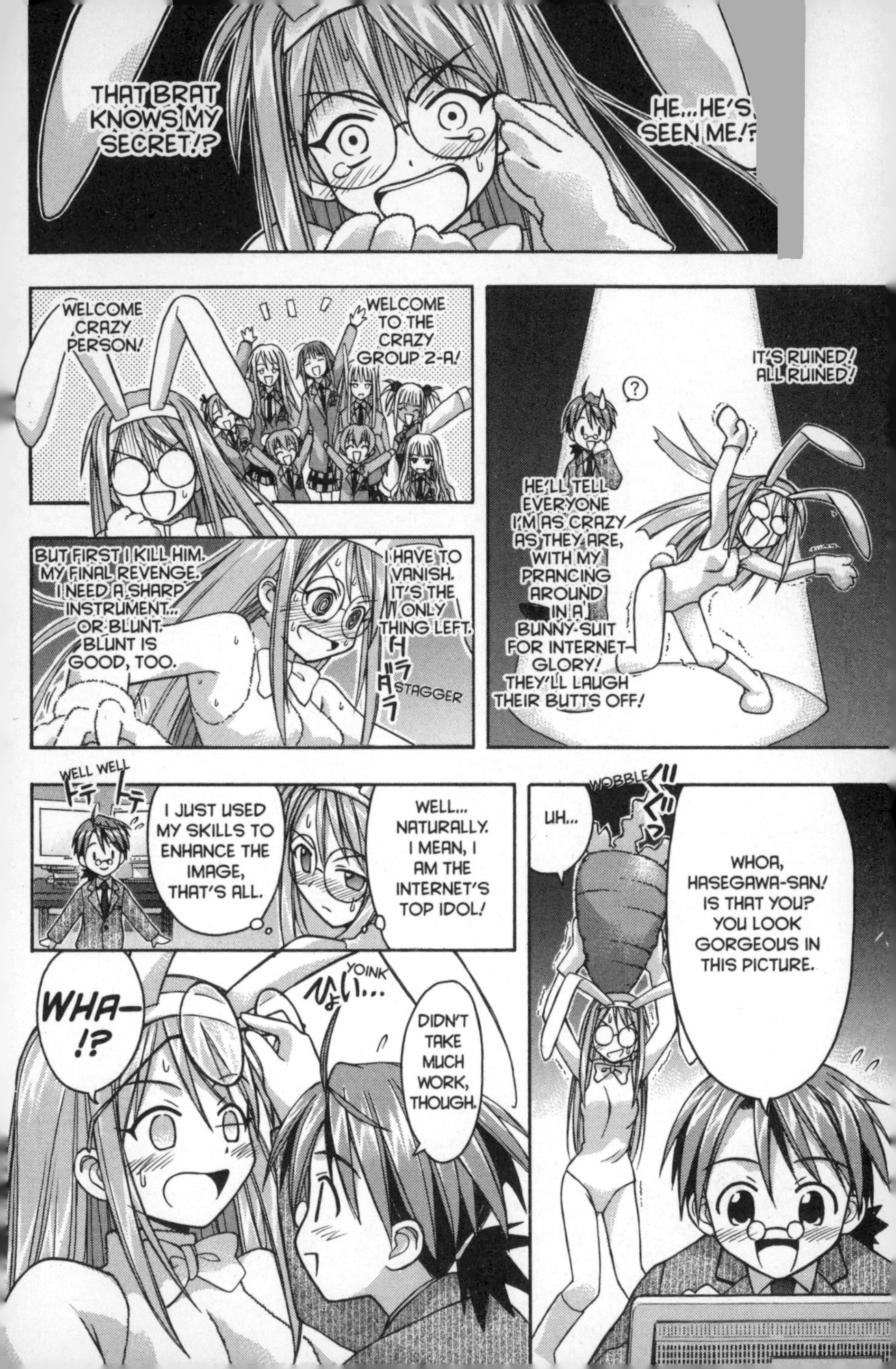

HE...HE'S SEEN ME!?
THAT BRAT KNOWS MY SECRET!?
IT'S RUINED! ALL RUINED!
?
HE'LL TELL EVERYONE I'M AS CRAZY AS THEY ARE, WITH MY PRANCING AROUND IN A BUNNY-SUIT FOR INTERNET GLORY! THEY'LL LAUGH THEIR BUTTS OFF!
WELCOME TO THE CRAZY GROUP 2-A!
WELCOME CRAZY PERSON!
I HAVE TO VANISH. IT'S THE ONLY THING LEFT.
STAGGER
BUT FIRST I KILL HIM. MY FINAL REVENGE. I NEED A SHARP INSTRUMENT... OR BLUNT. BLUNT IS GOOD, TOO.
WOBBLE
UH...
WHOA, HASEGAWA-SAN! IS THAT YOU? YOU LOOK GORGEOUS IN THIS PICTURE.
WELL WELL
WELL... NATURALLY. I MEAN, I AM THE INTERNET'S TOP IDOL!
I JUST USED MY SKILLS TO ENHANCE THE IMAGE, THAT'S ALL.
YOINK
DIDN'T TAKE MUCH WORK, THOUGH.
WHA-!?

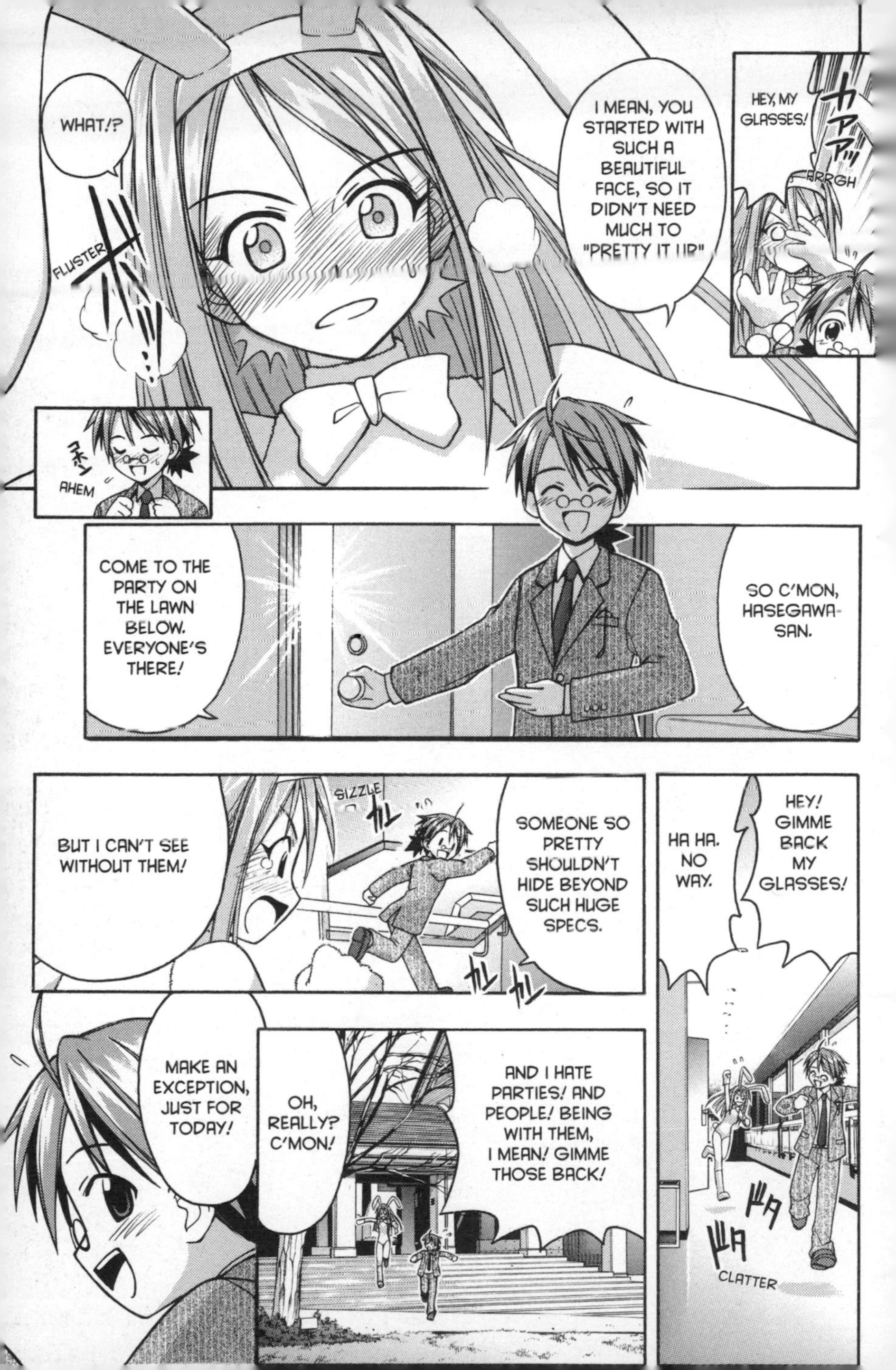
HEY, MY GLASSES!
ARRGH
I MEAN, YOU STARTED WITH SUCH A BEAUTIFUL FACE, SO IT DIDN'T NEED MUCH TO "PRETTY IT UP"
WHAT!?
FLUSTER
AHEM
SO C'MON, HASEGAWA-SAN.
COME TO THE PARTY ON THE LAWN BELOW. EVERYONE'S THERE!
HEY! GIMME BACK MY GLASSES!
HA HA. NO WAY.
SOMEONE SO PRETTY SHOULDN'T HIDE BEYOND SUCH HUGE SPECS.
SIZZLE
BUT I CAN'T SEE WITHOUT THEM!
CLATTER
AND I HATE PARTIES! AND PEOPLE! BEING WITH THEM, I MEAN! GIMME THOSE BACK!
OH, REALLY? C'MON!
MAKE AN EXCEPTION, JUST FOR TODAY!

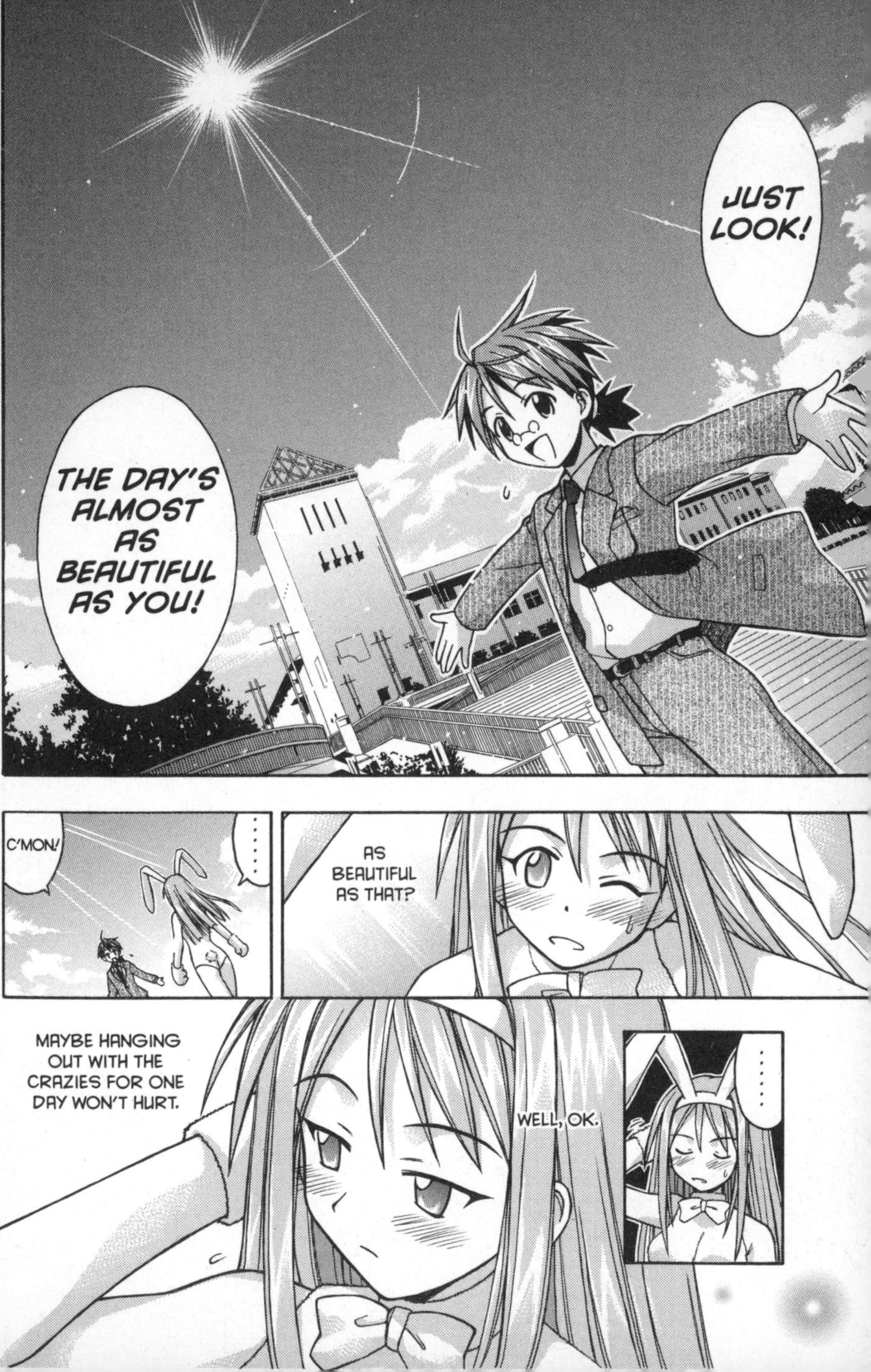
JUST LOOK!
THE DAY'S ALMOST AS BEAUTIFUL AS YOU!
AS BEAUTIFUL AS THAT?
......
C'MON!
......
WELL, OK.
MAYBE HANGING OUT WITH THE CRAZIES FOR ONE DAY WON'T HURT.

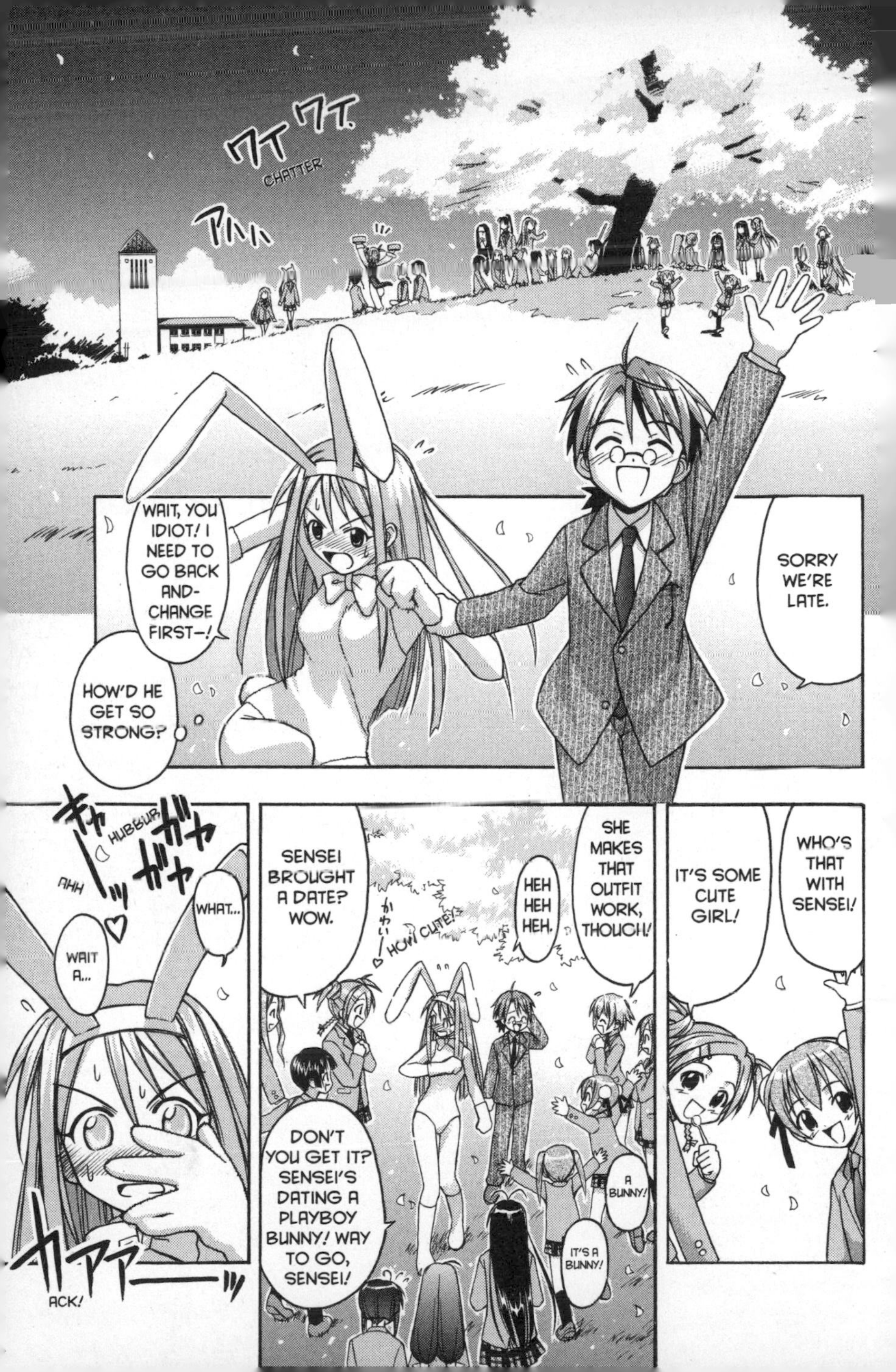

ワイワイ
CHATTER
アハハ
SORRY WE'RE LATE.
WAIT, YOU IDIOT! I NEED TO GO BACK AND- CHANGE FIRST--!
HOW'D HE GET SO STRONG?
WHO'S THAT WITH SENSEI!
IT'S SOME CUTE GIRL!
SHE MAKES THAT OUTFIT WORK, THOUGH!
HEH HEH HEH.
かわいー!
HOW CUTE!
SENSEI BROUGHT A DATE? WOW.
A BUNNY!
IT'S A BUNNY!
DON'T YOU GET IT? SENSEI'S DATING A PLAYBOY BUNNY! WAY TO GO, SENSEI!
ガヤガヤ
HUBBUB
キャーッ
AHH
WHAT...
WAIT A...
カアアーーッ
ACK!

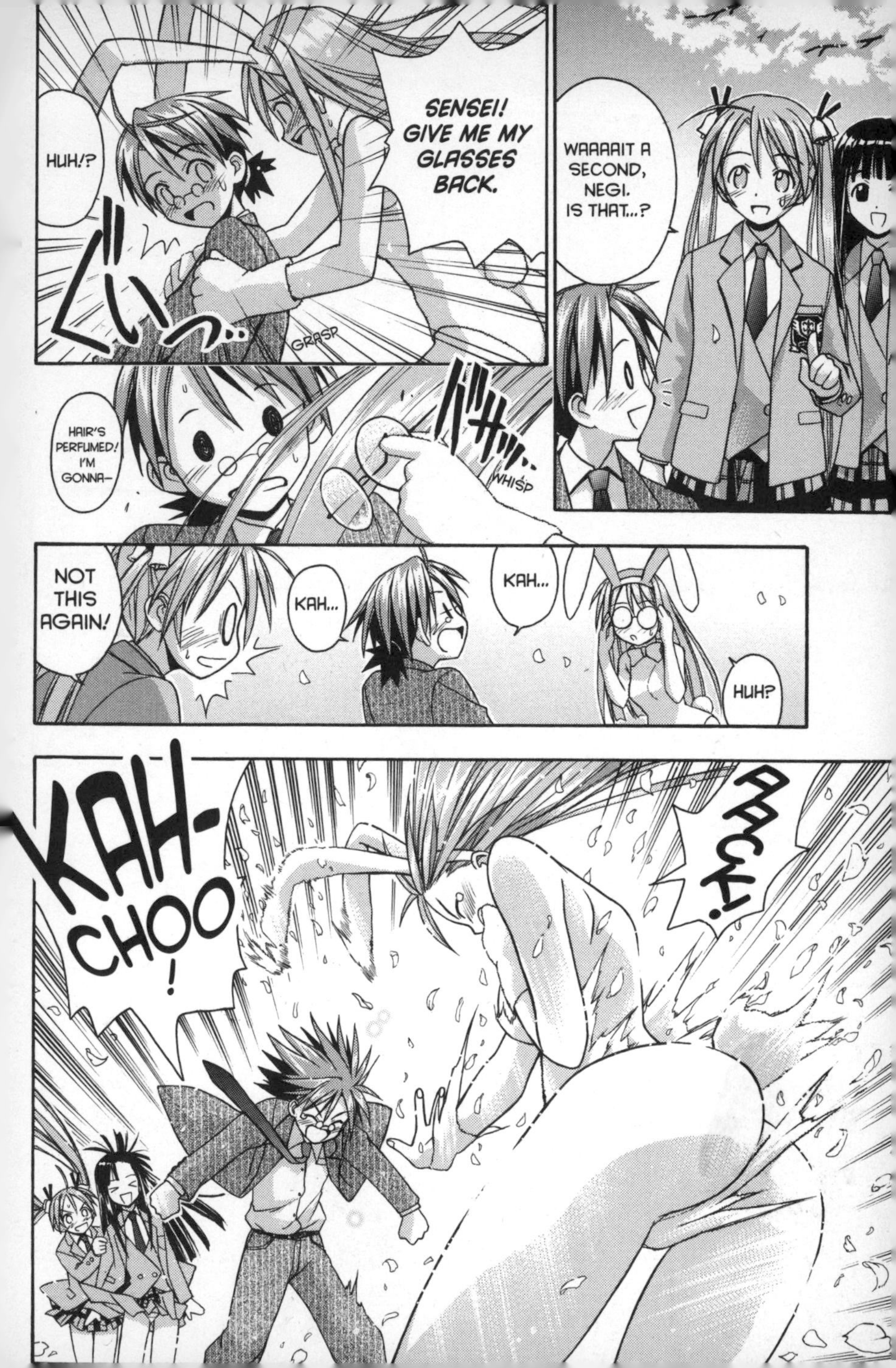

WAAAAIT A SECOND, NEGI. IS THAT...?
SENSEI! GIVE ME MY GLASSES BACK.
HUH!?
GRASP
WHISP
HAIR'S PERFUMED! I'M GONNA-
HUH?
KAH...
KAH...
NOT THIS AGAIN!
AACK!
KAH-CHOO!

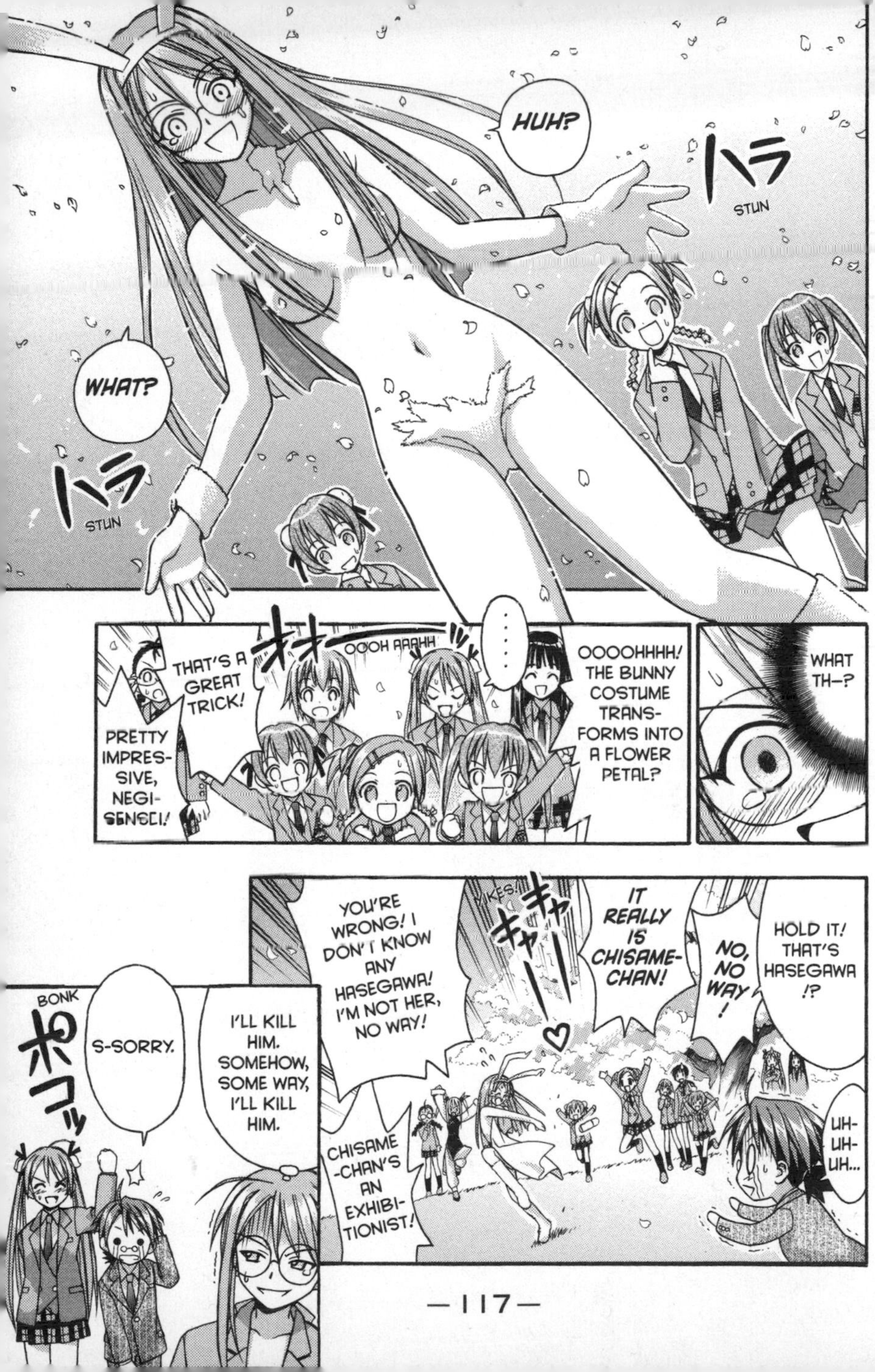

HUH?
ハラ
STUN
WHAT?
ハラ
STUN
WHAT TH–?
OOOOHHHH! THE BUNNY COSTUME TRANS-FORMS INTO A FLOWER PETAL?
......
ォォー
OOOH AAAHH
THAT'S A GREAT TRICK!
PRETTY IMPRES-SIVE, NEGI-SENSEI!
HOLD IT! THAT'S HASEGAWA!?
UH-UH-UH...
NO, NO WAY!
IT REALLY IS CHISAME-CHAN!
キャキャ
YIKES!
YOU'RE WRONG! I DON'T KNOW ANY HASEGAWA! I'M NOT HER, NO WAY!
CHISAME-CHAN'S AN EXHIBI-TIONIST!
I'LL KILL HIM. SOMEHOW, SOME WAY, I'LL KILL HIM.
S-SORRY.
ポコッ
BONK

STUDENT NUMBER 22
FUKA NARUTAKI (RIGHT)

BORN: DECEMBER 6, 1988
BLOOD TYPE: A
LIKES: PRANKS, SWEET THINGS
    DISLIKES: GHOSTS, KEEPING QUIET
    AFFILIATIONS: STROLLING CLUB
NOTE: EYESIGHT 1.2

STUDENT NUMBER 23
FUMIKA NARUTAKI (LEFT)

BORN: DECEMBER 6, 1988
BLOOD TYPE: A
LIKES: CLEANING, SWEET THINGS
DISLIKES: LONG, HAIRY THINGS
    (LIKE CATERPILLARS)
AFFILIATIONS: STROLLING CLUB, BEAUTIFICATION
    COMMITTEE

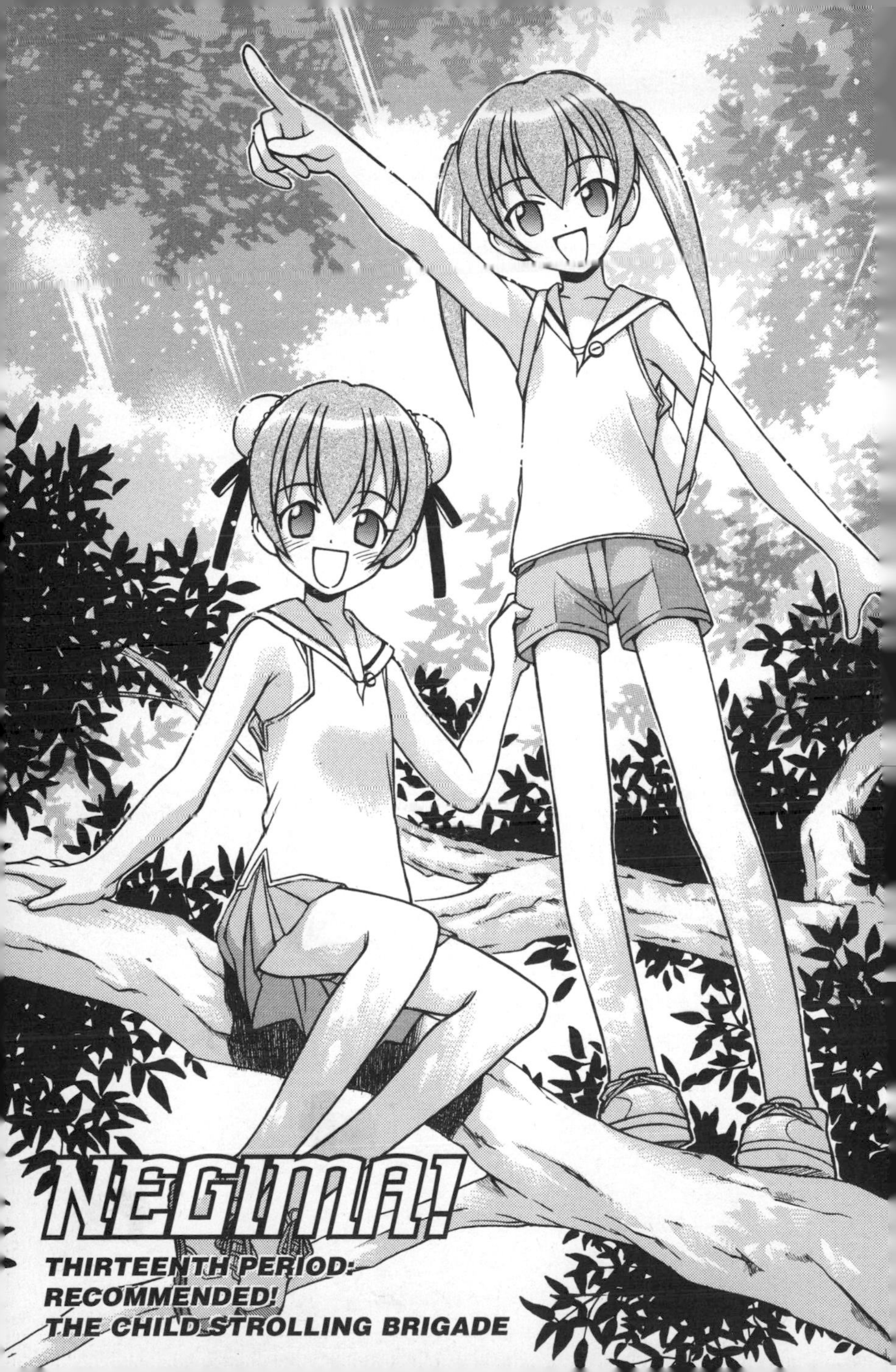
NEGIMA!
THIRTEENTH PERIOD:
RECOMMENDED!
THE CHILD STROLLING BRIGADE

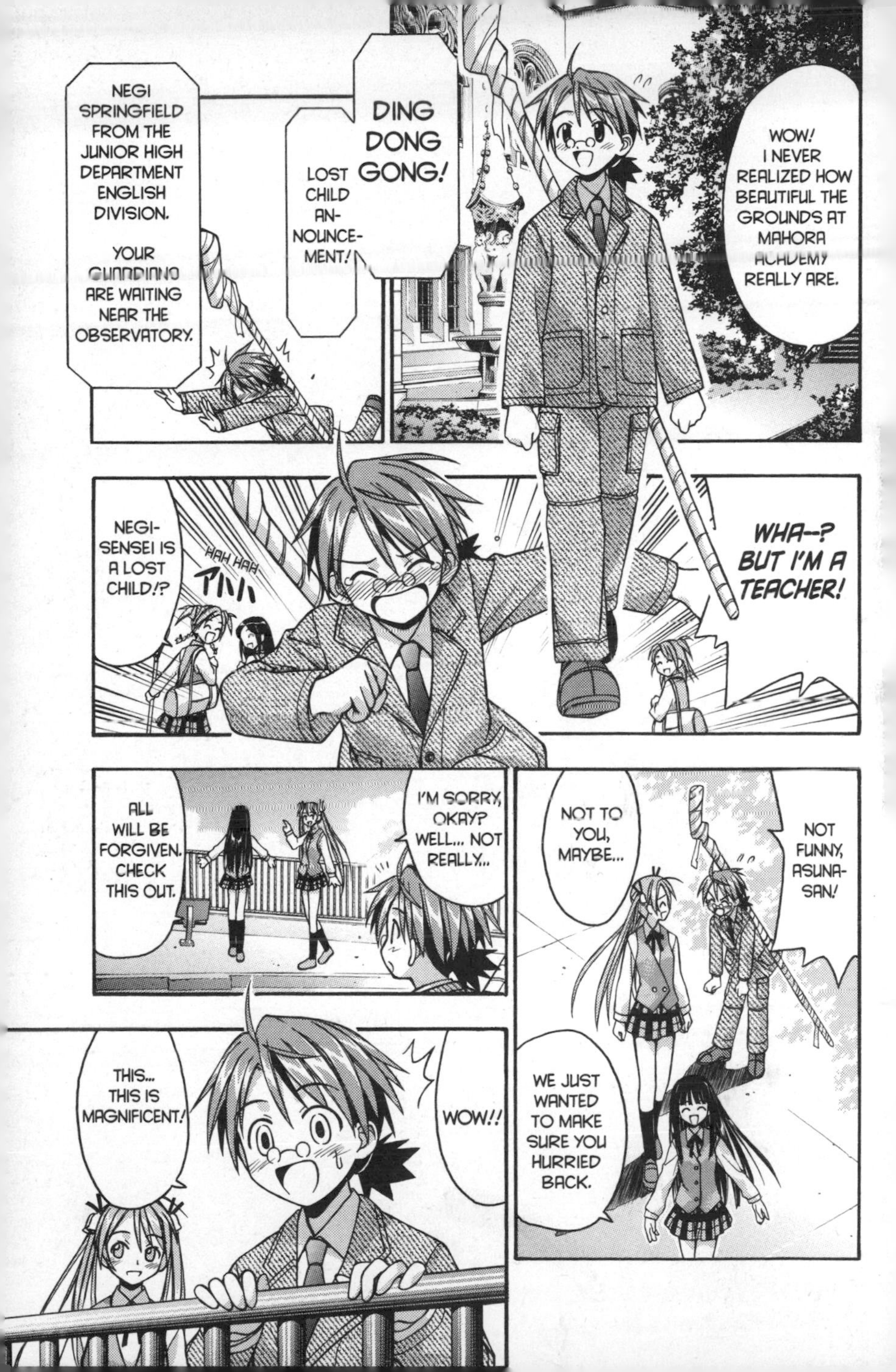
WOW! I NEVER REALIZED HOW BEAUTIFUL THE GROUNDS AT MAHORA ACADEMY REALLY ARE.
DING DONG GONG!
LOST CHILD AN-NOUNCE-MENT!
NEGI SPRINGFIELD FROM THE JUNIOR HIGH DEPARTMENT ENGLISH DIVISION.
YOUR GUARDIANS ARE WAITING NEAR THE OBSERVATORY.
WHA--? BUT I'M A TEACHER!
NEGI-SENSEI IS A LOST CHILD!?
HAH HAH
NOT FUNNY, ASUNA-SAN!
NOT TO YOU, MAYBE...
WE JUST WANTED TO MAKE SURE YOU HURRIED BACK.
I'M SORRY, OKAY? WELL... NOT REALLY...
ALL WILL BE FORGIVEN. CHECK THIS OUT.
WOW!!
THIS... THIS IS MAGNIFICENT!

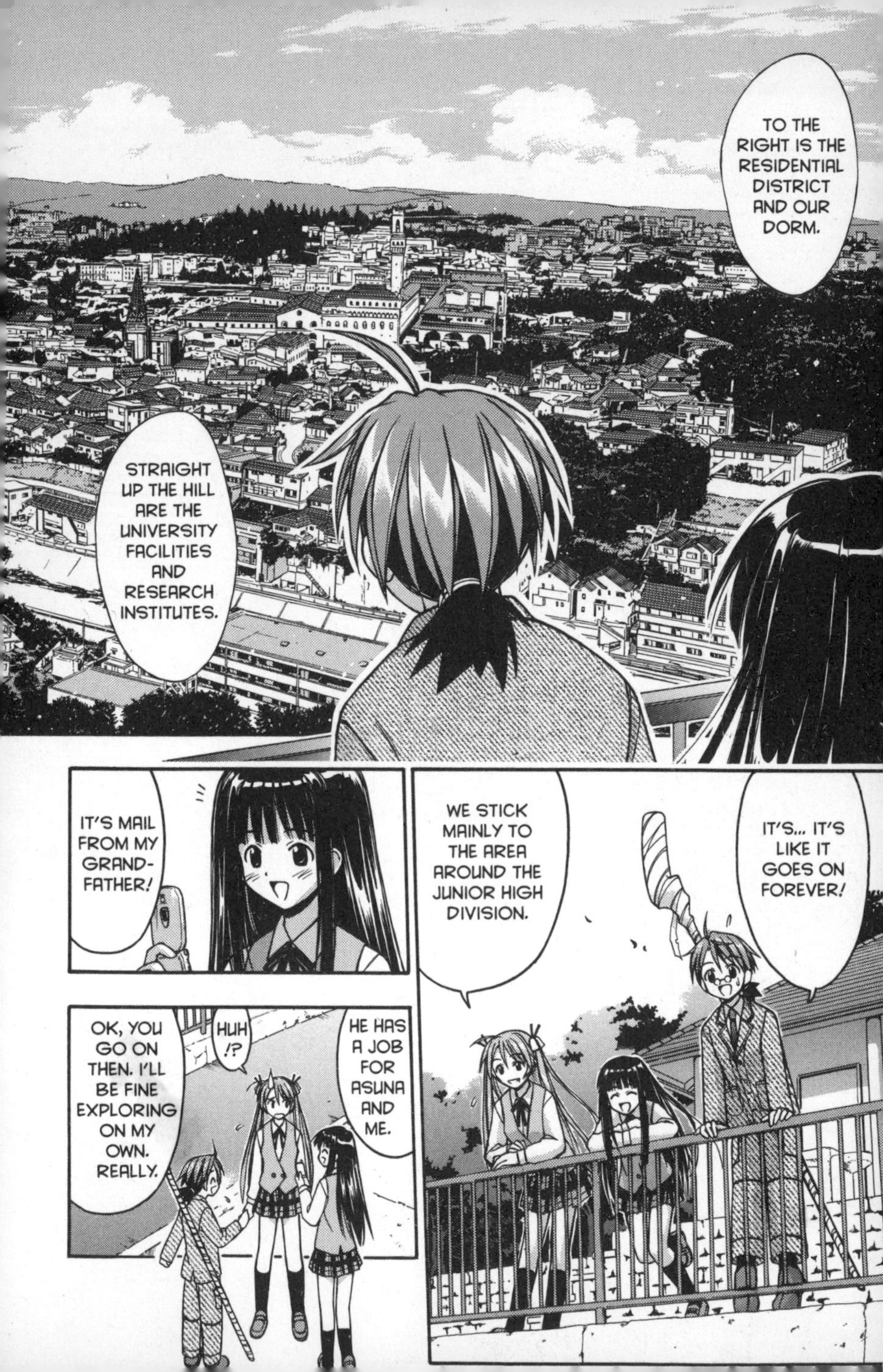
TO THE RIGHT IS THE RESIDENTIAL DISTRICT AND OUR DORM.
STRAIGHT UP THE HILL ARE THE UNIVERSITY FACILITIES AND RESEARCH INSTITUTES.
IT'S... IT'S LIKE IT GOES ON FOREVER!
WE STICK MAINLY TO THE AREA AROUND THE JUNIOR HIGH DIVISION.
IT'S MAIL FROM MY GRAND-FATHER!
HE HAS A JOB FOR ASUNA AND ME.
HUH!?
OK, YOU GO ON THEN. I'LL BE FINE EXPLORING ON MY OWN. REALLY.

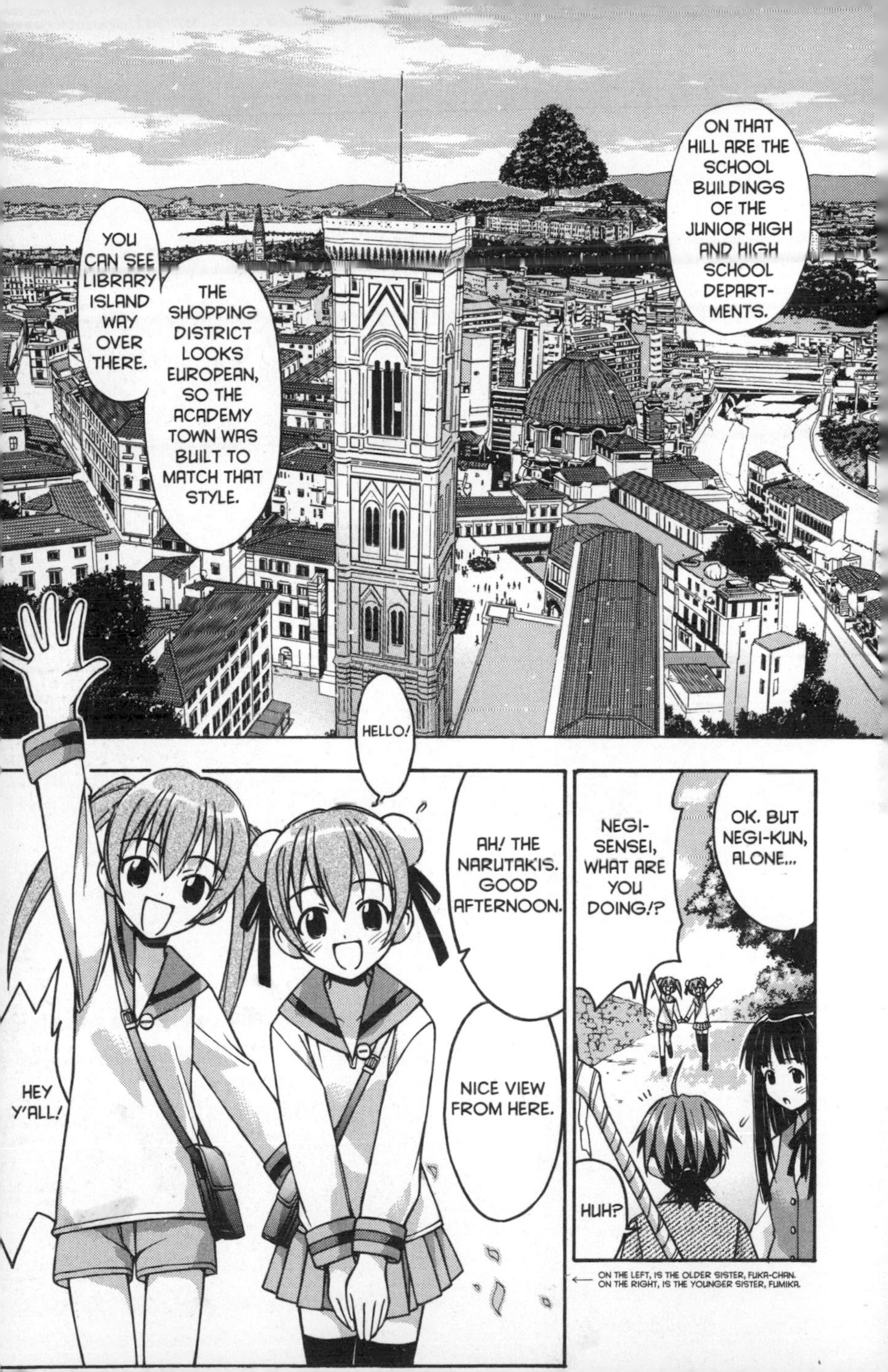

ON THAT HILL ARE THE SCHOOL BUILDINGS OF THE JUNIOR HIGH AND HIGH SCHOOL DEPART-MENTS.
YOU CAN SEE LIBRARY ISLAND WAY OVER THERE.
THE SHOPPING DISTRICT LOOKS EUROPEAN, SO THE ACADEMY TOWN WAS BUILT TO MATCH THAT STYLE.
OK. BUT NEGI-KUN, ALONE...
NEGI-SENSEI, WHAT ARE YOU DOING!?
HUH?
← ON THE LEFT, IS THE OLDER SISTER, FUKA-CHAN. ON THE RIGHT, IS THE YOUNGER SISTER, FUMIKA.
AH! THE NARUTAKIS. GOOD AFTERNOON.
NICE VIEW FROM HERE.
HELLO!
HEY Y'ALL!

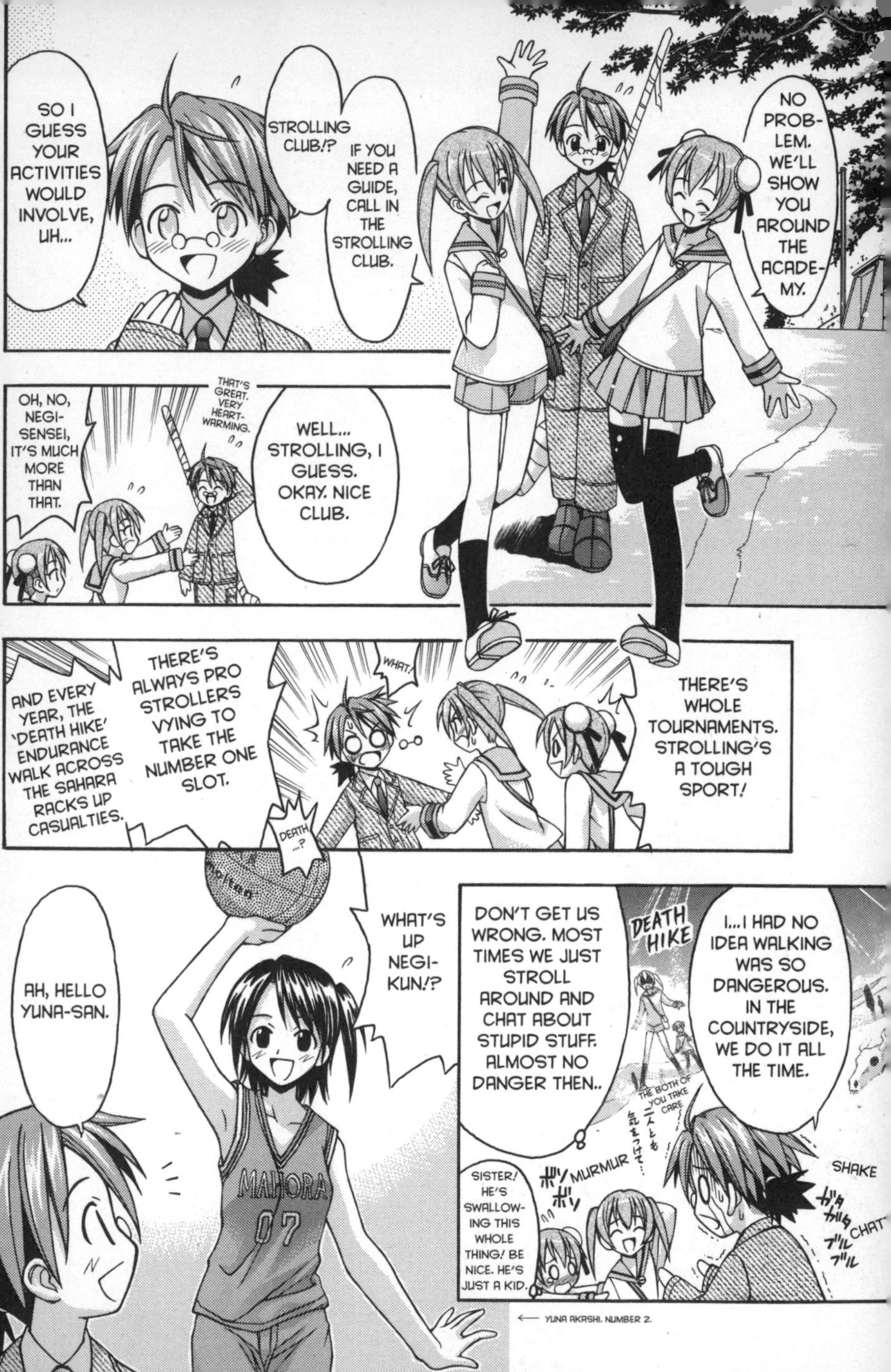

STROLLING CLUB!?
IF YOU NEED A GUIDE, CALL IN THE STROLLING CLUB.
NO PROBLEM. WE'LL SHOW YOU AROUND THE ACADEMY.
SO I GUESS YOUR ACTIVITIES WOULD INVOLVE, UH...
WELL... STROLLING, I GUESS. OKAY. NICE CLUB.
THAT'S GREAT. VERY HEART-WARMING.
OH, NO, NEGI-SENSEI, IT'S MUCH MORE THAN THAT.
THERE'S WHOLE TOURNAMENTS. STROLLING'S A TOUGH SPORT!
WHAT!
THERE'S ALWAYS PRO STROLLERS VYING TO TAKE THE NUMBER ONE SLOT.
AND EVERY YEAR, THE 'DEATH HIKE' ENDURANCE WALK ACROSS THE SAHARA RACKS UP CASUALTIES.
DEATH ...?
I...I HAD NO IDEA WALKING WAS SO DANGEROUS. IN THE COUNTRYSIDE, WE DO IT ALL THE TIME.
DEATH HIKE
DON'T GET US WRONG. MOST TIMES WE JUST STROLL AROUND AND CHAT ABOUT STUPID STUFF. ALMOST NO DANGER THEN..
二人とも気をつけて…
THE BOTH OF YOU TAKE CARE
ガタガタ
ブルブル
SHAKE
CHATT
ボソボソ
MURMUR
SISTER! HE'S SWALLOWING THIS WHOLE THING! BE NICE. HE'S JUST A KID.
WHAT'S UP NEGI-KUN!?
AH, HELLO YUNA-SAN.
MAHORA
07

← YUNA AKASHI. NUMBER 2.

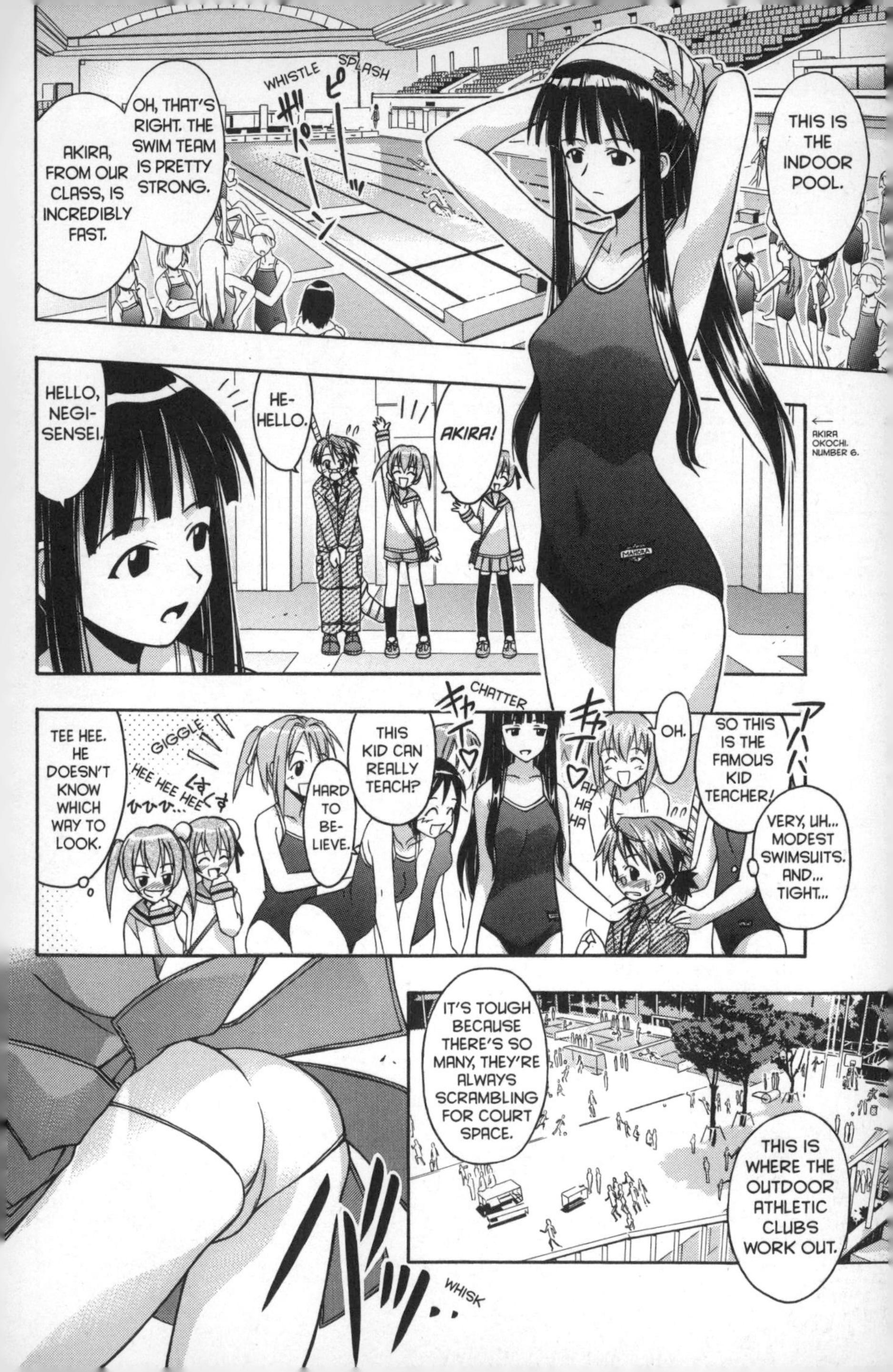
THIS IS THE INDOOR POOL.
WHISTLE
SPLASH
OH, THAT'S RIGHT. THE SWIM TEAM IS PRETTY STRONG.
AKIRA, FROM OUR CLASS, IS INCREDIBLY FAST.
AKIRA OKOCHI. NUMBER 6.
AKIRA!
HE-HELLO.
HELLO, NEGI-SENSEI.
SO THIS IS THE FAMOUS KID TEACHER!
OH.
CHATTER
VERY, UH... MODEST SWIMSUITS. AND... TIGHT...
AH HA HA
THIS KID CAN REALLY TEACH?
HARD TO BE-LIEVE.
GIGGLE
HEE HEE HEE
くすくす
ひひひ...
TEE HEE. HE DOESN'T KNOW WHICH WAY TO LOOK.
THIS IS WHERE THE OUTDOOR ATHLETIC CLUBS WORK OUT.
IT'S TOUGH BECAUSE THERE'S SO MANY, THEY'RE ALWAYS SCRAMBLING FOR COURT SPACE.
WHISK

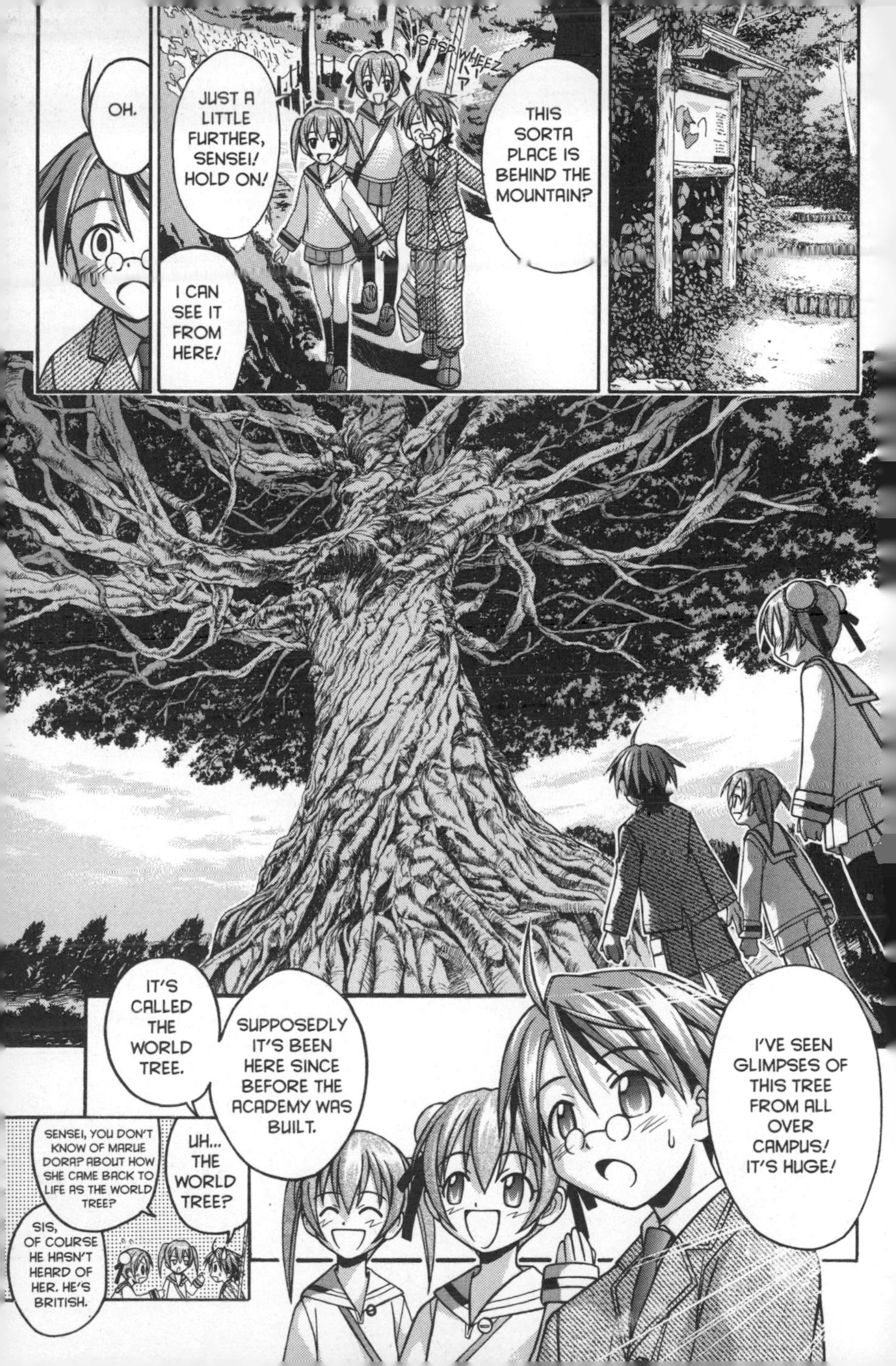
GASP WHEEZ
THIS SORTA PLACE IS BEHIND THE MOUNTAIN?
JUST A LITTLE FURTHER, SENSEI! HOLD ON!
I CAN SEE IT FROM HERE!
OH.
I'VE SEEN GLIMPSES OF THIS TREE FROM ALL OVER CAMPUS! IT'S HUGE!
SUPPOSEDLY IT'S BEEN HERE SINCE BEFORE THE ACADEMY WAS BUILT.
IT'S CALLED THE WORLD TREE.
UH... THE WORLD TREE?
SENSEI, YOU DON'T KNOW OF MARUE DORA? ABOUT HOW SHE CAME BACK TO LIFE AS THE WORLD TREE?
SIS, OF COURSE HE HASN'T HEARD OF HER. HE'S BRITISH.

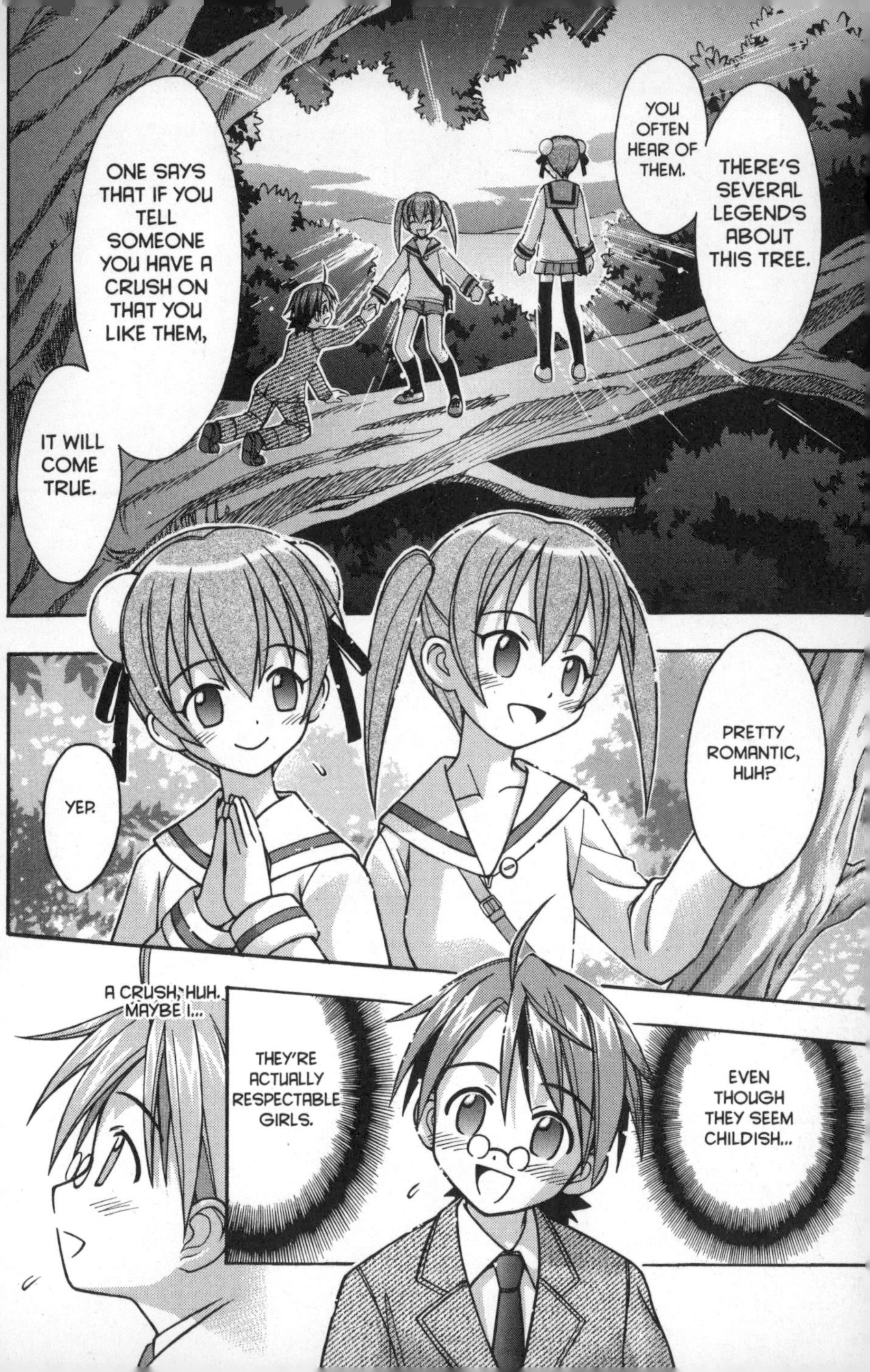
THERE'S SEVERAL LEGENDS ABOUT THIS TREE.
YOU OFTEN HEAR OF THEM.
ONE SAYS THAT IF YOU TELL SOMEONE YOU HAVE A CRUSH ON THAT YOU LIKE THEM,
IT WILL COME TRUE.
PRETTY ROMANTIC, HUH?
YEP.
EVEN THOUGH THEY SEEM CHILDISH...
THEY'RE ACTUALLY RESPECTABLE GIRLS.
A CRUSH, HUH. MAYBE I...

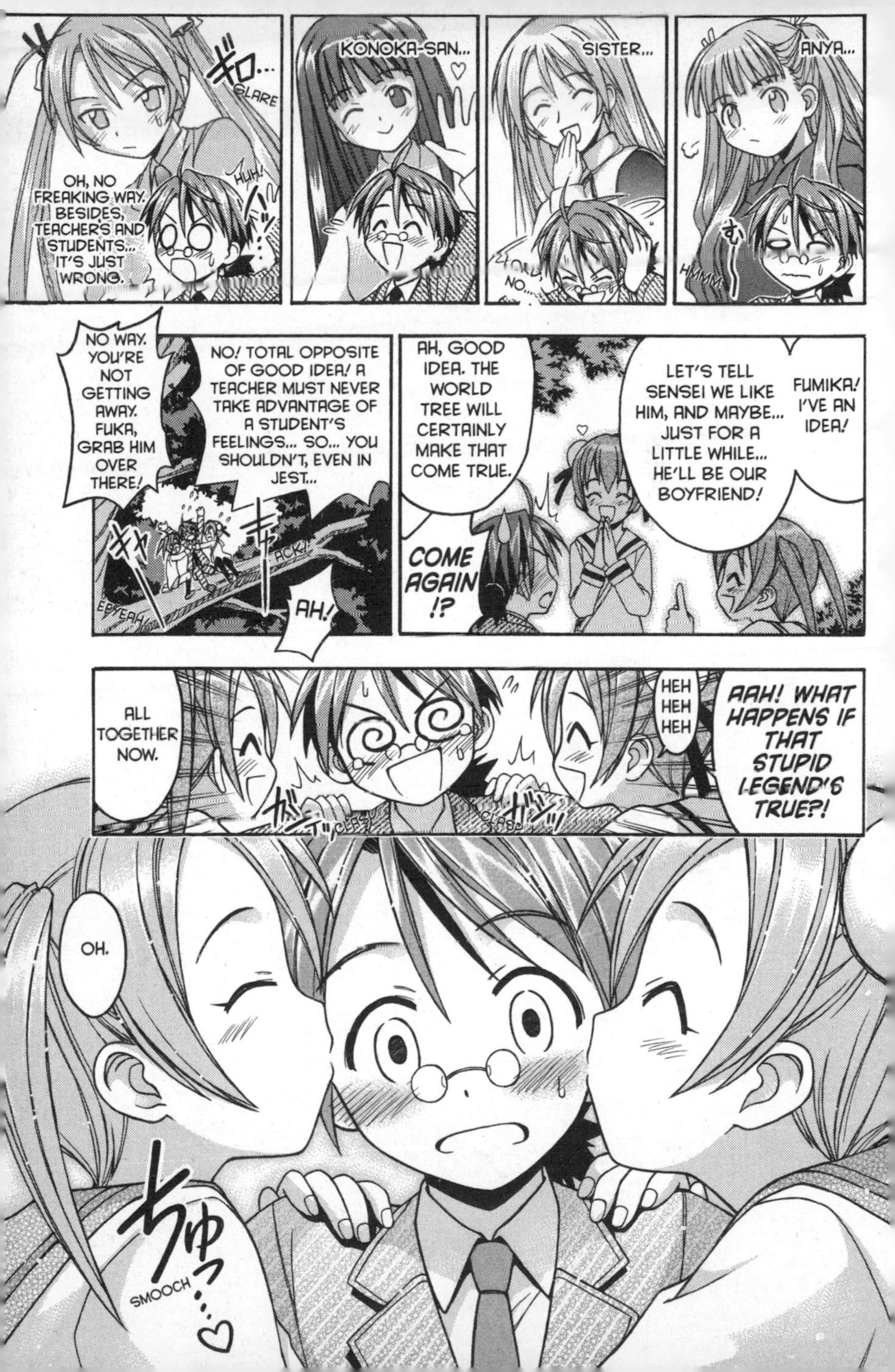
ANYA...
HMMM
SISTER...
NO...
KONOKA-SAN...
GLARE
OH, NO FREAKING WAY. BESIDES, TEACHERS AND STUDENTS... IT'S JUST WRONG.
HUH!
FUMIKA! I'VE AN IDEA!
LET'S TELL SENSEI WE LIKE HIM, AND MAYBE... JUST FOR A LITTLE WHILE... HE'LL BE OUR BOYFRIEND!
AH, GOOD IDEA. THE WORLD TREE WILL CERTAINLY MAKE THAT COME TRUE.
COME AGAIN!?
NO! TOTAL OPPOSITE OF GOOD IDEA! A TEACHER MUST NEVER TAKE ADVANTAGE OF A STUDENT'S FEELINGS... SO... YOU SHOULDN'T, EVEN IN JEST...
NO WAY. YOU'RE NOT GETTING AWAY. FUKA, GRAB HIM OVER THERE!
ACK!
EPYEAH
AH!
AAH! WHAT HAPPENS IF THAT STUPID LEGEND'S TRUE?!
HEH HEH HEH
ALL TOGETHER NOW.
CLASP
CLASP
OH.
SMOOCH

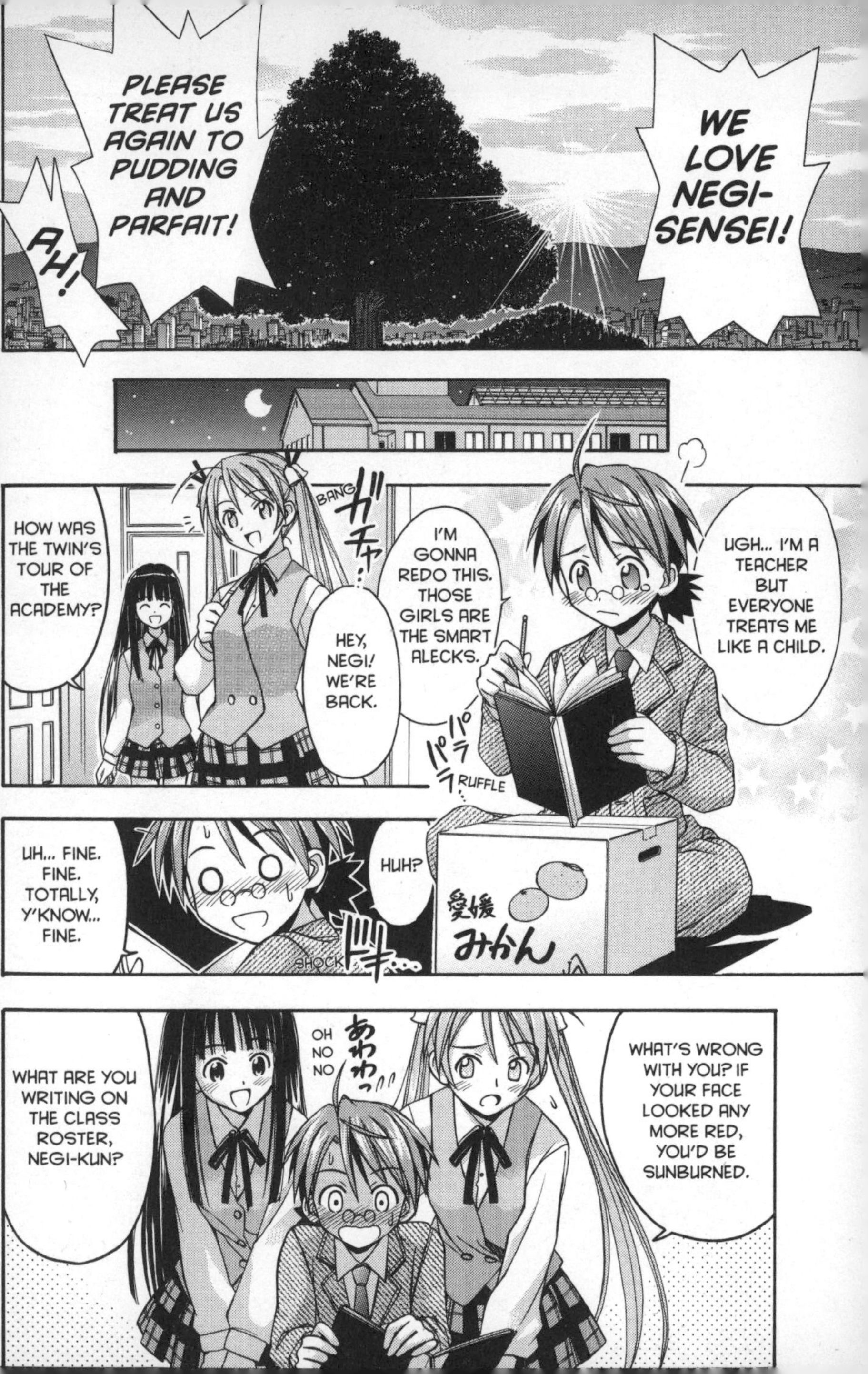
WE LOVE NEGI-SENSEI!
PLEASE TREAT US AGAIN TO PUDDING AND PARFAIT!
AH!
UGH... I'M A TEACHER BUT EVERYONE TREATS ME LIKE A CHILD.
I'M GONNA REDO THIS. THOSE GIRLS ARE THE SMART ALECKS.
パラ
パラ
RUFFLE
BANG
ガチャ
HEY, NEGI! WE'RE BACK.
HOW WAS THE TWIN'S TOUR OF THE ACADEMY?
愛媛
みかん
HUH?
ドキ
SHOCK
UH... FINE. FINE. TOTALLY, Y'KNOW... FINE.
WHAT'S WRONG WITH YOU? IF YOUR FACE LOOKED ANY MORE RED, YOU'D BE SUNBURNED.
あわわっ
OH NO NO
WHAT ARE YOU WRITING ON THE CLASS ROSTER, NEGI-KUN?

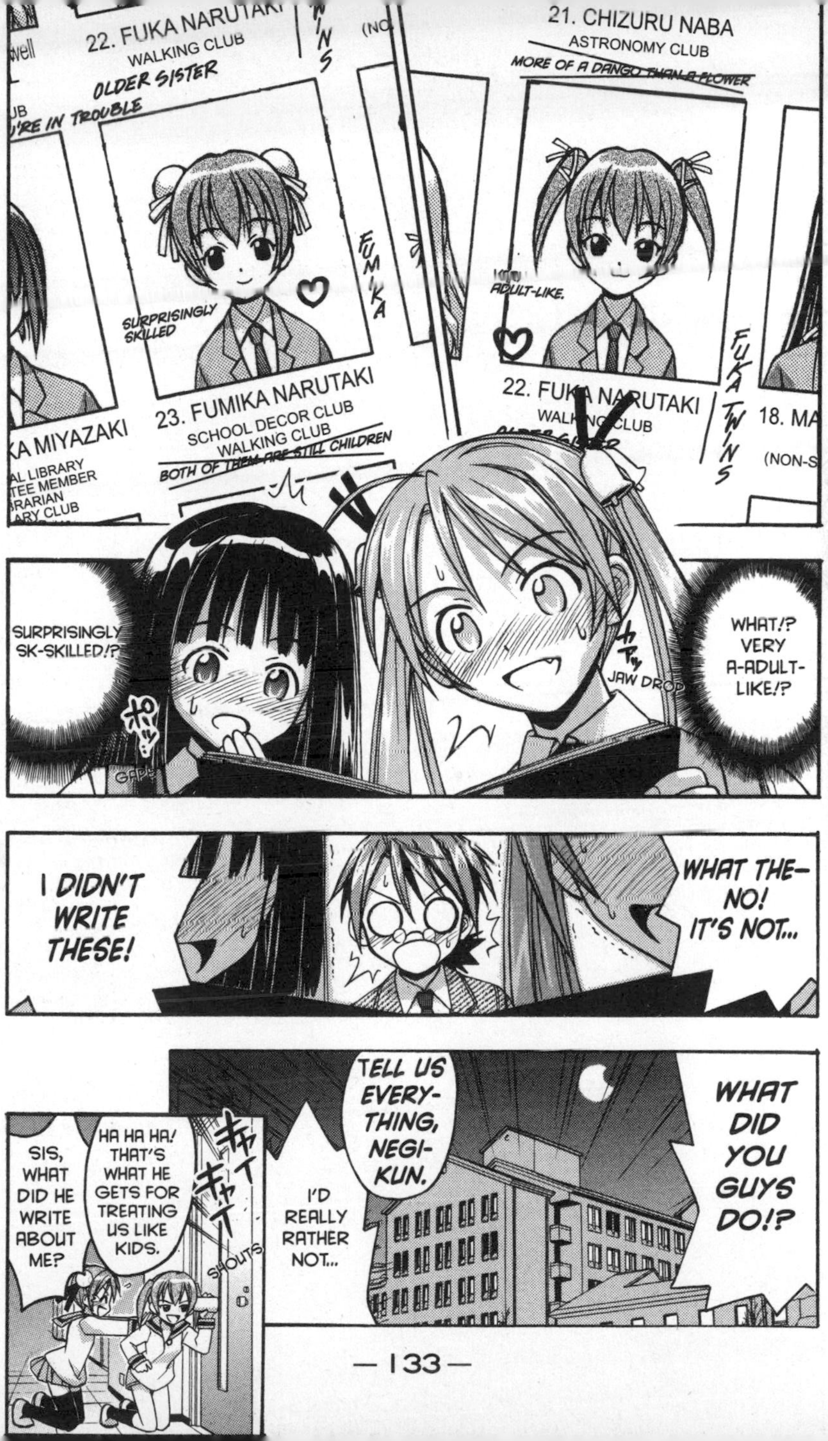

21. CHIZURU NABA
ASTRONOMY CLUB
MORE OF A DANGO THAN A FLOWER
FUKA TWINS
22. FUKA NARUTAKI
WALKING CLUB
ADULT-LIKE.
FUMIKA
22. FUKA NARUTAKI
WALKING CLUB
OLDER SISTER
SURPRISINGLY SKILLED
23. FUMIKA NARUTAKI
SCHOOL DECOR CLUB
WALKING CLUB
BOTH OF THEM ARE STILL CHILDREN
WHAT!? VERY A-ADULT-LIKE!?
JAW DROP
SURPRISINGLY SK-SKILLED!?
GAPE
WHAT THE— NO! IT'S NOT...
I DIDN'T WRITE THESE!
WHAT DID YOU GUYS DO!?
TELL US EVERYTHING, NEGI-KUN.
I'D REALLY RATHER NOT...
SHOUTS
HA HA HA! THAT'S WHAT HE GETS FOR TREATING US LIKE KIDS.
SIS, WHAT DID HE WRITE ABOUT ME?

STUDENT NUMBER 29
AYAKA YUKIHIRO

BORN: JULY 5, 1988
BLOOD TYPE: O
LIKES: NEGI-SENSEI, FLOWERS, PURE AND
     INNOCENT BOYS
DISLIKES: VIOLENT AND DISORDERLY PEOPLE
AFFILIATIONS: EQUESTRIAN CLUB, FLOWER
     ARRANGEMENT CLUB
NOTES: SECOND DAUGHTER OF THE YUKIHIRO
     ZAIBATSU, OWNER OF A BUSINESS
     MONOPOLY FORMED DURING WAR TIME.
     BEAUTIFUL APPEARANCE, CLEAR-HEADED
     (RANKED 4TH), IS MADLY IN LOVE
     WITH NEGI-SENSEI.

NEGIMA!

FOURTEENTH PERIOD: YESTERDAY'S ENEMY IS TOMORROW'S NEMESIS

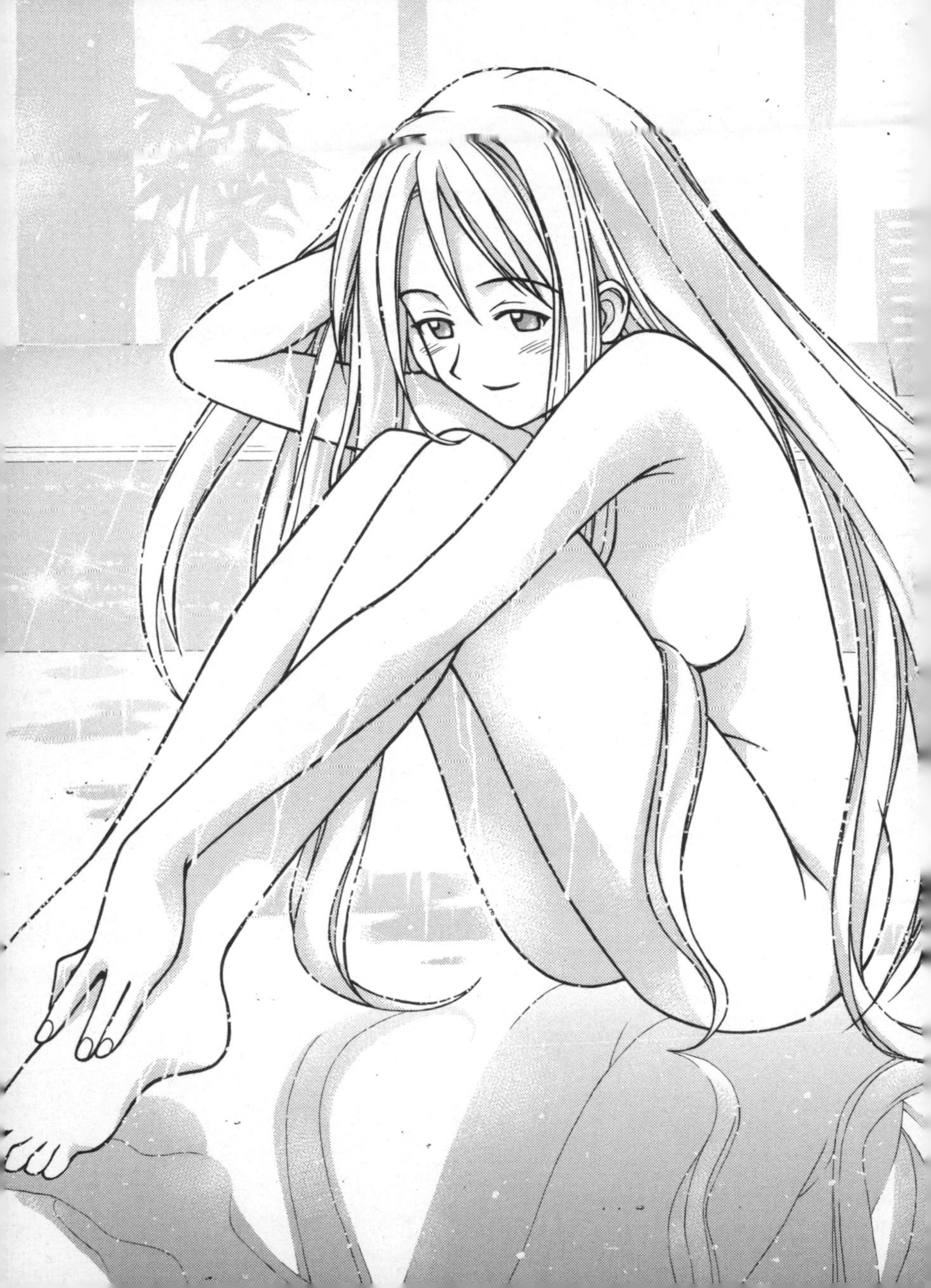

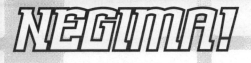

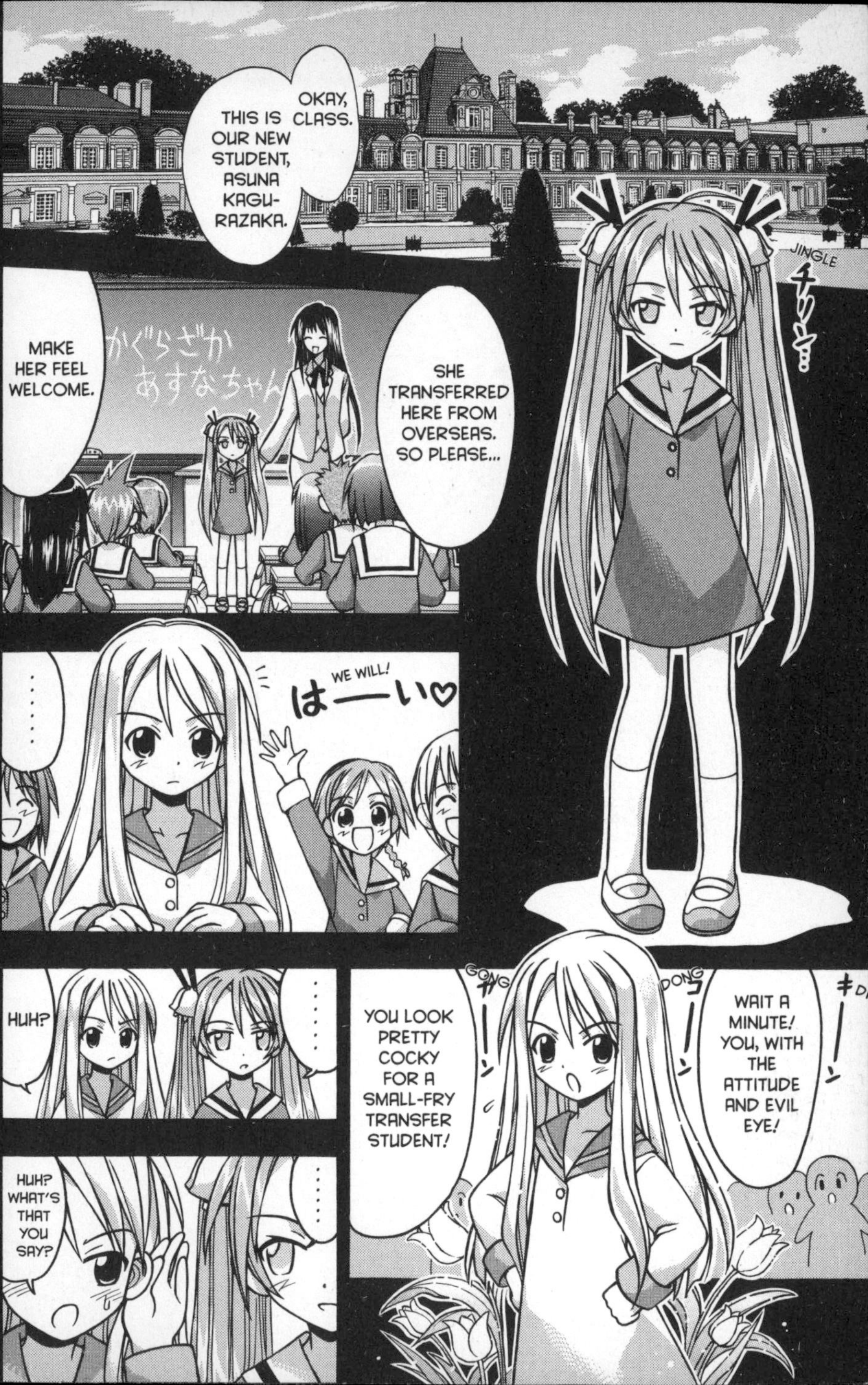
OKAY, CLASS.
THIS IS OUR NEW STUDENT, ASUNA KAGURAZAKA.
JINGLE
チリ〜ン…
かぐらざか
あすなちゃん
SHE TRANSFERRED HERE FROM OVERSEAS. SO PLEASE...
MAKE HER FEEL WELCOME.
WE WILL!
はーい♡
......
WAIT A MINUTE! YOU, WITH THE ATTITUDE AND EVIL EYE!
GONG
DONG
YOU LOOK PRETTY COCKY FOR A SMALL-FRY TRANSFER STUDENT!
......
HUH?
......
HUH? WHAT'S THAT YOU SAY?

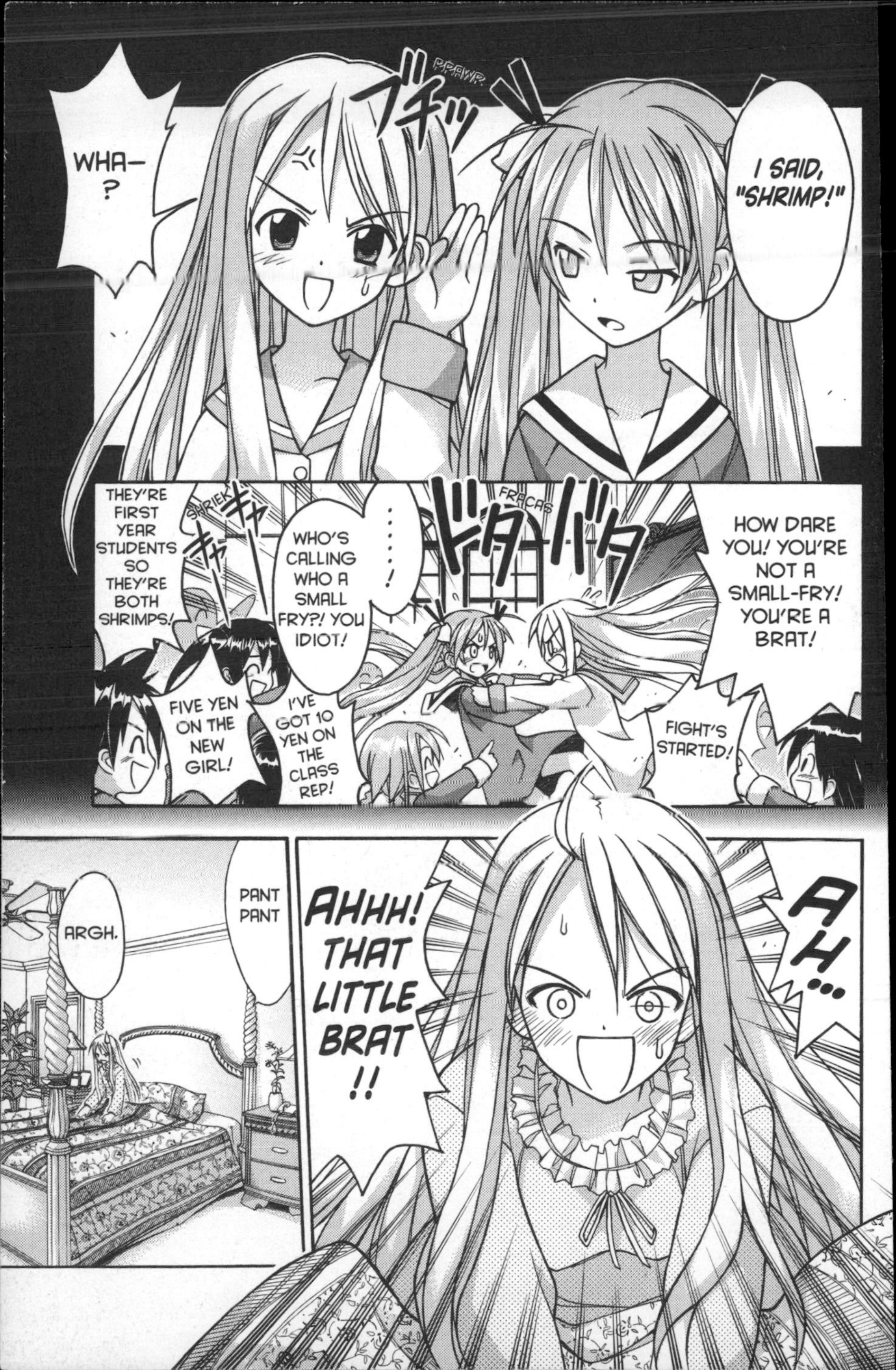

I SAID, "SHRIMP!"
PPRAWR
WHA—?
FRACAS
HOW DARE YOU! YOU'RE NOT A SMALL-FRY! YOU'RE A BRAT!
......!
WHO'S CALLING WHO A SMALL FRY?! YOU IDIOT!
SHRIEK
THEY'RE FIRST YEAR STUDENTS SO THEY'RE BOTH SHRIMPS!
FIGHT'S STARTED!
I'VE GOT 10 YEN ON THE CLASS REP!
FIVE YEN ON THE NEW GIRL!
AH...
AHHH! THAT LITTLE BRAT!!
PANT PANT
ARGH.

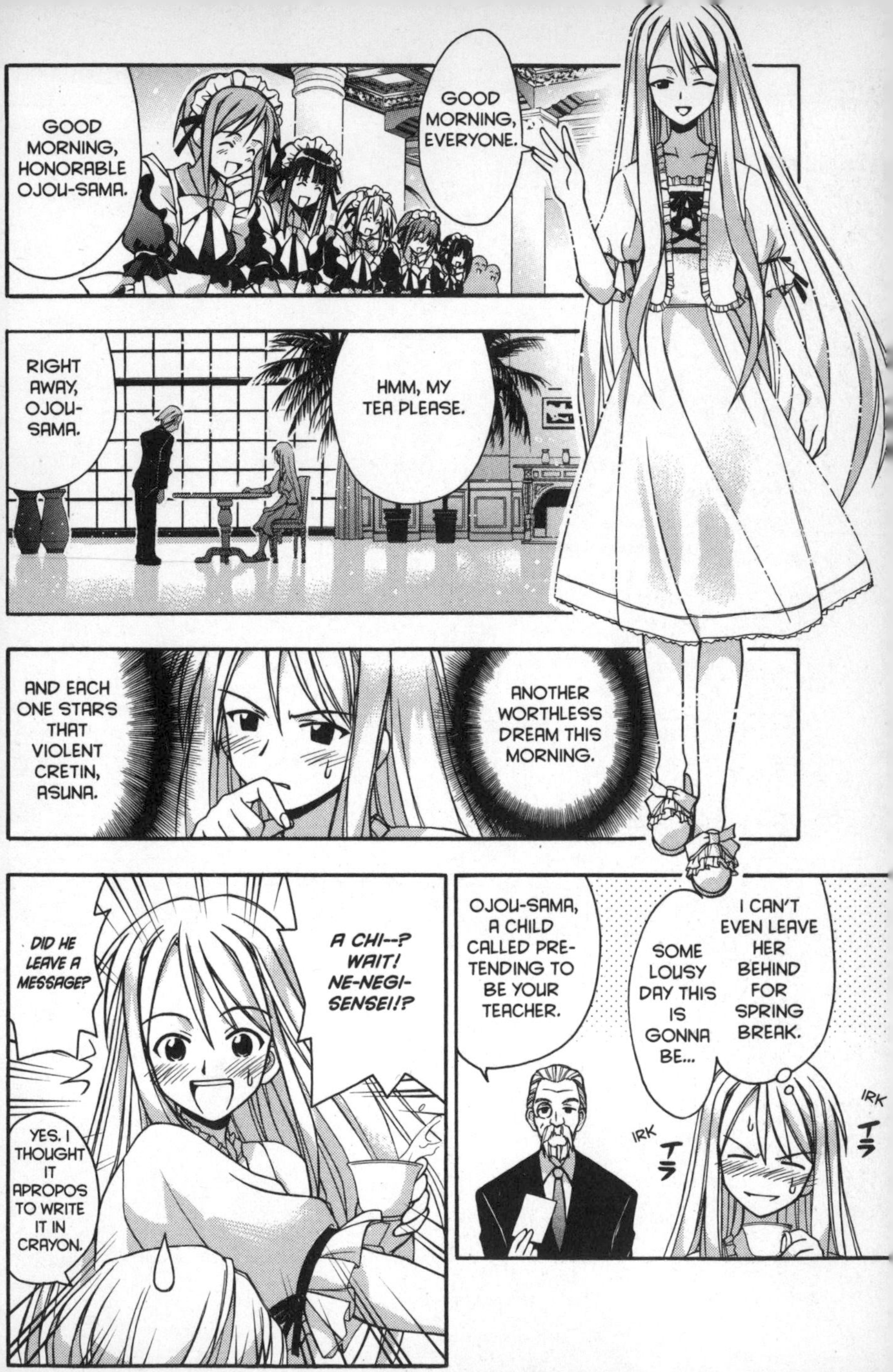
GOOD MORNING, EVERYONE.
GOOD MORNING, HONORABLE OJOU-SAMA.
HMM, MY TEA PLEASE.
RIGHT AWAY, OJOU-SAMA.
ANOTHER WORTHLESS DREAM THIS MORNING.
AND EACH ONE STARS THAT VIOLENT CRETIN, ASUNA.
I CAN'T EVEN LEAVE HER BEHIND FOR SPRING BREAK.
SOME LOUSY DAY THIS IS GONNA BE...
IRK
OJOU-SAMA, A CHILD CALLED PRE-TENDING TO BE YOUR TEACHER.
IRK
A CHI--? WAIT! NE-NEGI-SENSEI!?
DID HE LEAVE A MESSAGE?
YES. I THOUGHT IT APROPOS TO WRITE IT IN CRAYON.

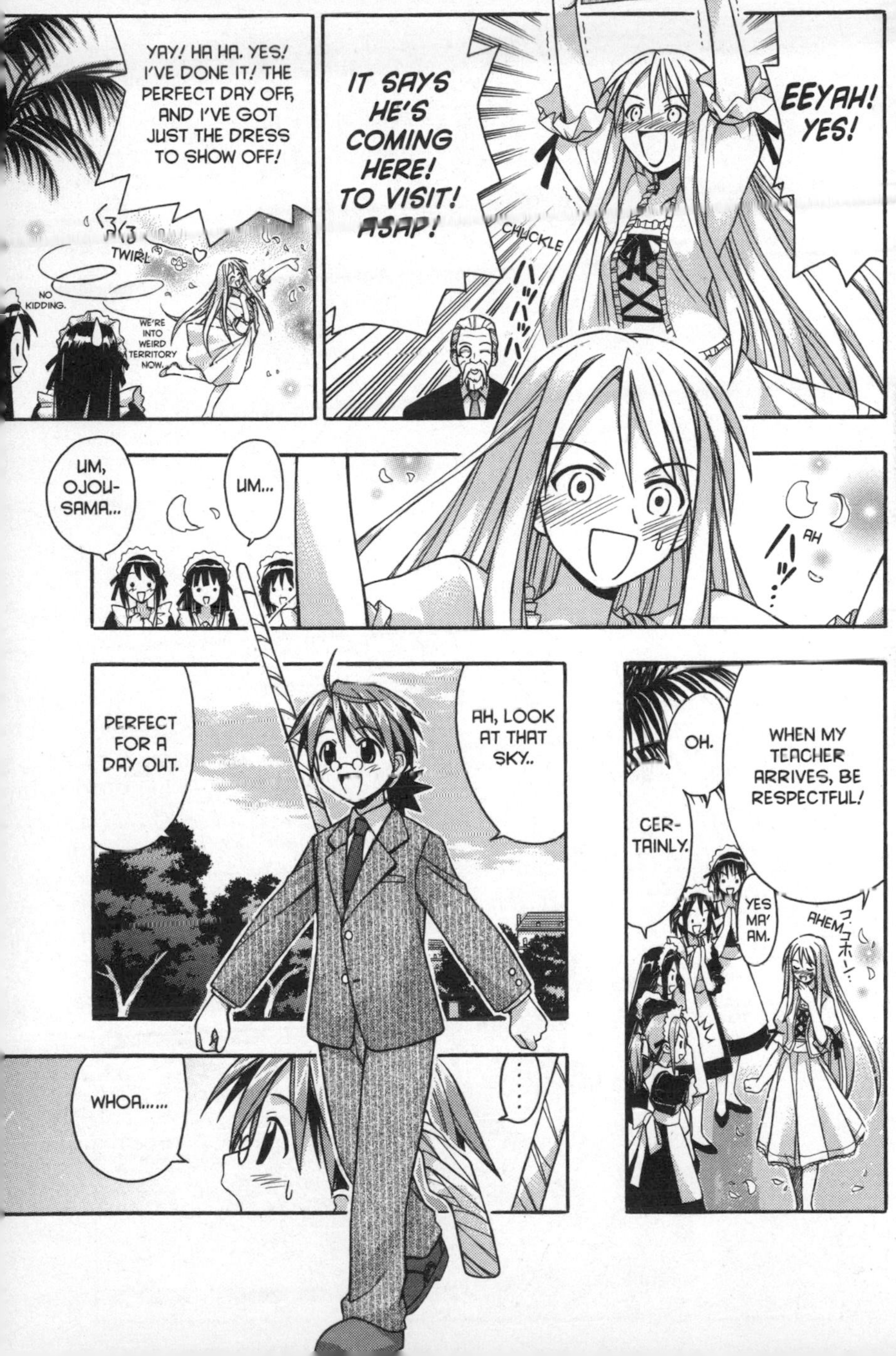
EEYAH! YES!
IT SAYS HE'S COMING HERE! TO VISIT! ASAP!
CHUCKLE
ハッハッハ
YAY! HA HA. YES! I'VE DONE IT! THE PERFECT DAY OFF, AND I'VE GOT JUST THE DRESS TO SHOW OFF!
TWIRL
NO KIDDING.
WE'RE INTO WEIRD TERRITORY NOW.
AH
UM...
UM, OJOU-SAMA...
OH.
WHEN MY TEACHER ARRIVES, BE RESPECTFUL!
CERTAINLY.
YES MA'AM.
AHEM
AH, LOOK AT THAT SKY..
PERFECT FOR A DAY OUT.
......
WHOA......

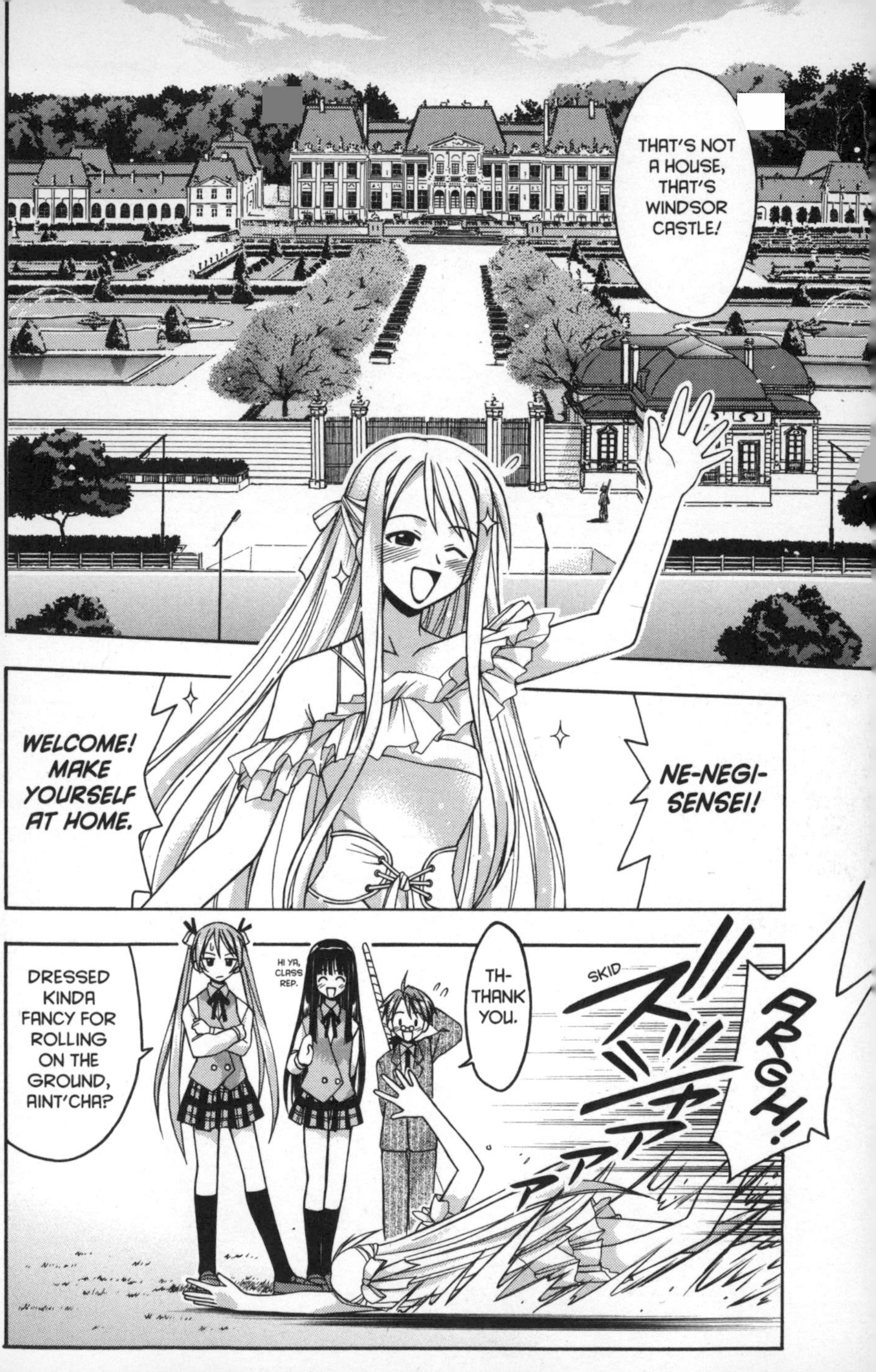

THAT'S NOT A HOUSE, THAT'S WINDSOR CASTLE!
NE-NEGI-SENSEI!
WELCOME! MAKE YOURSELF AT HOME.
ARGH!
SKID
TH-THANK YOU.
HI YA, CLASS REP.
DRESSED KINDA FANCY FOR ROLLING ON THE GROUND, AINT'CHA?

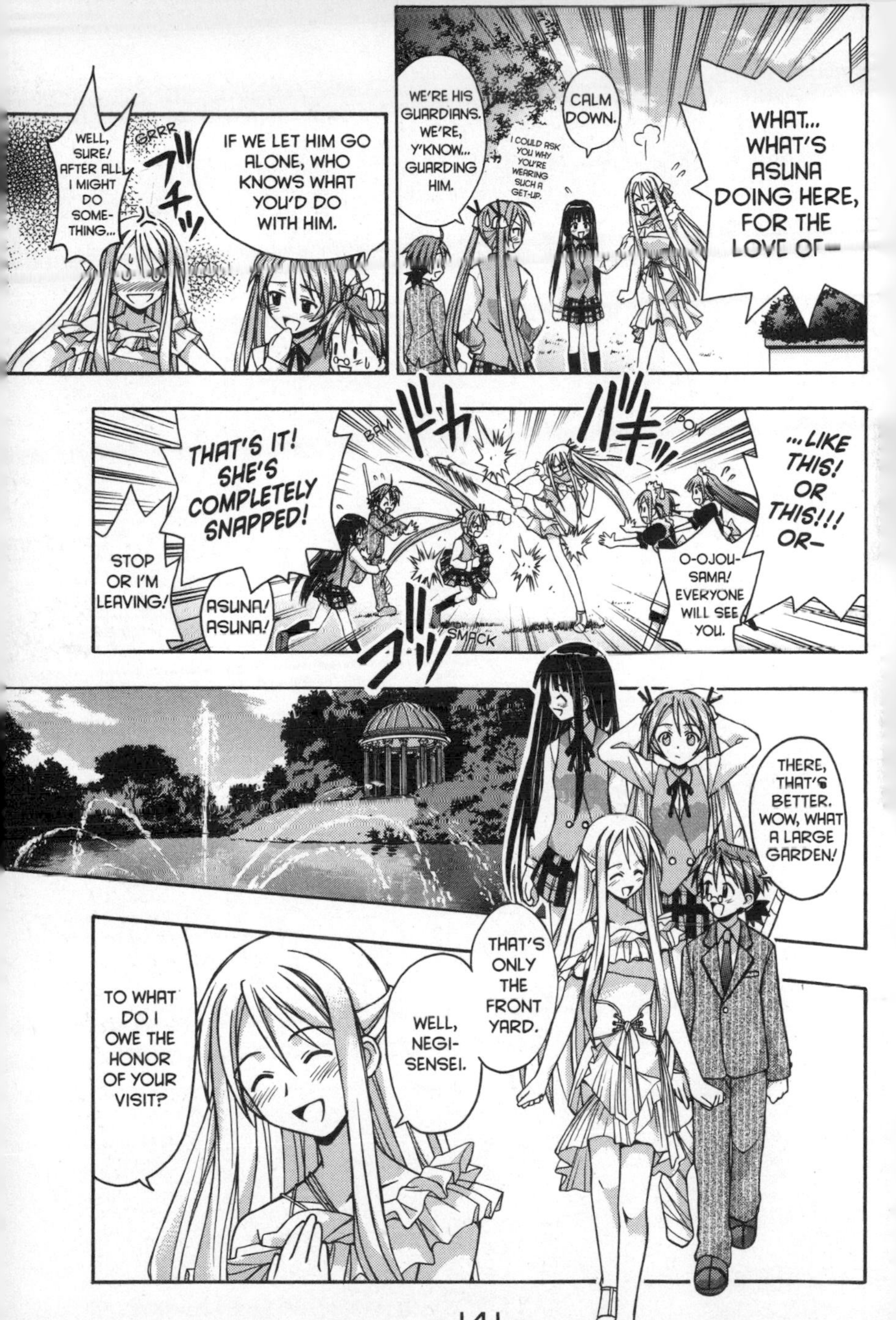
WHAT... WHAT'S ASUNA DOING HERE, FOR THE LOVE OF—
CALM DOWN.
I COULD ASK YOU WHY YOU'RE WEARING SUCH A GET-UP.
WE'RE HIS GUARDIANS. WE'RE, Y'KNOW... GUARDING HIM.
IF WE LET HIM GO ALONE, WHO KNOWS WHAT YOU'D DO WITH HIM.
GRRR
WELL, SURE! AFTER ALL I MIGHT DO SOME-THING...
...LIKE THIS! OR THIS!!! OR—
O-OJOU-SAMA! EVERYONE WILL SEE YOU.
PON
BAM
THAT'S IT! SHE'S COMPLETELY SNAPPED!
ASUNA! ASUNA!
STOP OR I'M LEAVING!
SMACK
THERE, THAT'S BETTER. WOW, WHAT A LARGE GARDEN!
THAT'S ONLY THE FRONT YARD.
WELL, NEGI-SENSEI.
TO WHAT DO I OWE THE HONOR OF YOUR VISIT?

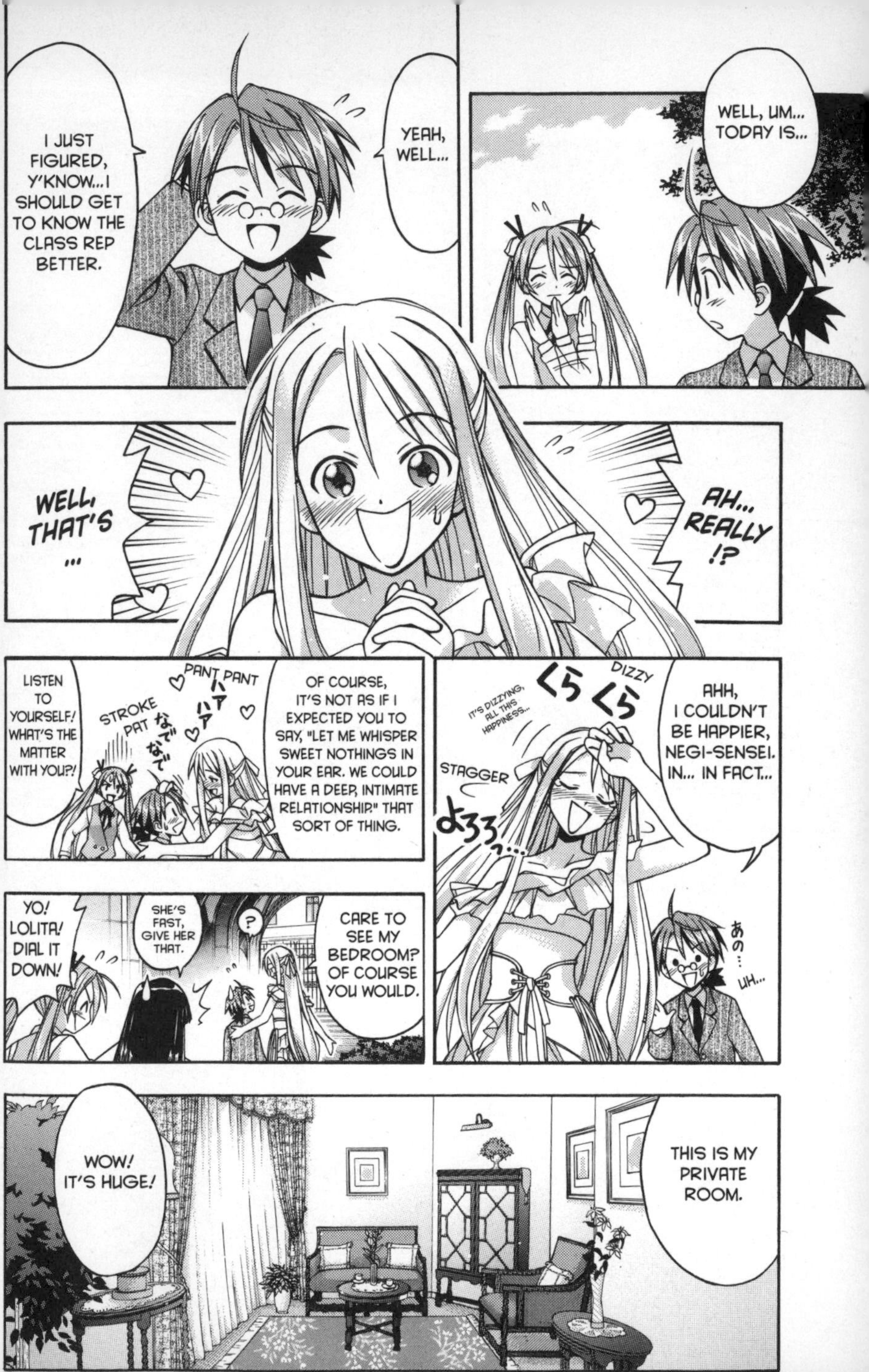

WELL, UM... TODAY IS...
YEAH, WELL...
I JUST FIGURED, Y'KNOW...I SHOULD GET TO KNOW THE CLASS REP BETTER.
AH... REALLY !?
WELL, THAT'S ...
AHH, I COULDN'T BE HAPPIER, NEGI-SENSEI. IN... IN FACT...
DIZZY
くら くら
IT'S DIZZYING, ALL THIS HAPPINESS...
STAGGER
よろろ…
あの… UH...
OF COURSE, IT'S NOT AS IF I EXPECTED YOU TO SAY, "LET ME WHISPER SWEET NOTHINGS IN YOUR EAR. WE COULD HAVE A DEEP, INTIMATE RELATIONSHIP." THAT SORT OF THING.
PANT PANT
ハアハア
STROKE PAT
なでなで
LISTEN TO YOURSELF! WHAT'S THE MATTER WITH YOU?!
CARE TO SEE MY BEDROOM? OF COURSE YOU WOULD.
?
SHE'S FAST, GIVE HER THAT.
YO! LOLITA! DIAL IT DOWN!
THIS IS MY PRIVATE ROOM.
WOW! IT'S HUGE!

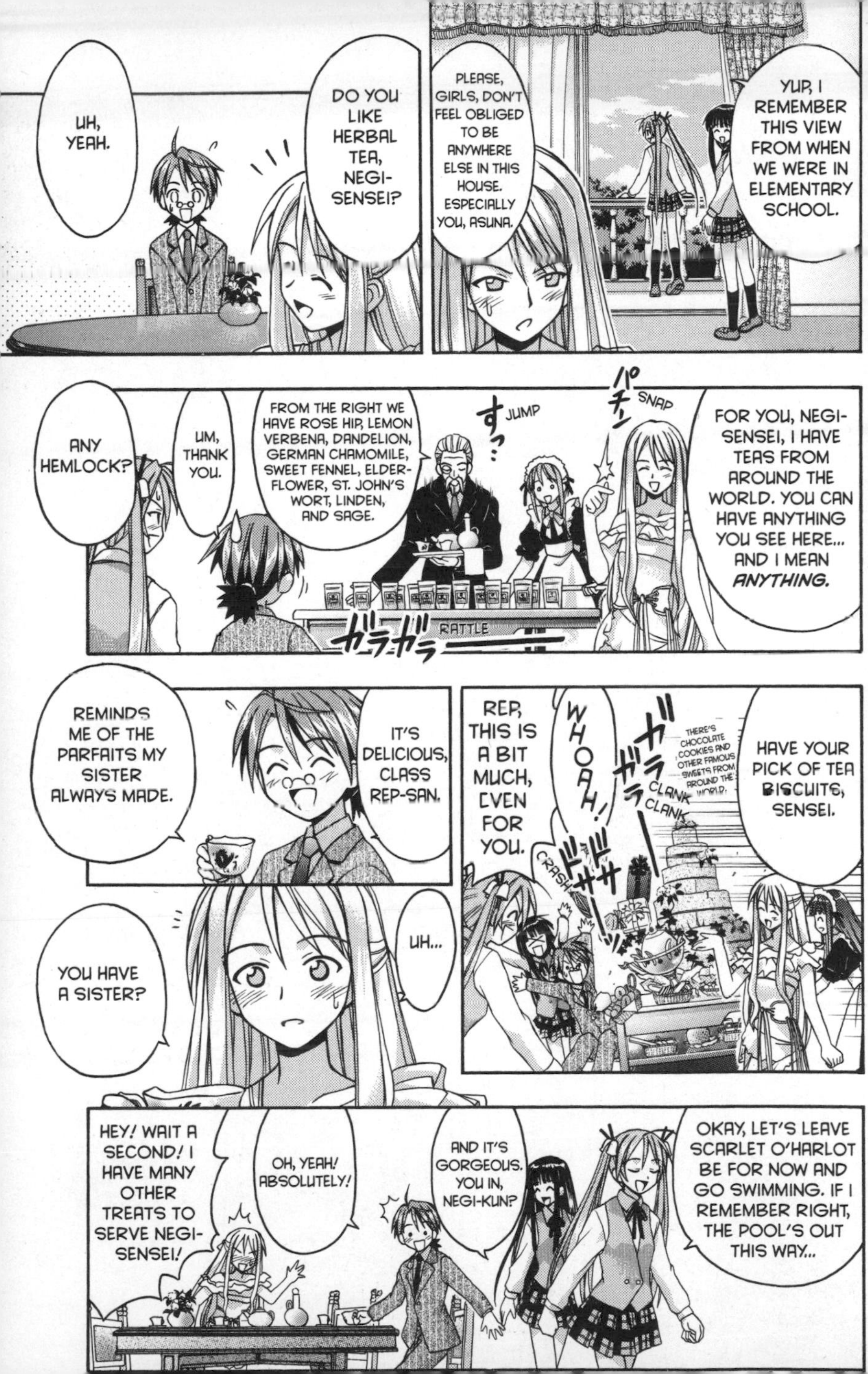
YUP, I REMEMBER THIS VIEW FROM WHEN WE WERE IN ELEMENTARY SCHOOL.
PLEASE, GIRLS, DON'T FEEL OBLIGED TO BE ANYWHERE ELSE IN THIS HOUSE. ESPECIALLY YOU, ASUNA.
DO YOU LIKE HERBAL TEA, NEGI-SENSEI?
UH, YEAH.
SNAP
FOR YOU, NEGI-SENSEI, I HAVE TEAS FROM AROUND THE WORLD. YOU CAN HAVE ANYTHING YOU SEE HERE... AND I MEAN ANYTHING.
JUMP
FROM THE RIGHT WE HAVE ROSE HIP, LEMON VERBENA, DANDELION, GERMAN CHAMOMILE, SWEET FENNEL, ELDER-FLOWER, ST. JOHN'S WORT, LINDEN, AND SAGE.
UM, THANK YOU.
ANY HEMLOCK?
RATTLE
HAVE YOUR PICK OF TEA BISCUITS, SENSEI.
THERE'S CHOCOLATE COOKIES AND OTHER FAMOUS SWEETS FROM AROUND THE WORLD.
CLANK CLANK
WHOAH!
CRASH
REP, THIS IS A BIT MUCH, EVEN FOR YOU.
IT'S DELICIOUS, CLASS REP-SAN.
REMINDS ME OF THE PARFAITS MY SISTER ALWAYS MADE.
UH...
YOU HAVE A SISTER?
OKAY, LET'S LEAVE SCARLET O'HARLOT BE FOR NOW AND GO SWIMMING. IF I REMEMBER RIGHT, THE POOL'S OUT THIS WAY...
AND IT'S GORGEOUS. YOU IN, NEGI-KUN?
OH, YEAH! ABSOLUTELY!
HEY! WAIT A SECOND! I HAVE MANY OTHER TREATS TO SERVE NEGI-SENSEI!

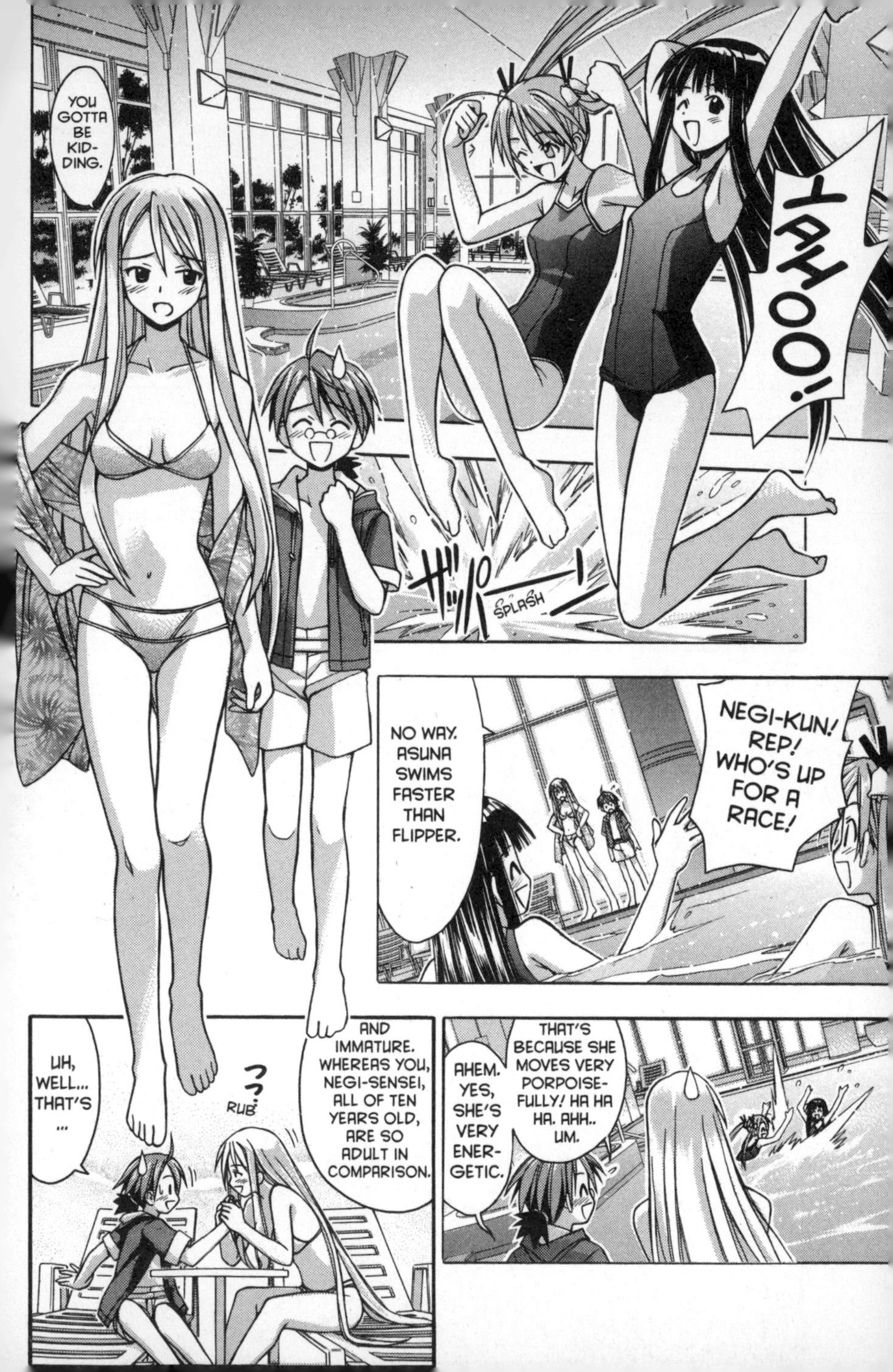
YAHOO!
SPLASH
YOU GOTTA BE KID-DING.
NEGI-KUN! REP! WHO'S UP FOR A RACE!
NO WAY. ASUNA SWIMS FASTER THAN FLIPPER.
THAT'S BECAUSE SHE MOVES VERY PORPOISE-FULLY! HA HA HA. AHH.. UM.
AHEM. YES, SHE'S VERY ENER-GETIC.
AND IMMATURE. WHEREAS YOU, NEGI-SENSEI, ALL OF TEN YEARS OLD, ARE SO ADULT IN COMPARISON.
RUB
UH, WELL... THAT'S ...

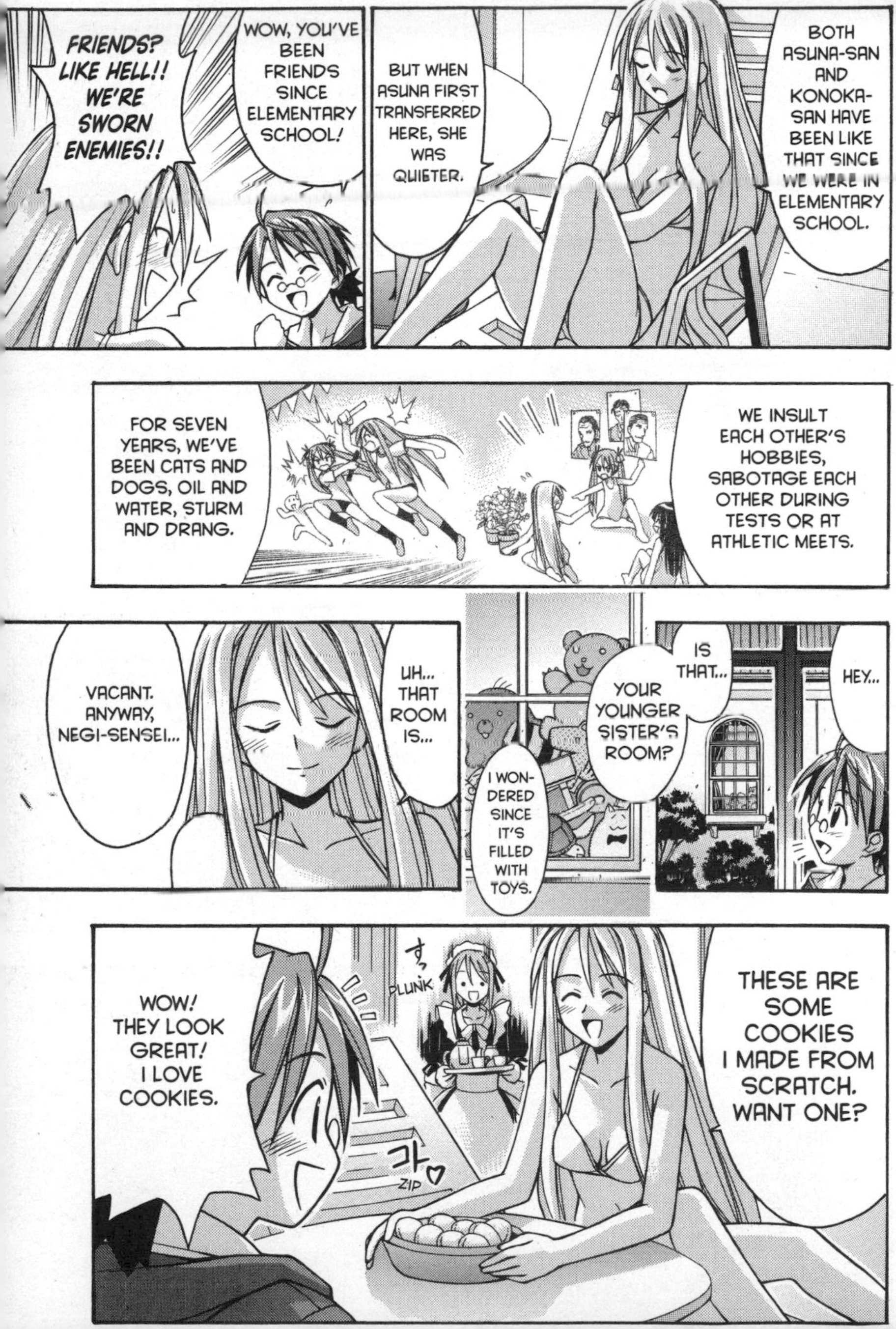
BOTH ASUNA-SAN AND KONOKA-SAN HAVE BEEN LIKE THAT SINCE WE WERE IN ELEMENTARY SCHOOL.
BUT WHEN ASUNA FIRST TRANSFERRED HERE, SHE WAS QUIETER.
WOW, YOU'VE BEEN FRIENDS SINCE ELEMENTARY SCHOOL!
FRIENDS? LIKE HELL!! WE'RE SWORN ENEMIES!!
WE INSULT EACH OTHER'S HOBBIES, SABOTAGE EACH OTHER DURING TESTS OR AT ATHLETIC MEETS.
FOR SEVEN YEARS, WE'VE BEEN CATS AND DOGS, OIL AND WATER, STURM AND DRANG.
HEY...
IS THAT...
YOUR YOUNGER SISTER'S ROOM?
I WONDERED SINCE IT'S FILLED WITH TOYS.
UH... THAT ROOM IS...
VACANT. ANYWAY, NEGI-SENSEI...
THESE ARE SOME COOKIES I MADE FROM SCRATCH. WANT ONE?
PLUNK
ZIP
WOW! THEY LOOK GREAT! I LOVE COOKIES.

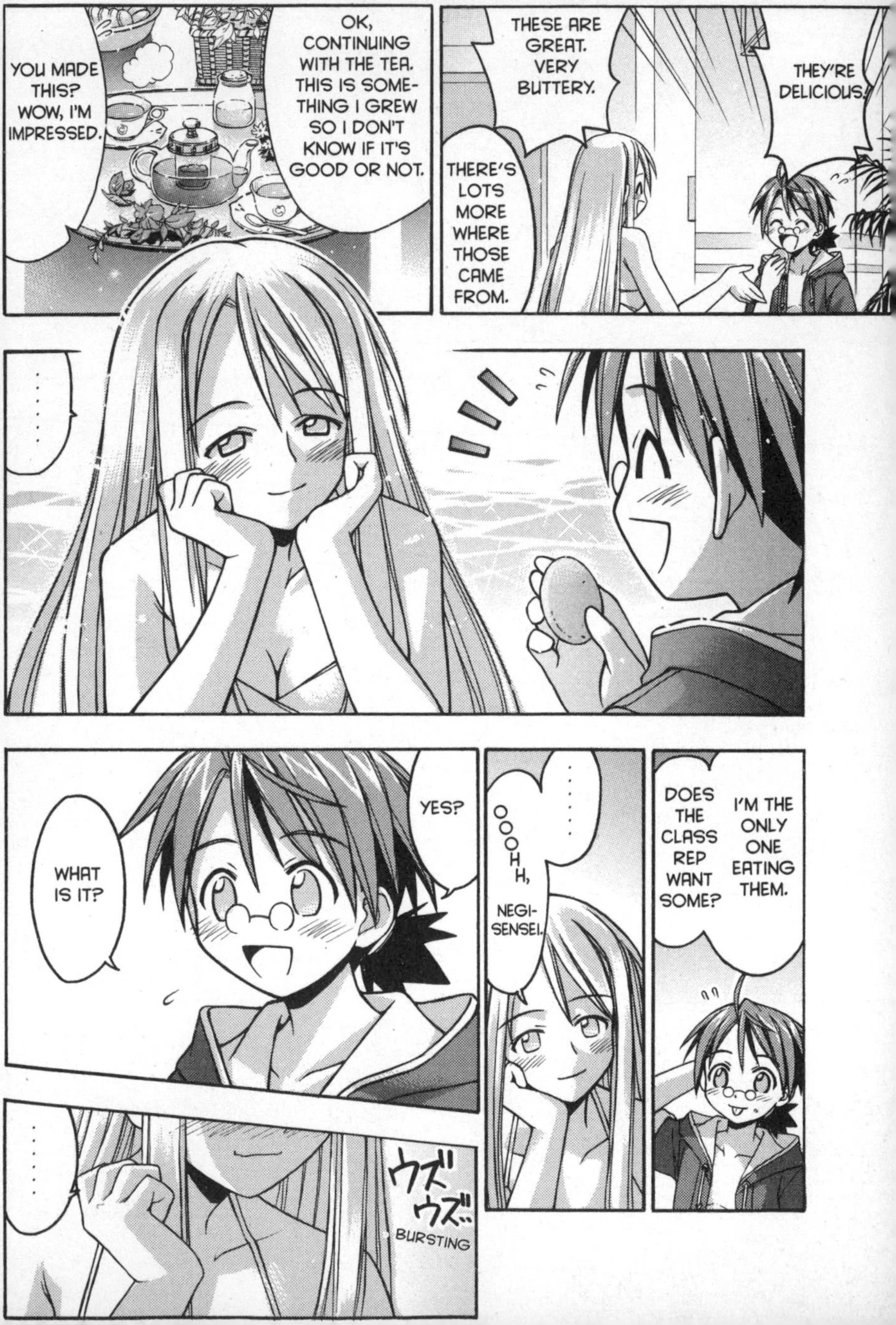
THEY'RE DELICIOUS!
THESE ARE GREAT. VERY BUTTERY.
THERE'S LOTS MORE WHERE THOSE CAME FROM.
OK, CONTINUING WITH THE TEA. THIS IS SOME-THING I GREW SO I DON'T KNOW IF IT'S GOOD OR NOT.
YOU MADE THIS? WOW, I'M IMPRESSED.
......
I'M THE ONLY ONE EATING THEM.
DOES THE CLASS REP WANT SOME?
......
OOOHH, NEGI-SENSEI.
YES?
WHAT IS IT?
......
ウズウズ
BURSTING

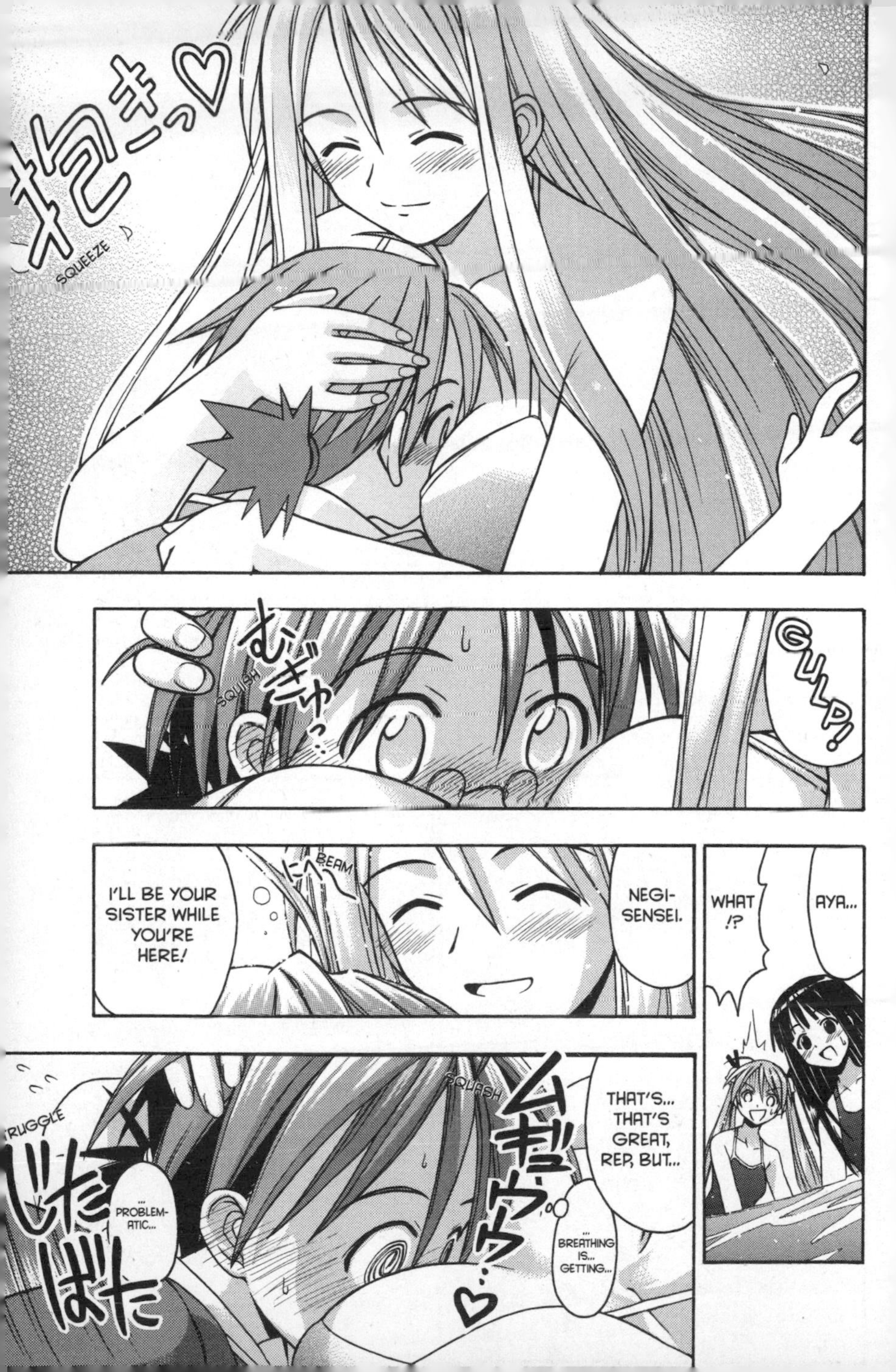
抱きっ♡
SQUEEZE
GULP!
むぎゅっ
SQUISH
NEGI-SENSEI.
I'LL BE YOUR SISTER WHILE YOU'RE HERE!
にへ
BEAM
AYA...
WHAT!?
THAT'S... THAT'S GREAT, REP, BUT...
ムギュウ
SQUASH
... BREATHING IS... GETTING...
... PROBLEMATIC...
じたばた
STRUGGLE

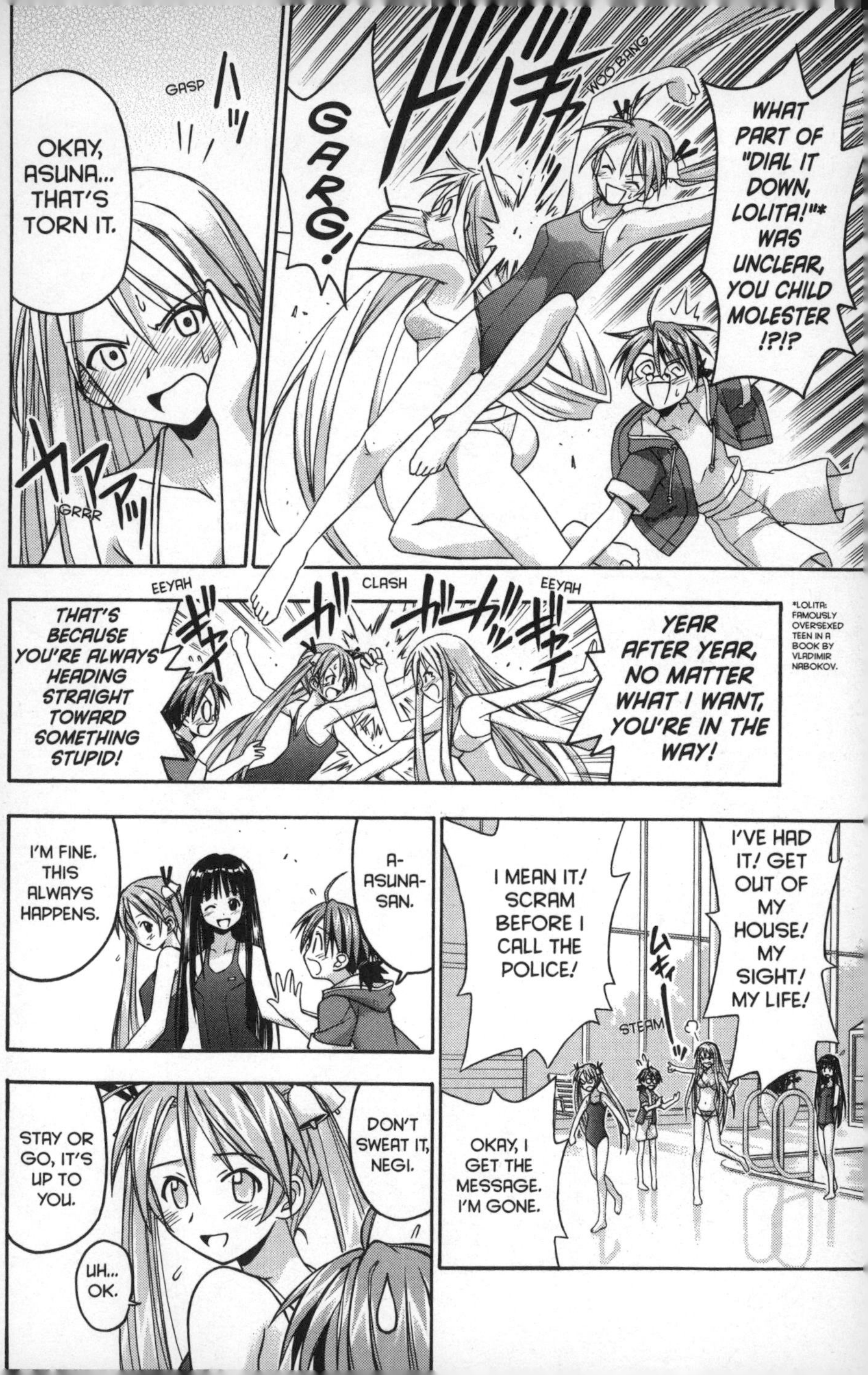
WHAT PART OF "DIAL IT DOWN, LOLITA!"* WAS UNCLEAR, YOU CHILD MOLESTER !?!?
WOO BANG
GARG!
GASP
OKAY, ASUNA... THAT'S TORN IT.
GRRR
YEAR AFTER YEAR, NO MATTER WHAT I WANT, YOU'RE IN THE WAY!
EEYAH
CLASH
EEYAH
THAT'S BECAUSE YOU'RE ALWAYS HEADING STRAIGHT TOWARD SOMETHING STUPID!
I'VE HAD IT! GET OUT OF MY HOUSE! MY SIGHT! MY LIFE!
I MEAN IT! SCRAM BEFORE I CALL THE POLICE!
STEAM
OKAY, I GET THE MESSAGE. I'M GONE.
A-ASUNA-SAN.
I'M FINE. THIS ALWAYS HAPPENS.
DON'T SWEAT IT, NEGI.
STAY OR GO, IT'S UP TO YOU.
UH... OK.

*LOLITA: FAMOUSLY OVERSEXED TEEN IN A BOOK BY VLADIMIR NABOKOV.

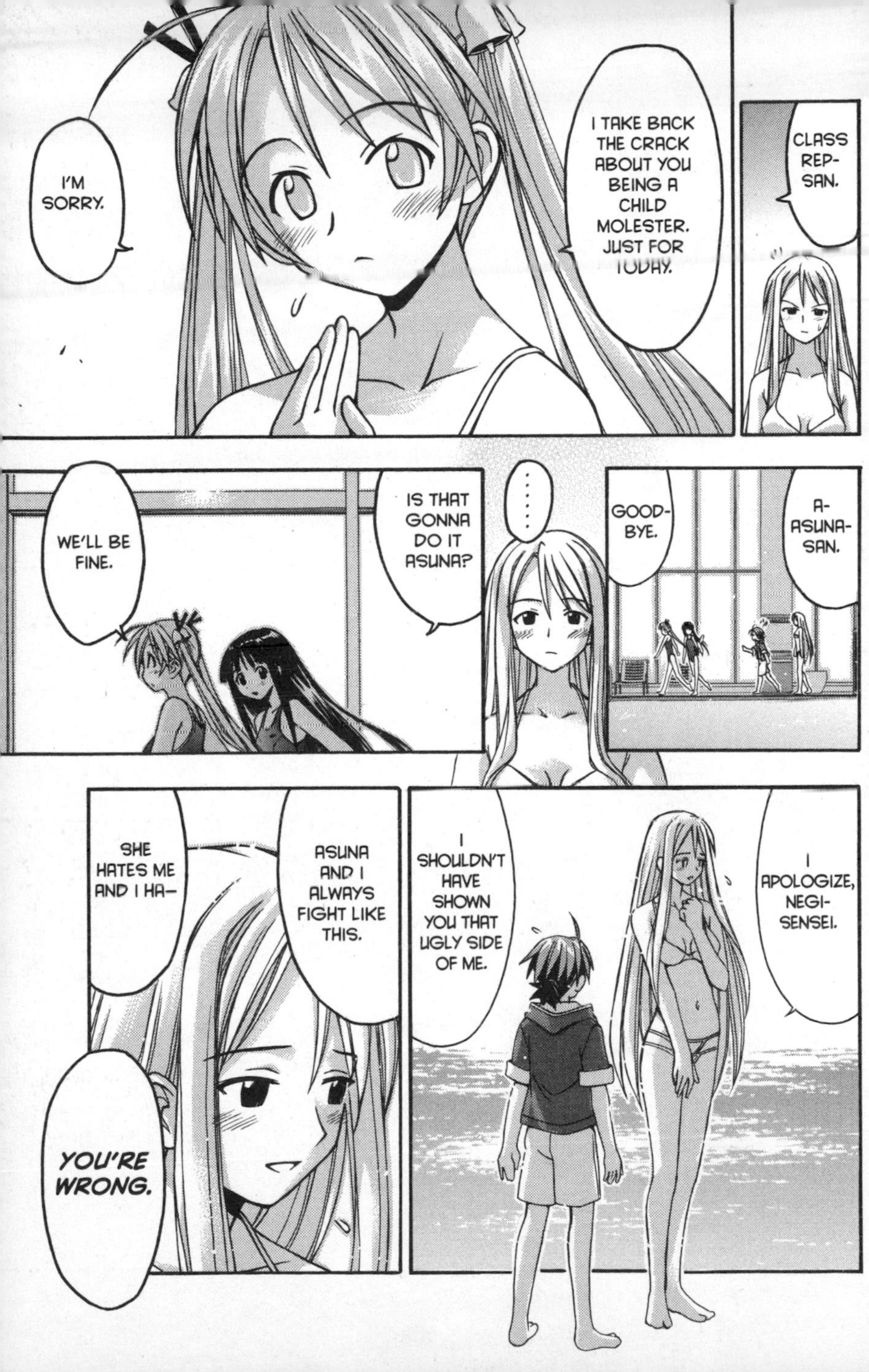

CLASS REP-SAN.
I TAKE BACK THE CRACK ABOUT YOU BEING A CHILD MOLESTER. JUST FOR TODAY.
I'M SORRY.
A-ASUNA-SAN.
GOOD-BYE.
......
IS THAT GONNA DO IT ASUNA?
WE'LL BE FINE.
I APOLOGIZE, NEGI-SENSEI.
I SHOULDN'T HAVE SHOWN YOU THAT UGLY SIDE OF ME.
ASUNA AND I ALWAYS FIGHT LIKE THIS.
SHE HATES ME AND I HA-
YOU'RE WRONG.

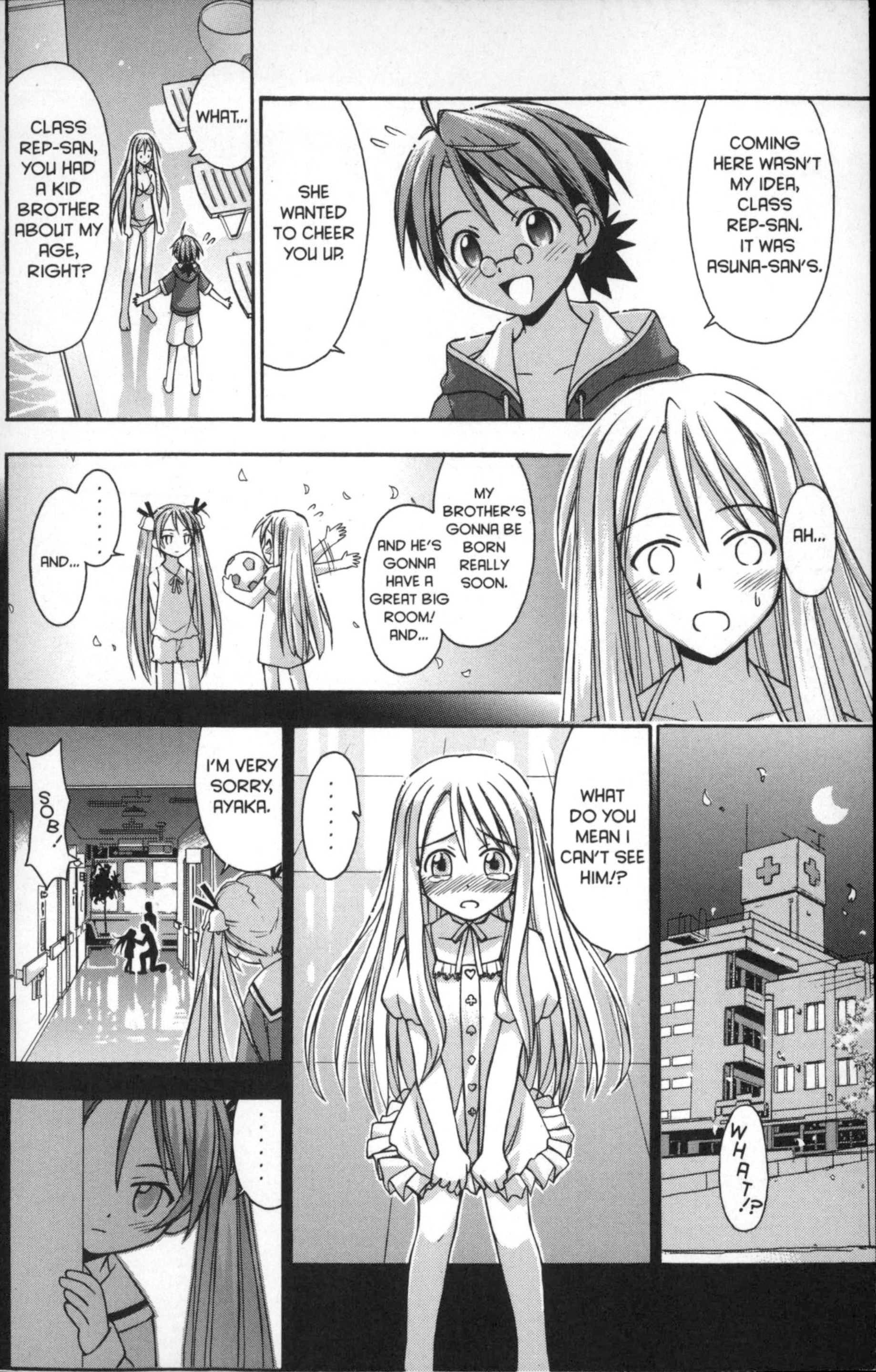
COMING HERE WASN'T MY IDEA, CLASS REP-SAN. IT WAS ASUNA-SAN'S.
SHE WANTED TO CHEER YOU UP.
WHAT...
CLASS REP-SAN, YOU HAD A KID BROTHER ABOUT MY AGE, RIGHT?
AH...
MY BROTHER'S GONNA BE BORN REALLY SOON.
AND HE'S GONNA HAVE A GREAT BIG ROOM! AND...
......
AND...
WHAT!?
WHAT DO YOU MEAN I CAN'T SEE HIM!?
......
I'M VERY SORRY, AYAKA.
SOB!
......

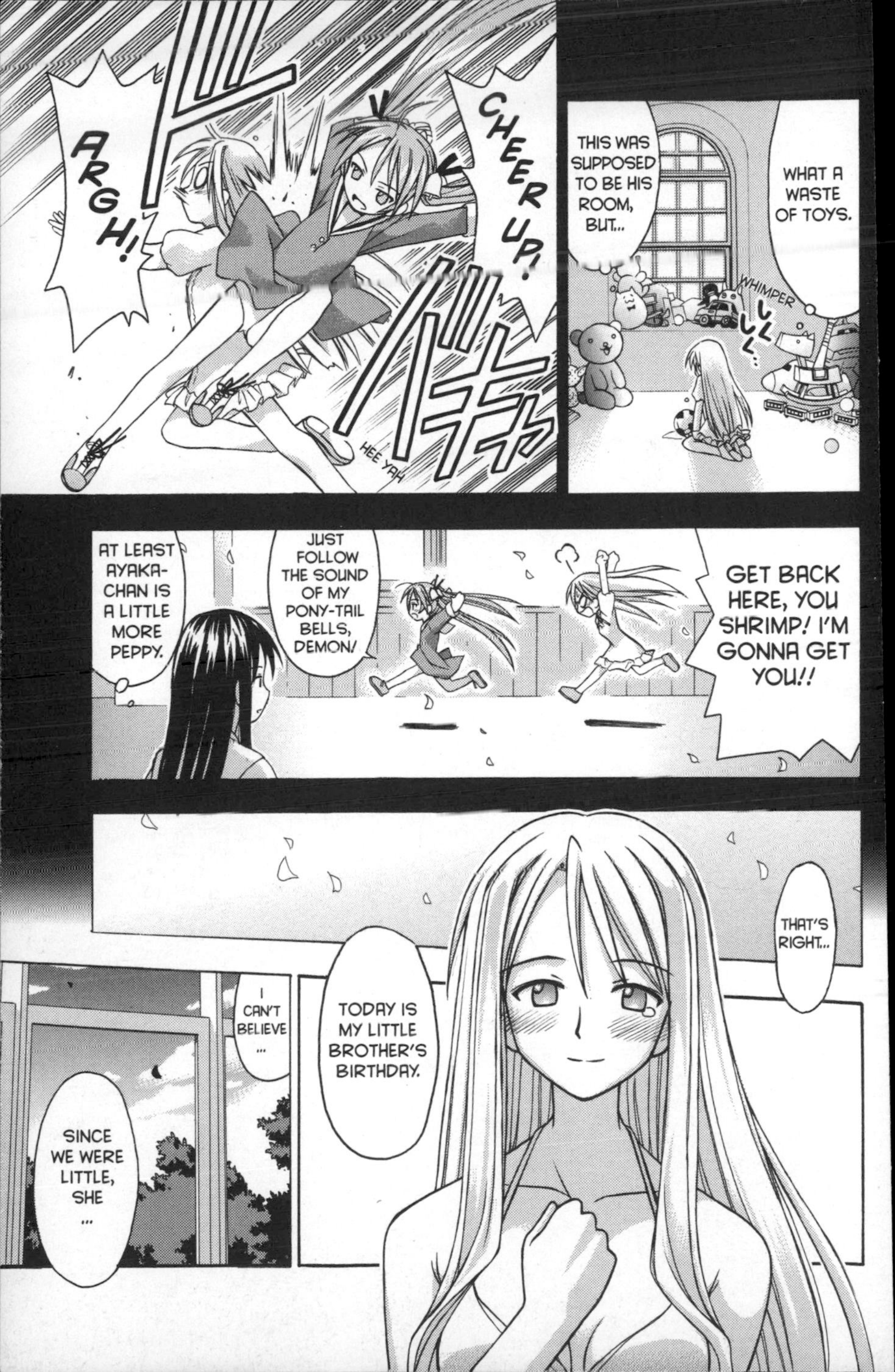
WHAT A WASTE OF TOYS.
THIS WAS SUPPOSED TO BE HIS ROOM, BUT...
WHIMPER
CHEER UP!
ARGH!
HEE YAH
GET BACK HERE, YOU SHRIMP! I'M GONNA GET YOU!!
JUST FOLLOW THE SOUND OF MY PONY-TAIL BELLS, DEMON!
AT LEAST AYAKA-CHAN IS A LITTLE MORE PEPPY.
THAT'S RIGHT...
TODAY IS MY LITTLE BROTHER'S BIRTHDAY.
I CAN'T BELIEVE ...
SINCE WE WERE LITTLE, SHE ...

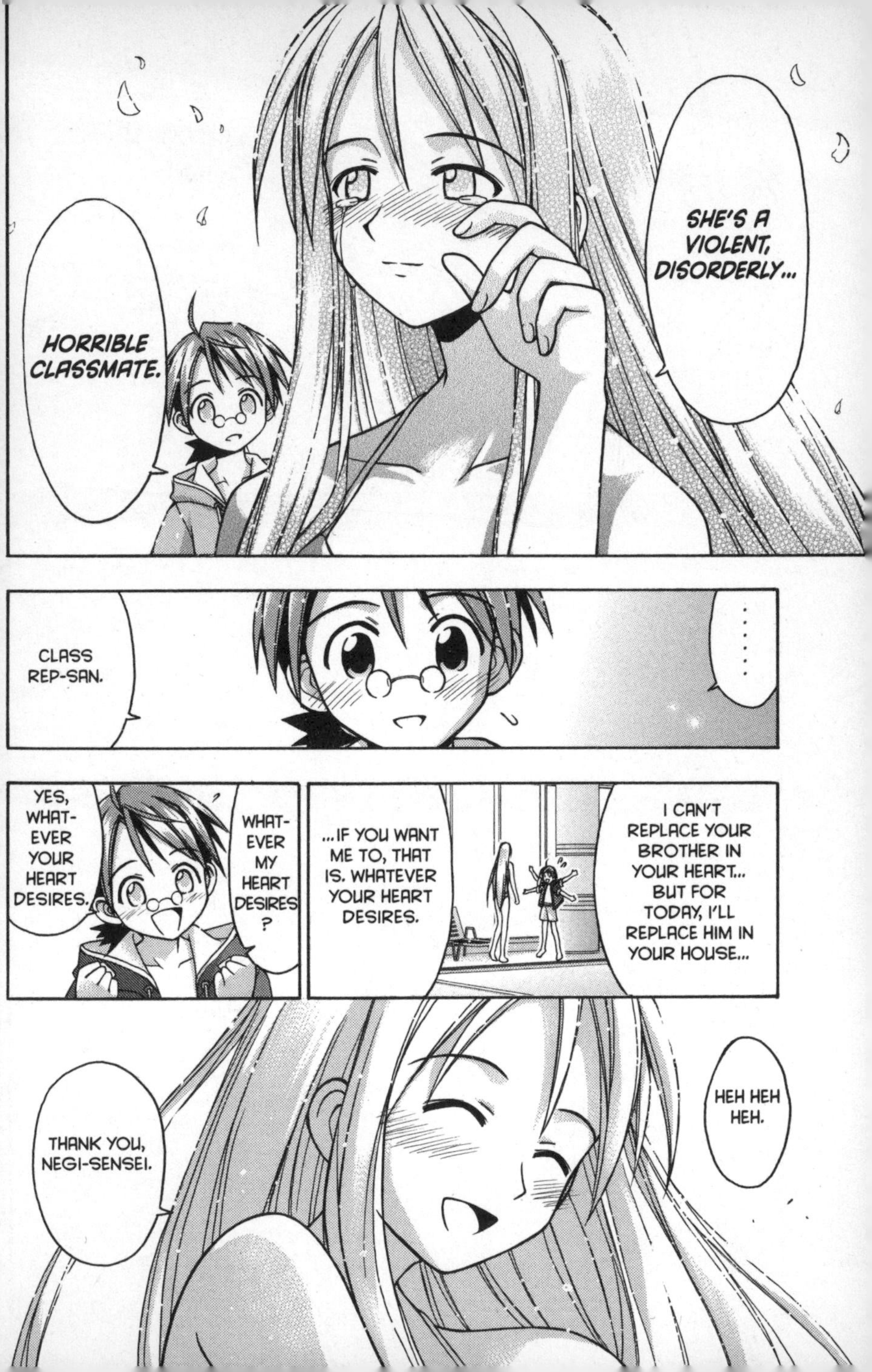
SHE'S A VIOLENT, DISORDERLY...
HORRIBLE CLASSMATE.
......
CLASS REP-SAN.
I CAN'T REPLACE YOUR BROTHER IN YOUR HEART... BUT FOR TODAY, I'LL REPLACE HIM IN YOUR HOUSE...
...IF YOU WANT ME TO, THAT IS. WHATEVER YOUR HEART DESIRES.
WHATEVER MY HEART DESIRES?
YES, WHATEVER YOUR HEART DESIRES.
HEH HEH HEH.
THANK YOU, NEGI-SENSEI.

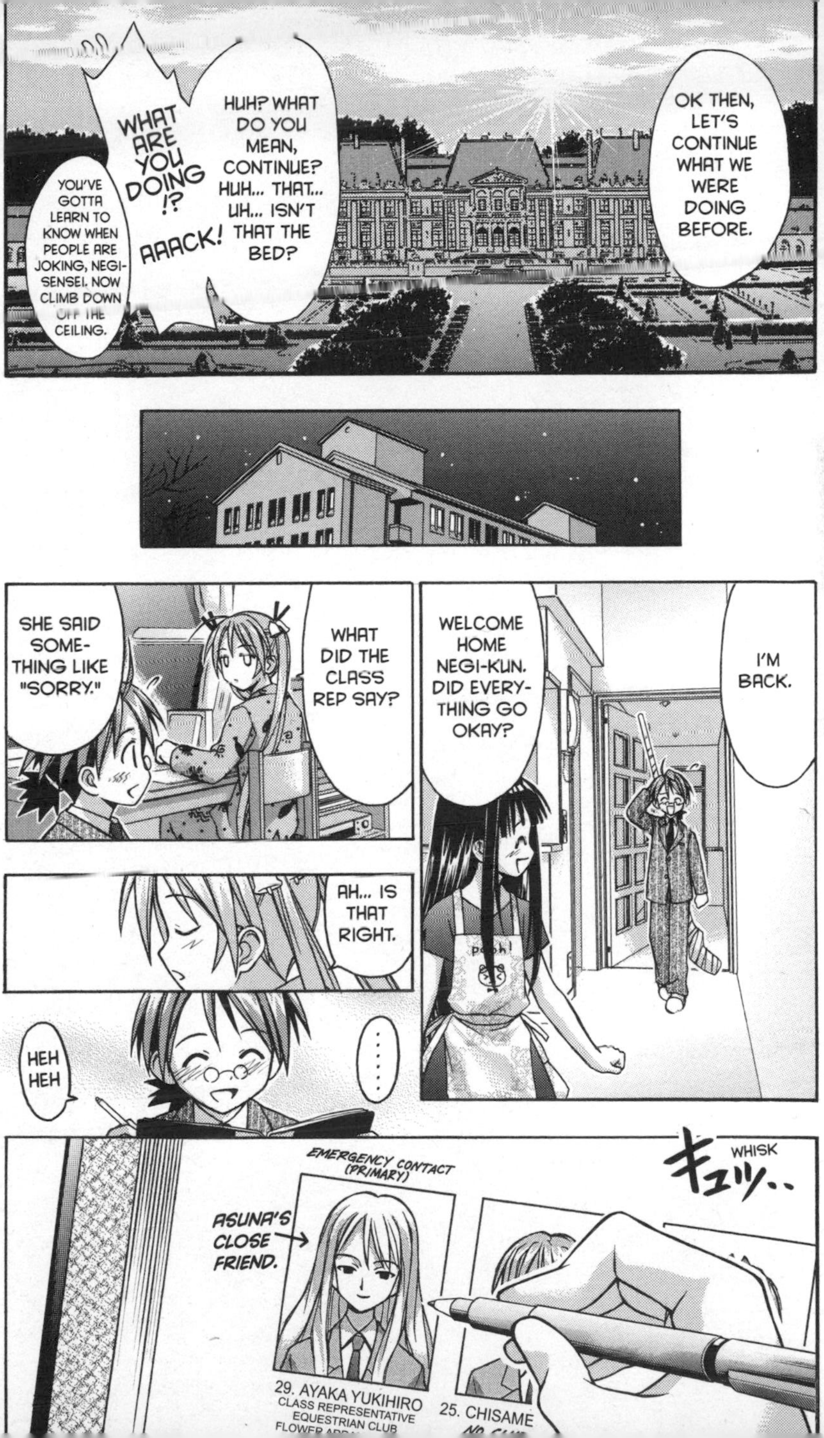
OK THEN, LET'S CONTINUE WHAT WE WERE DOING BEFORE.
HUH? WHAT DO YOU MEAN, CONTINUE? HUH... THAT... UH... ISN'T THAT THE BED?
WHAT ARE YOU DOING !?
AAACK!
YOU'VE GOTTA LEARN TO KNOW WHEN PEOPLE ARE JOKING, NEGI-SENSEI. NOW CLIMB DOWN OFF THE CEILING.
I'M BACK.
WELCOME HOME NEGI-KUN. DID EVERYTHING GO OKAY?
WHAT DID THE CLASS REP SAY?
SHE SAID SOMETHING LIKE "SORRY."
AH... IS THAT RIGHT.
......
HEH HEH
WHISK
EMERGENCY CONTACT (PRIMARY)
ASUNA'S CLOSE FRIEND.
29. AYAKA YUKIHIRO
CLASS REPRESENTATIVE
EQUESTRIAN CLUB
25. CHISAME

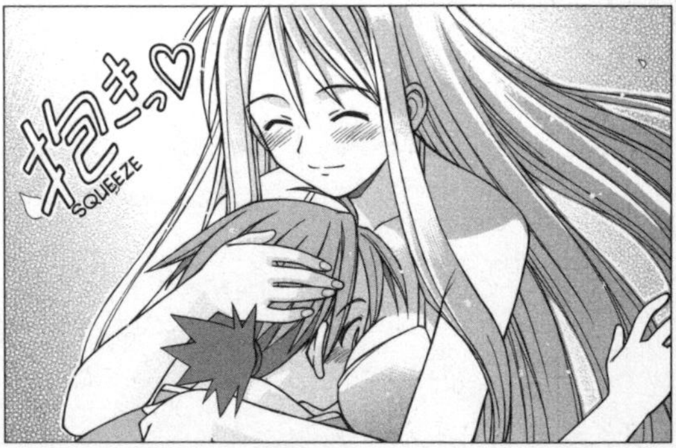
抱きっ♡
SQUEEZE

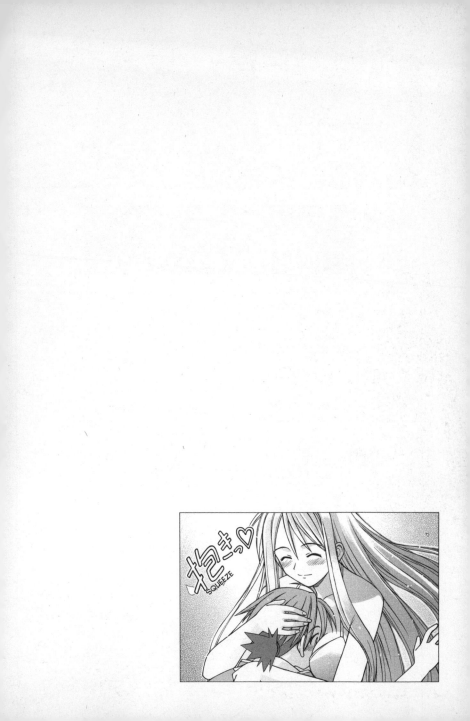

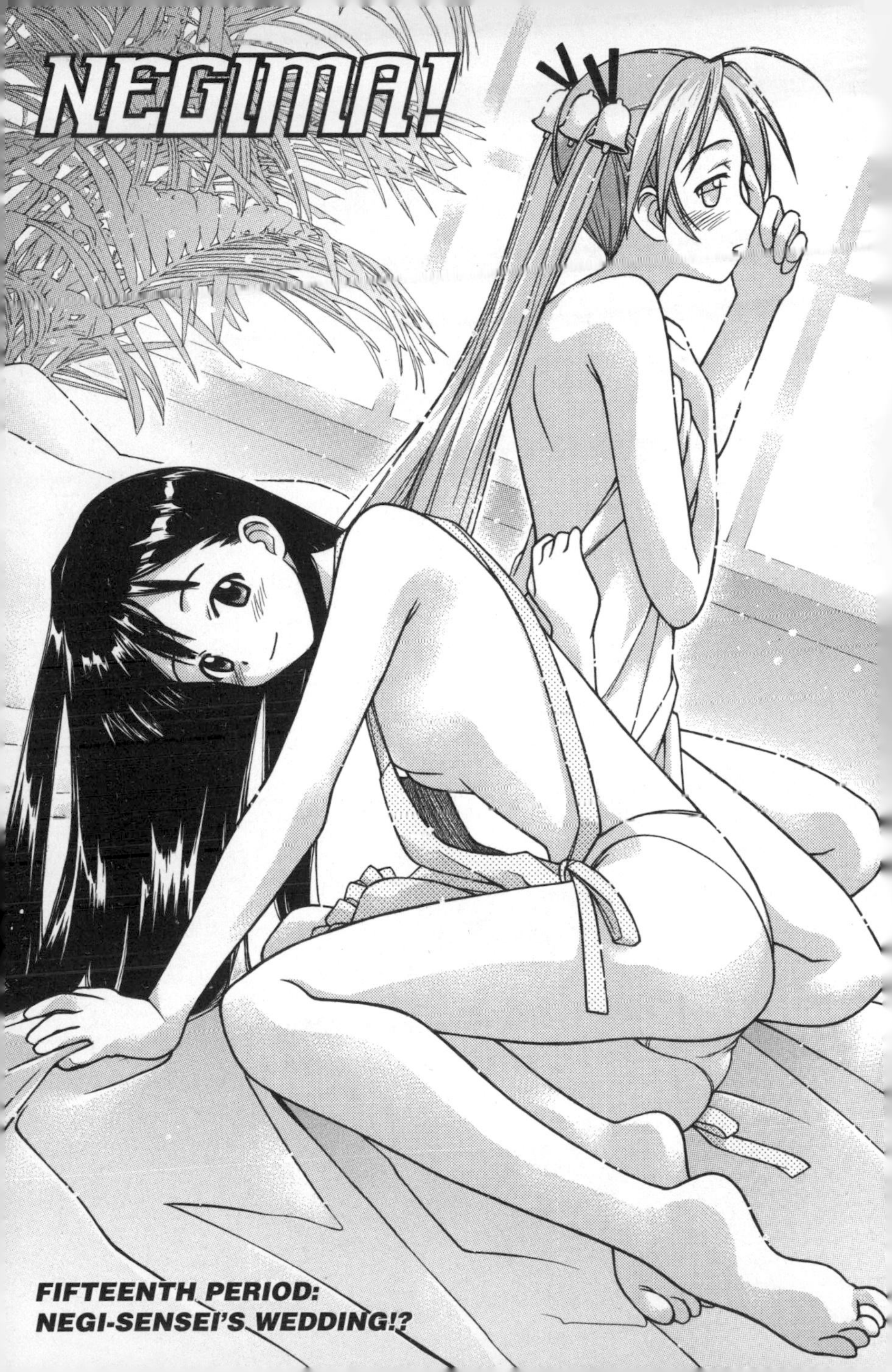
NEGIMA!
FIFTEENTH PERIOD:
NEGI-SENSEI'S WEDDING!?

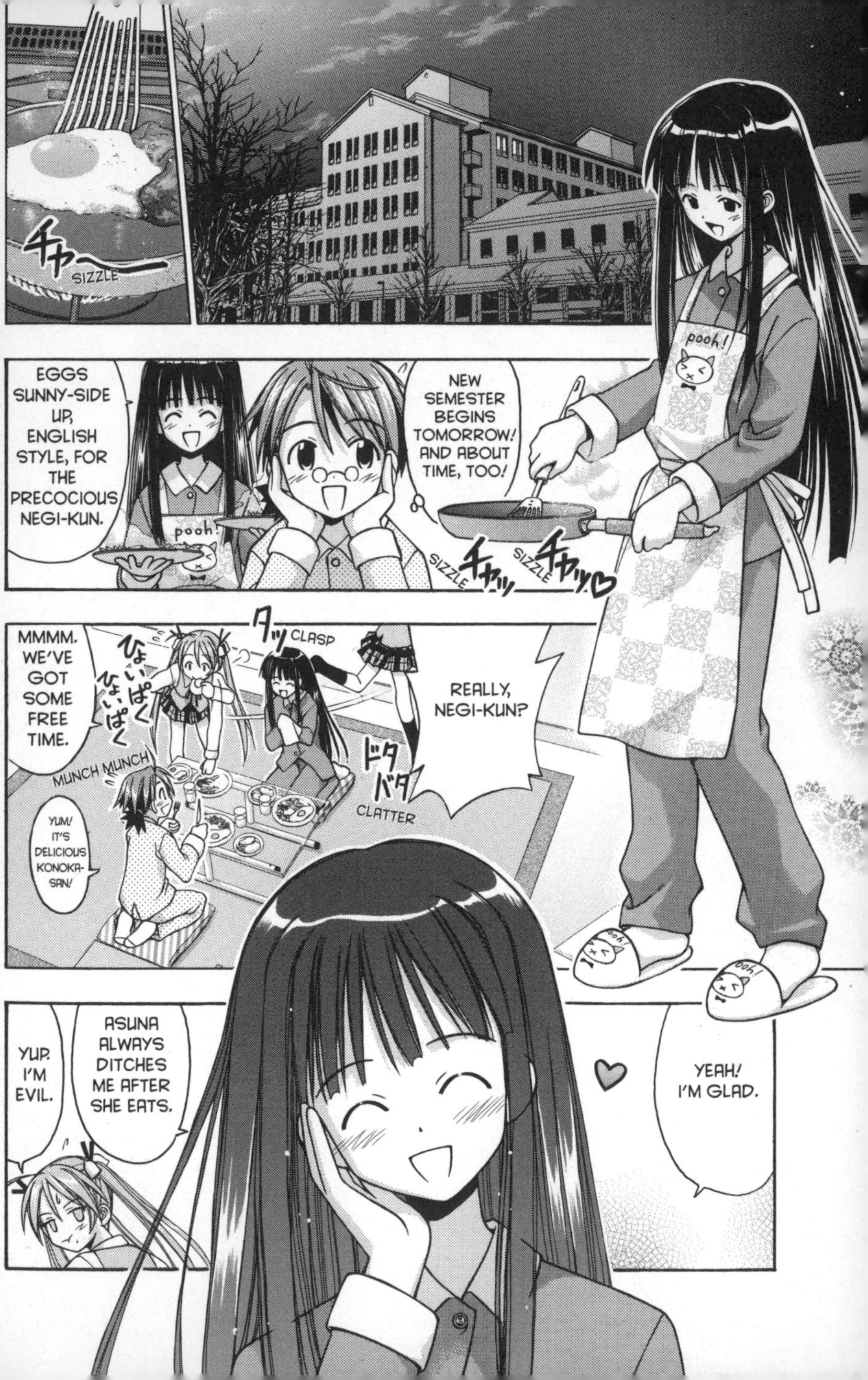

チャー
SIZZLE
NEW SEMESTER BEGINS TOMORROW! AND ABOUT TIME, TOO!
EGGS SUNNY-SIDE UP, ENGLISH STYLE, FOR THE PRECOCIOUS NEGI-KUN.
チャッ
SIZZLE
チャッ
SIZZLE
pooh!
REALLY, NEGI-KUN?
ドタバタ
CLATTER
タッ
CLASP
MMMM. WE'VE GOT SOME FREE TIME.
ひょいぱく ひょいぱく
MUNCH MUNCH
YUM! IT'S DELICIOUS KONOKA-SAN!
YEAH! I'M GLAD.
ASUNA ALWAYS DITCHES ME AFTER SHE EATS.
YUP. I'M EVIL.

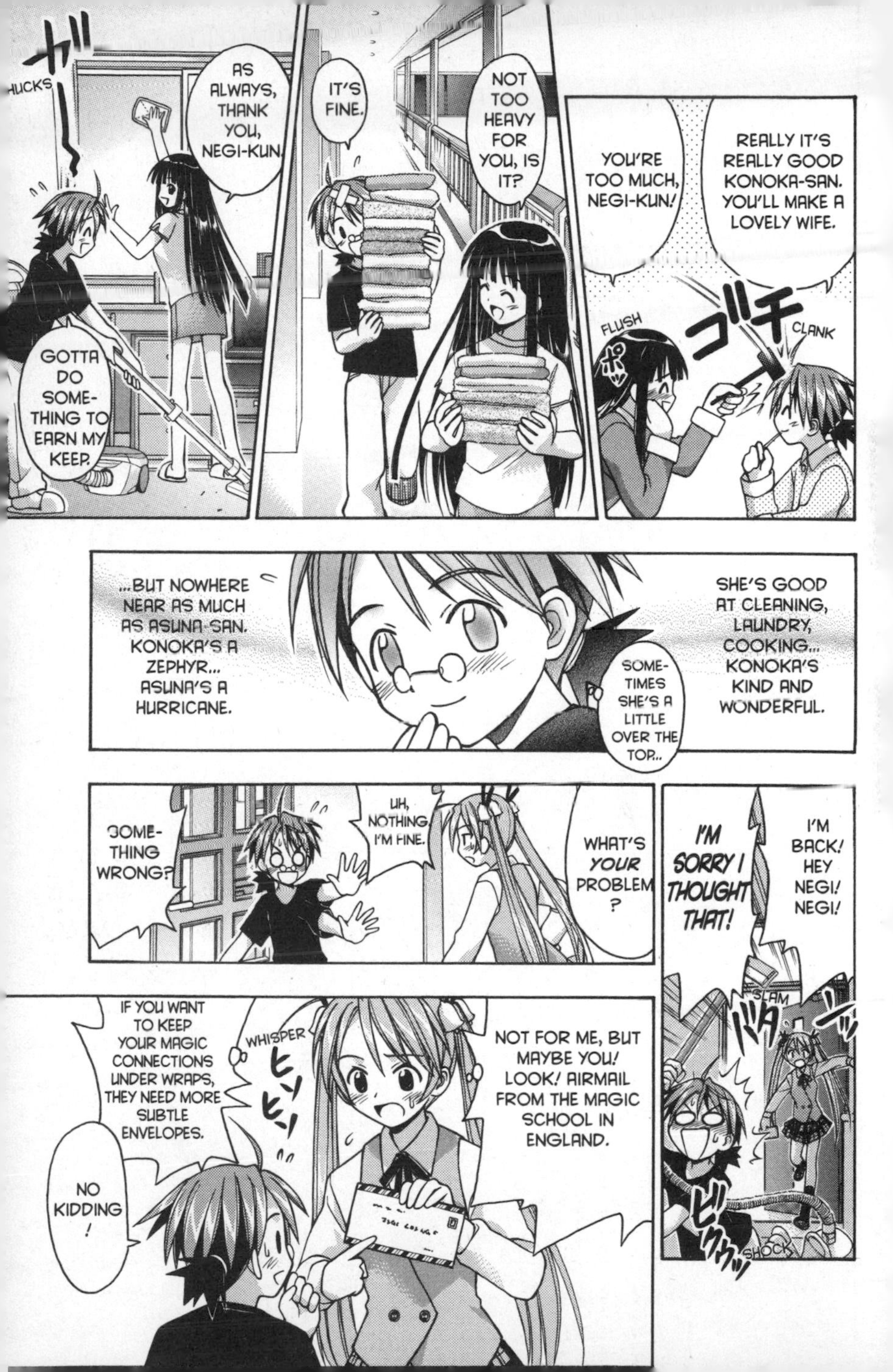
REALLY IT'S REALLY GOOD KONOKA-SAN. YOU'LL MAKE A LOVELY WIFE.
YOU'RE TOO MUCH, NEGI-KUN!
FLUSH
CLANK
NOT TOO HEAVY FOR YOU, IS IT?
IT'S FINE.
AS ALWAYS, THANK YOU, NEGI-KUN.
HUCKS
GOTTA DO SOME-THING TO EARN MY KEEP.
SHE'S GOOD AT CLEANING, LAUNDRY, COOKING... KONOKA'S KIND AND WONDERFUL.
SOME-TIMES SHE'S A LITTLE OVER THE TOP...
...BUT NOWHERE NEAR AS MUCH AS ASUNA-SAN. KONOKA'S A ZEPHYR... ASUNA'S A HURRICANE.
I'M BACK! HEY NEGI! NEGI!
I'M SORRY I THOUGHT THAT!
SLAM
SHOCK
WHAT'S YOUR PROBLEM?
UH, NOTHING. I'M FINE.
SOME-THING WRONG?
NOT FOR ME, BUT MAYBE YOU! LOOK! AIRMAIL FROM THE MAGIC SCHOOL IN ENGLAND.
WHISPER
IF YOU WANT TO KEEP YOUR MAGIC CONNECTIONS UNDER WRAPS, THEY NEED MORE SUBTLE ENVELOPES.
NO KIDDING!

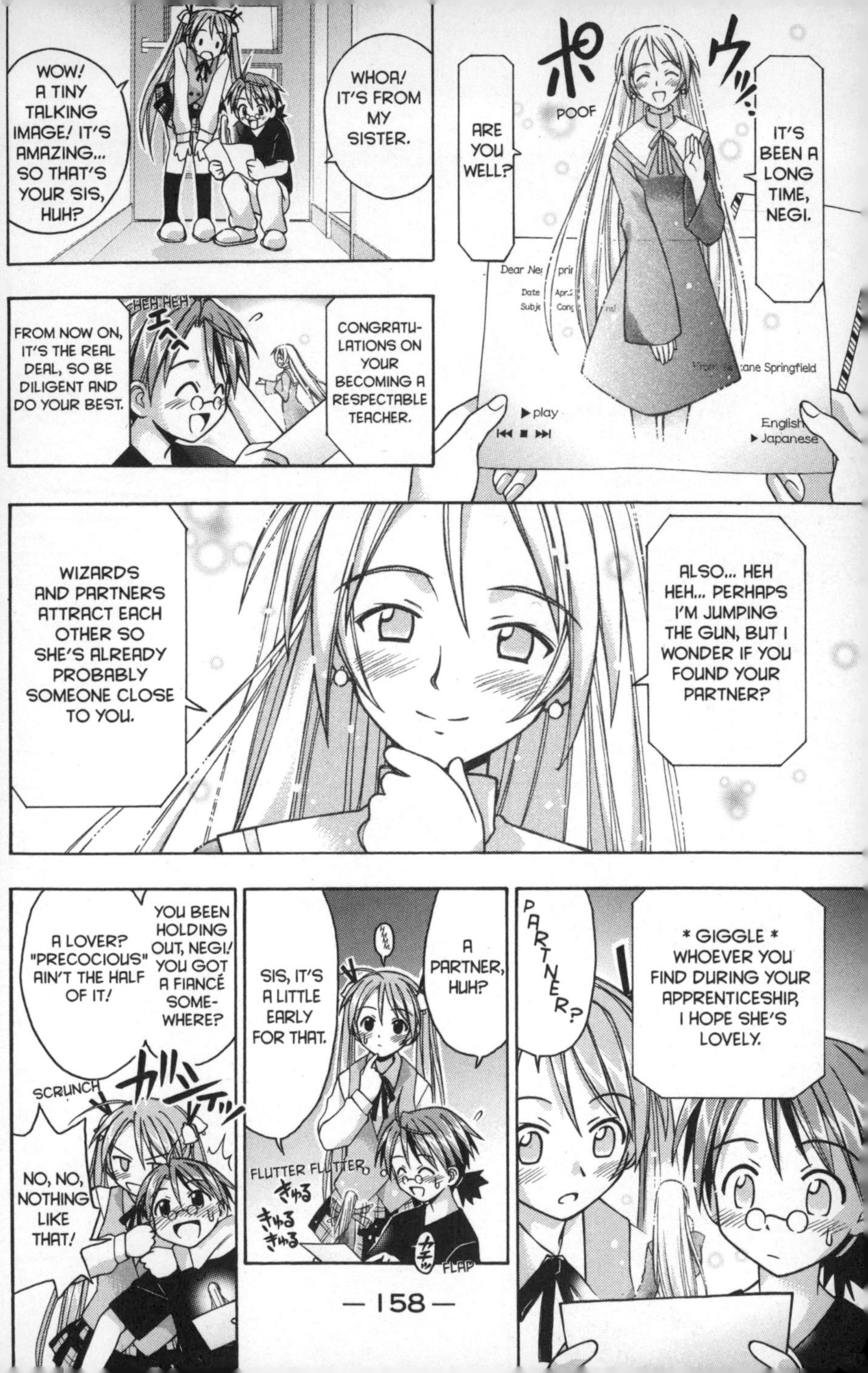
POOF
IT'S BEEN A LONG TIME, NEGI.
ARE YOU WELL?
play
English
Japanese
WHOA! IT'S FROM MY SISTER.
WOW! A TINY TALKING IMAGE! IT'S AMAZING... SO THAT'S YOUR SIS, HUH?
CONGRATULATIONS ON YOUR BECOMING A RESPECTABLE TEACHER.
HEH HEH
FROM NOW ON, IT'S THE REAL DEAL, SO BE DILIGENT AND DO YOUR BEST.
ALSO... HEH HEH... PERHAPS I'M JUMPING THE GUN, BUT I WONDER IF YOU FOUND YOUR PARTNER?
WIZARDS AND PARTNERS ATTRACT EACH OTHER SO SHE'S ALREADY PROBABLY SOMEONE CLOSE TO YOU.
* GIGGLE * WHOEVER YOU FIND DURING YOUR APPRENTICESHIP, I HOPE SHE'S LOVELY.
PARTNER?
A PARTNER, HUH?
SIS, IT'S A LITTLE EARLY FOR THAT.
FLUTTER FLUTTER
FLAP
YOU BEEN HOLDING OUT, NEGI! YOU GOT A FIANCÉ SOMEWHERE?
A LOVER? "PRECOCIOUS" AIN'T THE HALF OF IT!
SCRUNCH
NO, NO, NOTHING LIKE THAT!

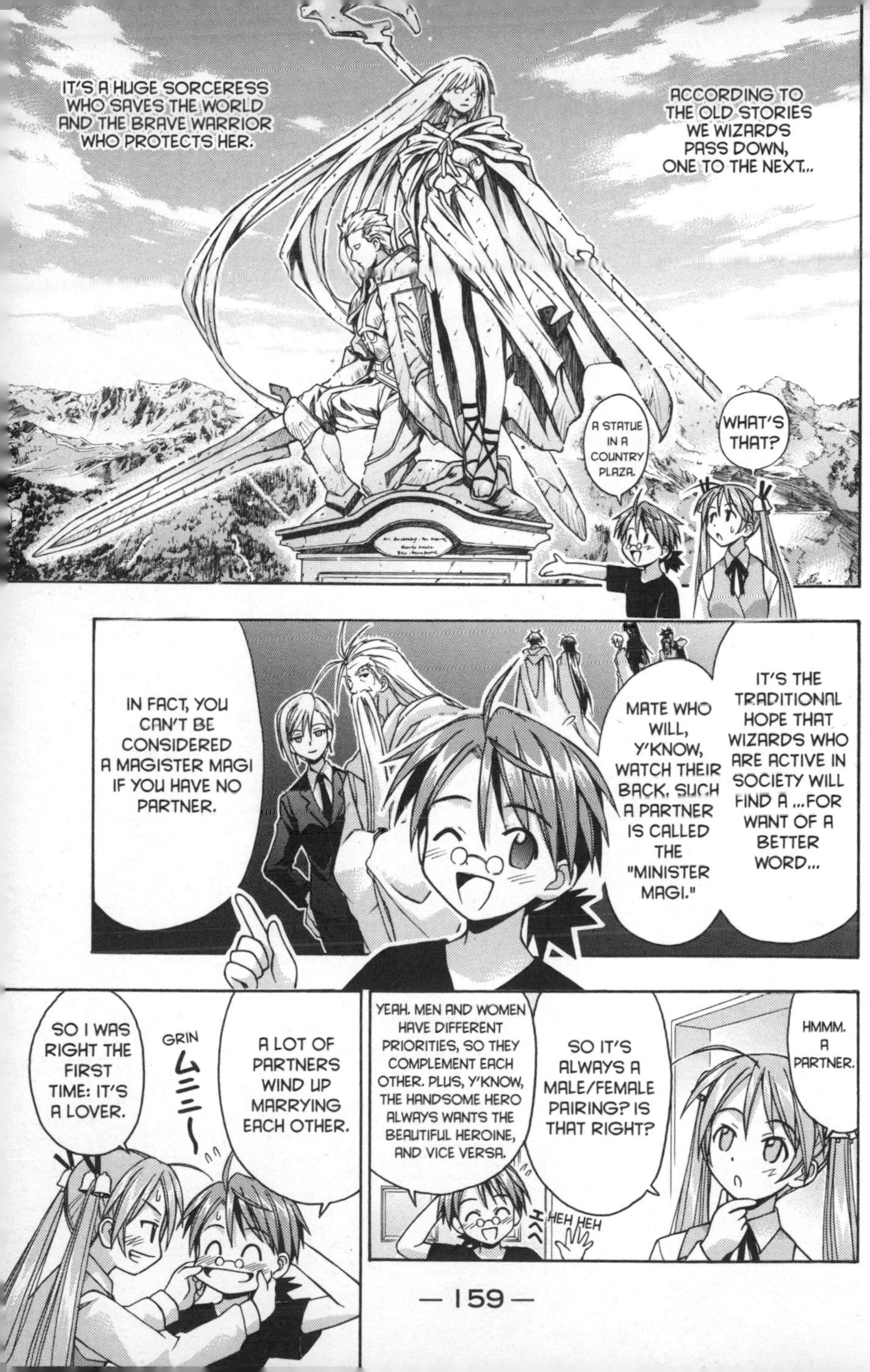
ACCORDING TO THE OLD STORIES WE WIZARDS PASS DOWN, ONE TO THE NEXT...
IT'S A HUGE SORCERESS WHO SAVES THE WORLD AND THE BRAVE WARRIOR WHO PROTECTS HER.
WHAT'S THAT?
A STATUE IN A COUNTRY PLAZA.
IT'S THE TRADITIONAL HOPE THAT WIZARDS WHO ARE ACTIVE IN SOCIETY WILL FIND A ...FOR WANT OF A BETTER WORD...
MATE WHO WILL, Y'KNOW, WATCH THEIR BACK. SUCH A PARTNER IS CALLED THE "MINISTER MAGI."
IN FACT, YOU CAN'T BE CONSIDERED A MAGISTER MAGI IF YOU HAVE NO PARTNER.
HMMM. A PARTNER.
SO IT'S ALWAYS A MALE/FEMALE PAIRING? IS THAT RIGHT?
YEAH. MEN AND WOMEN HAVE DIFFERENT PRIORITIES, SO THEY COMPLEMENT EACH OTHER. PLUS, Y'KNOW, THE HANDSOME HERO ALWAYS WANTS THE BEAUTIFUL HEROINE, AND VICE VERSA.
HEH HEH
A LOT OF PARTNERS WIND UP MARRYING EACH OTHER.
GRIN
ムニー
SO I WAS RIGHT THE FIRST TIME: IT'S A LOVER.

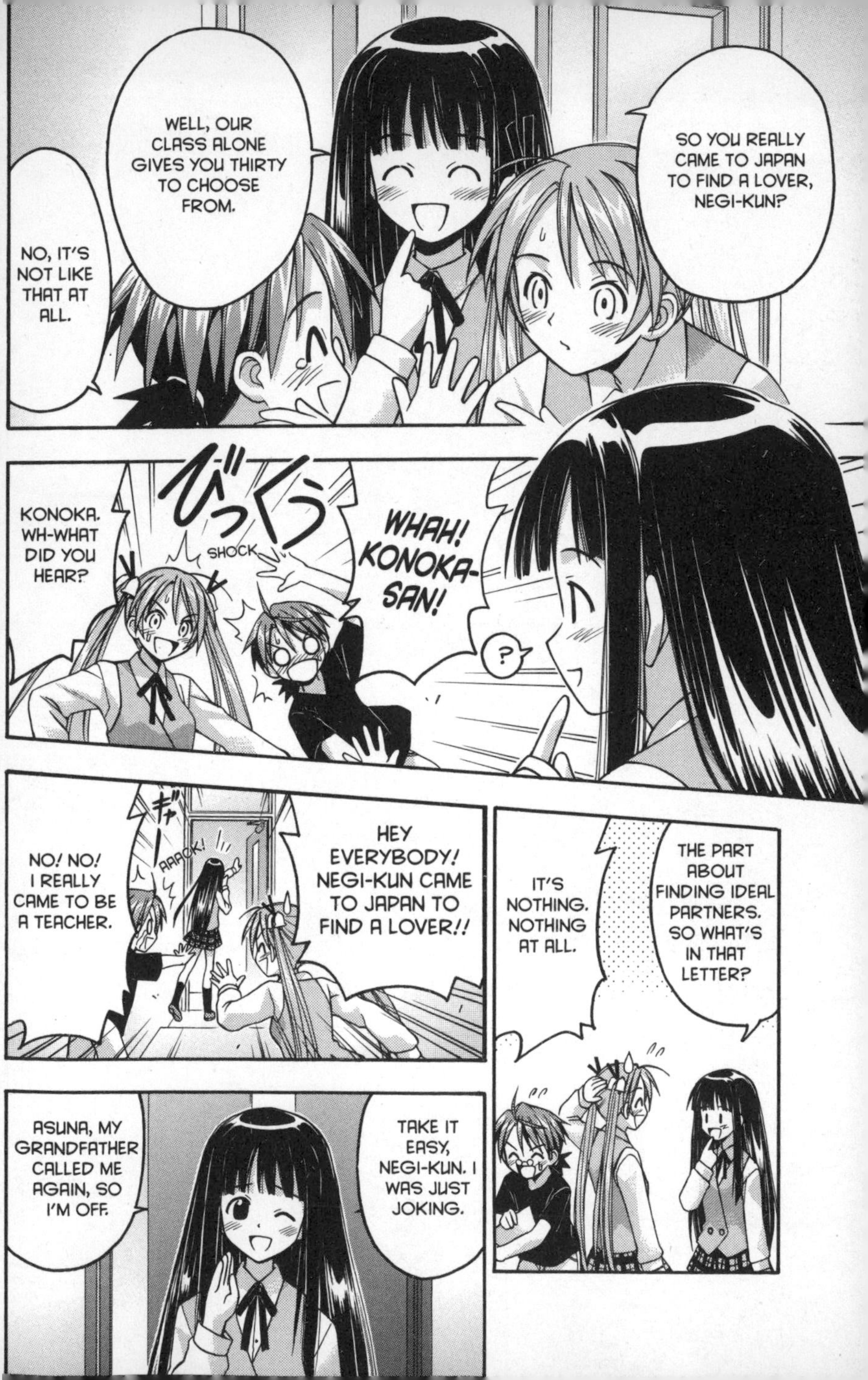
SO YOU REALLY CAME TO JAPAN TO FIND A LOVER, NEGI-KUN?
WELL, OUR CLASS ALONE GIVES YOU THIRTY TO CHOOSE FROM.
NO, IT'S NOT LIKE THAT AT ALL.
?
WHAH! KONOKA-SAN!
びっくぅ
SHOCK
KONOKA. WH-WHAT DID YOU HEAR?
THE PART ABOUT FINDING IDEAL PARTNERS. SO WHAT'S IN THAT LETTER?
IT'S NOTHING. NOTHING AT ALL.
HEY EVERYBODY! NEGI-KUN CAME TO JAPAN TO FIND A LOVER!!
ギャー
AAACK!
NO! NO! I REALLY CAME TO BE A TEACHER.
TAKE IT EASY, NEGI-KUN. I WAS JUST JOKING.
ASUNA, MY GRANDFATHER CALLED ME AGAIN, SO I'M OFF.

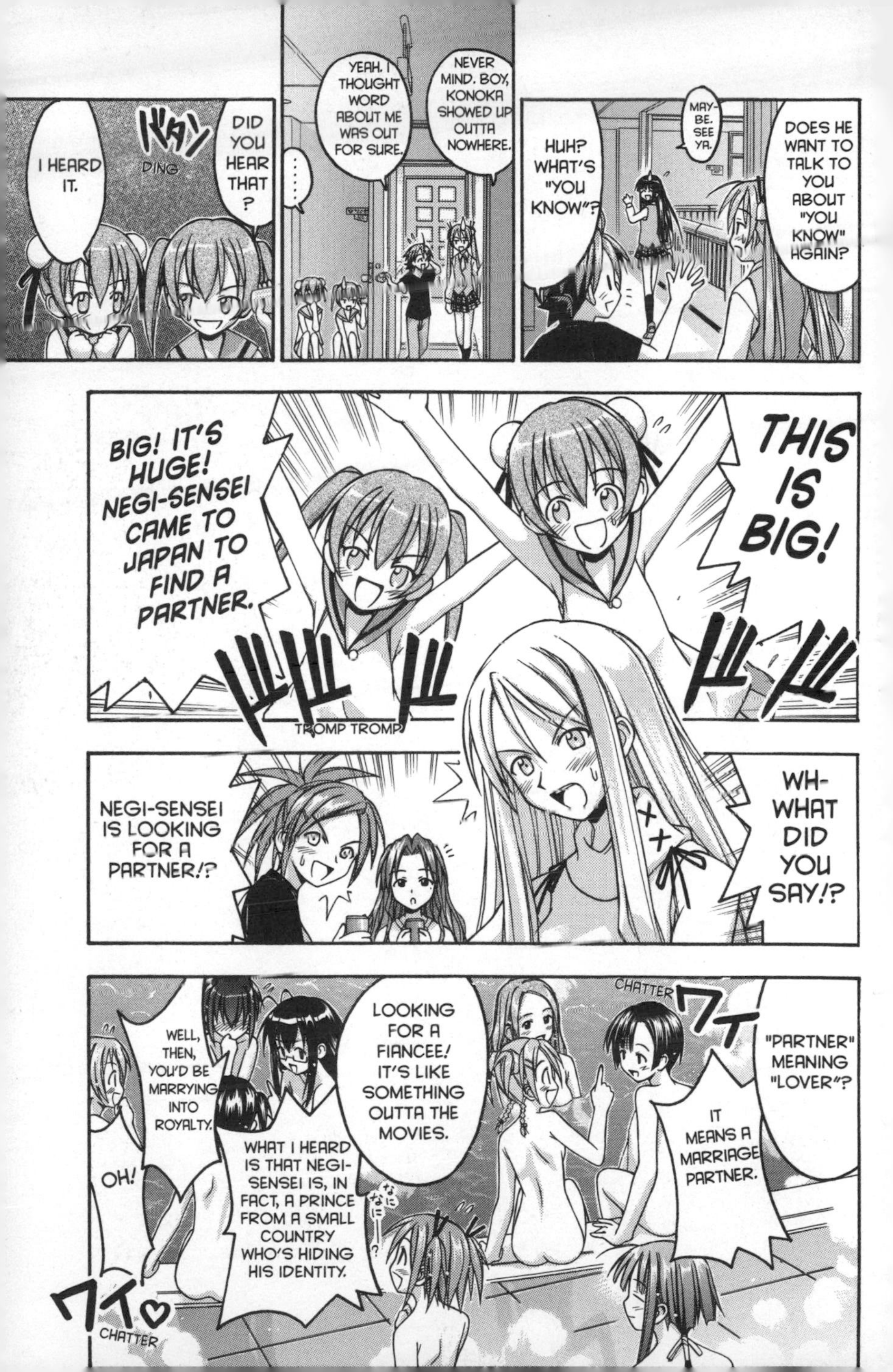

DOES HE WANT TO TALK TO YOU ABOUT "YOU KNOW" AGAIN?
MAY-BE. SEE YA.
HUH? WHAT'S "YOU KNOW"?
NEVER MIND. BOY, KONOKA SHOWED UP OUTTA NOWHERE.
YEAH. I THOUGHT WORD ABOUT ME WAS OUT FOR SURE.
......
DID YOU HEAR THAT?
バタン
DING
I HEARD IT.
THIS IS BIG!
BIG! IT'S HUGE! NEGI-SENSEI CAME TO JAPAN TO FIND A PARTNER.
TROMP TROMP
WH-WHAT DID YOU SAY!?
NEGI-SENSEI IS LOOKING FOR A PARTNER!?
ワイ
CHATTER
"PARTNER" MEANING "LOVER"?
IT MEANS A MARRIAGE PARTNER.
LOOKING FOR A FIANCEE! IT'S LIKE SOMETHING OUTTA THE MOVIES.
WELL, THEN, YOU'D BE MARRYING INTO ROYALTY.
なになに—?
WHAT I HEARD IS THAT NEGI-SENSEI IS, IN FACT, A PRINCE FROM A SMALL COUNTRY WHO'S HIDING HIS IDENTITY.
OH!
ワイ♡
CHATTER

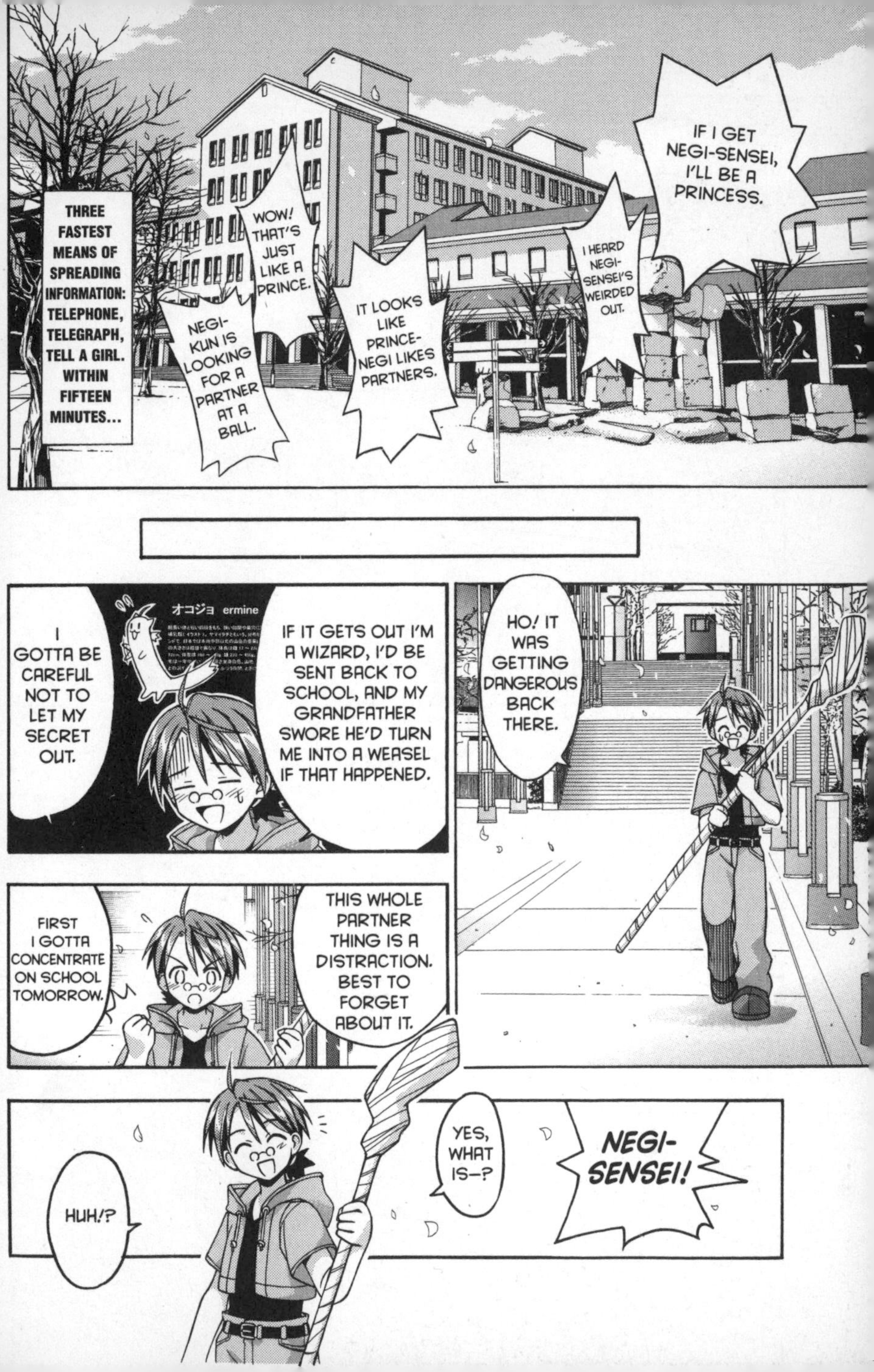

THREE FASTEST MEANS OF SPREADING INFORMATION: TELEPHONE, TELEGRAPH, TELL A GIRL. WITHIN FIFTEEN MINUTES...
IF I GET NEGI-SENSEI, I'LL BE A PRINCESS.
I HEARD NEGI-SENSEI'S WEIRDED OUT.
IT LOOKS LIKE PRINCE-NEGI LIKES PARTNERS.
WOW! THAT'S JUST LIKE A PRINCE.
NEGI-KUN IS LOOKING FOR A PARTNER AT A BALL.
HO! IT WAS GETTING DANGEROUS BACK THERE.
オコジョ ermine
IF IT GETS OUT I'M A WIZARD, I'D BE SENT BACK TO SCHOOL, AND MY GRANDFATHER SWORE HE'D TURN ME INTO A WEASEL IF THAT HAPPENED.
I GOTTA BE CAREFUL NOT TO LET MY SECRET OUT.
THIS WHOLE PARTNER THING IS A DISTRACTION. BEST TO FORGET ABOUT IT.
FIRST I GOTTA CONCENTRATE ON SCHOOL TOMORROW.
NEGI-SENSEI!
YES, WHAT IS—?
HUH!?

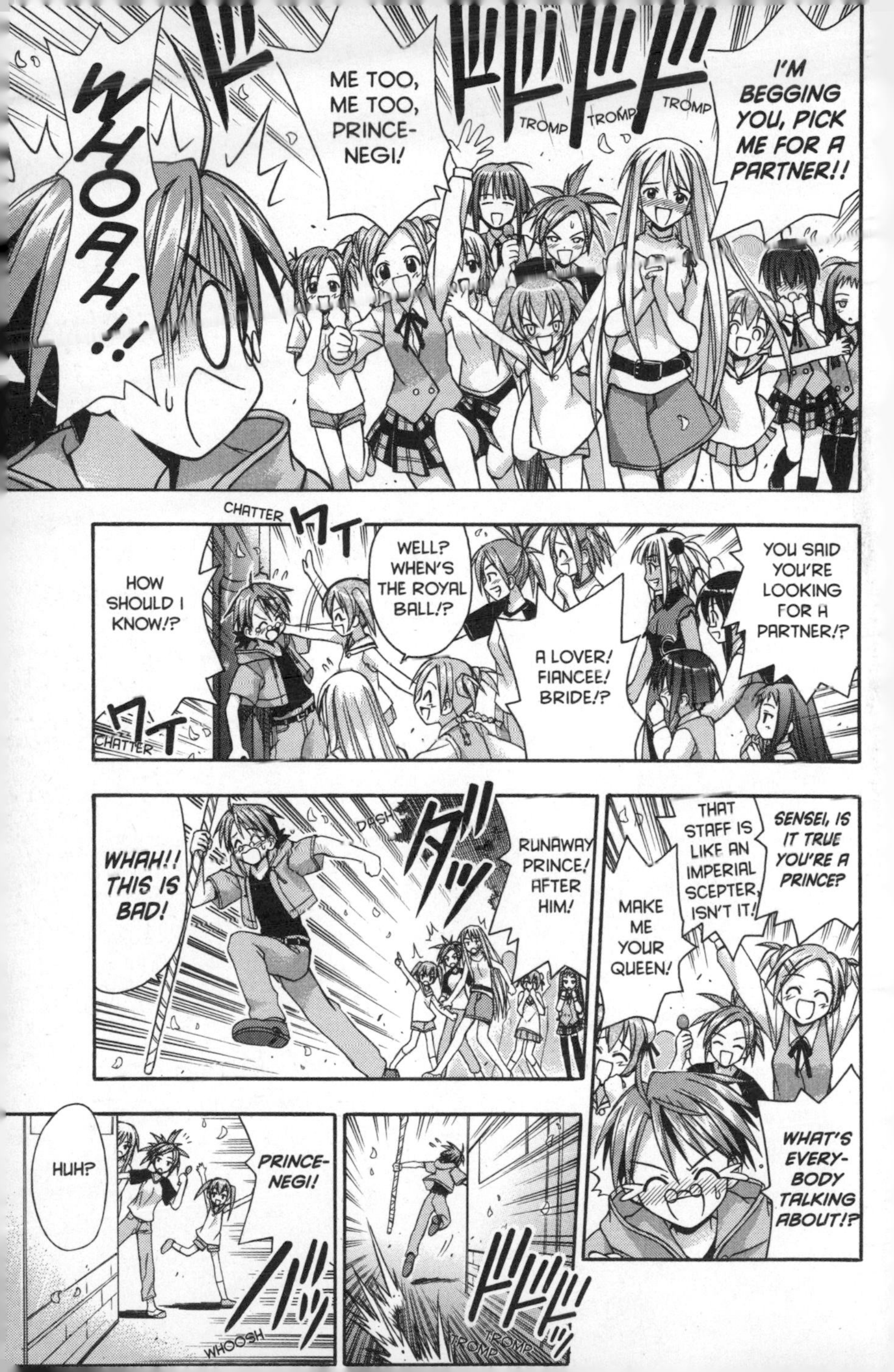
I'M BEGGING YOU, PICK ME FOR A PARTNER!!
TROMP TROMP TROMP
ME TOO, ME TOO, PRINCE-NEGI!
WHOAH!!
YOU SAID YOU'RE LOOKING FOR A PARTNER!?
A LOVER! FIANCEE! BRIDE!?
WELL? WHEN'S THE ROYAL BALL!?
CHATTER
HOW SHOULD I KNOW!?
CHATTER
SENSEI, IS IT TRUE YOU'RE A PRINCE?
THAT STAFF IS LIKE AN IMPERIAL SCEPTER, ISN'T IT!
MAKE ME YOUR QUEEN!
WHAT'S EVERYBODY TALKING ABOUT!?
RUNAWAY PRINCE! AFTER HIM!
DASH
WHAH!! THIS IS BAD!
TROMP TROMP
PRINCE-NEGI!
HUH?
WHOOSH

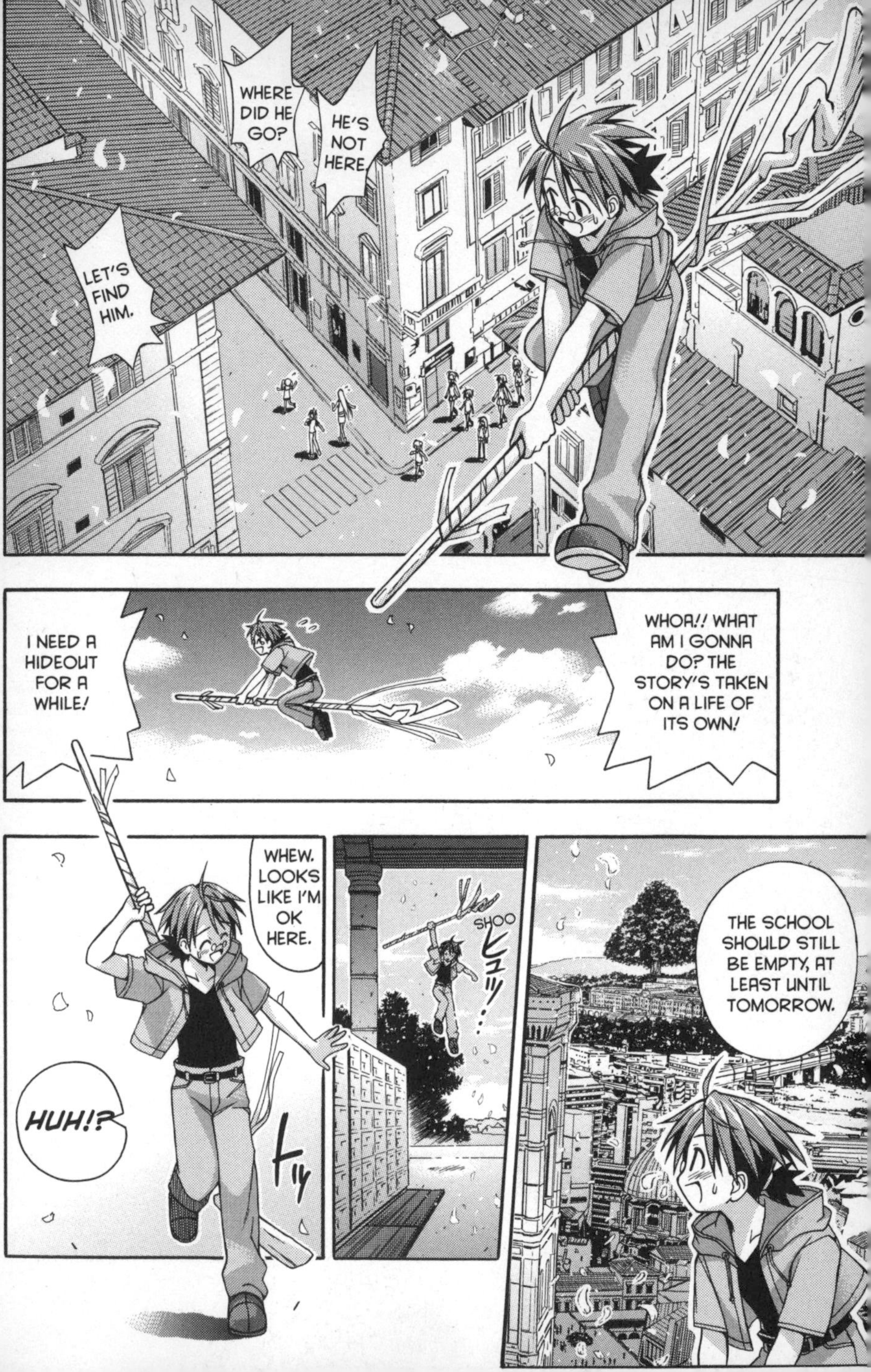
HE'S NOT HERE.
WHERE DID HE GO?
LET'S FIND HIM.
WHOA!! WHAT AM I GONNA DO? THE STORY'S TAKEN ON A LIFE OF ITS OWN!
I NEED A HIDEOUT FOR A WHILE!
THE SCHOOL SHOULD STILL BE EMPTY, AT LEAST UNTIL TOMORROW.
SHOO
ヒュッ
WHEW. LOOKS LIKE I'M OK HERE.
トッ
HUH!?

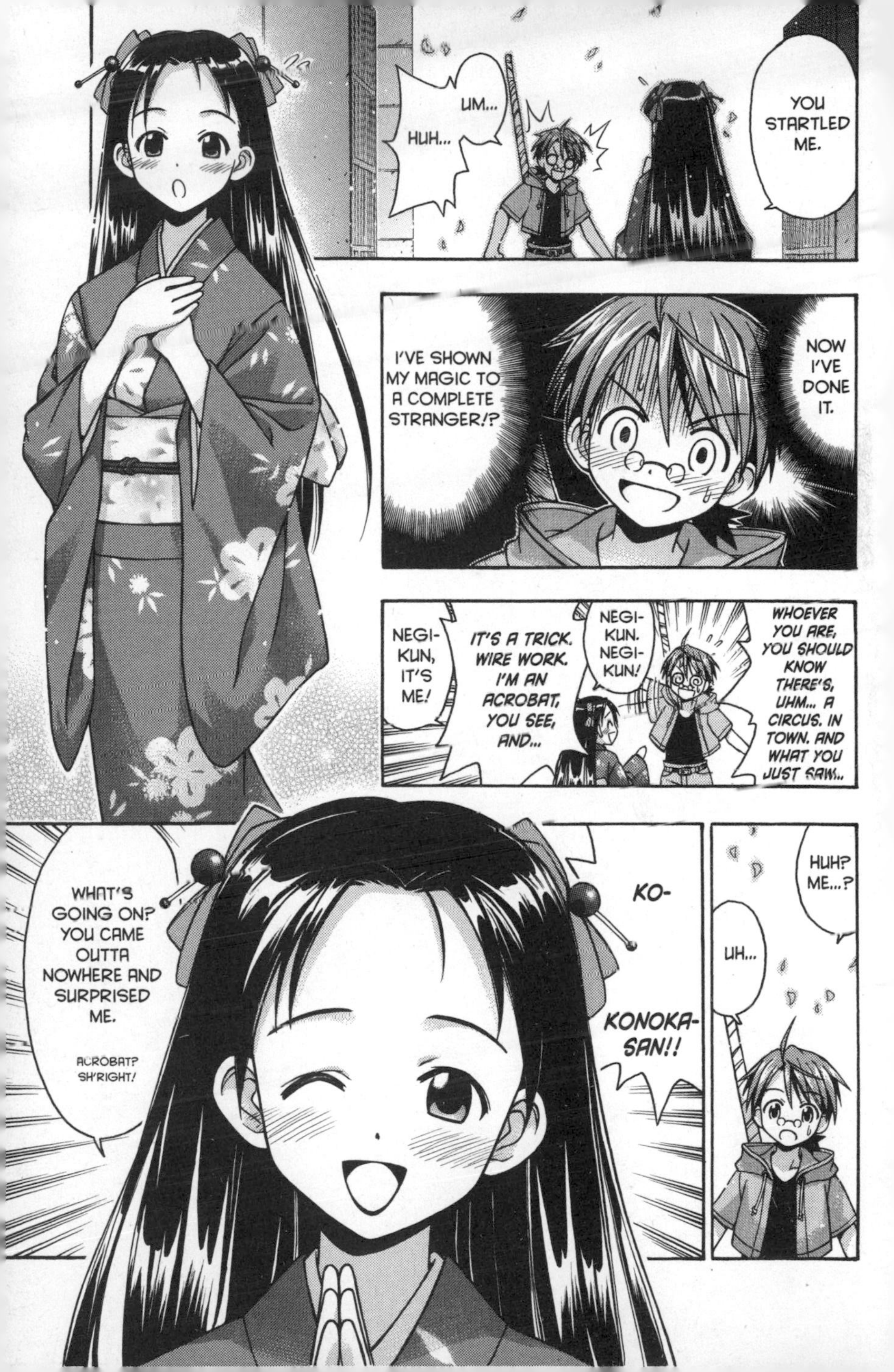
YOU STARTLED ME.
UM... HUH...
NOW I'VE DONE IT.
I'VE SHOWN MY MAGIC TO A COMPLETE STRANGER!?
WHOEVER YOU ARE, YOU SHOULD KNOW THERE'S, UHM... A CIRCUS. IN TOWN. AND WHAT YOU JUST SAW..
NEGI-KUN. NEGI-KUN!
IT'S A TRICK. WIRE WORK. I'M AN ACROBAT, YOU SEE, AND...
NEGI-KUN, IT'S ME!
HUH? ME...?
UH...
KO-
KONOKA-SAN!!
WHAT'S GOING ON? YOU CAME OUTTA NOWHERE AND SURPRISED ME.
ACROBAT? SH'RIGHT!

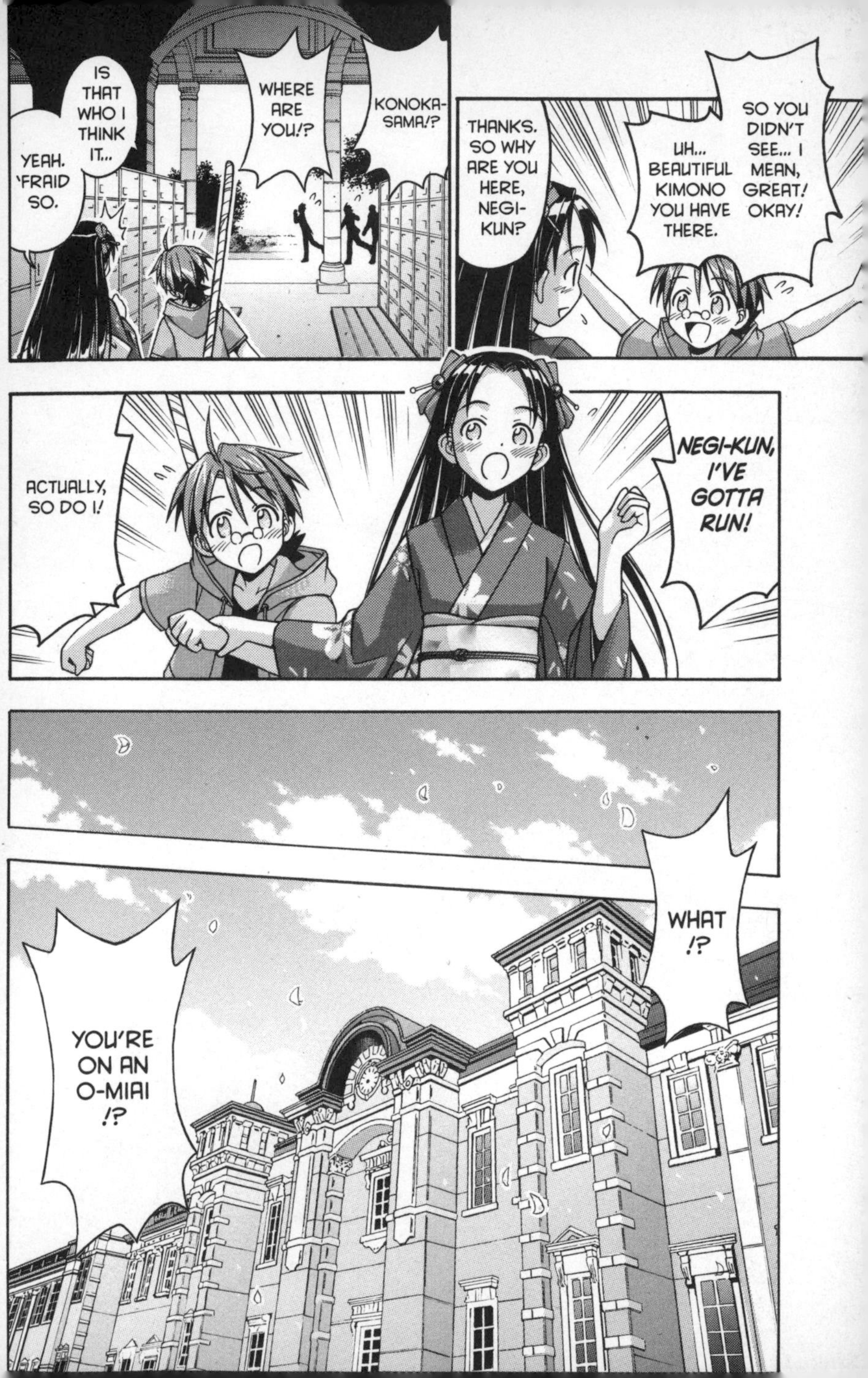
SO YOU DIDN'T SEE... I MEAN, GREAT! OKAY!
UH... BEAUTIFUL KIMONO YOU HAVE THERE.
THANKS. SO WHY ARE YOU HERE, NEGI-KUN?
KONOKA-SAMA!?
WHERE ARE YOU!?
IS THAT WHO I THINK IT...
YEAH. 'FRAID SO.
NEGI-KUN, I'VE GOTTA RUN!
ACTUALLY, SO DO I!
WHAT !?
YOU'RE ON AN O-MIAI !?

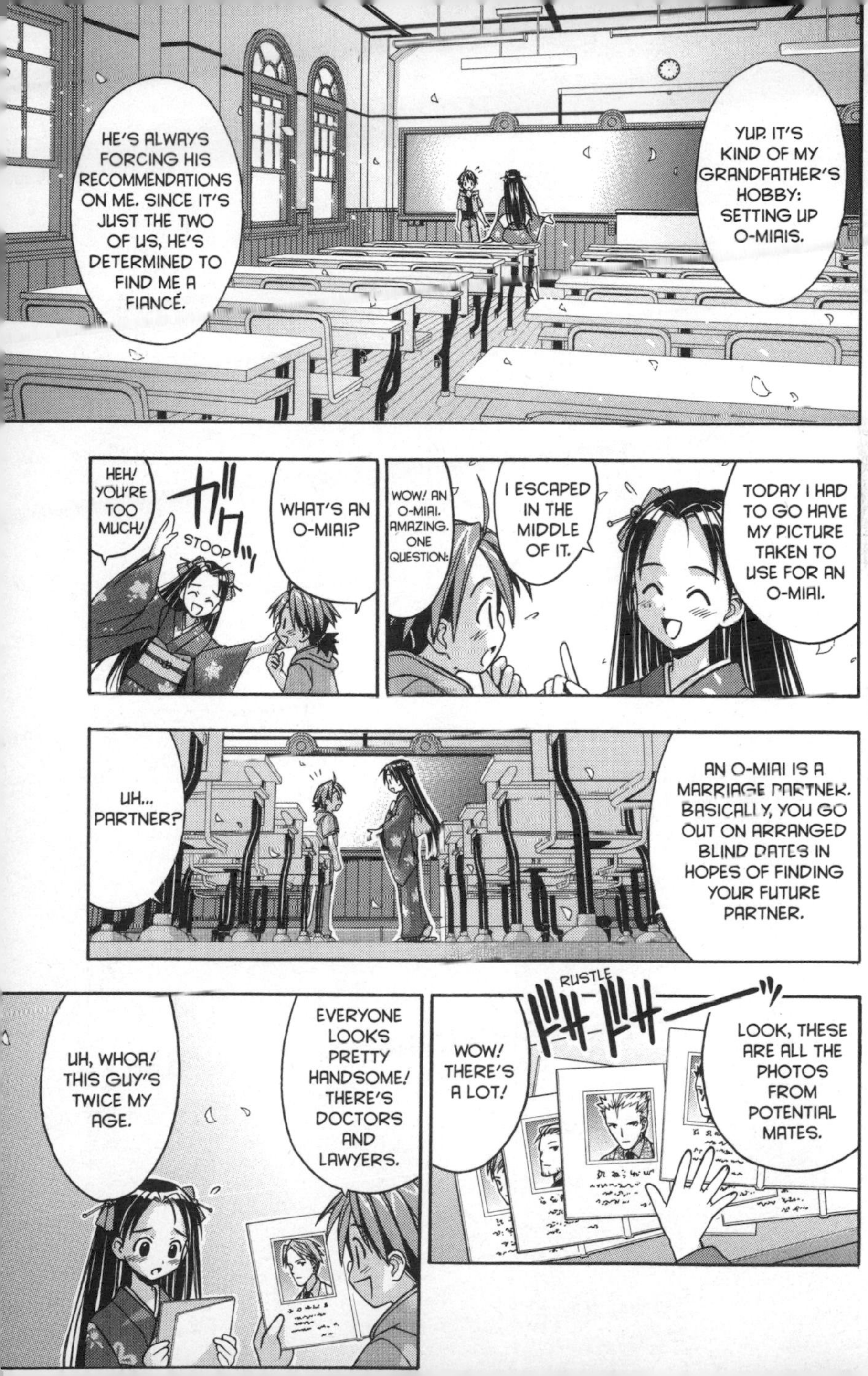

YUP. IT'S KIND OF MY GRANDFATHER'S HOBBY: SETTING UP O-MIAIS.
HE'S ALWAYS FORCING HIS RECOMMENDATIONS ON ME. SINCE IT'S JUST THE TWO OF US, HE'S DETERMINED TO FIND ME A FIANCÉ.
TODAY I HAD TO GO HAVE MY PICTURE TAKEN TO USE FOR AN O-MIAI.
I ESCAPED IN THE MIDDLE OF IT.
WOW! AN O-MIAI. AMAZING. ONE QUESTION:
WHAT'S AN O-MIAI?
HEH! YOU'RE TOO MUCH!
STOOP
AN O-MIAI IS A MARRIAGE PARTNER. BASICALLY, YOU GO OUT ON ARRANGED BLIND DATES IN HOPES OF FINDING YOUR FUTURE PARTNER.
UH... PARTNER?
RUSTLE
LOOK, THESE ARE ALL THE PHOTOS FROM POTENTIAL MATES.
WOW! THERE'S A LOT!
EVERYONE LOOKS PRETTY HANDSOME! THERE'S DOCTORS AND LAWYERS.
UH, WHOA! THIS GUY'S TWICE MY AGE.

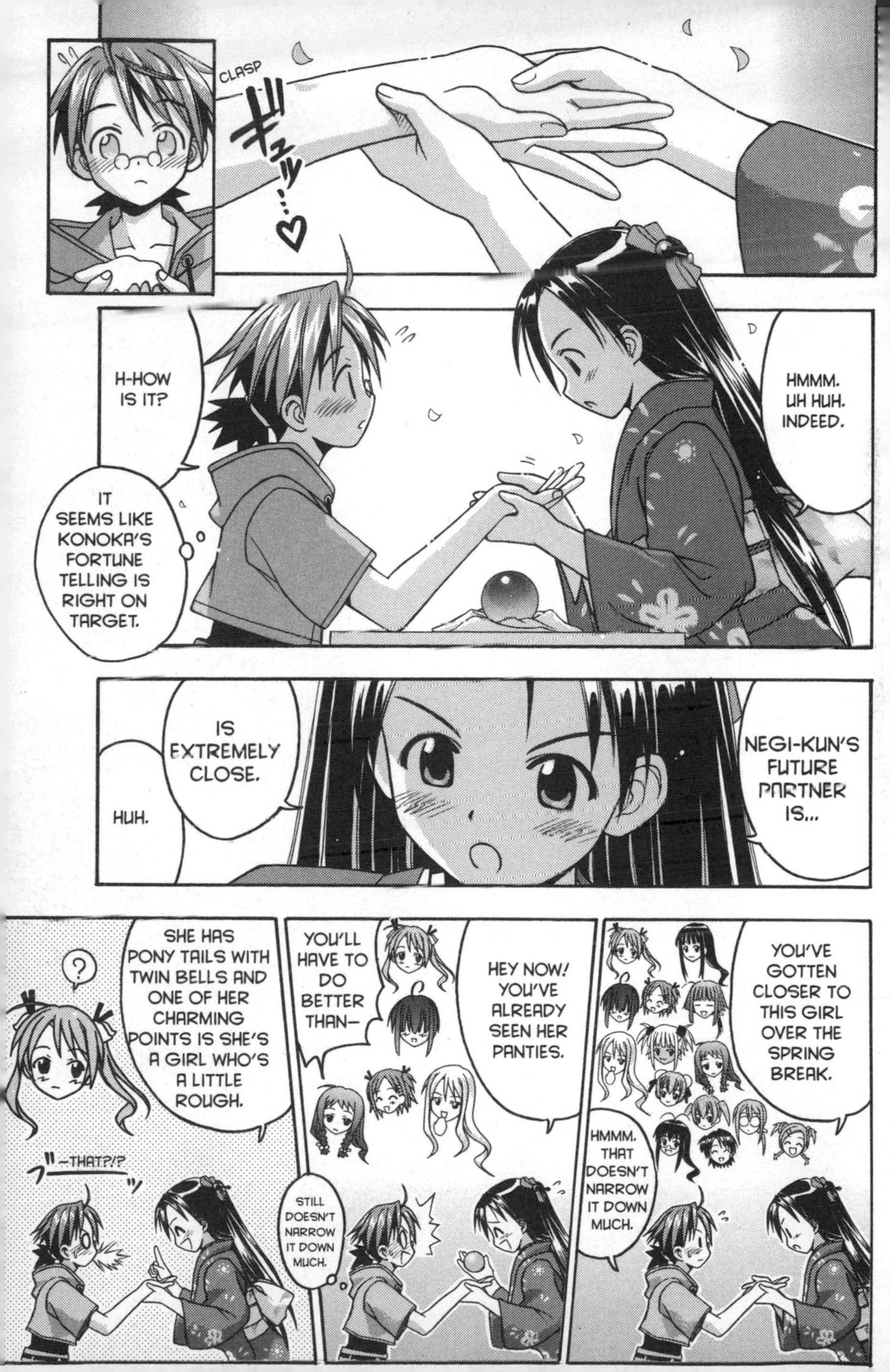
CLASP
HMMM. UH HUH. INDEED.
H-HOW IS IT?
IT SEEMS LIKE KONOKA'S FORTUNE TELLING IS RIGHT ON TARGET.
NEGI-KUN'S FUTURE PARTNER IS...
IS EXTREMELY CLOSE.
HUH.
YOU'VE GOTTEN CLOSER TO THIS GIRL OVER THE SPRING BREAK.
HMMM. THAT DOESN'T NARROW IT DOWN MUCH.
HEY NOW! YOU'VE ALREADY SEEN HER PANTIES.
YOU'LL HAVE TO DO BETTER THAN—
STILL DOESN'T NARROW IT DOWN MUCH.
SHE HAS PONY TAILS WITH TWIN BELLS AND ONE OF HER CHARMING POINTS IS SHE'S A GIRL WHO'S A LITTLE ROUGH.
?
—THAT?!?

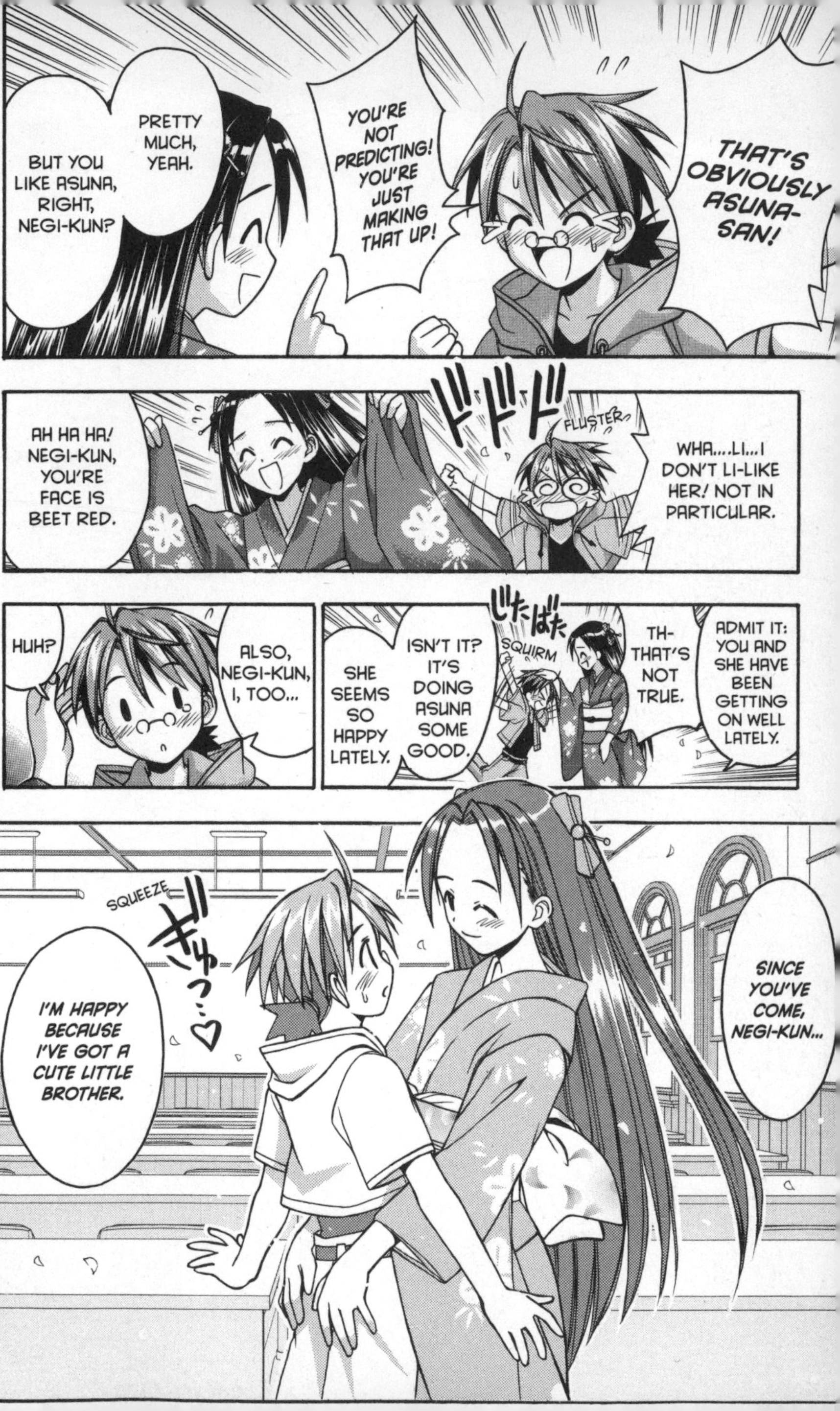
THAT'S OBVIOUSLY ASUNA-SAN!
YOU'RE NOT PREDICTING! YOU'RE JUST MAKING THAT UP!
PRETTY MUCH, YEAH.
BUT YOU LIKE ASUNA, RIGHT, NEGI-KUN?
ドドド
FLUSTER
WHA....LI...I DON'T LI-LIKE HER! NOT IN PARTICULAR.
AH HA HA! NEGI-KUN, YOU'RE FACE IS BEET RED.
ADMIT IT: YOU AND SHE HAVE BEEN GETTING ON WELL LATELY.
TH-THAT'S NOT TRUE.
じたばた
SQUIRM
ISN'T IT? IT'S DOING ASUNA SOME GOOD.
SHE SEEMS SO HAPPY LATELY.
ALSO, NEGI-KUN, I, TOO...
HUH?
SINCE YOU'VE COME, NEGI-KUN...
SQUEEZE
ぎゅっ…♡
I'M HAPPY BECAUSE I'VE GOT A CUTE LITTLE BROTHER.

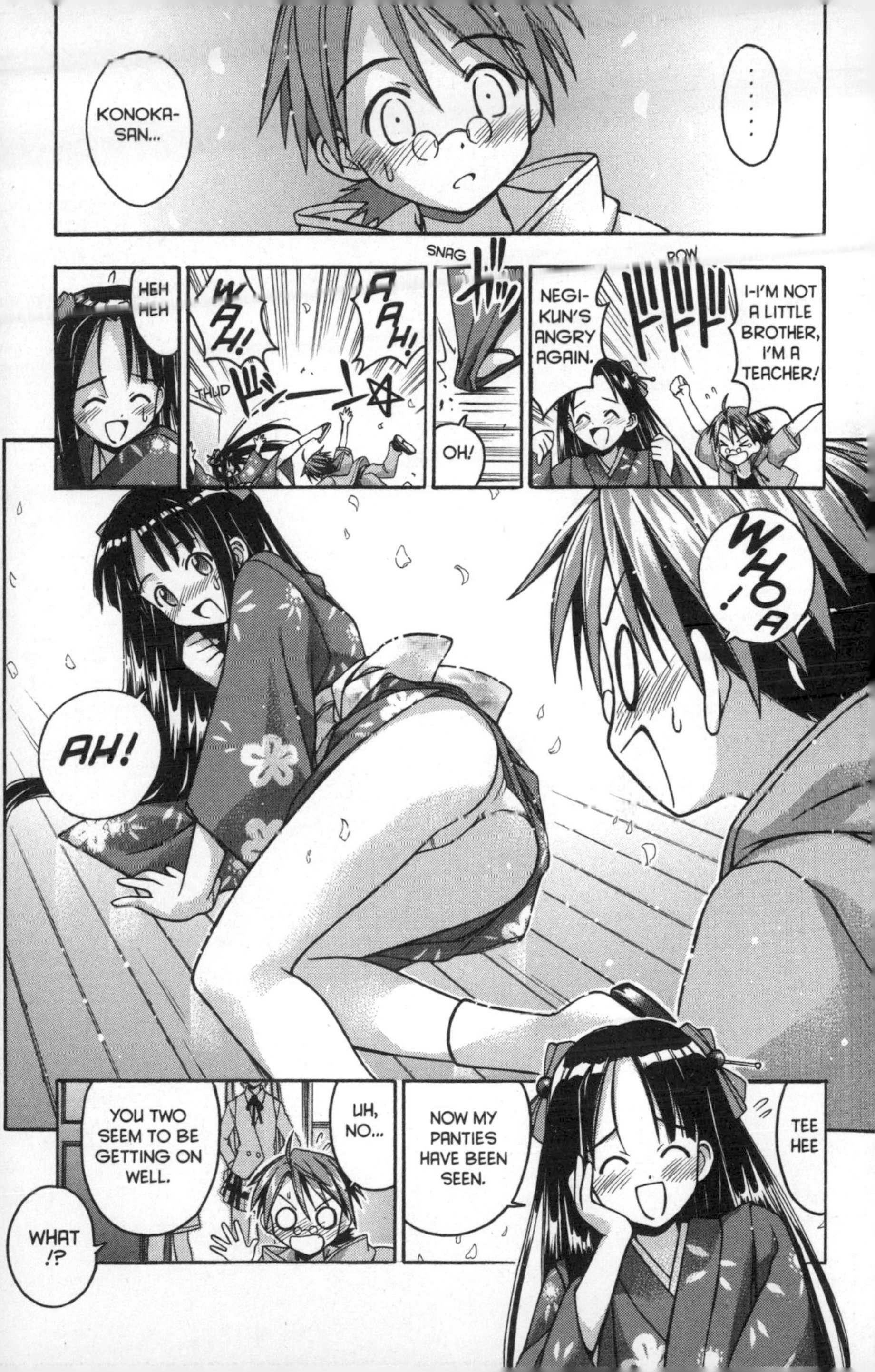
......
KONOKA-SAN...
I-I'M NOT A LITTLE BROTHER, I'M A TEACHER!
POW
NEGI-KUN'S ANGRY AGAIN.
SNAG
OH!
AAAH!
WAAH!
THUD
HEH HEH
WHOA!
AH!
TEE HEE
NOW MY PANTIES HAVE BEEN SEEN.
UH, NO...
YOU TWO SEEM TO BE GETTING ON WELL.
WHAT!?

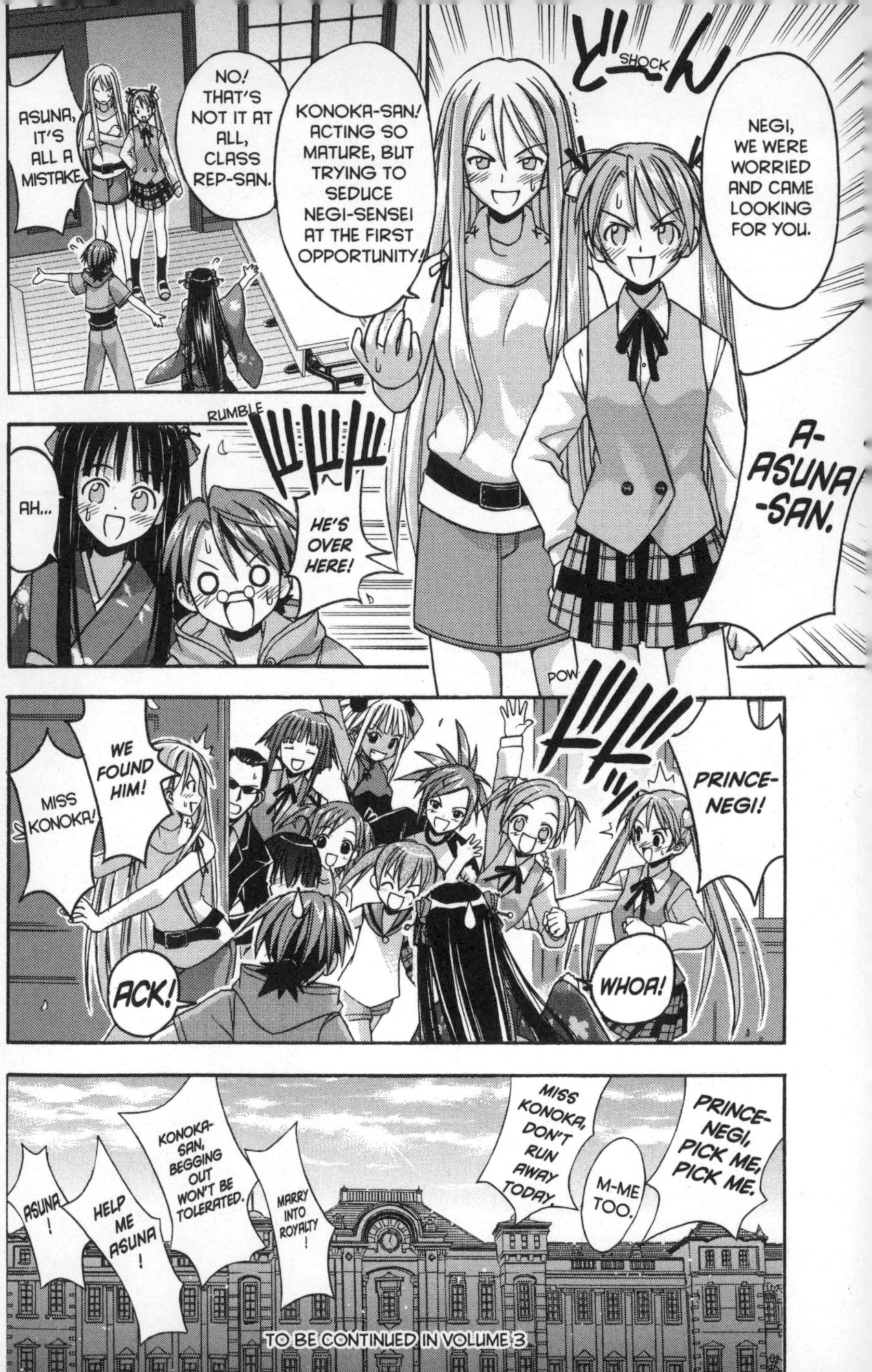
SHOCK
NEGI, WE WERE WORRIED AND CAME LOOKING FOR YOU.
KONOKA-SAN! ACTING SO MATURE, BUT TRYING TO SEDUCE NEGI-SENSEI AT THE FIRST OPPORTUNITY!
NO! THAT'S NOT IT AT ALL, CLASS REP-SAN.
ASUNA, IT'S ALL A MISTAKE.
A-ASUNA-SAN.
RUMBLE
HE'S OVER HERE!
AH...
POW
PRINCE-NEGI!
WE FOUND HIM!
MISS KONOKA!
WHOA!
ACK!
PRINCE-NEGI, PICK ME, PICK ME.
M-ME TOO.
MISS KONOKA, DON'T RUN AWAY TODAY.
MARRY INTO ROYALTY!
KONOKA-SAN, BEGGING OUT WON'T BE TOLERATED.
HELP ME ASUNA!
ASUNA!
TO BE CONTINUED IN VOLUME 3

- STAFF -

Ken Akamatsu
Takashi Takemoto
Kenichi Nakamura
Masaki Ohyama
Keiichi Yamashita
Chigusa Amagasaki
Takaaki Miyahara
Kei Nishikawa

Thanks To

Ran Ayanaga
Toshiko Akamatsu

About the Creator

Negima! is only Ken Akamatsu's third manga, although he started working in the field in 1994 with *AI Ga Tomaranai*. Like all of Akamatsu's work to date, it was published in Kodansha's *Shonen Magazine*. *AI Ga Tomaranai* ran for five years before concluding in 1999. In 1998, however, Akamatsu began the work that would make him one of the most popular manga artists in Japan: *Love Hina*. *Love Hina* ran for four years, and before its conclusion in 2002, it would cause Akamatsu to be granted the prestigious Manga of the Year award from Kodansha, as well as going on to become one of the known and bestselling manga in the United Kingdom.

Volumes 1, 2 and 3 of *Negima!* are avalaible now.

COMPILATION OF MATERIAL FOR THE BEGINNING SETTINGS OF NEGIMA!

THE ORIGINAL CHARACTER SKETCHES

THERE ARE MANY CHARACTERS THAT APPEAR IN NEGIMA! SO THREE ASSISTANTS AND I LIVE TOGETHER. WE DIVIDE THE WORK AND DECIDE THE MINUTE DETAILS OF THE SETTINGS. BECAUSE OF THIS, EVERY CHARACTER'S 'GROWING PAINS' ARE DIFFERENT. THIS TIME, WE'LL INTRODUCE THOSE SKETCH IDEAS.

—AKAMATSU.

MAGISTER NEGI MAGI

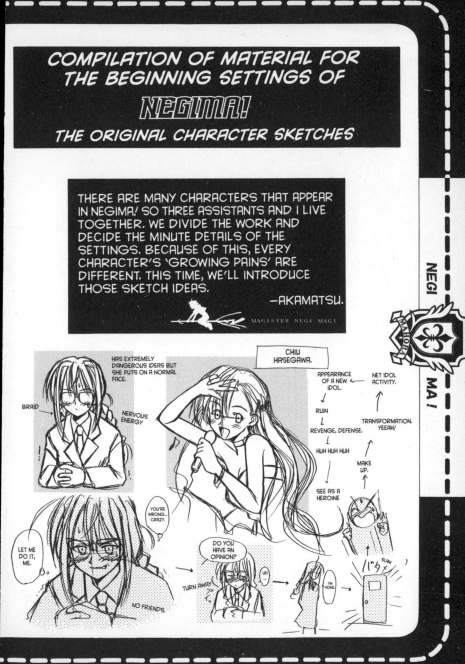

CHIU HASEGAWA.
HAS EXTREMELY DANGEROUS IDEAS BUT SHE PUTS ON A NORMAL FACE.
BRAID
NERVOUS ENERGY
APPEARANCE OF A NEW IDOL.
NET IDOL ACTIVITY.
RUIN
REVENGE, DEFENSE.
HUH HUH HUH
TRANSFORMATION. YEEAH!
MAKE UP.
SEE AS A HEROINE
YOU'RE WRONG... CRAZY.
LET ME DO IT, ME.
DO YOU HAVE AN OPINION?
UH ...
TURN AWAY
I'M HOME.
SLAM
NO FRIENDS.

THE STORY PLAN FOR CHISAME IS NOT WRITTEN (HA HA). WE'RE MAKING IT UP AS WE GO. AT THE BEGINNING, THE TWINS DIDN'T HAVE MUCH PERSONALITY. IN THE FINAL VERSION THEY'RE A COUPLE OF PRANKSTERS. BUT THIS IS ALSO INTERESTING.

MAGISTER NEGI MAGI

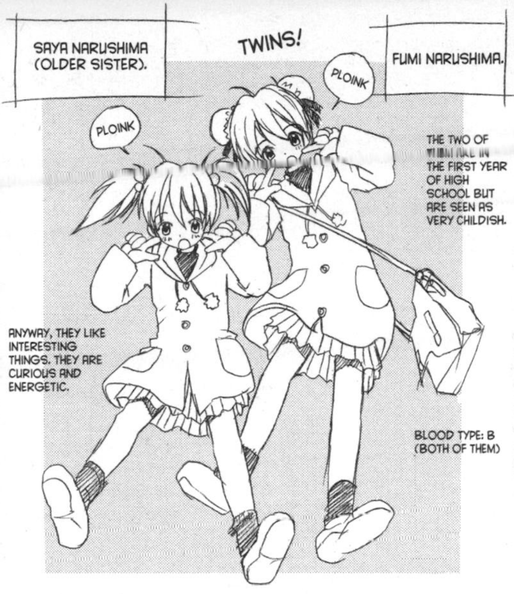
SAYA NARUSHIMA (OLDER SISTER).
TWINS!
FUMI NARUSHIMA.
PLOINK
PLOINK
THE TWO OF THEM ARE IN THE FIRST YEAR OF HIGH SCHOOL BUT ARE SEEN AS VERY CHILDISH.
ANYWAY, THEY LIKE INTERESTING THINGS. THEY ARE CURIOUS AND ENERGETIC.
BLOOD TYPE: B (BOTH OF THEM)

I'M NOT SURE WHAT TO DO ABOUT THEIR NAMES. THEY'RE TWO PEOPLE WHO DON'T THINK ALIKE ABOUT ANYTHING. OCCASIONALLY, THEY CHUCKLE AND LAUGH TOGETHER.

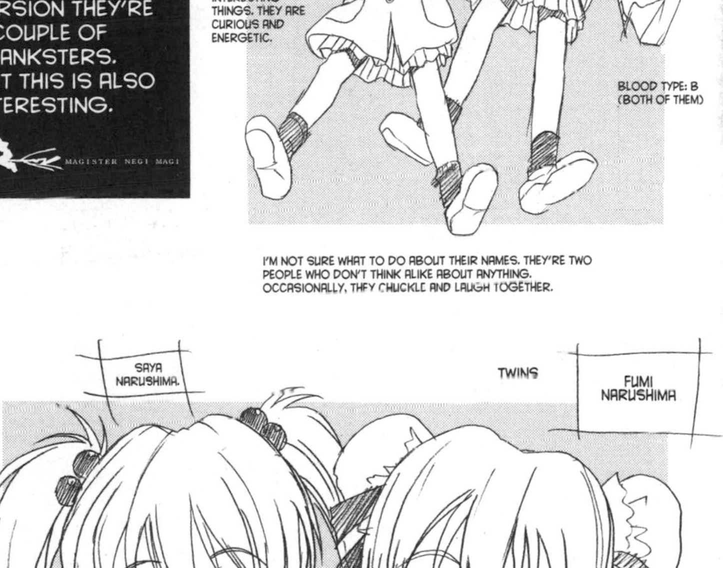
SAYA NARUSHIMA.
TWINS
FUMI NARUSHIMA
SURPRISED.
LAUGHING.

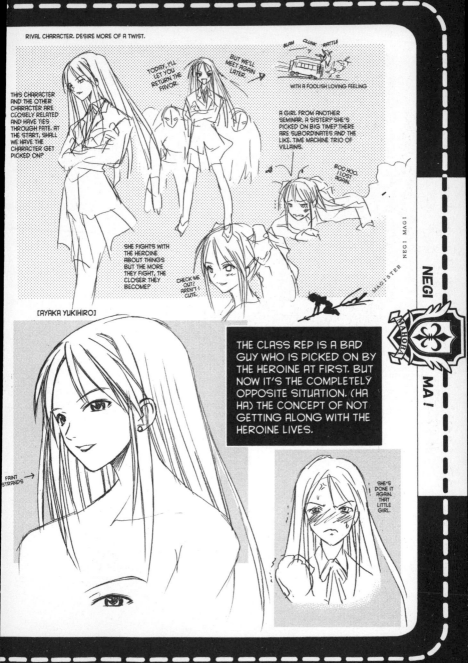

RIVAL CHARACTER. DESIRE MORE OF A TWIST.

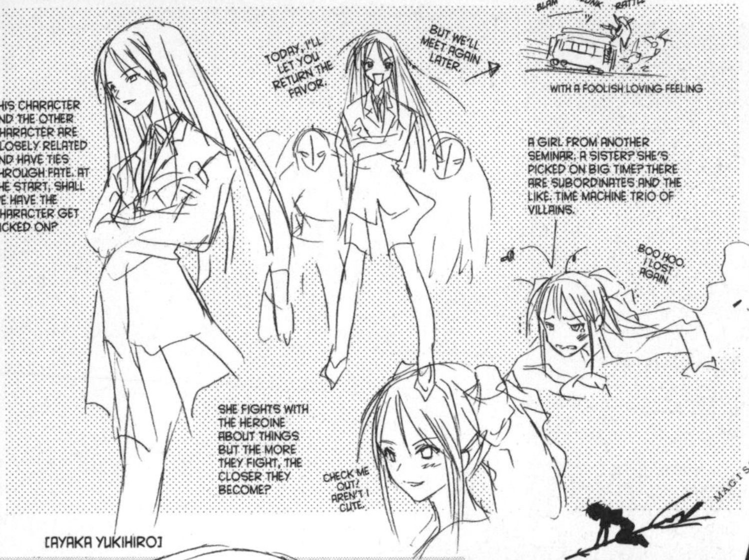

BLAM
CLUNK
RATTLE
BUT WE'LL MEET AGAIN LATER.
TODAY, I'LL LET YOU RETURN THE FAVOR.
WITH A FOOLISH LOVING FEELING
THIS CHARACTER AND THE OTHER CHARACTER ARE CLOSELY RELATED AND HAVE TIES THROUGH FATE. AT THE START, SHALL WE HAVE THE CHARACTER GET PICKED ON?
A GIRL FROM ANOTHER SEMINAR; A SISTER? SHE'S PICKED ON BIG TIME? THERE ARE SUBORDINATES AND THE LIKE. TIME MACHINE TRIO OF VILLAINS.
BOO HOO, I LOST AGAIN.
SHE FIGHTS WITH THE HEROINE ABOUT THINGS. BUT THE MORE THEY FIGHT, THE CLOSER THEY BECOME?
CHECK ME OUT! AREN'T I CUTE.
NEGI MAGI
MAGISTER

[AYAKA YUKIHIRO]

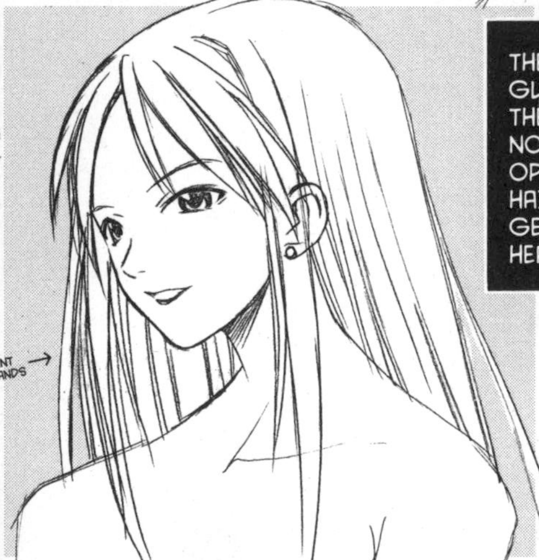

FAINT STRANDS

THE CLASS REP IS A BAD GUY WHO IS PICKED ON BY THE HEROINE AT FIRST. BUT NOW IT'S THE COMPLETELY OPPOSITE SITUATION. (HA HA) THE CONCEPT OF NOT GETTING ALONG WITH THE HEROINE LIVES.

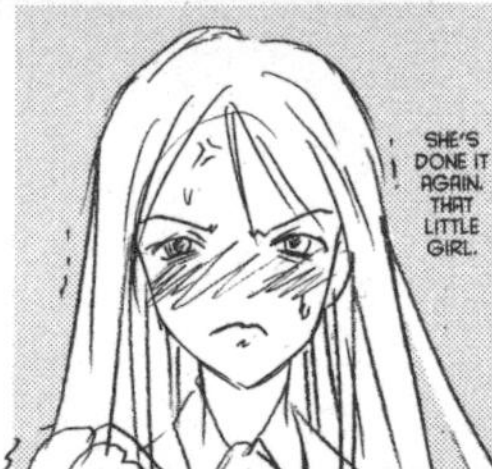

SHE'S DONE IT AGAIN. THAT LITTLE GIRL.

[KOZUE MIGARA]

A GENERAL PERSON. THE HEROINES CLOSE FRIEND WHO PLAY A FORCEFUL ROLE.

LIGHT FLUFFY HAIR RUSTLING IN THE WIND

THIS IS CHARACTER DESIGNED AS THE ORIGINAL "HEROINE'S PAL". IT BECAME THE ORIGINAL PLAN FOR "MAKIE". SAKURAKO SPRANG FROM THE LACROSSE CLUB. HER POPULARITY WITH THE STAFF IS HIGH.

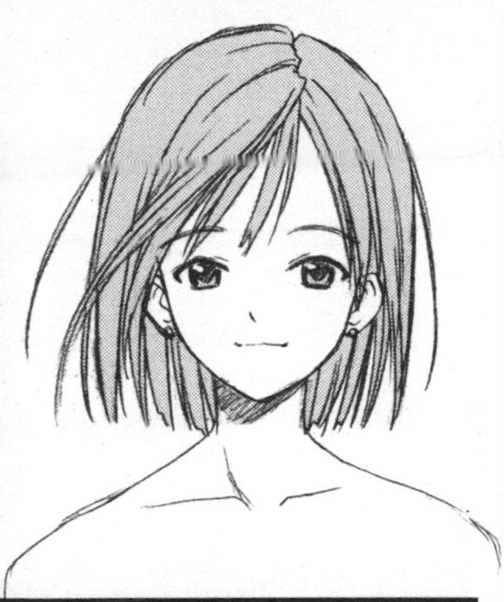

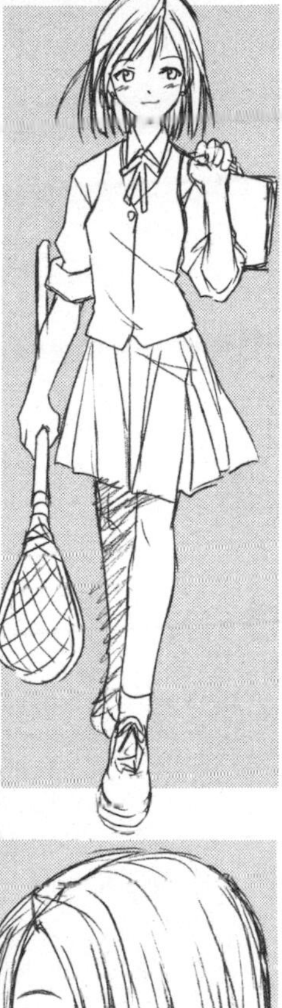

BY THE WAY, THE SERIAL NEGIMA! IN THE CHUKAN SHOUNEN MAGAZINE OFTEN HAS A CHARACTER POPULARITY VOTE. DEPENDING ON THIS, THEIR APPEARANCE FLUCTUATES SO EVERYONE PLEASE PARTICIPATE!

MAGISTER NEGI MAGI

A GENERAL STUDENT. A GOOD FRIEND OF THE HEROINE. SEVERAL STRANGE INCIDENTS THAT THEY'RE THRUST INTO (IN THEIR HEARTS) APPEAR IN THE THIRD STORY. YOU CAN FEEL THE FATIGUE OF BEING INVOLVED. WHY THE SCHOOL IS THIS STRANGE IS IN QUESTION. INCREASINGLY, IT BECOMES AN ISSUE THAT MUST BE DEALT WITH.

LACROSSE CLUB

AN EXTREMELY NORMAL, REALISTIC PERSON WITH REGARDS TO BEING AWARE OF LOVE ETC.

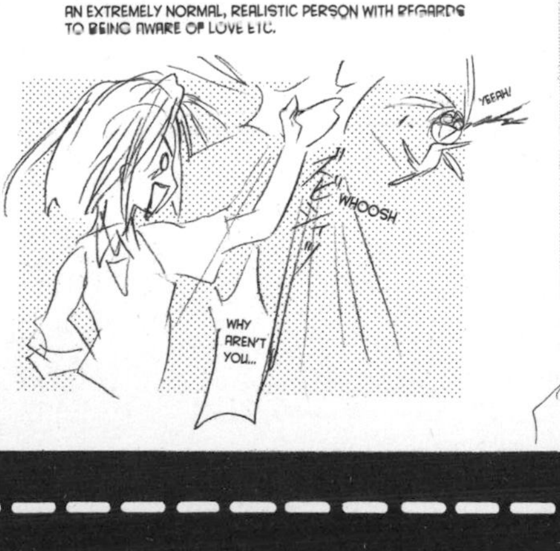
YEEAH!
WHOOSH
WHY AREN'T YOU...

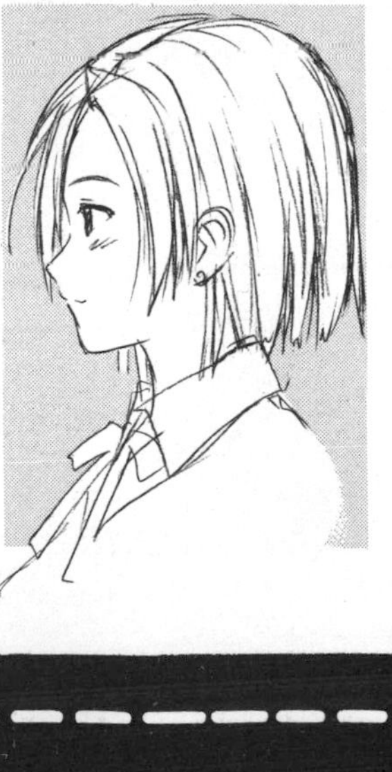

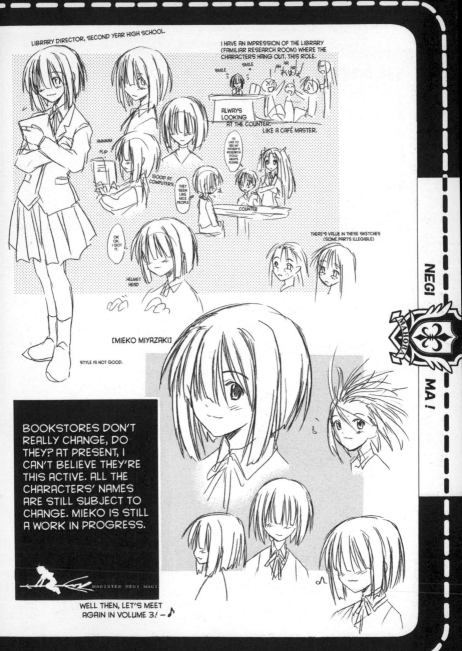

LIBRARY DIRECTOR, SECOND YEAR HIGH SCHOOL.
I HAVE AN IMPRESSION OF THE LIBRARY (FAMILIAR RESEARCH ROOM) WHERE THE CHARACTER'S HANG OUT. THIS ROLE.
SMILE
SMILE
HA HA HA
ALWAYS LOOKING AT THE COUNTER.
LIKE A CAFÉ MASTER.
HMMMM
FLIP
I'D LIKE TO SEE MY FATHER'S RESEARCH DOCU- MENTS PLEASE.
GOOD AT COMPUTERS
THEY SEEM LIKE NICE PEOPLE
COUNTER
OK OK. I GOT IT.
HELMET HEAD
THERE'S VALUE IN THESE SKETCHES (SOME PARTS ILLEGIBLE)
[MIEKO MIYAZAKI]
STYLE IS NOT GOOD.
MAGISTER NEGI MAGI

BOOKSTORES DON'T REALLY CHANGE, DO THEY? AT PRESENT, I CAN'T BELIEVE THEY'RE THIS ACTIVE. ALL THE CHARACTERS' NAMES ARE STILL SUBJECT TO CHANGE. MIEKO IS STILL A WORK IN PROGRESS.

WELL THEN, LET'S MEET AGAIN IN VOLUME 3! –♪

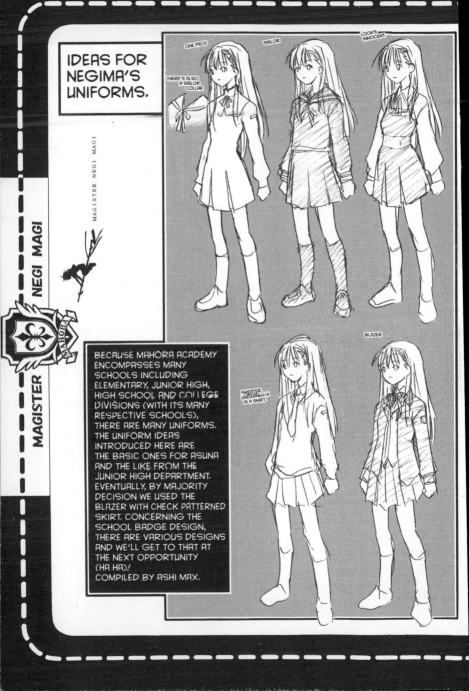

IDEAS FOR NEGIMA'S UNIFORMS.

ONE PIECE

THERE'S ALSO A SAILOR COLLAR

SAILOR

LOOKS INNOCENT.

BLAZER

SWEATER UNDERNEATH IS A SHIRT.

BECAUSE MAHORA ACADEMY ENCOMPASSES MANY SCHOOLS INCLUDING ELEMENTARY, JUNIOR HIGH, HIGH SCHOOL AND COLLEGE DIVISIONS (WITH ITS MANY RESPECTIVE SCHOOLS), THERE ARE MANY UNIFORMS. THE UNIFORM IDEAS INTRODUCED HERE ARE THE BASIC ONES FOR ASUNA AND THE LIKE FROM THE JUNIOR HIGH DEPARTMENT. EVENTUALLY, BY MAJORITY DECISION WE USED THE BLAZER WITH CHECK PATTERNED SKIRT. CONCERNING THE SCHOOL BADGE DESIGN, THERE ARE VARIOUS DESIGNS AND WE'LL GET TO THAT AT THE NEXT OPPORTUNITY (HA HA)! COMPILED BY ASHI MAX.

LATIUM LEXICON NEGIMARIUM

Compiled by Minoru Ashi

- **Magister Negi Magi.** Magic-Sensei Negima is the subtitle in the Japanese edition. Well, Latin is used everywhere in the world. Here, *magister* means *sensei*. *Negi* is a proper name. *Magi* means *magical*. Basically, it translates to Wizard Negi-Sensei. (So what in the world does the 'ma' in *Negima!* mean?)

- The Latin used in *Negima!* has cases where the long vowels are not extended owing to the convenience of rhythm. For example, *magi* is actually pronounced *ma-gee* but as he is often called *ma-jai* so he comes to be called *magi*.

- **Magister Magi** also means magical people. Magi is the plural case of *wizard*. The singular nominative case is *magus*. Magister here means *people*. As written above, it also means *sensei* and is equivalent to the English *master* and the German *meister*.

- **Melchizedek.** The Vulgata translation of the Bible (Genesis 14:17-20) says that upon returning from the subjugation of Cherdorlaomer and the kings who were allied with him, King Sodom came to meet Abram in Valley Shaveh. The king of Salem, Melchizedek, a priest of the supreme god, came there bringing bread and wine. Melchizedek said blessings to Abram. The blessing asked of the supreme god, creator of heaven and earth, was for Abram. The blessing also promised to deliver the enemy into the clutches of the supreme god. In Hebrew, it's Melchizedek. It's not written in the canons or Apocrypha, but there's a legend of our ancestor Abraham being granted the secret of cabala. (Eighth Period.)

- **Minister magi** means a 'follower of magic' and is equivalent to the English term *minister*. In the case of women, they are called *ministra magi*. The relationship between the magi as an individual and as a master of magic has many factors, and the role the minister plays varies in response to that. Today, there are a lot of partners who become lovers and spouses, but partners aren't always limited to the opposite sex. For more on this, refer to Negima Volume 3.

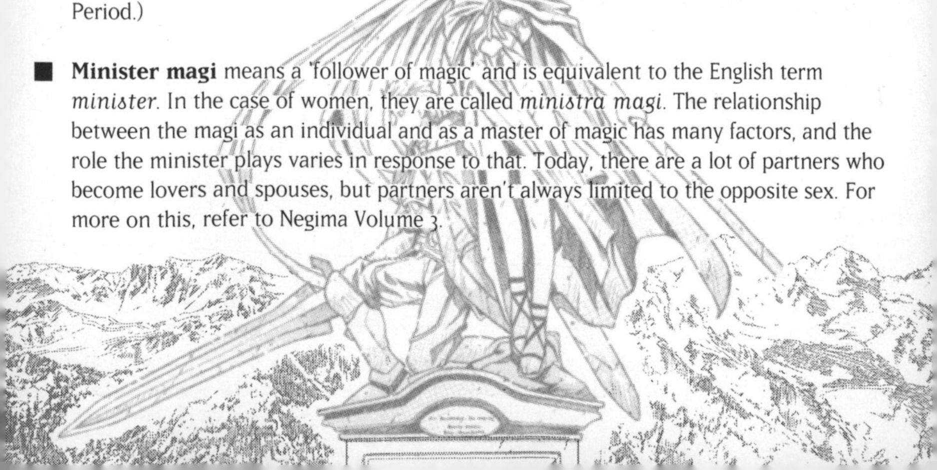

Spells

■ **Rastel maskil magister.** This is not Latin (and that language is the key to releasing magic), and it seems like it's a code with no meaning. *Rastel maskil magister* is the exclusive incantation for Negi Springfield. Each and every wizard thinks of one for themselves, and Negi came up with his own when he graduated from magic school. In the case of simple magic, you can abbreviate it. (First used in Second Period.)

■ **Age nascatur, potio amoris.** Literally: well, in life, a love potion. This is a spell for the preparation of magic medicine. *Potio* means potion in Latin. Used for the purification of love potions. (Second Period.)

■ **Aer aer amplificet mammas.** Air, atmosphere, breasts expand. Negi calls on the power of a friendly air spirit to manipulate the air. In this case, it created an air bubble around Asuna's chest, making it seem like she had huge breasts. To actually change Asuna's appearance, Negi would have needed to use the spell *mammae crescant*, which means, in short, "breasts become larger!" (Third Period.)

■ **Salent, penicili.** Dance, brushes. Making things move is basic magic. (Fourth Period.)

■ **Aer...** Magic word meaning air. Used by Negi, angry at the attack by Black Lily from the dodge ball club, to call on the air spirit. In the previous panel, an air current was starting to happen. However, in the middle of the incantation he was hit by Asuna, so just how powerful the spell is remains a mystery. (Sixth Period.)

■ **Tria fila nigra prommissiva, mihi limitationem per tres dies.** Three black pledge strings, a restriction on myself for three days. A spell that Negi cast on himself, bottling up his own magic power. Can also be used to contain the magic of enemies who possess magic powers. (Seventh Period.)

■ **Undecim spiritus lucis, coeuntes segittant inimicum, sagitta magica.** The 11 pillars of spirit light! Come gather and light up my enemy, magic archer. *Sagitta magica* means magic arrow. *Spiritus* is 'spirit' in English. Calling on a minor spirit, it's a spell that shoots the enemy you're facing. Depending on the spirit you call on, the effect is different. A rudimentary battle spell, but the scope of its application is wide. (Tenth Period.)

■ **Fragrantia floris, amicis vigorem, vitalitatem, auram salutarem refectio.** The fragrance of a flower, a wind that will fill my friends with energy, vitality, and health. Complete energy recovery. The flower that Negi uses is the catalyst. That catalyst makes it easier to cast the spell and heightens the effect. A spell that refreshes one's mood.

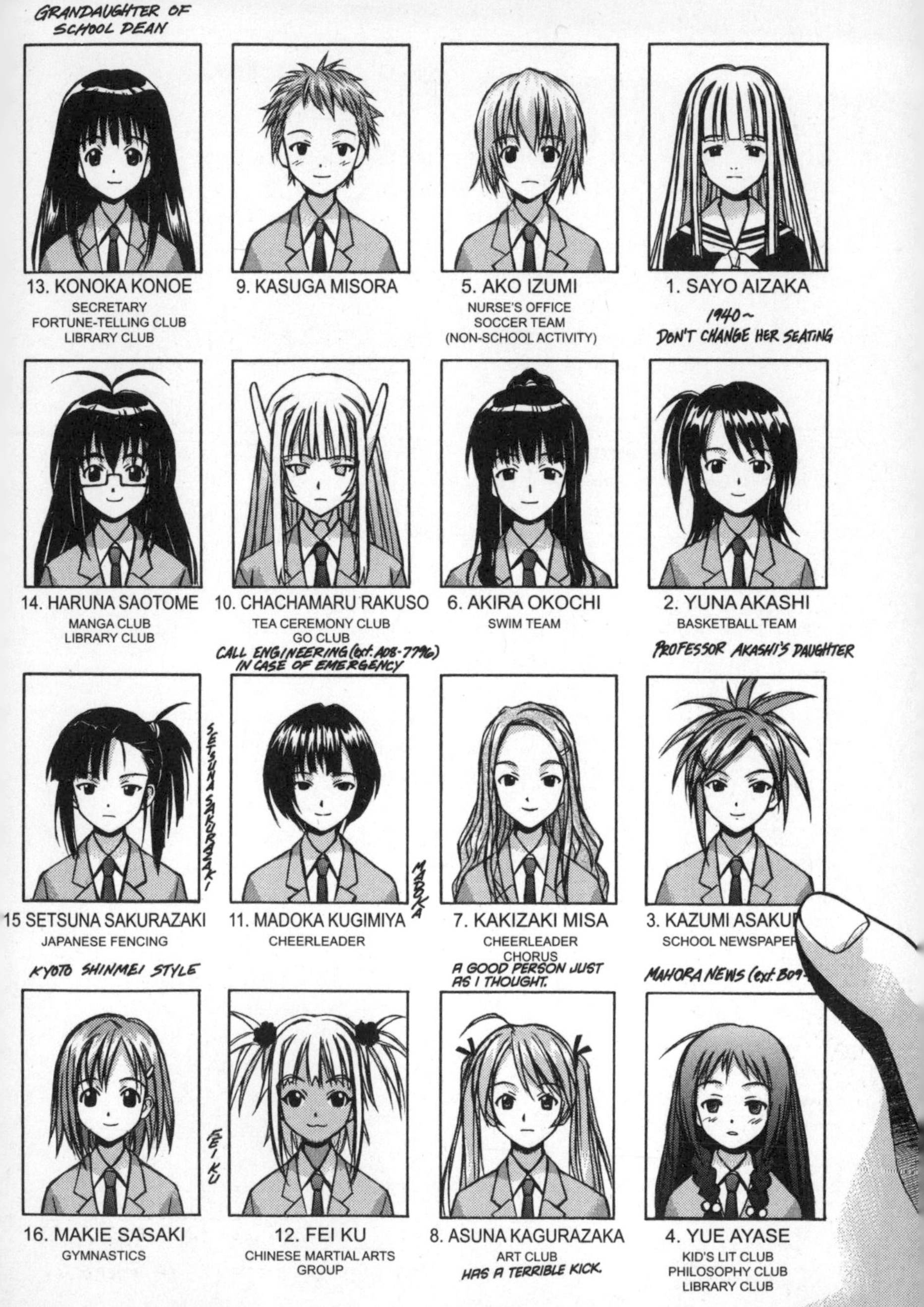

GRANDAUGHTER OF SCHOOL DEAN
1. SAYO AIZAKA
1940~
DON'T CHANGE HER SEATING
5. AKO IZUMI
NURSE'S OFFICE
SOCCER TEAM
(NON-SCHOOL ACTIVITY)
9. KASUGA MISORA
13. KONOKA KONOE
SECRETARY
FORTUNE-TELLING CLUB
LIBRARY CLUB
2. YUNA AKASHI
BASKETBALL TEAM
PROFESSOR AKASHI'S DAUGHTER
6. AKIRA OKOCHI
SWIM TEAM
10. CHACHAMARU RAKUSO
TEA CEREMONY CLUB
GO CLUB
CALL ENGINEERING (ext. A08-7796) IN CASE OF EMERGENCY
14. HARUNA SAOTOME
MANGA CLUB
LIBRARY CLUB
3. KAZUMI ASAKU
SCHOOL NEWSPAPE
MAHORA NEWS (ext. 809-
7. KAKIZAKI MISA
CHEERLEADER
CHORUS
A GOOD PERSON JUST AS I THOUGHT.
11. MADOKA KUGIMIYA
CHEERLEADER
MADOKA
15 SETSUNA SAKURAZAKI
JAPANESE FENCING
SETSUNA SAKURAZAKI
KYOTO SHINMEI STYLE
4. YUE AYASE
KID'S LIT CLUB
PHILOSOPHY CLUB
LIBRARY CLUB
8. ASUNA KAGURAZAKA
ART CLUB
HAS A TERRIBLE KICK.
12. FEI KU
CHINESE MARTIAL ARTS GROUP
FEI KU
16. MAKIE SASAKI
GYMNASTICS

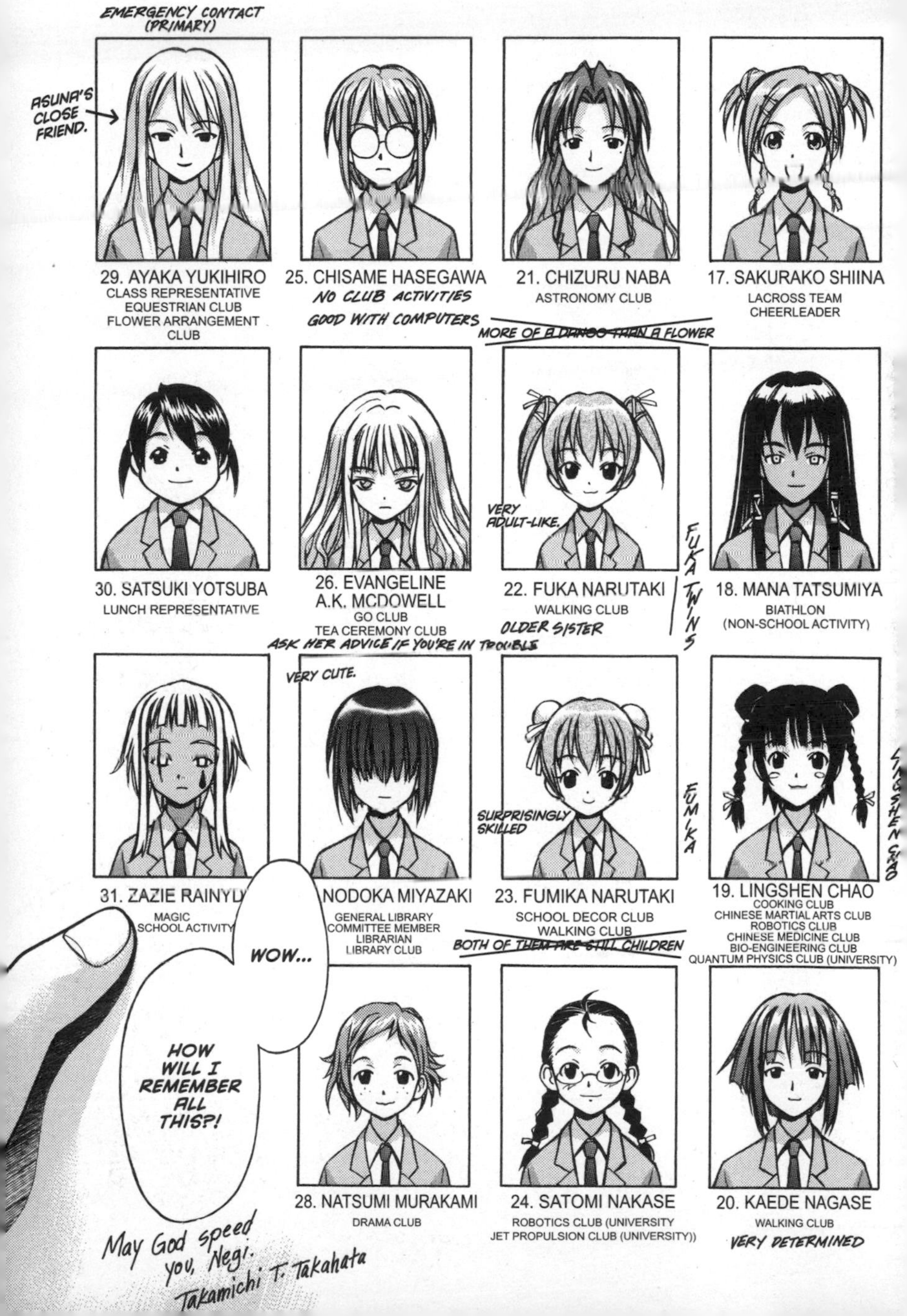
EMERGENCY CONTACT (PRIMARY)
ASUNA'S CLOSE FRIEND.
29. AYAKA YUKIHIRO
CLASS REPRESENTATIVE
EQUESTRIAN CLUB
FLOWER ARRANGEMENT CLUB
25. CHISAME HASEGAWA
NO CLUB ACTIVITIES
GOOD WITH COMPUTERS
21. CHIZURU NABA
ASTRONOMY CLUB
MORE OF A DANGO THAN A FLOWER
17. SAKURAKO SHIINA
LACROSS TEAM
CHEERLEADER
30. SATSUKI YOTSUBA
LUNCH REPRESENTATIVE
26. EVANGELINE A.K. MCDOWELL
GO CLUB
TEA CEREMONY CLUB
ASK HER ADVICE IF YOU'RE IN TROUBLE
VERY ADULT-LIKE.
22. FUKA NARUTAKI
WALKING CLUB
OLDER SISTER
FUKA TWINS
18. MANA TATSUMIYA
BIATHLON
(NON-SCHOOL ACTIVITY)
31. ZAZIE RAINYD
MAGIC
SCHOOL ACTIVITY
VERY CUTE.
NODOKA MIYAZAKI
GENERAL LIBRARY
COMMITTEE MEMBER
LIBRARIAN
LIBRARY CLUB
SURPRISINGLY SKILLED
FUMIKA
23. FUMIKA NARUTAKI
SCHOOL DECOR CLUB
WALKING CLUB
BOTH OF THEM ARE STILL CHILDREN
19. LINGSHEN CHAO
COOKING CLUB
CHINESE MARTIAL ARTS CLUB
ROBOTICS CLUB
CHINESE MEDICINE CLUB
BIO-ENGINEERING CLUB
QUANTUM PHYSICS CLUB (UNIVERSITY)
LINGSHEN CHAO
WOW...
HOW WILL I REMEMBER ALL THIS?!
28. NATSUMI MURAKAMI
DRAMA CLUB
24. SATOMI NAKASE
ROBOTICS CLUB (UNIVERSITY
JET PROPULSION CLUB (UNIVERSITY))
20. KAEDE NAGASE
WALKING CLUB
VERY DETERMINED
May God speed you, Negi.
Takamichi T. Takahata

Translation Notes

Japanese is a tricky language for most westerners, and translation is often more art than science. For your edification and reading pleasure, here are notes on some of the places where we could have gone in a different direction in our translation of the work, or where a Japanese cultural reference is used.

Half and Half, page 6

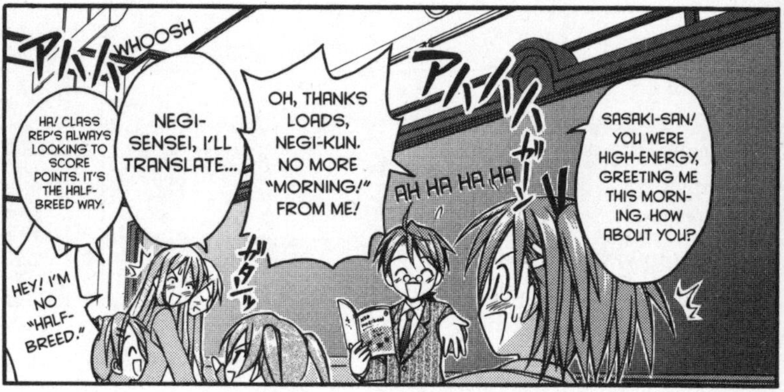
SASAKI-SAN! YOU WERE HIGH-ENERGY, GREETING ME THIS MORNING. HOW ABOUT YOU?
AH HA HA HA
OH, THANKS LOADS, NEGI-KUN. NO MORE "MORNING!" FROM ME!
NEGI-SENSEI, I'LL TRANSLATE...
WHOOSH
HA! CLASS REP'S ALWAYS LOOKING TO SCORE POINTS. IT'S THE HALF-BREED WAY.
HEY! I'M NO "HALF-BREED."

In this context in Japanese, the term "half" used here indicates mixed ancestry, so we gave it the closest English translation: "half-breed."

Baseball Janken, page 11

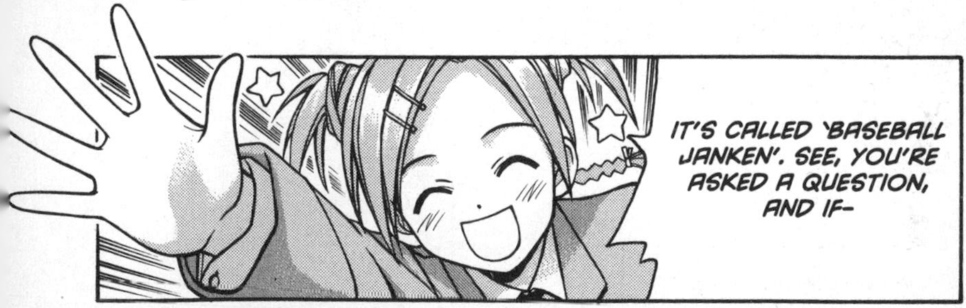
IT'S CALLED 'BASEBALL JANKEN'. SEE, YOU'RE ASKED A QUESTION, AND IF-

Janken is the Japanese name for "rock, paper, scissors," but this version is usually played as a drinking game accompanied by a song about baseball that incorporates the "safe" and "out" rules used in baseball. If one loses, or gets out, you have to remove articles of clothing so it's something like strip janken.

Mattcha Cola, page 19

Mattcha is a high-grade green tea used in the traditional Japanese Tea Ceremony.

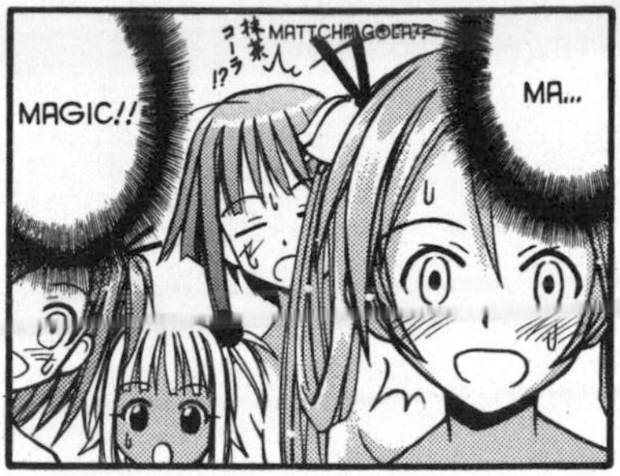
MA...
抹茶コーラ!?
MAGIC!!

Safe! page 25

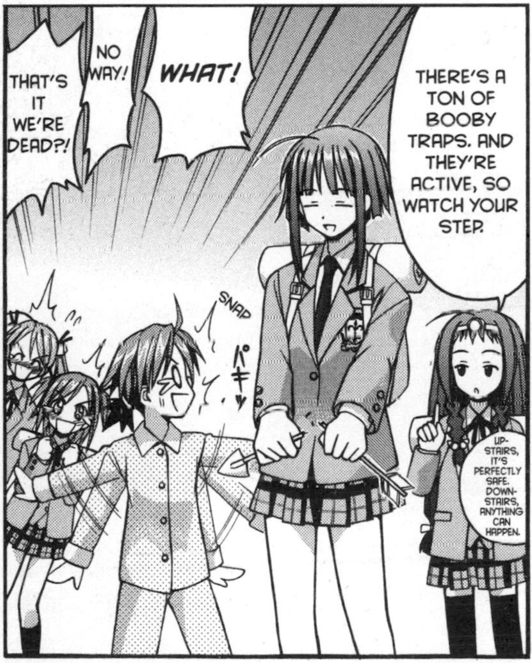
THERE'S A TON OF BOOBY TRAPS. AND THEY'RE ACTIVE, SO WATCH YOUR STEP.
WHAT!
NO WAY!
THAT'S IT WE'RE DEAD?!
UP-STAIRS, IT'S PERFECTLY SAFE. DOWN-STAIRS, ANYTHING CAN HAPPEN.
SNAP
パキッ

The word being used to describe the library in Japanese is *matomo*, which means honest, decent or proper, not safe. But because Japanese is such a contextual language, it's meant to indicate that the library is free of traps, or safe.

Kotatsu, page 29

A *kotatsu* is a low table with a blanket placed under it that covers the legs. A small heater is underneath the table keeping your feet warm. Older *kotatsus* have a sunken floor where you can stretch your legs.

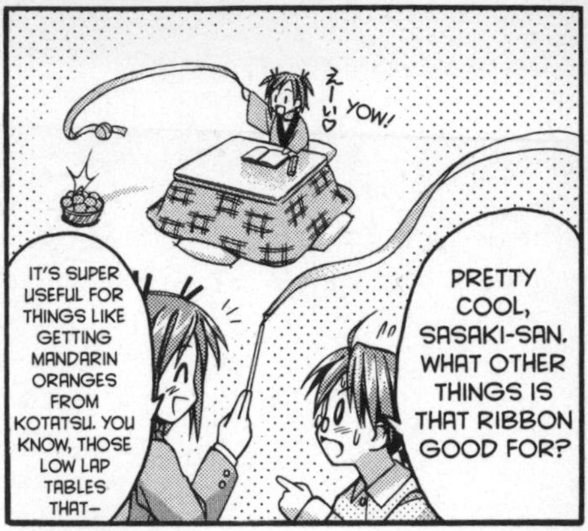
YOW!
PRETTY COOL, SASAKI-SAN. WHAT OTHER THINGS IS THAT RIBBON GOOD FOR?
IT'S SUPER USEFUL FOR THINGS LIKE GETTING MANDARIN ORANGES FROM KOTATSU. YOU KNOW, THOSE LOW LAP TABLES THAT—

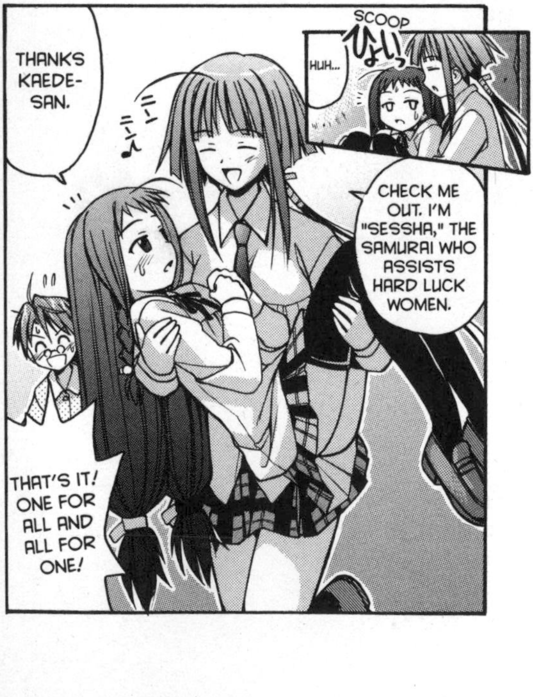
SCOOP
HUH...
CHECK ME OUT. I'M "SESSHA," THE SAMURAI WHO ASSISTS HARD LUCK WOMEN.
THANKS KAEDE-SAN.
THAT'S IT! ONE FOR ALL AND ALL FOR ONE!

Sessha, page 71

Sessha is a condescending word that samurais used to refer to themselves. It also refers to a character from a book written in the 17th century that assisted women down on their luck.

Make Cake, Not Love, page 128

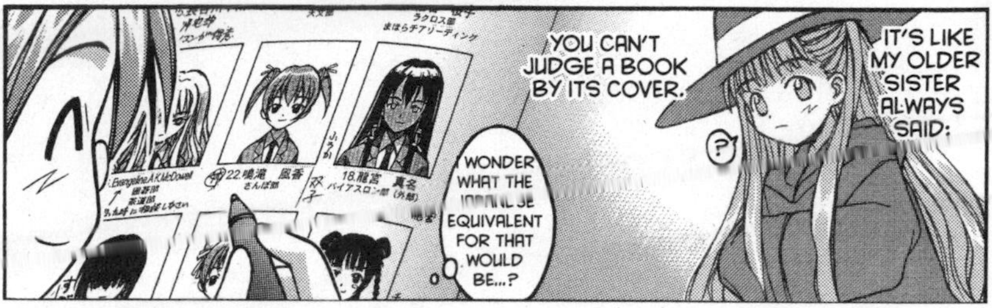
IT'S LIKE MY OLDER SISTER ALWAYS SAID:
YOU CAN'T JUDGE A BOOK BY ITS COVER.
WONDER WHAT THE EQUIVALENT FOR THAT WOULD BE...?

The literal translation of what Negi's sister said to him was "Love cake rather than love make," which means eating (or surviving) is more important than other things like love. In this context, however, it means "you can't judge a book by its cover."

Dango, page 133

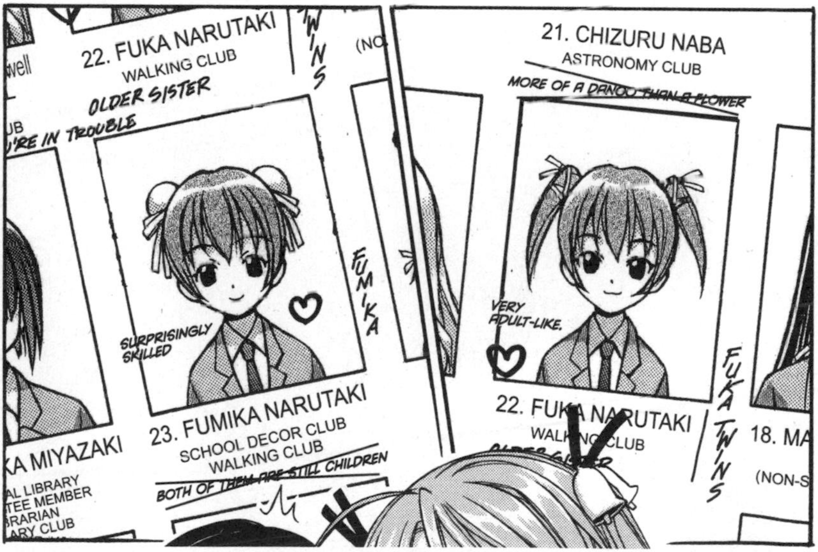
21. CHIZURU NABA
ASTRONOMY CLUB
MORE OF A DANGO THAN A FLOWER
VERY ADULT-LIKE.
22. FUKA NARUTAKI
WALKING CLUB
FUKA TWINS
22. FUKA NARUTAKI
WALKING CLUB
OLDER SISTER
TWINS
FUMIKA
SURPRISINGLY SKILLED
23. FUMIKA NARUTAKI
SCHOOL DECOR CLUB
WALKING CLUB
BOTH OF THEM ARE STILL CHILDREN

Actually, what this said in Japanese was "More like a dango than a flower." A *dango* is a roasted rice ball that comes on a stick, usually three at a time.

Ojou-sama, page 138

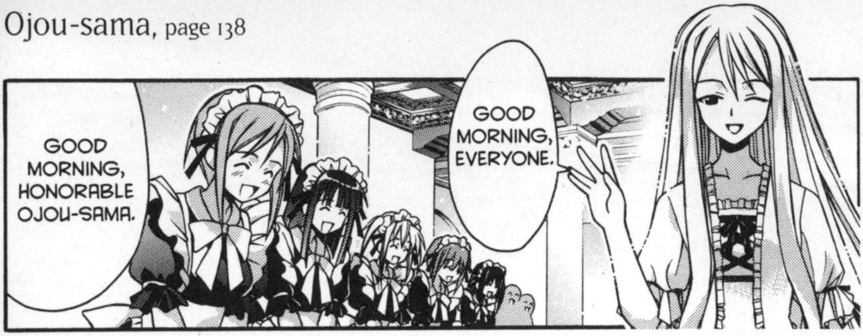
GOOD MORNING, EVERYONE.
GOOD MORNING, HONORABLE OJOU-SAMA.

Ojou-sama is a way of referring to the daughter or sister of someone with high political or social status.

O-miai, page 166

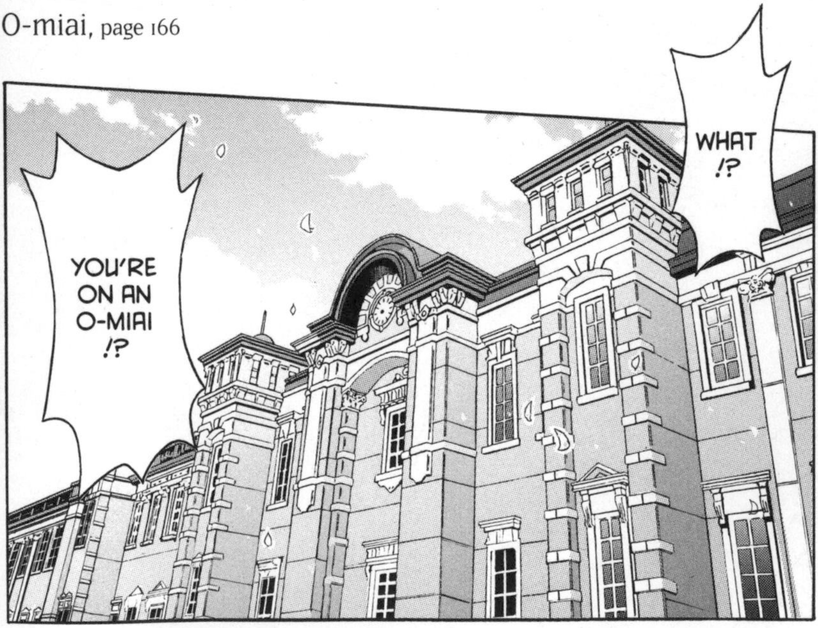
WHAT !?
YOU'RE ON AN O-MIAI !?

An *O-miai* is a date set up usually by one's parents, where information about each person is exchanged. Kind of like a blind date. Ideally, it leads to marriage. *O-miai* are becoming less popular in Japan as people seek to find their own partners. However, they are still used for people who for some reason or another have trouble finding a mate.

Preview of Volume Three

We` re pleased to present you a preview of Volume 3. This volume is available in English, but we thought you might like to see a preview in the original Japanese.

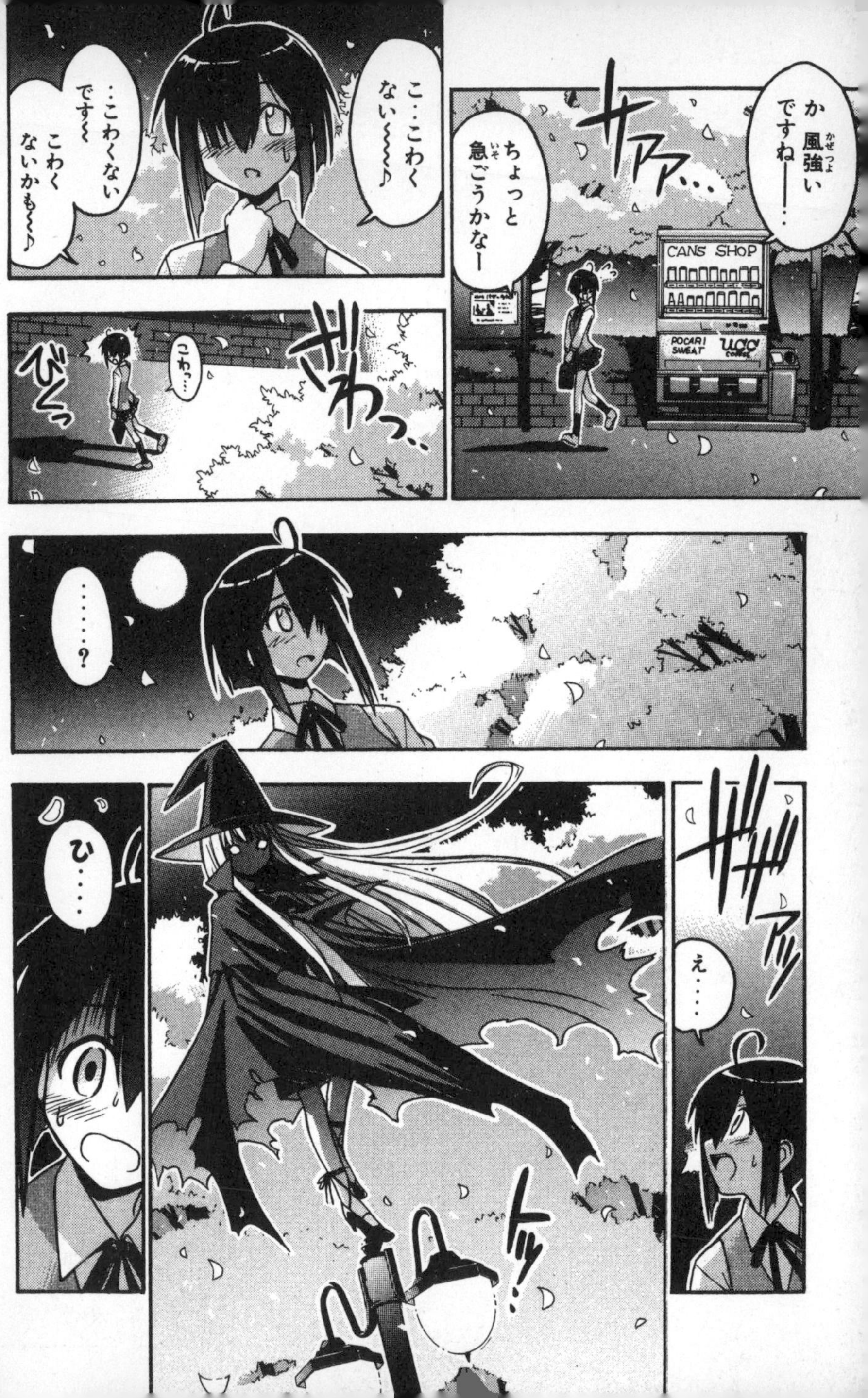
か風強いですね――…
サァア…
ちょっと急ごうかなー
CANS SHOP
POCARI SWEAT
UCC COFFEE
こ…こわくない〜〜〜♪
…こわくないです〜
こわくないかも〜〜♪
ざわっ…
こわっ…
びくっ
……?
ザザァァッ
え……
トッ!!
ひ……

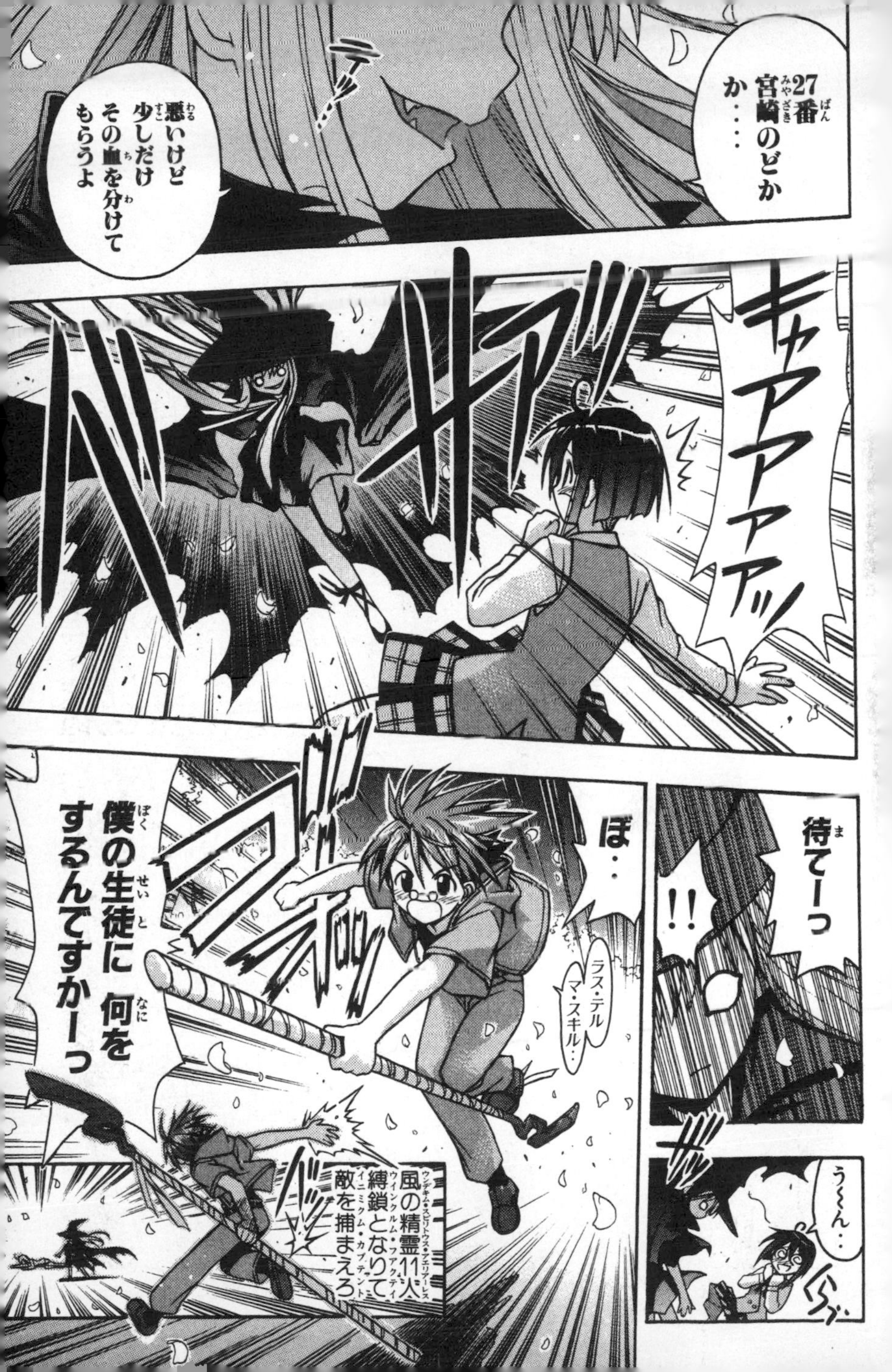
27番
宮崎のどか
か・・・・
悪いけど
少しだけ
その血を分けて
もらうよ
キャアアアアアッ
バサァッ
待てーっ
!!
ぼ・・
僕の生徒に 何を
するんですかーっ
ラス・テル
マ・スキル・・
風の精霊11人
縛鎖となりて
敵を捕まえろ
うくん・・

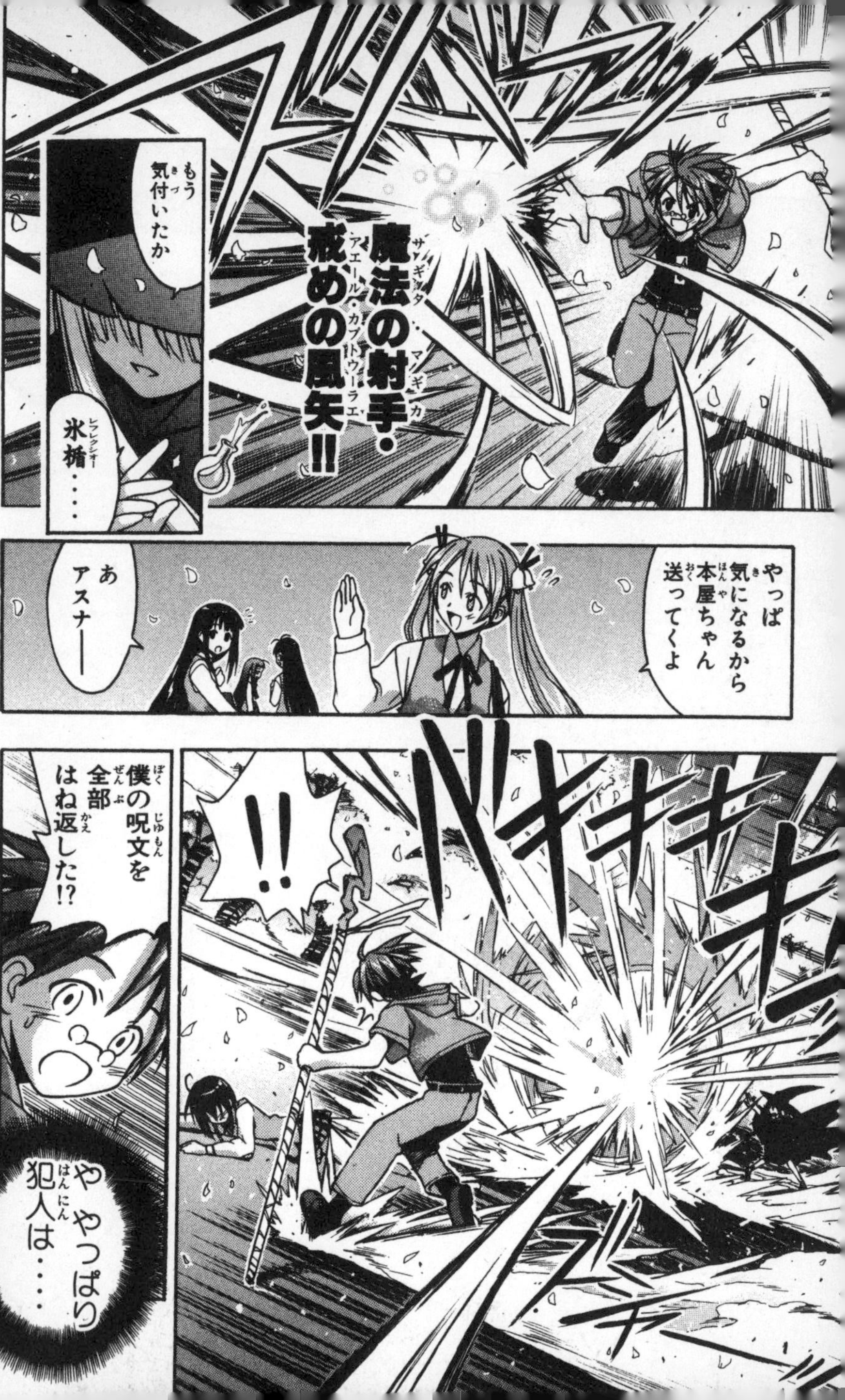

魔法の射手・戒めの風矢!!
もう気付いたか
氷楯・・・・
やっぱ気になるから本屋ちゃん送ってくよ
あアスナー
バキキキキ
!!
僕の呪文を全部はね返した!?
ややっぱり犯人は・・・・

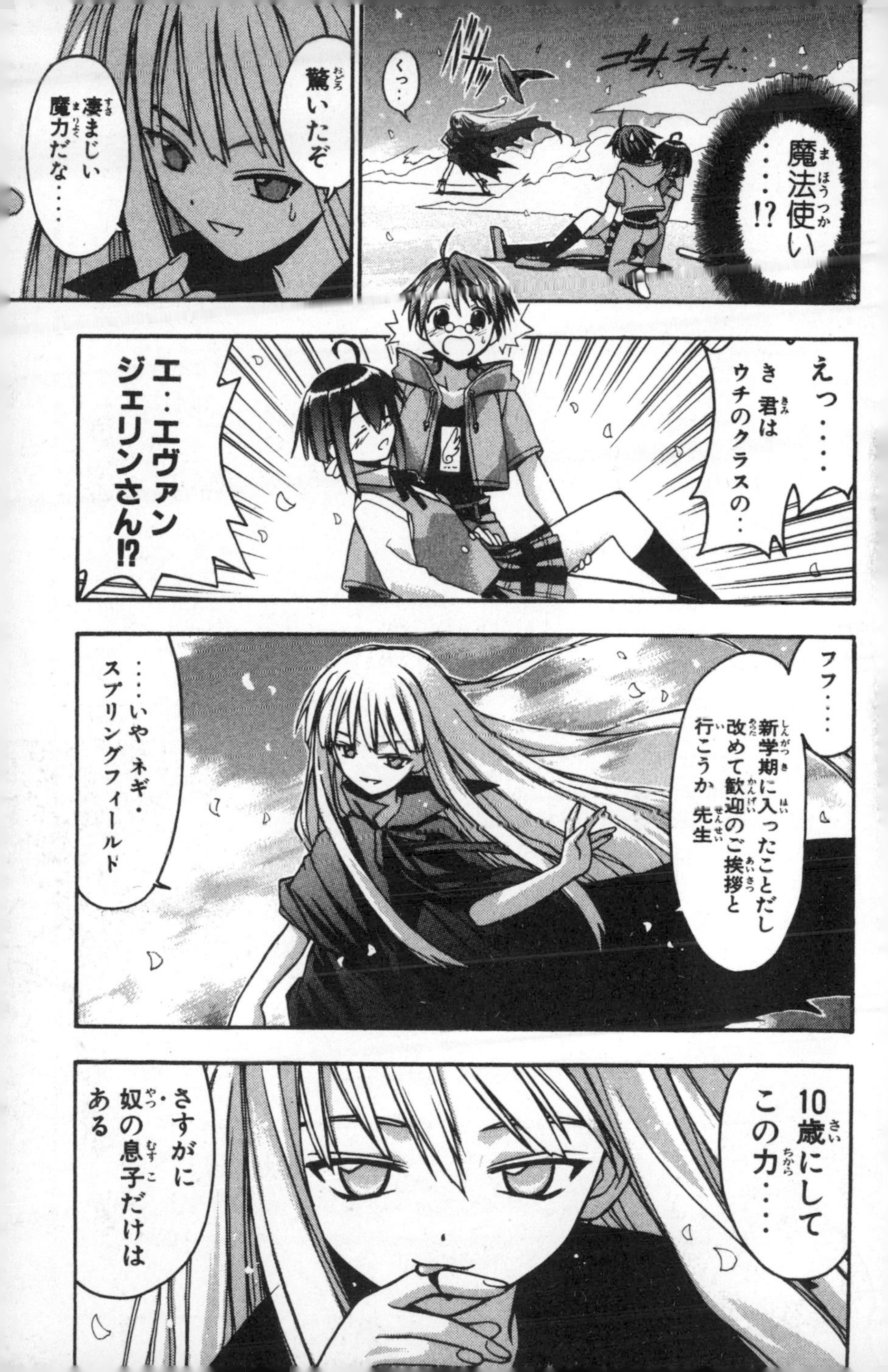
魔法使い……!?
くっ…
驚いたぞ
凄まじい魔力だな……
えっ……き 君はウチのクラスの…
エ・エヴァンジェリンさん!?
フフ……
新学期に入ったことだし改めて歓迎のご挨拶と行こうか 先生
……いや ネギ・スプリングフィールド
10歳にしてこの力……
さすがに奴の息子だけはある

BY CLAMP

Watanuki Kimihiro is haunted by visions. When he finds himself irresistibly drawn into a shop owned by Yûko, a mysterious witch, he is offered the chance to rid himself of the spirits that plague him. He accepts, but soon realizes that he's just been tricked into working for the shop to pay off the cost of Yûko's services! But this isn't any ordinary kind of shop . . . In this shop, Yûko grants wishes to those in need. But they must have the strength of will not only to truly understand their need, but to give up something incredibly precious in return.

Ages: 13+

Special extras in each volume! Read them all!

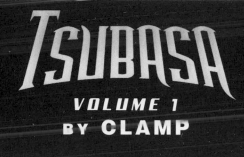

TSUBASA

VOLUME 1
BY CLAMP

SAKURA AND SYAORAN RETURN!

But they're not the people you know. Sakura is the princess of Clow—and possessor of a mysterious, misunderstood power that promises to change the world. Syaoran is her childhood friend and leader of the archaeological dig that took his father's life. They reside in an alternate reality . . . where whatever you least expect can happen—and does. When Sakura ventures to the dig site to declare her love for Syaoran, a puzzling symbol is uncovered—which triggers a remarkable quest. Now Syaoran embarks upon a desperate journey through other worlds—all in the name of saving Sakura.

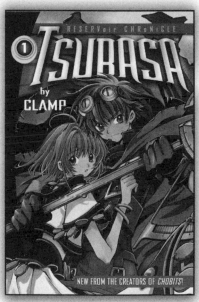

Ages: 13+

Includes special extras after the story!

School Rumble

BY JIN KOBAYASHI

SUBTLETY IS FOR WIMPS!

She . . . is a second-year high school student with a single all-consuming question: Will the boy she likes ever really notice her?

He . . . is the school's most notorious juvenile delinquent, and he's suddenly come to a shocking realization: He's got a huge crush, and now he must tell her how he feels.

Life-changing obsessions, colossal foul-ups, grand schemes, deep-seated anxieties, and raging hormones—School Rumble portrays high school as it really is: over-the-top comedy!

School Rumble
Jin Kobayashi
Vol. 1

Ages: 16 +

Coming soon in January 2007!

Special extras in each volume! Read them all!

tanoshimi

AIR GEAR

BY OH!GREAT

Itsuki Minami needs no introduction—everybody's heard of the "Babyface" of the Eastside. He's the strongest kid at Higashi Junior High School, easy on the eyes but dangerously tough when he needs to be. Plus, Itsuki lives with the mysterious and sexy Noyamano sisters. Life's never dull, but it becomes downright dangerous when Itsuki leads his school to victory over vindictive Westside punks with gangster connections. Now he stands to lose his school, his friends, and everything he cares about. But in his darkest hour, the Noyamano girls give him an amazing gift, one that just might help him save his school: a pair of Air Trecks. These high-tech skates are more than just supercool. They'll enable Itsuki to execute the wildest, most aggressive moves ever seen—and introduce him to a thrilling and terrifying new world.

AIRGEAR
1
Oh!great

Ages: 16+

Coming in October 2006!
Special extras in each volume! Read them all!

tanoshimi

Basilisk

ORIGINAL STORY BY FŪTARO YAMADA
MANGA BY MASAKI SEGAWA

THE BATTLE BEGINS

The Iga clan and the Kouga clan have been sworn enemies for more than four hundred years. Only the Hanzo Hattori truce has kept the two families from all-out war. Now, under the order of Shogun Ieyasu Tokugawa, the truce has been dissolved. Ten ninja from each clan must fight to the death in order to determine who will be the next Tokugawa Shogun. The surviving clan will rule for the next thousand years.

But not all the clan members are in agreement. Oboro of the Iga clan and Gennosuke of the Kouga clan have fallen deeply in love. Now these star-crossed lovers have been pitted against each other. Can their romance conquer a centuries-old rivalry? Or is their love destined to end in death?

Mature: Ages 18+

Special extras in each volume! Read them all!